BENGAL DISTRICT GAZETTEERS

MĀNBHUM

BENGAL DISTRICT GAZETTEERS

MĀNBHUM

By

H. Coupland

GYAN

Published by

Gyan Publishing House
5, Ansari Road
Daryaganj, New Delhi-110002
Phone: 011-47034999, 9811692060
E-mail: books@gyanbooks.com

Distribution Network
gyanbooks.com
India, USA, Canada, UK, Australia, France

ISBN : 978-81-212-6785-4 (PB)
First Published, 1911

2nd Impression 2022

Printed at: Gyan Press, Delhi.

BENGAL DISTRICT GAZETTEERS MANBHUM
Author: H. COUPLAND

BENGAL DISTRICT GAZETTEERS.

MĀNBHUM.

BY

H. COUPLAND,

INDIAN CIVIL SERVICE.

1911.

PREFACE.

THE account of Mānbhum district contained in this volume has been compiled from the Statistical Account of Bengal, volume XVII, by Sir W. W. Hunter, and from materials gathered from local records. In the sections dealing with history and ethnology frequent reference has been made to Colonel E. T. Dalton's Descriptive Ethnology of Bengal and various articles by the same author in the Journals of the Asiatic Society, to Mr. J. D. Beglar's Report of a Tour through the Bengal Provinces in 1872-73, published in the Archæological Survey of India Reports, and also to the various reports and letters (unpublished) of Sir H. H. Risley (Superintendent of Ghātwāli Survey, 1880-1884), Sir E. N. Baker (Deputy Commissioner), Colonel Dalton, Messrs. Hewett, Forbes and Gait (at various times Commissioners of the Chota Nagpur Division) on the subject of the ghātwāls of the district.

For the Chapter on Geology I am indebted to Mr. E. W. Vredenburg of the Geological Survey of India; for the article on economical products and also for much assistance and advice elsewhere in the volume, to the Revd. A. Campbell, D.D., of Pokhuria. I desire also to acknowledge gratefully the assistance received from Rai Nanda Gopal Banerji Bahadur in obtaining materials for and revising various articles in regard to which his detailed knowledge of the district extending over 33 years was invaluable, and to express my thanks to Mr. J. H. Lindsay, I.C.S., Subdivisional Officer of Dhanbaid, for revising the Chapter on the Coal-fields of Mānbhum.

H. COUPLAND.

The 24th December 1910.

PLAN OF CONTENTS.

Chapter.		Pages.
I.	Physical aspects	1–25
	Appendix—geology by E. W. Vredenburg ...	26—46
II.	History	47—68
III.	The people	69—97
IV.	Public health	98—112
V.	Agriculture	113—127
VI.	Natural calamities	128–142
VII	Rents, wages and prices	143—156
VIII.	Occupations, manufactures and trade ...	157–169
IX.	The coal-fields of Mnbhum	170—182
X.	Means of communication	183–186
XI.	Land revenue administration	187—212
	Appendix—A note on the police tenures in Manbhum	213—245
XII	General administration	246—253
XIII.	Local self-government	254—257
XIV.	Education	258—262
XV.	Gazetteer	263—289
	Index	291—298

TABLE OF CONTENTS.

CHAPTER I.

PHYSICAL ASPECTS.

PAGES.

GENERAL DESCRIPTION—Origin of name—Boundaries—Configuration—NATURAL DIVISIONS AND SCENERY—HILLS—RIVERS—Barākhar—Dāmodar—Dhalkisor and Silai—Kāsai—Subarnarekha—LAKES AND MARSHES—GEOLOGY—Minerals—BOTANY—Trees and vegetation—Economic uses—FAUNA—Game Birds—Fish—Reptiles—CLIMATE—Rainfall ... ... 1—25

APPENDIX TO CHAPTER I.

GEOLOGY.

GENERAL FEATURES—Geological constitution of the district—Faulted fractures—Absence of well-marked topographical features—Long-continued subaerial denudation—Topography depending solely on differences of hardness of rocks—Structure of Gondwāna basins—Influence of Gondwāna rocks on drainage—Intrusive rocks—Structural directions—Fault-rock—THE GONDWĀNA COAL-FIELDS—Tālcher stage—Boulder-beds—Permian ice-age—Tālcher fossils—Dāmodar stage—Barākhar sub-stage—Ironstone shales—Rāniganj sub-stage—Dāmodar fossils—Intrusive rocks in Gondwāna coal-fields—Mica-peridotite—Exceptional richness in phosphorus—Dolerite dykes—The Gondwāna coal—Hot springs along faulted boundaries—THE DHĀRWĀR SYSTEM—Northern boundary of main outcrop of Dhārwārs—Constitution of Dhārwārs—Calcareous jasper—Potstone—Sequence amongst Dhārwārs—Fault-rocks along boundary of Dhārwārs—Physical features of Dhārwār outcrop The Dalma Trap—Degree of metamorphism of Dhārwārs—Auriferous veins—Dhārwār outliers near Mānbazar—Susunia hill—Altered rocks perhaps referable to the Dhārwārs—Alluvial gold—Magnetic sands—ARCHÆAN GNEISSES—Distribution of Archæan gneisses—The Bengal gneiss—Constitution of gneisses—Composition of porphyritic gneiss—Garnet and pyroxene gneisses—ANCIENT INTRUSIVE ROCKS—The "dome-gneiss"—Distribution of granitic intrusions—Constitution of "dome-gneiss"—Pegmatite veins—EXCEPTIONAL ROCKS—Kyanite and corundum veins—Calcareous schists—Fault rock and dykes—Epidiorites—Anorthosite—Pyroxene-gneiss of Parasnath—Felspar porphyry—LATERITE AND CLAY—VALUABLE MINERALS—Coal—Iron—Building stones—Limestone—Lead ... 26—46

CHAPTER II.

HISTORY.

PAGES.

EARLY HISTORY—The Jain or Buddhistic era—Mr. Beglar's theory—Colonel Dalton's theory—MUHAMMADAN RULE—Pānchet estate—EARLY ENGLISH ADMINISTRATION—Barābhum in 1800—Ganga Nārāyan's rebellion—Causes and results of the outbreak—MUTINY OF 1857—LATER HISTORY—Formation of the district—ARCHÆOLOGICAL REMAINS ... ... 47—68

CHAPTER III.

THE PEOPLE.

GROWTH OF POPULATION—CENSUS OF 1901—MIGRATION—GENERAL CHARACTERISTICS—Density of population—Towns and villages—LANGUAGE—RELIGION—Hindus and Animists—The Sun God and other local deities—Gramya Devata—Witchcraft—Festivals—Muhammadans—Christians—CASTES AND TRIBES—Kurmis—Santhals—Bhumij—Bauris—Brāhmans—Kāmārs and Lohārs—Bhuiyas—Other Kolarian tribes—Kora—Mahli—Mundas and Kharias—Mallik—Pahira—Sārāks—VILLAGE OFFICIALS—VILLAGE SOCIAL LIFE—General appearance of the village—Dwellings—Furniture—Dress—Bedding—Village festivals—Pastimes ... 69—97

CHAPTER

PUBLIC HEALTH.

GENERAL CONDITIONS—VITAL STATISTICS—Births—Deaths—Infantile mortality—DISEASES—Fever—Cholera—Small-pox—Bowel complaints—Plague—Infirmities—VACCINATION—SANITATION—In Purulia—In the villages—In the coal-fields—Necessity for legislation—MEDICAL INSTITUTIONS—Indigenous system of medicine—Leper asylum ... ... 98—112

CHAPTER V.

AGRICULTURE.

GENERAL CONDITIONS—INFLUENCE OF RAINFALL—IRRIGATION—Wells—Extension of irrigation—SOILS—Scientific classification—Popular classification—EXTENSION OF CULTIVATION—PRINCIPAL CROPS—Extent of cultivation—Rice—Maize—Other crops—Outturn of crops—IMPROVEMENTS IN CULTIVATION—CATTLE ... ...113—127

CHAPTER VI.

NATURAL CALAMITIES.

LIABILITY TO FAMINE—FAMINE OF 1770—FAMINE OF 1866—FAMINE OF 1874—SCARCITY IN 1892—FAMINE OF 1897—DISTRESS IN 1908—General conclusions—FLOODS, EARTHQUAKES, LOCUSTS ... ...128—142

CHAPTER VII.

RENTS, WAGES AND PRICES.

PAGES.

CASH RENTS—Prevalence of customary or quit rents—*Nāyabādi* settlements—Produce rents—*Abwāb*—*Bāstu* rent—Miscellaneous—WAGES—Village labourers—SUPPLY OF LABOUR—PRICES—MATERIAL CONDITION OF THE PEOPLE—Landlords—Increasing improvidence—Indebtedness ... ...148—156

CHAPTER VIII.

OCCUPATIONS, MANUFACTURES AND TRADE.

OCCUPATIONS—MANUFACTURES AND INDUSTRIES—FACTORIES—Iron and steel—Pottery—Lac—Silk and tasar weaving—Cotton weaving—Ironware and cutlery—Stone carving—Gold washing—Other industries—TRADE—Weights and measures ... ...157—169

CHAPTER IX.

THE COAL-FIELDS OF MANBHUM.

EARLY DISCOVERIES—Mr. Rupert Jones' enquiry—Early developments in Mānbhum—The Rāniganj field—The Jharia field—Geology of the Jharia field—Composition—Method of working—Labour—Inspection ...170—182

CHAPTER X.

MEANS OF COMMUNICATION.

DEVELOPMENT OF MEANS OF COMMUNICATION—ROADS—RAILWAYS—Extensions of the railway system—RIVERS—FERRIES—STAGING AND INSPECTION BUNGALOWS—POSTAL COMMUNICATIONS ... ...183—186

CHAPTER XI.

LAND REVENUE ADMINISTRATION.

DIVISION INTO ESTATES—Probable origin—Suzerainty of Pānchet—The permanent settlement—BARABHUM—Form of agreement, 1776—Meaning of "Zamindar"—Other estates—PANCHET—Muhammadan era—Early British era—TEMPORARILY SETTLED ESTATES—Mātha—Kailāpal—LATER HISTORY—The rule of primogeniture—Exemption of estates from sale for arrears and debt—The Encumbered Estates Act—REVENUE-FREE PROPERTIES—DIGWARI ESTATES—SUBORDINATE TENURES—Shikmi taluks—Patni taluks—Mankiāri and Murāri tenures—Mokrari—Panchaki Brahmottars, etc.—Ijāra—Maintenance tenures—Cultivating tenures—Rent-free grants for religious or charitable purposes—SERVICE TENURES—Minor service tenures ...187—212

APPENDIX TO CHAPTER XI.

A NOTE ON THE POLICE TENURES IN MĀNBHUM.

PAGES.

POLICE TENURES IN MĀNBHUM—Colonel Dalton's account of their origin—Early police arrangements in Panchet—Digwārs—Digwārs of Mahal and Sankhandi—Ghatwals subordinate to the digwārs—Panchet jaigirs—Digwārs in Jharia, Pandra, Jhalda, and Begunkodar—Digwārs without tenures—Service tenures in Mānbhum, Barābhum, Kailāpāl, and Pātkum—Kailāpāl—Mānbhum—Barābhum—The ghātwāli survey, 1880-83—The compromise of 1884—The results of the compromise—The compromise overruled by the Court—Documentary evidence of early origin—Sardārs and paiks in 1800 and earlier years—Identity of the sardārs and paiks with the later ghātwāls—Existence of certain of the tenures in 1789—Their entry in the ekjai papers of 1205 as mahāl Bhumijāni—And in those of 1206, 1207—The four major tarafs definitely recognized as tenures prior to and immediately after the Permanent Settlement—Meaning of Bhumijāni—The Bhumijāni tenure not distinct from the ghātwāli or jaigir—Origin of the so-called minor tarafs—Bangurda—Kumāripar—Sarberia—Other ghātwāli tenures in the chākrān lists—Vague distinction between mahāl Bhumijāni and chākrān—The isamnavisis of 1824 and 1833—Rent and panchak in the 1833 isamnavisi—Mamul khajana—The village list of 1870—Ultimate origin in the Mundāri village system—Tenures in Pātkum—Conclusion ... ...213—245

CHAPTER XII.

GENERAL ADMINISTRATION.

ADMINISTRATIVE STAFF—Revenue—Land Revenue—Excise—Stamps—Income Tax—Cess—Registration—ADMINISTRATION OF JUSTICE—Criminal justice—Civil justice—EMIGRATION—POLICE—JAILS ... ...246—253

CHAPTER XIII.

LOCAL SELF-GOVERNMENT.

DISTRICT BOARD—Income—Expenditure—LOCAL BOARD—MUNICIPALITIES—Purulia—Income and expenditure—Jhalda—Raghunathpur ... ...254—257

CHAPTER XIV.

EDUCATION.

PAGES.

PROGRESS OF EDUCATION—GENERAL STATISTICS—SECONDARY EDUCATION—PRIMARY EDUCATION—FEMALE EDUCATION—SPECIAL SCHOOLS—INDUSTRIAL EDUCATION—NIGHT OR CONTINUATION SCHOOLS—OTHER SCHOOLS—BOARDING HOUSES—EDUCATION OF DIFFERENT RACES—Aboriginals—LIBRARIES AND NEWSPAPERS ... ... 258—262

CHAPTER XV.

GAZETTEER.

Adra— Balarāmpur— Barābāzār— Borām— Buddhpur— Chākultor— Charra—Dalmi—Dhanbaid—Dhanbaid Subdivision— Gobindpur— Jhalda—Jharia—Kātras or Kātrasgarh—Mānbāzār—Pabanpur—Pakbira—Pānchet or Pānchkot—Pāra—Purulia—Purulia Subdivision—Raghunāthpur—Telkupi ... 263—289

INDEX ... ... 291—298

GAZETTEER

OF THE

MANBHUM DISTRICT.

CHAPTER I.

PHYSICAL ASPECTS.

General description. THE district of Mānbhum forms the eastern part of the Chota Nāgpur Division and lies between 22° 43′ and 24° 4′ North Latitude, and 85° 49′ and 86° 54′ East Longitude. It contains an area of 4,147 square miles and a population, according to the census of 1901, of 1,301,364 souls. The principal town and administrative head-quarters is Purūlia situated some three miles north of the Kāsai River in 23° 20′ N. and 86° 22′ E.

Origin of name. The district takes its name from one of its most easterly Parganas, at the chief place in which, Mānbazār or Mānbhum Khas, was the head-quarters of the Jungle Mahals district from 1833 to 1838, in the earlier of which years the Mānbhum district was constituted. Of the origin of the name it is difficult to speak with any certainty; the apparently obvious derivation from *mān* (Bengali) "the land of honour" may, at once, be rejected as the Bengali connection with the Pargana and district can hardly date back much more than two centuries. Dr. Hunter prefers "the land of the wrestlers" (*malla* or *mala*). Other authorities, including Mr. W. B. Oldham and Sir H. H. Risley, follow General Cunningham and ascribe the origin of the name to the Dravidian tribe of Māl referred to by Pliny as Mālli and identical apparently with the Sauri, the Saurian family to which the Rājmahāl Pahārias, the Orāons and the Sabārs belong, and neighbours of the Mandei or Monodes, identified with the Munda Kols. The tribal name Māl, Māle, or Maler is variously derived from a Dravidian root meaning a hill, (c. f. Pahāria, the hillmen), and from *male* "a man," the tribe speaking of themselves as "men" just as the Kolarian tribes, Sonthals, Mundas and Larka Kols (Hor, ho) do at the present day. That the district name is derived from non-Aryan sources is the more probable as a very large number of the village names and several of the pargana names (*e.g.*, Pātkum) undoubtedly come from one or other of the aboriginal dialects, though some of them have within recent times adopted a more Aryan appearance.

Boundaries. The district is bounded on the north by the districts of Hazāribagh and the Sonthal Parganas; on the east by Burdwan, Bānkura, and Midnapore; on the south by Singhbhum, and on the west by Rānchi and Hazāribagh. The whole of the northern boundary is marked by the Barākhar river; on the north-east the Barākhar and Dāmodar separate the district from Burdwan, and on the west and south the Subarnarekha river flows along the boundary for short distances.

Configuration. In shape Mânbhum is an irregular parallelogram, having a length of 90 miles from north to south and a breadth of 60 miles from west to east, with Purulia, its administrative head-quarters, situated a little south of the centre. The Dāmodar river divides the district into two unequal portions, the northern portion corresponding to the Dhânbāid, until recently the Gobindpur, sub-division with an area of 803 square miles, and the southern to the Sadār subdivision of 3,344 square miles.

Natural divisions and scenery. The district has been described as the first step of a gradual descent from the table land of Chota Nāgpur to the delta of Lower Bengal; more properly it is the last step in the descent from the great elevated high lands of Central India, the Chota Nāgpur plateau with its general elevation of 2,000 to 2,500 feet forming the intermediate stage. The general characteristics are those of an upland district, consisting, as it does, in great measure, of metamorphic rocks, spurs projected from the table-land on the west, and swelling ridges of laterite. Towards the east, as the metamorphic rocks thin out, the laterite ridges thicken, the undulations so characteristic of Chota Nāgpur are less pronounced, and the dips between the ridges are broader and more level; the country is more open, and presents the appearance of a series of rolling downs, dotted here and there with isolated conical hills. This description applies generally to the north and east of the district, including the valleys of the Dāmodar and Kāsai rivers, with their various affluents. In the north-western corner, however, a double spur of hills branches out from the range of which Parasnāth is the most striking feature and, extending across Pargana Tundi, forms the watershed between the Dāmodar and Barākhar rivers. In the adjoining Pargana of Nāwagarh, to the west, the lower slopes of the Parasnāth range extend well into the district, and outlying ridges and isolated hills, locally known as *dungris*, extend in more or less parallel lines along the Jamunia river to the banks of the Dâmodar.

South of this again spurs from the Hazāribagh part of the Chota Nāgpur plateau abut on or extend short distances into the western parts of Parganas Khāspel and Jainagar. In the adjoining Pargana of Jhalda, there begins a series of isolated groups of hills and isolated peaks, some of them of considerable elevation, which still further south form a regular range known as the Bāghmundi or Ajodhya range, which in places reaches an elevation of over 2,000 feet and forms the water-shed between the Subarnarekha and Kāsai rivers. This range which, indeed, is rather a plateau of considerable extent, on which there are a number of flourishing villages, than a mere range of hills, ends somewhat abruptly in Pargana Mātha, but numerous isolated peaks and groups of low hills connect it with the spurs from the Rānchi plateau on the west, and the range separating Pargana Pātkum from the Kharsāwan State in the south-west. Practically continuous with the last, save for the very narrow valley of the Subarnarekha, is another range extending along the Singhbhum boundary known by the name of its highest peak, Dalma. This, like the Bāghmundi range, marks the division between the watersheds of the Subarnarekha and the various feeders of the Kāsai, of which the Nengsai, the Kumāri and the Tatko are the most prominent. Of picturesque scenery the more level portions furnish but little in the dry months of the year except where the Parasnāth or Tundi ranges in the north, the Bāghmundi range in the centre and west, and Dalma in the south give a striking background to the picture. The general absence of trees in this part of the country, and the fact that cultivation is almost entirely confined to the rice crop, gives in the dry season the general appearance of a barren waste. In the rains the prospect is more pleasing when the fresh green of the young rice shades off into the darker greens of the grass which springs up everywhere when the first showers fall, and contrasts with the browns of the ripening crops on the high lands, and of the bare gravel ridges, varied here and there by black masses of exposed rock. These effects are naturally enchanced when the hills give a background of mingled jungle growth and enormous masses of rock of quaint shapes and varying shades of colour. In the early hot weather the jungle-covered areas, whether on the hills or in the plain, present for a time a brilliant spectacle, the red blossom of the *palās* (Butea frondosa) contrasting in striking fashion with the fresh green of the new leaves. Generally it may be said of the district that, from the point of view of the picturesque, the seasons of the new leaves and the *palās* blossom, that is to say the early hot weather, and of the young rice, August-September, are the two most favourable; of the constantly picturesque and of the grand there is little or none in comparison with the more favoured high lands to the west.

Hills. The general trend of the hill system has been described in the previous paragraph, and it remains only to notice the more prominent peaks. Of these Parasnāth, though not actually within the district, forms unquestionably the most conspicuous feature of the landscape throughout the northern and western parts of the district. Compared with its commanding height (4,480 feet) and generally striking appearance all other hills in this neighbourhood are dwarfed; on clear days in the rains and early cold weather it is a prominent object even so far south as Purūlia, a distance of some 70 miles; its southern and eastern lower slopes are within the district and it is the great hill (the Marang Buru) of the Sonthals who constitute nearly one-sixth of the whole population, and consequently it may be claimed as to some extent appertaining to, though not within, the district. Highest within the district itself is the crowning peak of the Dalma range (3,407 feet), but it is in no sense the rival of Parasnāth; it wants the bold precipices and commanding peaks of that hill, and its height loses effect from the fact that it is merely the highest point in a long rolling ridge reached by a gradual rise from the lower hills on either side. The slopes of the hill are still covered with dense jungle, though much of the big timber has been cut away within recent years; its summit is accessible to men and beasts of burden. Sawai (2,637 feet) and Chārājural (2,412 feet) in the extreme south-western corner of the district are even less conspicuous in proportion to their height than Dalma, shut off as they are by a group of hills on the Mānbhum side of which Auli (2,108 feet), Karānti (1,932 feet), Chātam (1,766 feet) with others ranging from 1,100 to 1,300 to the north and east are sufficiently high to take from the effect. Ganga Buru (or Gaj Buru) the highest peak in the Bāghmundi range makes much more of its 2,220 feet, but the chief features of this range are several more or less detached lower peaks of which one at the north-east corner, in shape like an irregular church steeple or a gigantic tooth, is a very conspicuous object for miles around. At the northern end of the same range but detached from it, not far from Jhalda, Bānsa (1,789 feet) attracts some attention rising up abruptly nearly 1,000 feet from the general level of the plain in the shape of huge sugarloaf. Pānchkot or Pānchet (1,600 feet) is the most conspicuous object in the north-east of the district, in Pargana Chaurāsi, some 35 miles north of Purūlia. In shape it is a long crescent like ridge rising to its highest point at its eastern extremity; it is covered with small but dense jungle, with some fine clumps of mango and mahua scattered over the low foot hills at its base. At the foot of its eastern face are the ruins of the old palace and fort of the Pānchet Rājas, and above and also below them, of some ancient temples, an account of which will be given in a later chapter. A few miles south of Pānchet is a picturesque group of rocky hills of bold irregular formation with great masses of grey black boulder jutting out above the scanty scrub jungle which clothes the lower slopes. One more precipitous than the rest with a clear drop of several hundred feet from an immense boulder on the top is known as Execution Hill, the story being that from this spot the Rāja of Pānchet used, in ancient days, to have his enemies as well as detected evil-doers hurled over the face of the cliff to be dashed to pieces on the rough stones at the foot. In the extreme north of the district the only peak of any prominence, apart from Parasnāth, is the curious double-peaked hill in the Tundi range, known as Dumunda; its height is inconsiderable, but its appearance makes it a conspicuous object.

Following the natural slope of the district all the rivers which intersect or take their rise within it, have an easterly or south-easterly course. They have the usual characteristics of hill-fed streams; their beds are entirely or almost dry during the greater part of the cold season, and the whole of the hot season; they are not navigable during any portion of the year with the single and intermittent exception of the Dāmodar, and are subject to sudden and violent freshets which are usually of very short duration. Except where they run over exposed rock, their beds are usually deep in gravel and sand; their banks are abrupt and broken into deep cuts wherever the drainage from the surrounding country finds its way to the level of the stream. Cases of alluvion are very rare, and the only notable instance is the small island thrown up at the junction of the Dāmodar and Barākhar rivers. Diluvion on a small scale is on the other hand constant; huge masses of gravelly soil are constantly being undermined and detached from the banks, and every heavy fall of rain scours out the small cuts and channels which feed the larger RIVERS.

streams. There is no regular system of river-cultivation, and as a general rule the banks are covered with low scrub jungle.

Barākhar. The northernmost river in Mānbhum is the Barākhar, which skirts Parganas Tundi and Pāndra and forms the northern and north-eastern boundary of the district. Running at first in a south-easterly direction, it suddenly sweeps round the low group of hills to which Durgāpur (1,186 feet) gives its name, and runs due south with several bends and turns till it joins the Dāmodar a few miles south of Chirkunda and Barākhar, at the trijunction of Parganas Domurkonda, Chaurāsi, and Shergarh. Just above this point it receives from the west its only important tributary, the Khudia, which takes its rise in the extreme west of the district between the Parasnāth and Tundi ranges, and drains the whole country between that range and the high ridge which marks the nothern limit of the Jharia coal-field.

Dāmodar. The Dāmodar, as already stated, divides the Dhānbāid from the Sadar Division; its course through the district is almost due east. On its entry into the district it receives from the north the waters of the Jamunia, a considerable stream which marks the boundary between the Hazāribagh and Mānbhum districts along almost the whole length of Pargana Nāwagarh. Of its other affluents from the north the Katri, which takes its rise in the foot hills below Parasnāth and cuts through the coal-field area, is the most important. From the south its main affluent is the Gowai which before its junction with the Dāmodar just east of Bhojudih itself receives the waters of the Ijri and the Harâi which drain practically the whole country east of the Jhalda hills, north of the Rānchi Road and north and west of the Purūlia-Asansol Railway line as far up as the Pānchet hill. The watershed between this and the Kāsai river is somewhat inconspicuously marked by a line of high ridges, occasionally rising to sufficient height to be designated hills, running across the district in an easterly and later northerly direction as far as the Pānchet hill.

The Dāmodar receives the waters of the Barākhar on the Burdwan border, and here, as well as near the confluence with the Gowai, a small island is formed in a loop of the stream. Navigation of the Dāmodar even in the rainy season is difficult owing to the sudden changes in depth due to freshets, and the violence of the current which tends to throw up sand banks in constantly shifting sites. Rafts of timber still come down from the jungle areas higher up, but since the opening of the Railway the conveyance of coal in country boats by this route has practically ceased.

South of the Dāmodar and between it and the Kāsai, the Dhalkisor and the Silai, which become important streams lower down, drain a large portion of Pargana Ludhurka in which they take their rise. Within the district they are short streams of no particular importance; their watershed is marked off from that of the affluents of the Dāmodar by the high ridge of which the isolated peaks at Raghunāthpur are the only prominent feature. Between the two and between them and the Kāsai the watershed is even less distinctly marked by the Magura hill just south of Hura. Dhalkisor and Silai.

The Kāsai is the most important river of the centre portion of the district. It takes its rise on the extreme west in the hills north of Jhalda and, flowing in a south-easterly direction, leaves Purūlia a few miles on the north and finally passes out into the Bānkura district at a point some 60 miles from its source, and after draining practically the whole of the centre and south-eastern portion of the district east of the Bāghmundi and north of the Dalma range. Just outside the district beyond Mānbazar it receives the waters of the Kumari which, with its affluents the Tatko and the Nengsai, drains the whole of the northern slope of the Dalma range. Within the district it is quite impossible for navigation; it is particularly liable to sudden and violent freshets and in the year 1898 it overflowed its banks, which are generally of very considerable height, and near Purūlia, where in the dry weather it is a stream at most a foot deep and 15 or 20 feet in width, it presented a breadth of over 2,700 feet. Villages situated on the high banks were washed away and crops destroyed by this flood, which is still remembered as the great flood of 1304 (Bengali year). Kāsai.

West of the Bāghmundi range and south of Dalma the only river of importance is the Subarnarekha. For 35 miles it follows a tortuous course along the district border from Bhojpura, some 10 miles north-west of Jhalda, to Jojodih on the borders of Pātkum and Bāghmundi Parganas where it turns towards the east, its general direction previously having been due south, and intersects the former Pargana till it meets the district border a few miles south of Chandil. It then flows for some miles along the Singhbhum-Mānbhum border in an easterly direction, skirting the Dalma range, and finally leaves the District near Kapāli. Its only affluent of any size or importance within the district is the Karkari, which rises in the Rānchi District and bisects the Pātkum Pargana for some 20 miles, meeting the Subarnarekha a few miles east of Ichāgarh. Subarnarekha.

Lakes and Marshes.

There are no large marshes in the district, nor are there any natural lakes. Artificial lakes of considerable size have, however, been formed in several places by running dams across small ravines or valleys, so that the enclosed space is filled by the natural drainage from above. Of such, the most noticeable example is the Sāhib-bāndh at Purūlia the water in which, when full in the rains, covers over 50 acres, and even at the lowest some 30 or 35 acres. The dam or *bāndh* was constructed about 1848 mainly by convict labour, and according to local tradition the then Deputy Commissioner refused to consider any petition filed unless the petitioner had first done a day's hard labour on the *bāndh*. There are avenues of trees on three sides, and a couple of wooded islands which greatly add to the general picturesqueness. From a utilitarian point of view the lake is the chief source of drinking water for the western half of the town, and it is under contemplation at present to construct another *bāndh* or tank below it for bathing and the washing of clothes, and reserve the Sāhib-bāndh entirely for drinking purposes. At Gobindpur there is a similar bāndh on a smaller scale known as the Risley Bāndh; others constructed by private enterprise are the Rāni-Bāndhs at Pāndra and Jaypur; the Bābir-Bāndh at Bābudih, the Jobūna-Bāndh near Rangāmati, and the large railway *bāndh* recently made by the Bengal-Nāgpur Railway Company near Adra to provide the railway settlement with pure drinking water. The construction of similar *bāndhs* forms the main part of the district programme of village famine works, their economic value as reservoirs of drinking water being at any rate equalled by their value for irrigation purposes, the fields lying immediately at the foot of the dams being kept constantly moist by percolation of the water, and forming ideal rice-growing land. Canals and artificial water courses are practically unknown.

Geology.

The geological formations are the Archæan and the Gondwāna. The Archæan rocks consist of gneiss and crystalline schists, the gneiss occupying by far the largest portion of the district. It belongs principally to the group known as Bengal gneiss, which is remarkable for its varied composition, consisting of successive bands of intermixed granitic, granulitic and dioritic gneisses, and micaceous chloritic and hornblendic schists, with a laminated or foliated structure striking usually east and west. About the centre of the district is a great belt of unfoliated or only slightly foliated granitic intrusions, also striking east and west, and extending westwards into the adjacent district of Rānchi. Crystalline limestones occasionally occur. Along the southern boundary there exists a group of rocks resembling the

Dharwār schists of Southern India, which were originally sedimentary and volcanic, but have been altered into quartzites, quartzitic sandstones, slates of various kinds, hornblendic mica, and talcose and chloritic schists, the latter passing into potstones, green stones and epidiorites.

Quite close to the southern boundary of Mānbhum, the schists are invaded by a gigantic dyke of basic igneous rock forming an imposing east and west range, which culminates in the lofty Dalma hill. The schists are here more metamorphosed than elsewhere with a considerable development of iron ores; in this neighbourhood, moreover, the rocks are richest in gold.

The Gondwānas, whose age as determined by fossil plants, is partly upper palaeozoic and partly mesozoic, are the principal rocks from an economic point of view. They occur along the Dāmodar river and form the Rānīganj coal-field, the western portion of which lies in Mānbhum, and the rich Jharia coal-field almost entirely situated within the district. The Gondwāna rocks comprise the Māhādeva, Pānchet, Rānīganj, ironstone shales, Barākhar and Tālcher divisions, of which all but the first belong to the lower Gondwānas. The series consists throughout almost exclusively of shales and sandstones. The coal seams are restricted to the Barākhar and Rānīganj divisions.

The coal-fields owe their preservation from denudation and their present situation to a system of faults that has sunk them amidst the surrounding gneiss. The faults are easily recognized along their boundaries, especially on the south, and sulphurous hot springs are often situated in their neighbourhood. Innumerable fissures are occupied by intrusive dykes of basalt and of mica-apatite-peridotite, the latter being frequently detrimental to the coal seams which have often been burnt away by it. These intrusions are of the same age as the volcanic rocks of the Rājmahāl hills.*

The most important mineral found in Mānbhum is coal of which a more detailed account will be found in a later Chapter. The whole of the Jharia field, 180 square miles in extent, lies within the district, besides portions of the Rānīganj-Barākhar field. On its western border, the Jharia field practically joins on to the Bokāru-Rāmgarh field which is now being exploited in Hazāribagh. Minerals.

Iron is plentiful in several parts of the district, and the Barākhar iron and steel works have in the past obtained much

* A fuller account of the geology of this district which has been specially written by Mr. E. Vredenburg of the Geological Survey of India for this volume is printed as an Appendix to this Chapter.

of their ore from Malti and Cheliāma in Barābhum and Pātkum in the south and from various places within the limits of the Rānīganj coal-field in the north-east of the district There a clay iron-stone, which constitutes a large proportion of the iron-stone shales, is especially rich and plentiful, and is sometimes associated with carbonaceous matter forming a black-band iron ore. Magnetic and titaniferous iron ores are also found among the gneissose and schistose rocks; red hematite occurs in the siliceous fault breccias of the same areas, and lateritic iron ores also exist. Iron is worked on a small scale, principally by the aboriginal tribes, in various places among which may be mentioned Ajodhya on the Bāghmundi plateau, and Akro and other villages in the south of Pargana Mānbhum. The rocks on the southern boundary of the district constitute part of the northern edge of the auriferous tract of Chota Nāgpur. They are traversed by innumerable gold-bearing quartz veins, from which has been derived the alluvial gold obtained in all the rivers that drain the schist area. The Pātkum prospecting syndicate attempted to work the gold on an extensive scale but failed, and the careful investigation to which the area has been subjected of late years leaves very little hope of extracting the gold at a profit. An attempt has also been made to work gold at Akro in the south of Mānbhum Pargana but so far the result has not been very successful. Washing for gold goes on at a number of places along the Subarnarekha river in Pargana Pātkum; the results are, however, very small, the average earnings of a washer being not more than four or five annas a day.

Lead ores (principally argentiferous) are found near Dhādka in south-eastern Barābhum, the amount of silver per ton of lead in two samples tested being 119 and 99 ounces. Copper ores are found at Purda 30 miles south, and at Kaliānpur 32 miles due west from Purūlia. Traces of corundum have been found in the Tinsāya Ghātwāli tenure in Barābhum, where also various superior clays including kaolin are also said to exist in workable quantities. Chalk, red ochre and traces of mica are found here and there, but the only attempt to work the last named commercially (in Pāndra in the north of the district) failed. Soap-stone quarries are worked at several places in the south of the district, particularly round about Pātkum, and the stone produced is fairly extensively employed for the manufacture of idols, plates, bowls and the like. The process of manufacture is simple, the blocks being roughly dressed by hand and then cut into form in a rude lathe, and finished off with a smooth surface. Kankar suitable for the manufacture of lime is found in most parts of the district, and rubble, quartz, sand-stone, trap and basalt are quarried for building purposes, road metal and ballast.

BOTANY Trees and vegetation.

It is only in respect of a comparatively limited area, namely, along the hill ranges to the north-west, south and south-west of the district, that Mānbhum can now be described as a well wooded country, and even in these parts denudation has gone on to such an extent that the amount of large timber left, except in the most inaccessible places, is very small. There are small areas of protected forest in the Mātha and Kailapāl estates which, in course of time (they have only been under protection since 1892), should develop into fairly useful forests, and here and there zamindars and others have made special efforts to preserve some small patches usually as a shooting preserve (shikar jungal or mahal). In ghātwāli villages some sort of protection is nominally enforced, but the strict application of rules in the case of villages nearer the centres of civilization or in the midst of a fairly thick population has, in practice, been impossible and only a small percentage of the ghātwāli jungles is now, in consequence, worthy of the name of forest. Of the four sections, therefore, into which Mr. V. Ball* in 1869 divided the district, the first, *i.e.*, "original jungle land in which trees are of large size" has almost entirely disappeared. The second "stunted jungle land from which timber is regularly cut, and where the trees are never allowed to attain respectable dimensions" describes accurately the bulk of the jungle that survives The third and fourth classes, "dry, gravelly and rocky ground cut up by ravines, incapable of supporting a tree cultivation", and "land under cultivation" have proportionately increased; the former, owing to the practice of "jhuming" or bringing under cultivation jungle areas not suited for permanent cultivation, and which are necessarily denuded of soil once cultivation, or the attempt at cultivation, ceases, has probably increased at least as rapidly, if not more rapidly than the actual permanently cultivated area. Mr. Ball gives as among the most characteristic trees in his first division the *Sāl* (*Shorea robusta*), *Asan* (*Terminalia tomentosa*), *Kusum* (*Schleichera trijuga*), *Kend* (*Melanoxylon*) and *Piar* (*Buchanania latifolia*). On the higher hills the bamboo as a rule takes the place of other trees. Herbaceous plants are comparatively scarce, but there are numerous large scandent creepers among which the *Butea superba* with its magnificent orange-red flowers, and the *Bauhinia Vahlii* are the

---

* Flora of Manbhum—J. A. S., 1869.

most conspicuous; parasites and epipytes are represented by several species of loranthus and of orchids. Mr. Ball's second and third divisions have no very characteristic vegetation; stunted *sāl*, the result of cutting the original too high from the ground, the *palās* (*Butea frondosa*) and various grasses and more or less dwarfed bushes of different species form the ordinary vegetation; timber trees of any size are ordinarily conspicuous by their absence, though in the areas nearer the hills the general appearance of open forest or park like country is preserved by the presence of numerous *mahua* (*Bassia latifolia*). These, as well as *palās* besides the various fig trees, the mango, *nim*, *bair* or plum tree, *jamun* and jack with very occasional date palms, are the principal varieties found in and near the cultivated tracts.

Economic uses.

Of trees and plants yielding good timber, or of which various parts and products serve useful economic purposes, Dr. A. Campbell, of Pokhuria, gives the following account of the most important; he mentions at the outset that the list is not exhaustive, and that, apart from the trees and shrubs referred to, there are over 90 species of plants which minister to the necessities of the people by providing food of a sort during scarcity or famine.

Dilleniaceæ.—Two species of the genus Dillenia, are fairly common. Dillenia indica, Linn, (Chalta, Beng., Korkot, Sant.) and D. pantagyna, Roxb., (Sahar, Sant.). The former yields a good timber and fruit of the latter is eaten. *Anonaceæ.*—Miliusa velutina, Horssk. fil and Thoms, (Kāre, Beng., Ome, Sant.) is a middle sized tree, the timber of which is used for yokes and axles and the fruit is edible. Anona squamosa, Linn., (Sārpha, Beng., Mandargom, Sant.,) the custard apple, and A. reticulata, Linn., (Mandal, Beng., Gom, Sant.,) the Bullock's heart, are found cultivated and in a semi-wild state. Both yield edible fruit.

Capparidaceæ.—Caparis horrida, Linn., (Buru asaria, Sant.,) a scrambling shrub is met with. *Bixineæ.*—Cochlospermum gossypium, D.C., (Golgol, Beng., Hopo, Sant.,) is remarkable for its large, handsome yellow flowers, which appear before the leaves. It yields a gum, known commercially as Hog-gum, and from the seeds a soft silk cotton is obtained which is known by its trade name of *Kopok* fibre. Flacourtia Ramontchi, L'Herit., (Obir, Beng., Merlec, Sant.,) yields an edible fruit. *Dipterocarpaceæ.*—Shorea robusta, Gaertn., (Sāl, Sakhua, Beng., Sarjom, Sant.,) is a large gregarious tree yielding a heavy, strong, tough timber, which is valuable for all purposes where a smooth polished surface is not required. There seem to be two forms of this tree, the most prevalent having a dark-brown heart-wood, while that of the other is white slightly tinged with red. The fruit is eaten, the resin is used locally for several purposes but does not appear to be exported, the bark serves as a tan. This is the sacred tree of the Sonthals, the tribal deities being worshipped under its shade. —*Malvaceæ.* Is important for the number of fibre-yielding plants embraced in it. Bombax malabaricum, D.C., the cotton tree (Shimal, Beng., Edel, Sant.,) attains to a very large size. The wood is white and soft, and as broad planks can be had from it, it is in much request for doors. The seeds yield a fine silky cotton, which is in demand for stuffing, and large quantities are exported under the trade name of *Kopok* fibre. Kydia calycina, Roxb., is a large shrub or small tree from the bark of which a serviceable fibre is procured. Other wild *Malvaceæ* which yield fibre are mostly small shrubs, many of which, such as Thespasia Lampas, Dals. et Gibbs.; Abutilon indicum, Don.; Urena repanda, Roxb.; U. sinuāta, Linn.; U. lobata, Linn.; Sida mysurensis, Wight; S. carpinifolia Linn; S. rhombifolia, Linn., yield fibre deserving attention. *Sterculiaceæ* embraces many trees and shrubs among which the following are worthy of note:—Sterculia urens, Roxb. (Telhor, Beng., Telhec, Sant.), S. villosa, Roxb., (Udal, Beng. Ganjher, Sant.), and S. colorata, Roxb., are middle sized deciduous trees, all of which yield a very strong bast fibre. Helicteres Isora, Linn. (Maronphol, Beng., Petchamra, Sant.,) is a large shrub with a spirally twisted fruit, which is given medicinally in colic, etc. The bark yields a bast fibre. Pterospermum acerifolium, Willd. (Makchan, Beng., Machkunda, Sant.) is a tall ever-green tree, not very common, the large white flowers of which are used as a disinfectant. *Tiliaceæ*—Grewia hirsuta, Vahl. (Kukurbicha, Beng., Seta andir, Sant.), G. tiliæfolia, Vahl. (Jang olat Sant.), G. sapida, Roxb., var. Campbellii, Watt.; G. vestita, Wall., (Kœluta, Beng., Olat, Sant.), G. scabrophylla, Roxb., (Tarse kotap, Sant.), G. lævigata, Wall., are all shrubs or small trees. The timber of these which attain to the size of trees is remarkably strong, tough and light, and is used for purposes where these qualities are in request. All yield a strong bast fibre. *Rutaceæ.*—Ægle marmelos, Correa., (Bel, Beng., Sinjo, Sant.) is found wild and is also planted largely for its fruit, which possesses a high medicinal value. Feronia Elephantum, Correa (Katbel, Beng., Kochbel, Sant.) is not common, but probably indigenous. *Burseraceæ.*—Boswellia serrata, Roxb. (Salga, Beng., Sant.) yields an aromatic gum. Garuga pinnata, Roxb., (Kanwer, Sant.); Bursera serrata, Colebr. (Armu, Sant.), all three species are deciduous and the timber is of little value. *Meliaceæ* Azadirachta indica, A. Juss., Syn. Melia Azadirachta, Linn. (Nim, Beng., Sant,) a large evergreen tree naturalized all over the district. The seeds yield a medicinal oil. Melia Azadarach, Linn., (Bakain, Beng, Bokom, Sant.) the Persian Lilac. A middle-sized tree, not indigenous. Soymida febrifuga, Adr. Juss. (Rohan, Beng., Ruhen, Sant.), is a large tree with tall, straight trunk, heart-wood dark reddish-brown, and very durable. Cedrela Toona, Roxb., (Tun, Beng., Sant) yields a very fair timber for finer carpentry. *Olacineæ.*—Two species may be mentioned :—Olax scandens, Roxb., a small bush or climber; and O. nana, Wall., a medium-sized shrub. *Celastrineæ.*—Celastrus paniculatus, (Willd. Kujri, Beng, Sant.), the seeds of which yield a medicinal oil; Elæodendron Roxburghii, W. and A (Raj jehul, Beng, Neuri, Sant.) *Rhamneæ.*—Ventilago madras patana, Gaertn., Syn. Ventilago calyculata, Tulasne (Raerui-Beng., Bonga Sarjom, Sant.) is a large climber, the seeds of which yield an oil in taste approaching *ghee*, used for culinary purposes. The bark yields a bast fibre. There are four species of Zizyphus: Zizyphus Jujuba, Lam. (Kul bair, Beng., Jom, janum, dodhaori janum, Sant.). There are two forms of this, one cultivated, which grows to be a good sized tree, the fruit of which is very palatable, the other, the wild form, is a small gregarious bush, the fruit of which, though sour, is largely eaten. Zizyphus xylopyra, Willd. (Korkot, Beng., Karkat Sant.); Z. oxyphylla, Edgew., (Seakul Beng., Kurit rama, Sant.); Z. rugosa, Lam. (Sahra, Beng., Sahra, Sant.); all yield edible fruits.

Ampelideæ—Is represented by several genera, mostly climbing plants, with a few shrubs, none of which is of any economic value. *Sapindaceæ.*—Schleichera trijuga, Willd. (Kusum, Beng., Baru, Sant.), the only species of any importance in the district, is a large tree valued mainly for the oil yielded by its seeds and for the superior quality of lac procured from it.

Anacardiaceæ.—Odina Wodier, Roxb. (Kasmala, Beng., Doka, Sant.) is a large deciduous tree, the wood of which is said to be suitable for making bobbins. Spondias mangifera, Willd. (Amra, Beng. Sant.) the Hog-plum, is a large deciduous tree, fruit edible. Buchanania latifolia, Roxb. (Pial, piar, Beng. Tarop, Sant.) is a middle sized tree, the fruit and gum of which are eaten. Mangifera indica, Linn. (Am, Beng, Ul, Sant.) the mango tree; a large evergreen tree, apparently indigenous, but largely planted as groves near villages and on road sides The fruit of the cultivated tree is highly esteemed, but that of the wild is sour and stringy. Semecarpus Anacardium, Linn. f., var. cuneifolia (Bhelwa, Beng., Soso, Sant.) the marking nut tree. The drupe is about one inch in length, the pericarp is full of an acrid juice, which takes the place of marking ink, the hypocarp when ripe is of a bright orange colour and is edible. *Moringeæ.*—Moringa pterygosperma, Gaertn. (Sogna sag, Beng., Munga arak, Sant.) the Horse raddish tree. This small tree does not seem to be indigenous, but is largely cultivated, leaves, flowers and fruit eaten

Leguminosæ - Is represented by a large number of genera and species comprising many large timber trees, but the majority are shrubs or climbers. There are five species of Crotalaria; two of Indigofera; seven of Desmodium; one of Ouginia, O. Dalbergioides, Benth.; one of Abrus, A. precatorius, Linn.; one of Mucuna; one of Erythrina, E. indica, Lam.; one of Pueraria; one of Spatholobus, S Roxburghii, Benth., a large climber yielding a strong bast fibre; two of Butea, B. frondosa, Roxb., (Palas, Beng., Murup, Sant.), a fairly large tree, gregarious in its habits, noted for its brilliant orange, red flowers, and as a large producer of lac. B. superba, Roxb, a large climber with flowers of a flaring orange colour, larger than those of B. frondosa; three species of Flemingia, all small shrubs; three of Dalbergia, D. lanceolaria, Linn. (Siris, Beng., Chapot Siris, Sant.), D. latifolia, Roxb. (Sotsal, Beng., Satsayar, Sant), both large deciduous trees yielding good timber; D. volubilis, Roxb., a large scrambling shrub; one of Pterocarpus, P. marsupium Roxb. (Murga, Beng., Murga Sant.) a large deciduous tree with a brownish heart wood; one of Pongamia, P. glabra, Vent (Kurunj, Beng., Sant.) probably introduced into the district, but has been long naturalized, seeds yield a useful oil and fruits edible; one species of Tamarindus, T. indica, Linn (Tetul, Beng., Jojo, Sant.) yielding an edible fruit; of Cassia five, C. Fistula, Linn. (Bandarlœ, Beng., Nuruic, Sant.), flowers in large pendulous racemes of a bright yellow, known as the Indian Laburnam; of Bauhinia seven, B. malabarica, Roxb., B purpurea Linn., B. variegata, Linn., B. retusa, Ham., B acuminata, Linn., B. racemosa. Lam., B. vahlii, Wight et Arn., the first six species are medium sized trees, the last is a gigantic climber (Chikor, Beng., Lamak lar, Jom lar, Sant), yielding an excellent bast fibre and an edible bean; one of Adenanthera, A. pavonia, Linn., not indigenous; of Mimosa, one, M. rubicaulis, Lam.; of Acacia, five, A. Farnesiana, Willd., A. pennata, Willd., A. cæsia, Willd., A. Catechu, Willd., A. arabica, Willd.; Of Albizzia four, A. myriophylla, Bl., A. odoratissisma, Benth., A. Lebbek, Benth.,

A. procera, Benth. (commonly known in the ver. as Siris), all large trees yielding excellent timber; *Combretaceæ.*—The most important are Terminalia belerica, Roxb. (Behra, Beng., Lopong Sant.); T. Chebula, Retz. (Harla, Beng., Rol. Sant.) yields the myrabolams of commerce; T. tomentosa, W. et Arn. (Asan, Beng., Atnak, Sant.), Tasar silkworm is largely reared on this species; T. Arjuna, Bedd. (Arjun, Beng., Kauha, Sant.) all four species are large trees and are very common. *Myrtaceæ.*—The principal are Eugenia operculata, Roxb., E. Jambolana, Lam. (Jamun, Beng., So kod, Sant.), E. caryophyllifolia, Lmk., all yield edible fruits; Barringtonia acutangula, Gærtn., (Kumia Beng., Hinjor, Sant.); Carea arborea, Roxb. (Kumbhir, Beng., Kumbir, Sant.). *Lythraceæ*—The most important species are Lagerstrœmia parviflora, Roxb. (Sidha, Beng., Sokroe, Sant.), a large gregarious tree, which coppices well, the gum is edible. Lawsonia alba, Lam. (Mihendi, Beng., Sant.), a shrub never found in a wild state, makes a good hedge, the leaves yield the "henna" dye which is used to colour the skin and hair. Woodfordia floribunda, Salisb. (Dhatki, Beng., Ichak, Sant.) a small bush, which is extensively used in house-building, being placed above the rafters to support the thatch. The flowers yield a dye and, before the aniline dyes were introduced, were exported in large quantities to Patna and Cawnpore. *Samydaceæ.*—Casearia tomentosa, Roxb. (Chorcho, Beng., Sant.), a small tree, the fruit is employed to poison fish. *Cornaceæ.*—Alangium Lamarckii, Thws. (Akura, Beng., Dhela, Sant.), a small deciduous tree, with a hard, close and even-grained heartwood. *Rubiaceæ*—Embraces about 18 genera, of which the following are the most important:—Anthocephalus Cadamba, Miq. (Kadam, Beng., Sant.), a large deciduous tree of rapid growth, the fruit is eaten and the flowers offered in worship. Adina cordifolia, Hook. f. and Benth., (Karam, Beng., Sant.), a large deciduous tree, a branch of which is fixed by the Hindus in the courtyard of the house during the observance of the *Karam* festival. Sonthals also dance round a branch of it at their *Karam* festival. Stephegyne parvifolia, Korth, syn. Nauclea parvifolia, Willd. (Gulikodom, Beng., Gore, Sant.), a large deciduous tree, the bark of which yields a good bast fibre. Hymenodictyon excelsum, Wall. (Bhorkond, Beng., Sant.), a large deciduous tree, the inner bark of which is in repute as a febrifuge. Wendlandia tinctoria, D. C. and W. exserta, D.C., are small bushes, fairly common, but without any economic value. Gardenia latifolia, Ait. (Pepra, Beng., Popro, Sant.), a small deciduous tree whose fruit is edible. There are two species of Randia, R. dumetorum,

Lamk., and R. uliginosa, D.C., both small trees which yield edible fruits. Canthium didymum, Roxb. (Garbagoja, Beng., Garbhagoja, Sant.), is a small or medium-sized tree with no particular economic use. Pavetta indica, Linn., and P. indica, Linn., var. tomentosa, Roxb., are small bushes. Ixora parviflora, Vahl., is a common, but, from an economic point of view, an unimportant tree. Morinda tinctoria, Roxb., syn. M. exserta, Roxb. (Chaili, Beng., Sant.) is a moderate sized deciduous tree seldom, if ever found in a purely wild state. This at one time was a most important tree as the bark of the root was extensively used to dye yellow and red. There are five species of Oldenlandia, all small unimportant shrubs with the exception of O. corymbosa, Linn., which is the Madras red dye known as chey root in commerce. There are several other plants belonging to this order, but they serve no economic uses and are not therefore noted. *Compositæ.*—A large number of plants found in the district belong to this order, but as all are herbs or shrubs with little economic value they are passed over. *Myrsineæ.*—Embelia robusta, Roxb., is a large shrub or small tree, with wood of a reddish hue.

Sapotaceæ.—Bassia latifolia, Roxb. (Mahua, Mahul, Beng., Matkom, Sant.) is a very large deciduous tree with reddish-brown, very hard heartwood. The timber is used for many purposes, but it is not lightly cut down. The flowers are an important article of food. When dry they store well, keeping in good condition for a very long time. The trees in most villages are divided among the ryots in proportion to the area they cultivate, but landless labourers generally are in possession of one or more trees. When the owner does not collect the produce himself, he as a rule engages another to do so, allowing him sometimes a third and sometimes a half thereof in return for his labour in collecting. *Mahua* is cooked and eaten by preference along with rice or rice water. Eaten alone it is said not to digest readily. A coarse spirit distilled from *Mahua* is the liquor most generally consumed in the district. The fruit (Kochra, Beng., Kuindi, Sant.) when unripe is eaten as a vegetable cooked. When ripe the pulp is only eaten. It is generally infested by a small white worm and can only be consumed by the less fastidious. The kernel of the fruit yields an oil which is used for culinary purposes, for lamps and anointing the person. To extract the oil the kernels are split and dried in the sun. They are then pounded into coarse flour in the *dhenki*, put into an airtight basket and steamed. The material is then wrapped up tightly and carefully with *sabee* grass and placed in the press which is worked with a lever. The oil as it readily solidifies is often used to adulterate *ghee*.

Ebenaceæ.—Three or four species of Diospyros are found within the district, the most important being Diospyros tomentosa, Roxb., which some botanists include in Diospyros Melanoxylon, Roxb. (Kend, Beng., Terel, Sant.), a small or medium sized tree never entirely leafless. The heartwood is very dark coloured, resembling ebony in hardness, and is considered to be of great value. The fruit when fully ripe is very palatable. *Styraceæ* —Symplocos racemosa, Roxb. (Lodh, Beng., Lodam, Sant.), is a small tree, the leaves and bark of which are used in dyeing. *Oleaceæ.*—Nyctanthes arbortristis, Linn. (Sitik, Beng., Saparom, Sant.), is a large shrub or small tree, generally gregarious in dry situations. It is sometimes cultivated on account of the fragrance of its flowers which open in the evening and drop off at sunrise. Jasminum arborescens, Roxb., is a scandent shrub frequenting the vicinity of streams. *Apocinaceæ.*—Carissa Carandas, Linn., Alstonia scholaris, R. Br., Holarrhena antidysenterica, Wall., Wrightia tomentosa, R. and S., Nerium odorum, Soland., Thevetia Neriifolia, Jus., are probably the most important species. *Asclepiadeæ.*—Calotropis gigantea, R. Br. (Akand, Beng., Akaona, Sant), a common gregarious bush, in flower all the year round. Its inner bark gives a fibre of fine silky texture, which is very strong and is used for bow strings, etc. The seeds are surrounded by silky hair which is used for stuffing pillows, the root is used to dye with. Calotropis procera, R. Br., fibre, silk from the seeds, and root are used in the same way as those of C. gigantea. Dregea volubilis, Benth., is a twining shrub, which yields an extremely strong fibre, from which Brāhmans make the *poita* or sacred thread. *Boragineæ.*—Cordia Myxa Linn.) Buch, Beng., Buch, Sant.), and C. Macleodii, H. F. and T. (Jugia, Sant.), are medium sized trees, the wood is valued for the purpose of making cattle yokes. Ehretia lævis, Roxb. (Pusi pan, Sant.), is a middle sized tree, of no particular economic use. *Convolvulaceæ.*—Ipomæa is represented by seven species. Erycibe paniculata, Roxb., is the only species which attains to any size, the others are herbs. *Solanaceæ.*—Datura fastuosa, Linn. (Dhatura, Beng., Sant.) is common, growing on waste places. Solanum xanthocarpum, Schrad. et Wendl., is a common procumbent thorny plant. *Scrophularineæ.*—There are two species of Torenia, one of Vandellia, two of Ilysanthes, one of Sopubia, one of Bonnaya, three of Limnophylla, one of Dopatrium, etc. *Bignonaceæ.*—Oroxylum indicum, Benth. (Sonae, Beng., Bana hatak, Sant.), a small tree remarkable for its long, flat, sword-like capsule and large flowers. The bark and fruit are used in tanning and dyeing. Stereospermum suaveolens, D. C. (Padal, Beng., Pader, Sant.) is a large deciduous tree, the wood of which is durable and easy to work. The tree is not common. *Acanthaceæ.*—Contains mostly herbs, among which the following are represented :—Barleria, Dædalacanthus, Strobilanthes, Ruellia, Peristrophe, Hemigraphis. Hygrophila, Rungia, Andrographis, etc., etc. *Verbenaceæ.*—Vitex Negundo, Linn. (Sindwari, Beng., Sinduari, Sant.), is a large shrub or small tree. V. piduncularis, Wall., Syn. Vitex alata, Roxb. (Bhade, Beng., Bhadu, Marak, Sant.), is a middle sized tree, with a hard, close grained timber. Gomelina arborea, Linn. (Gamhar, Beng., Kasmar, Sant.) is a large quick growing deciduous tree, with a close and even-grained wood, which is used largely in making the finer parts of palanquins. Two species of Callicarpa, two of Premna, and five of Clerodendron are found within our area. *Labiatæ.*—There are several plants belonging to this genus found in the district, but all are herbaceous. Three species of Leucas afford food in times of famine. *Amarantaceæ.*—Represented only by herbs, but these are important from an economic point of view as they afford sustenance to the poor in times of scarcity. The following may be noted in this connection :—Celocia argenta, Moq., Ærua lanata Linn., Amarantus gangeticus, Linn., Digera arvensis, Forsk., and Acternanthera sessilis, R. Br. *Polygonaceæ.*—With the exception of Polygonum glabrum, Willd., the leaves of which are used as a pot-herb, this contains no species of any importance.

Urticaceæ.—This contains many valuable species, but there is space only for the following :—Artocarpus integrifolia, Linn. (Kathal, Beng., Kanthar, Sant.), the jack tree is a large evergreen tree planted extensively for its fruit which is highly valued. The wood which is durable and takes a fine polish is largely employed for all kinds of carpentry. A. Lakoocha, Roxb., (Dahua, Beng., Dahu, Sant.), is a large tree, the male flower buds and fruit are eaten. Ficus bengalensis, Linn. (Bor, Beng., Bare, Sant.), the banyan, is a large evergreen tree, which throws down aerial roots from the branches, the fruit is eaten, and the wood which is of little value is mainly used to make solid cart wheels. F. infectoria, Willd. (Pakare, Beng., Sant.), F. religiosa, Linn., (Pipar, pipal, Beng., Hesak, Sant.), F. cordifolia, Roxb., (Sunum jor, Sant.), F. Cunia, Buch. (Bhoka dumbar, Beng., Horpodo, Sant.), F. glomerata, Roxb. (Dumbor, Beng., Loa, Sant.), F. tomentosa, Willd. (Chapakia baro, Sant.), F. scandens, Roxb. yield edible fruits. *Euphorbiaceæ.*—The more important species are Phyllanthus Emblica, Linn. (Aura, Beng., Meral, Sant.), P. multilocularis Mull. Arg. Putranjiva Roxburghii, Wall., Briodelia retusa, Spreng. (Kadrupala, Beng., Karke, Sant.), Croton oblongifolius, Roxb. (Putol, Beng., Goto, Sant.), and Mallotus philippinensis, Mull. Arg. (Rohra, Beng., Rora Sant.). This latter is a gregarious shrub or small tree and yields the *kamela* dye of commerce. *Palmæ.*—Borassus flabelliformis, Linn. (Tal, Beng., Tale, Sant.), the palmyra palm, and Phœnix sylvestris, Roxb., (Khajur, Beng., Khijur Sant.), the wild date palm, are the only species indigenous to the district. The palmyra palm seems to flourish everywhere, but the wild date palm does not grow so readily in all situations.

Gramineæ.—Of these the first to be noted is Dendrocalamus strictus, Nees. (Bans, Beng., Mat, Sant.), the male bamboo. This is apparently the only bamboo indigenous to Manbhum. Bambusa Tulda, Roxb., (Ropa bans, Beng., ropa mat, Sant.), the bamboo of Bengal, clumps of this bamboo are becoming increasingly frequent in the vicinity of villages. It grows readily when transplanted and is a source of considerable profit to the villagers. Of fodder grasses the best known is Cynodon Dactylon, Pers. (Dub, Beng., Dhobighas Sant.), Pollinia eriopoda, Hance. (Baboe, saboe, Beng., Bachkom, Sant.). The supply of this grass from wild sources being limited owing to the decrease of jungle it is now being largely cultivated. It is used for all kinds of rough twine and cordage and is of very great importance. Cattle eat it when young. A species of Aristida (Bhalki, Beng., kharang, Sant.), supplies the material from which house brooms are made. Heteropogon contortus, R. & S. (Khar, Kher, Beng. Sauri, Sant.), (is the principal thatching grass of the district. It grows to a height of two feet or over and lasts longer than rice straw. Andropogon muricatus, Retz. (Bena, Beng., Sirom, Sant.) is common, found in moist situations. The fragrant roots known under the name of *khaskhas* are used in the manufacture of *tatties*. The brush (Konch) with which a weaver applies starch to the warp of a web is made from the roots of this grass. Besides these there are many others in the plains and hills comprising species of Andropogon, Setaria, Pennisetum, Panicum, Paspalum, Eragrostis, Oplismenus, Perotis, Spondiopogon, Chrysopogon, Pollinia, Eleusine, Apluda, Sporobolus, Agrostis, Chloris, Aristida, Pogonatherum, Elytrophorus, Leersia, Ischæmum, Heteropogon, Isachne, Arundinella and others.

unua. Though the physical features of the district resemble so closely those of the adjoining districts of Chota Nāgpur, and though it shared till comparatively recent times their reputation as a happy hunting ground, this reputation is no longer deserved, and, speaking generally, the district is now singularly destitute of wild animals and game of all descriptions. The causes are not far to seek; cultivation and the clearing of jungles for this purpose has widely extended during the last 20 years, and denudation of the jungles, even where the land is not required or suitable for cultivation, almost as if not more, rapidly. Moreover, the Sonthal population has rapidly increased, and, as is well known, their hunting habits very quickly denude the country in their immediate neighbourhood of all small and ground game, both fur and feathered, deer, pig and hare, and birds, both game and non-game, and in the absence of their natural food the larger carnivorous animals must necessarily die out or remove to more favoured parts. It is possible now to travel through and to beat miles of jungle covered hill and see not a single head of game of any description; country eminently fitted for the smaller varieties of deer, for wild pig, for hare, for partridge, the jungle fowl or the pea fowl is untenanted save by the squirrel and the owl, and the natural habitation of the tiger, the leopard and the bear may, perchance, produce a stray hyæna or jackal. The larger game that are still occasionally seen or shot are the exception. Wild elephants have within recent years been seen in the jungles on the Dalma range in the south, visitors no doubt from Dhalbhum, where a small herd is known to survive. A stray tiger or two occasionally kill in the same area, or in the hills south of Pātkum, or on the Bāghmundi range, and within the last few years several visitors from the Hazāribagh jungles have been shot near Jhalda. Leopards (felis pardus) are somewhat less rare in the same areas, and are also met with at times in the jungles which run up the banks of the Kāsai river through Parganas Māubhum and Kāsaipar. They are also to be found, as also a very occasional tiger, on the Tundi range and on the foot hills of Parasnāth in the north. Other felines are represented by two or more varieties of wild cat, specimens of which though rarely seen are probably fairly numerous.

During the ten years ending 1908, 65 human beings and 2,181 cattle were reported to have been killed by tigers and leopards, and rewards were paid for the destruction of 3 tigers and 79 leopards.

The bear—the common black or sloth bear—is rather more common, and is still to be found in most of the wooded hills on the north, west and south of the district. On the Tundi and

Parasnāth hills on the north they must at one time have been very numerous as it is on record that one Sub-divisional Officer, who was at Gobindpur for several years in the eighties, shot over a hundred. During the ten years ending 1908, 11 human beings and 57 cattle were killed by bears and 45 bears were brought in for reward.

Wolves are said to be fairly numerous on and near the Pānchet hill, and are practically the sole relic of wild game in that neighbourhood; they are also met fairly frequently in other hilly and jungly parts of the district. Hyænas are to be found in the same regions and are apparently somewhat more numerous. Wolves and hyænas accounted during the last ten years for 16 human beings and 3,312 cattle and rewards were paid for the destruction of 45 wolves and 273 hyænas.

Jackals are, of course, numerous, but not nearly so common as might be expected from the general appearance of the country.

Of herbivorous quadrupeds the Sambar is almost extinct except on the Parasnāth and Dalma ranges where occasional specimens are seen; the spotted deer survives in certain more or less preserved jungles near Jhalda, Bāghmundi and Mánbazar, and a small herd is said to exist still in the jungles surrounding some low hills north-west of Balarampur. The barking deer is found occasionally in the same areas and in the Dalma range. The *chinkara* is practically unknown, and the four-horned antelope hardly survives except in the preserved jungles of the Pānchet zamindar near Kesargarh.

Wild pig are rarely to be found except in the dense jungles adjoining the Parasnāth and Dalma ranges; they do considerable damage to the crops grown on small patches of cleared land in and near the jungles, but in the struggle for survival they have little chance against the Sonthal or the Bhumij. The langur (*Semnopithecus entillus*) is to be found in the hills near Jhalda and elsewhere at various places but in no great numbers. One tribe or family visits Purūlia in the mango season and does some damage to the little fruit there is, until driven away.

The Indian fox is common throughout the district. The short-tailed Indian pangolin (*Manis crassicaudata*) an animal almost peculiar to this and the Singhbhum district of which a picturesque account is given in Hunter's Statistical Account of the district is not yet extinct though but rarely seen; a specimen was killed in Purūlia in 1907 while attempting to burrow its way into the local Post Office, and after seriously frightening the whole postal establishment. More recently another specimen was captured near Dhānbāid. Hares are very rare except where there are large areas of scrub jungle and broken ground, their habits making them a very easy prey for the aboriginal tribes, armed with bows, sticks or stones.

The game birds of Mānbhum are few in number and variety; jungle, spur, and pea fowl can now but rarely be found and only in the wildest parts of the district; the grey partridge is fairly common in suitable country, the black is only very occasionally seen. Pigeon, both rock and green, are fairly common. Of cold weather visitors the snipe is the most numerous, and from November till May a wisp or two can usually be found in the rice fields immediately below most *bandhs*. Towards the end of the season when suitable grounds are less numerous and of smaller area it is possible to get a fair bag. Wild geese resort regularly to the beds of the larger rivers, the Dāmodar, Kāsai and Subarnarekha, and a fair number of duck and teal are to be found on the larger *bandhs* throughout the district particularly in the later months of the season. The most common varieties are the common or blue winged teal, the pintail, the white-eyed, common and red-crested pochards, the gadwal and the shoveller; whistling teal both great and lesser are found occasionally and a fair number of cotton teal stay through the year on some of the larger tanks, near which there is cover for their breeding. Mānbhum is mentioned by Mr. E C. Stuart Baker* among the habitat of the Nullah teal or comb-bill, but no specimen has been seen or shot of recent years. Golden plovers are seen occasionally in considerable flights on the high *tanr* lands where also the common plover is fairly common. Of other birds the most common are the crow, the *maina*, the sparrow and the paddy-bird. Game Birds.

Many of the tanks and irrigation bandhs are regularly stocked with fry of the *rui*, *mirgel* and *katla* species, and various small species are to be found in almost every piece of water. *Hilsa* and *bachwa* are caught in the Dāmodar and Subarnarekha during the rains and both these rivers are said to contain mahseer. Fish.

Snakes are not specially numerous; of the poisonous varieties the cobra and the karait are fairly common; of others the most frequently seen is the *dhaman* which grows to a considerable size. In the hilly areas an occasional python is met with; and various harmless and grass snakes are generally common. During the ten years ending in 1908, 1,022 persons were reported to have been killed by snakes, and 3,859 snakes were destroyed. Reptiles.

* The Indian Ducks and their Allies. Bombay, 1908.

Climate. The climate is generally much drier than that of Eastern Bengal, though less so than that of the plateau of Chota Nāgpur proper. From early in March till the end of May or the beginning of June hot westerly winds ordinarily prevail, and the heat during the day is oppressive, the thermometer in the shade constantly rising as high as 110° and not infrequently several degrees higher. Towards evening the west wind usually drops, or dies away altogether, and there is a considerable fall in temperature. The nights during March are still cold, during April usually bearable, but towards the end of May the minimum night temperature is frequently above 90°. Occasional relief is afforded during these months by nor'-westers, which, even when not accompanied by rain, reduce the temperature by several degrees, and relieve the general feeling of oppression With June the wind veers to the south or east, the actual temperature drops, but the air becomes saturated with moisture, and, until the rain actually comes, the climate is unpleasant in the extreme.

During the rains which normally set in about the middle of June, and last till the middle of September, the climate is on the whole pleasant; the country being naturally well-drained, and the soil mainly composed of sand and gravel, the air is comparatively dry in the intervals between the rain, and the sultry, damp and steamy atmosphere of a Bengal district at the same season of the year is comparatively uncommon.

The end of September with a hot midday sun and the air still moist is fairly trying, but with October cooler currents of air from the north and west set in, and by the end of the month the cold weather is ordinarily well established.

From November to mid February the days are not unpleasantly warm, and the nights cool; the air is ordinarily dry and bracing, and a healthier or more enjoyable climate could hardly be wished for. Extreme cold is rare, and frost except on the higher hills practically unknown.

The range of temperature during the year is considerable. The mean maximum temperature, which is between 76° and 79° during December and February, rises to 89° in March, and in April and May to 103°. Throughout the rains it averages about 90° dropping to 88° in October and 84° in November.

The mean minimum temperature varies from as low as 52° in January to 79° in June, the mean for the cold weather months being about 58° and for the hot weather 76°. The mean temperature for the year is 77°.

RAINFALL.

The average monthly rainfall from seven reporting stations (Purūlia, Gobindpur, Raghunâthpur, Barâbhum, Jhalda, Chās and Pāndra) is shown in the annexed statement. Besides these there are registering stations more recently established at Manbazar, Bandwân, Kailāpal, and Dhânbâid. Between the different stations the differences are not very marked, the total rainfall of the year varying only between 49½ and 55½ inches.

Statement showing the average rainfall month by month for each reporting station.

Serial No.	Name of rain reporting stations.	AVERAGE RAINFALL MONTH BY MONTH.												
		January.	February.	March.	April.	May.	June.	July.	August.	September.	October.	November.	December.	Total.
1	Purūlia ...	0·44	1·02	0·98	0·99	2·94	10·09	12·23	12·26	8·14	3·24	0·24	0·18	52·77
2	Gobindpur ...	0·59	0·80	0·[illegible]7	0·69	2·60	9·34	14·12	13·40	8·92	3·49	0·22	0·16	55·19
3	Raghunāthpur	0·47	0·54	0·74	0·75	3·60	7·47	13·25	12·78	7·95	1·72	0·47	0·06	49·77
4	Barābhum ...	0·25	0·65	0·94	1·32	2·61	10·04	12·92	11·78	9·36	2·3[illegible]	0·53	0·13	53·67
5	Jhalda ...	0·49	0·80	1·23	1·30	2·58	10·21	12·56	15·00	7·06	2·71	0·27	0·14	55·20
6	Chās ...	0·63	0·48	0·74	1·07	2·74	8·06	12·13	12·46	8·34	2·43	0·32	0·14	49·54
7	Pāndra ...	0·41	0·78	0·33	1·00	3·25	11·00	12·51	11·86	8·94	2·09	0·14	0·04	52·33
		0·46	0·73	0·81	1·01	2·80	9·68	12·80	12·78	8·51	2·58	0·31	0·12	52·85

As might be anticipated, the rainfall is heaviest near the hilly areas in the north, west and south, and lightest in the comparatively level central area. In respect of variation from year to year the range is considerable; just under 100 inches were recorded at Gobindpur in 1893, in which year the average for the district was 73½ inches; two years later, in 1895, the average fall was only 34½ inches, and in 1896 barely 37 inches.

The cold and hot weather rains are usually very light, less than 3½ inches being ordinarily precipitated in the six months, November to April. The fall in May averages just under 3 inches, and the burst of the monsoon in June gives some 9½ inches; July and August with nearly 13 inches each are the wettest months; in September the fall averages about 8½ inches, and the final effort of the monsoon gives another 2½ inches in October. It is this final rain which in an otherwise normal year makes the difference between a full and an average, or even a comparatively poor crop.

APPENDIX TO CHAPTER I.

GEOLOGY.

E. W. Vredenburg.

General Features.

Geological constitution of the district.

From the point of view of the geologist Mānbhum can be divided from north to south into three successive belts, each of which stretches across the entire width of the district in an east and west direction. The northern belt is occupied mainly by the two great coal-basins of Rāniganj and Jharia, separated by an intervening area of crystalline rocks. The middle belt, which is broadest, is occupied almost exclusively by crystalline rocks The southern belt includes a series of ancient slates with associated volcanic rocks belonging to the group of rocks known to Indian geologists as the Dhārwār System.

Consequently the district includes a very great variety of different rocks, and it is a patchwork of formations which differ widely in age, in structure, and in history. The crystalline gneisses and the sedimentary Dhārwārs belong to the oldest formations known in India. They have been extensively disturbed and altered since their original formation. The rocks of the coal-basins in the northern belt of the district are less ancient and belong partly to the end of the period known to geologists as the "primary" or "palæozoic", partly to the beginning of the succeeding period known as "secondary" or "mesozoic". They constitute a portion of the group of rocks classified by Indian geologists as the "Gondwāna System" which consists of fluviatile sandstones and shales with intercalated coal-seams. These rocks have not been subjected to disturbances and alteration to the same extent as the older gneisses and Dhārwārs, and being usually far less indurated than those older formations, would have been mostly denuded away were it not that they have been let in amongst the older rocks

Faulted fractures.

along a series of faulted fractures, some of which indicate an enormous amount of subsidence.

The faulted fractures which affect the Gondwāna rocks of the coalfields are the latest disturbances of this kind which one observes in the district. Evidence of older faulted fractures abound in the gneissose and Dhārwār areas.

Absence of well-marked topographical features.

The extreme variety and checkered geological history of the rocks of this district are only very feebly expressed by its topographical features. Most of the structural features of the rocks exhibit an east and west trend; but this structure has very little influence upon the direction of the lines of drainage, most of which flow obliquely to the strike of the rocks, and are scarcely deflected to any appreciable extent when they pass from one formation to another. Some of the great structural faults are of enormous "throw", for instance, that forming the southern border of the Rāniganj coalfield which represents a subsidence of the Gondwāna strata of nearly two miles. Yet these great fractures are without any effect on the topography.

The only rivers whose course has been materially influenced by the nature and structure of the rocks are the Dāmodar, and to a minor extent some of its tributaries where they traverse the Gondwāna basins, as will be explained when dealing with the structure of the coal-fields.

It is the protracted denudation to which the region has been subject that accounts for the want of correspondence generally observed between its structural features and the directions of drainage. The district has been a dry land area subjected to atmospheric weathering and denudation since a very early geological period, and it has not been subjected to any earth-crust movements capable of influencing appreciably the shape of its surface since the completion of the great faulted fractures that limit the Gondwāna areas. These date back to a time previous to the close of the secondary era, and most parts of the earth's surface that have been dry land from so early a geological time have had the irregularities of their topography similarly reduced: the great mountain ranges, such as the Alps and Himalayas, owe their strong relief to the fact that they were uplifted only at a late period of the Tertiary era. In the case of a region subjected to denudation since a very early date, like that of Mānbhum, the

Long-continued sub-aerial denudation.

levelling action of denudation has been so protracted that, with the exception of a general seaward slope towards the Bay of Bengal, the only differences of level observed are due to relative differences in hardness of the rocks, without any reference to former movements of upheaval or subsidence. The extent to which the present topographical features are disconnected from the former geological history of the region is well illustrated in the case of Pānchet hill, and a few other hills along the southern border of the Rāniganj coal-fields. They owe their present relief to the fact they consist of hard sandstones and conglomerates that have resisted denudation better than the softer surrounding rocks; yet they occur on the downthrow side of one of the greatest faulted fractures of the district, and have sunk to a depth of almost two miles relatively to the older crystalline rocks which they overlook on their southern aspect. Ages of denudation have so equalised the level of the surface on the downthrow and upthrow sides of the fault that it is the sunken portion that now exhibits the strongest relief.

Topography depending solely on differences of hardness of rocks.

The other outstanding hills of the district all owe their preservation similarly to the relative hardness of the rocks constituting them; such are Dalma hill, at the southern border of the district, consisting of a great mass of "epidiorite"; Parasnāth hill, whose lower spurs touch the north-western edge of the district, consisting of a compact augite-enstatite granulite similar to the pyroxene granulites of the "Nilgiri gneiss" that constitute the loftiest hills in Southern India: the Bāghmundi plateau in the south-western part of the district, consisting of compact granite or granitite gneiss.

Structure of Gondwāna basins.

The geological formation that has attracted more attention than any other owing to its economic importance is the coal-bearing Gondwāna formation which occupies the Rāniganj and Jharia coalfields in the northern belt of the district. The Gondwāna rocks consist essentially of a succession of fluviatile sandstones and shales with intercalated coal-seams, which exhibit a general southerly dip, in such a manner that the oldest beds outcrop at the northern edge of the coal-basins, and the newest beds at its southern edge, where the succession is abruptly interrupted by the great structural fault that constitutes the main southern boundary of each of the coalfields. With few exceptions the Gondwāna rocks are moderately indurated and easily denuded away, and, owing to this relatively easy weathering, the larger channels of drainage have established themselves on their surface more easily than on the adjoining rocks. This is why the course of the largest river of the region, the Dāmodar, coincides with the position of the coal-basins. Moreover, the general southerly dip of the coal-bearing strata has had the effect of constantly displacing the main channel towards the south, so that the Dāmodar generally follows at a short distance the main southern faulted boundary of the coal-fields. Similar features are observed in all the coal-basins of India, which always exhibit the same unsymmetrical structure as the Rāniganj and Jharia basins, and almost invariably have their main boundary fault approximately coinciding with a great channel of drainage: a conspicuous instance is that of the Gondwāna basin of the lower Godāvari.

Influence of Gondwāna rocks on drainage.

In addition to the three great systems of rocks that make up the Mānbhum district, that is, the Gondwāna, the crystalline gneisses and the Dhārwār slates, there are numerous igneous intrusions varying in composition from acid (highly siliceous) to basic (comparatively poor in silica, but rich in lime, iron, and magnesia). The basic intrusions being more easily recognised have more particularly attracted attention, and generally have the shape of elongated linear vertical "dykes" representing fissures that have been filled up from below with a molten material of volcanic origin. Some of these basic intrusions are of very ancient date, almost or quite as old as the Dhārwār slates, and are probably contemporaneous with the ancient "basic" rocks of Dalma hill They are observed principally in the gneiss areas, and having shared in the disturbance that has affected the gneiss and the Dhārwār slates, they have been affected by alterations which considerably disguise the original character of their minerals. The later set of basic dykes is contemporaneous with the volcanic eruptions of the Rājmahal hills in Bengal. They are posterior to the latest dislocations that have affected the region, and except where acted upon by atmospheric weathering close to the surface, are quite unaltered. They are observed cutting through the Gondwāna rocks and also through the surrounding crystalline rocks, but are much more abundant within the Gondwāna areas than through the surrounding country because the soft Gondwāna sandstones and shales have afforded an easier path to the injected material than the harder surrounding crystalline rocks

Intrusive rocks.

The main structural features of the district as expressed by the strike of the rocks are directed from east to west, with some subsidiary deflections to north-west and south-east. The same directions are reflected in the faulted fractures so frequent

Structural directions.

throughout the district: the main directions of faulting are also east-west and north-west to south-east. Both directions are conspicuously exhibited in the main faults of the Rāniganj coalfields. Both inside and outside the coalfields, the north-west to south-east direction is that most frequently followed by the great intrusive dolerite dykes of Rājmahal age.

Fault-rock.

One of the most noteworthy rocks of Mānbhum, not from its bulk but for its wide distribution, is a peculiar siliceous and sometimes ferruginous rock which accompanies lines of faulting.

The Gondwāna Coalfields.

Though occupying less superficial extent than the gneiss and Dhārwār formations, the Gondwāna is the most important of the geological formations represented in Mānbhum on account of the immense value of its associated coal seams. Indian geologists have divided the Gondwāna system into a lower, a middle, and an upper series, of which the two first-named are exhibited in the Mānbhum coalfields.

The Gondwāna rocks occurring in Mānbhum include the following subdivisions:—

Middle Gondwāna	Kāmthi.	
	Pānchet.	
Lower Gondwāna	Dāmodar	Rāniganj.
		Ironestone shales.
		Barākhar.
	Tālcher.	

Tālcher stage.

The Tālcher subdivision is of moderate and rather uniform thickness, about 500 to 800 feet. It consists of fine-grained arenaceous shales of greenish grey, more rarely of red colour, and fine-grained soft sandstones, greenish-grey or reddish, consisting of quartz and undecomposed felspar. The shales are greatly jointed and break up into angular, often pencil-shaped, fragments. They are frequently calcareous. The sandstones are somewhat thickly, though distinctly, bedded, occasionally interstratified with shales, and often break up into cubic pieces for which reason they have received the name of "tesselated sandstones." The sandstones usually predominate in the upper portion of the Tālchers, there being a gradual increase in the coarseness of the sediments as one ascends through the section. Pebbles of various dimensions, sometimes reaching the size of large boulders, are frequently scattered through the fine shales or mudstones towards the base of the series, and constitute the Tālcher "boulder-beds." The pebbles often consist of rocks that do not occur in the neighbourhood of the Tālcher exposures in which they are found, and which must have been carried from a distance by glaciers. Similar indications of extensive glaciation have been detected in many other parts of the world amongst rocks of the same geological age as the Tālchers, that is, belonging to the passage zone between "Carboniferous" and "Permian." At that period the world must have passed through an ice-age somewhat similar to the one which immediately preceded the present era.

Boulder-beds.

Permian ice-age.

The Tālcher beds are usually barren of coal-seams. The lower strata of the Tālcher shales are unfossiliferous, as though, at the time they were deposited, the climate were still too severe for a luxurious development of vegetable life. The upper strata of the Tālcher are sometimes fossiliferous and contain a flora which is markedly dfferent from that of the overlying Dāmodar, the leading forms being various species of a fossil fern known as *Gangamopteris*.

Tālcher fossils.

In the Rāniganj and Jharia coalfields, the Tālcher is succeeded with varying degrees of overlap and unconformity by the coal-measures of the Dāmodar division. The Dāmodar stage is most completely represented in the Rāniganj coalfield which may be taken as the type for this division, the differences in other areas consisting principally in the absence or less complete development of the newer sub-stages.

Dāmodar stage.

The three sub-stages exhibited in the Rāniganj field are in ascending order, the Barākhar, ironstone shales, and Rāniganj.

The Barākhars, with a thickness of about 2,000 feet, consist of coarse conglomerates with white or buff sandstones and numerous coal-seams, the lowermost of which are often very thick. The pebble beds are particularly frequent towards the base of the sub-stage, the sediments becoming gradually finer in an upward direction. The Barākhar sandstones are sometimes felspathic, but the felspar grains are kaolinised, instead of being undecomposed, as in the case of the Tālchers.

Barākhar sub-stage.

The ironstone shales, about 1,400 feet thick, are black carbonaceous shales, with numerous bands of clay ironstone, the ferruginous element occurring in the form of iron carbonate. They

Ironstone shales.

sometimes constitute valuable iron-ores. The average amount of metallic iron in the clay-ironstones is 39 per cent. Some of the richer bands in the Rāniganj coalfield contain as much as 54 per cent.

Rāniganj sub-stage.

The Rāniganj sub-stage, with a maximum thickness of 5,000 feet, which it attains only in the Rāniganj coalfield, consists of sandstones, both coarse and fine-grained, mostly felspathic and false-bedded, intercalated with a large proportion of shales, together with coal-seams. The coal seams are thinner, but more constant than in the Bārakhar.

Dāmodar fossils.

Fossil plants occur abundantly in some of the Dāmodar strata. The leading fossils belong to the genera *Glossopteris*, *Schizoneura*, *Phyllotheca* and *Sphenophyllum*, the first of which is allied to the ferns, the other three to the *Equisetaceæ*.

All three subdivisions of the Dāmodar, together with the underlying Tālcher, are exposed both in the Rāniganj and Jharia coalfields. The overlying Pānchet beds are absent from the Jharia coalfield, but are well exposed in the Rāniganj coalfield where they occupy a considerable area in the southern part of the coal-basin, and constitute the underscarp of Pānchet hill, the upper crags of which consist of Kāmthi sandstone. In the Rāniganj field they attain a total thickness of about 1,500 feet consisting principally of very false-bedded coarse sandstones and red clays, with the exception of the lowest 250 or 300 feet which consist of grey and greenish-grey sandstones and shales, often micaceous and very thin-bedded, and not unlike some of the Tālcher beds.

Pānchet stage.

Vertebrate fossils.

The Pānchet beds are barren of coal-seams. Sometimes they contain poorly preserved impressions of fossil plants, which, when recognisable, appear to be closely related to or identical with common Dāmodar forms. They have also yielded remnants of labyrinthodont amphibians belonging to the genera *Gonioglyptus*, *Clypotognathus* and *Pachygonia*. and primitive reptiles of the genera *Dycinodon* and *Epicampodon*.

Intrusive rocks in Gondwāna coalfields.

Both in the Rāniganj and Jharia coalfields the Gondwāna strata are penetrated by numerous igneous intrusions, principally in the form of dykes, which usually stop short at the faulted boundaries of the coal-basins, although they occasionally extend beyond them. They are mostly or entirely of later age than the faults. Their preponderance within the Gondwana areas probably stands in relation to the fractured condition of the earth's crust in these sunken areas, and also with the greater ease with which the relatively soft sediments of the Gondwānas could be rent asunder by intrusive masses as compared with the much more compact surrounding gneisses and schists.

These intrusions are connected with the Rājmahal period of volcanic activity, probably of liassic age. They belong to two distinct types:—

(1) A group of mica-peridotites remarkable for the amount of apatite they contain.

(2) Large dykes of ordinary basalt or dolerite.

Both sets of intrusions belong to one geological epoch, though the mica-peridotites are more frequently observed crossing the dolerite ones than the reverse.

Mica-peridotite.

The dykes of mica-peridotite are generally narrow, not exceeding 3 to 5 feet, and at the surface are always decomposed to a soft buff-coloured crumbling earth, which is often vesicular and contains remnants of partially decomposed bundles of mica. The vesicular appearance is caused by the removal of some of the minerals by superficial weathering. Traced below the surface in the colliery workings, the rocks where unaffected by surface alteration, have a very different aspect, appearing as compact, tough and almost black rocks with spangles of biotite, glassy-looking porphyritic crystals of olivine, and large numbers of acicular crystals of apatite. They are seen to send out ramifications into the surrounding coal and sandstones and in some places they thicken out into boss-like masses or even spread out in wide sheets along the bedding planes, coking the coal with the production of remarkable columnar structures, baking the shales, and partially fusing the felspathic sandstones into compact rocks.

Fresh specimens of these mica-peridotites have a specific gravity of nearly 3. The primary minerals of the unaltered rocks, arranged in their order of crystallisation, are apatite, olivine, magnetite with varying amounts of chromite and ilmenite, biotite, a brown hornblende which has been regarded as antho phyllite, augite. The secondary minerals developed by the contact with the coal-seams are serpentine, secondary magnetite, a titaniferous mineral which has been regarded as perofskite, rhombohedral carbonates, chiefly dolomite, pyrites,

A constant character of these remarkable rocks is the exceptional quantity of apatite (phosphate of lime) which they contain, amounting in some of the freshest specimens from underground workings to as much as 11·5 per cent. of the rock.

Exceptional richness in phosphorus.

The basalt and dolerite dykes are easily distinguished from the associated intrusions of mica-peridotite, by their physical and mineralogical characters and their frequently much greater dimensions. They display a more or less columnar or polyhedral jointing, and the spheroidal jointing that usually characterise such rocks. They sometimes attain a thickness of 100 feet, and yet the action on the adjacent strata is in no way comparable to the effects of the much narrower intrusions of mica-peridotite. They do not penetrate the coal-seams like the mica-peridotites, and have never been observed to spread out into sills parallel with the stratification.

Dolerite dykes.

The specific gravity of these rocks averages 2·99. They consist chiefly of olivine, plagioclase felspar, and augite.

The Gondwāna coal has a very pronounced laminated appearance, owing to its being invariably composed of layers of varying thickness, which consist alternately of a bright jet-like black substance, and of a dull lustreless material. The brighter portions consist of very pure coal, while the dull portions are nothing more than an extremely carbonaceous shale. Hence the value of any Gondwāna coal depends mainly on the proportion of bright laminæ. In many instances the carbonaceous coal constituting the dull layers is too impure to soften by heat and constitutes an impediment to the manufacture of coke. Nevertheless excellent coke is obtained from many Gondwāna coals.

The Gondwāna coal.

The disturbed condition of the earth's crust along the main lines of faulting of the great coalfields, is revealed by the presence of mineral springs. Those situated near the Dāmodar river have especially attracted attention, such as the one situated below Chānch, on the faulted boundary of the Rāniganj coalfield, Two miles south-west of the Chānch spring is that of Tentulia on the south bank of the Dāmodar river, which is sulphurous and is said to have a temperature of 190° F. (88° C.). There is another hot spring on the north bank of the Dāmodar, situated 5 miles east by north of the

Hot springs along faulted boundaries.

eastern termination of the Jharia coalfield along the eastern continuation of the main boundary fault of that coal-basin.

A hot or tepid spring is said to flow at the south-west corner of Susunia hill where the quarries of "Burdwan stone" are situated.

The Dhārwār system.

The next older group of rocks anterior to the Gondwānas is the Dhārwār system which is indeed considerably more ancient, since it includes the oldest undoubted sediments met with in India.

Northern boundary of main outcrop of Dharwars.

The main outcrop of the Dhārwārs forms the southernmost belt of Mānbhum district. The northern boundary of this outcrop is described as a fault. The most eastern point where it has been observed is along the borders of the alluvium near Bheläidiha in Bānkura district, and from there it has been followed westwards to a point beyond Bāndgaon in Rānchi district, for a total distance of more than 100 miles. The faulted boundary runs just north of the towns of Ambikānagar and Barābhum, and crosses the Subarnarekha river six miles north-west of its confluence with its important tributary, the Karkari. The town of Barābhum, though situated south of the northern boundary of the Dhārwār belt, is not built on Dhārwār rocks, but on an inlier of granitic gneiss.

Constitution of Dhārwārs.

The Dhārwārs consist of quartzites, quartzitic sandstones, slates of various kinds, shales, hornblendic, mica, talcose and chloritic schists, the latter passing into potstones, and interstratified greenstones or diorites with what appear to be interstratified volcanic ash beds.

Calcareous jasper.

A particularly noteworthy rock amongst the Dhārwārs is a distinctly bedded siliceous rock having the appearance of black chert or Lydian stone or jasper. Its surface, under the influence of weathering, assumes a white crust, due to the removal of a small quantity of carbonate of lime. The colour is an intense black and the fracture conchoidal. These jaspidous rocks sometimes graduating into limestone are frequently observed amongst the ancient sediments of India.

Potstone.

Throughout the area of the Dhārwār rocks, magnesian schists are of common occurrence; they vary considerably in texture and composition. There are talcose and chloritic schists, soapstones, and potstones; many of the varieties are quarried and manufactured by means of rude lathes into plates, curry-dishes basins, and Mahadeos. One variety is not much esteemed owing to its inability to sustain heat. This is probably due to the presence of chlorite which contains a larger percentage of water of combination than the talcose minerals. The cracking of this variety is, therefore, doubtless caused by the liberation of this water when heat is applied.

Sequence amongst Dhārwārs.

So far as any regular sequence can be made out amongst the Dhārwār beds, it would seem as though the lowest strata consist of chloritic schists and potstones accompanied by hornblendic rocks and quartzites. A somewhat higher zone appears to consist of slates, schists, and of particular earthy shales closely resembling those of the Tālcher series, and, like them, perhaps indicating the former existence of glacial conditions at a still more remote period of the earth's history.

Fault-rocks along boundary of Dharwars.

Along the faulted northern boundary, the line of fracture has become, by means of infiltration, the receptacle of various mineral substances, principally silica and ores of iron. In many places the iron ore first deposited has subsequently been replaced by fine-grained quartz, some of the pseudomorphic plates of which show the delicate etching which occurs on "specular iron", while in other cases the iron has not been completely removed, but is retained in the interstices. Sometimes the quartz occurs massive but penetrated by numerous intersecting veins. The line of fracture is particularly evident to the north and north-east of Ambikānagar, near the eastern border of the district, where it is marked by deposits of hæmatite which appear to contain a great abundance of rich ore. In the hills between Balarāmpur and Bauch, nine miles west by north of Ambikānagar, there is, along the same line of fracture, another strong deposit of hæmatite, beyond which, and on the same disturbed line, there is an old worked-out copper mine in which traces of malachite and azurite are still to be found as encrustations on the neighbouring rocks. In its vicinity there is a vein of coarse crystalline dolomitic limestone. Further west, again, the fault is marked for a distance of 10 miles towards Barābhum by a range of hills 250 to 300 feet high, and striking 25° north of west, which consist of pseudomorphic quartz. Exposures of fault rock are also observed at a distance of 18 miles west of Barābhum. West of the Subarnarekha river, the western continuation of the fault has been traced into Ranchi district.

Physical features of Dhārwār outcrop.

The Dhārwārs constitute a region of jungle-clad hills, the lines of height generally following an east-west trend concording with the strike of the stratification. It is the harder bands amongst the strata which are particularly adapted to stand out as hills, and the succession of hill-formers is best seen in the neighbourhood of the Subarnarekha river; the northernmost range consists of a cherty quartzite which rises into saddle-shaped hummocks, then follow two chains of truncated or perfectly conical hills formed of slate, then a massive range of irregular elevation composed of basic volcanic or intrusive rock whose highest part forms the fine hill of Dalma. South of the igneous range are two more ranges, one of felspathic quartzite, and the other of talcose and micaceous schists of tolerably equable elevations throughout.

The Dalma Trap.

The Dalma trap forms, as it were, the backbone of the hilly region in southern Mānbhum and separates this district from that of Singhbhum situated next to the south.

The exact relation of the Dalma trap to the associated rocks is not quite clear owing to their disturbed condition and to the amount of alteration which they have suffered. The rock constituting the "Dalma Trap" is not a continuous compact intrusion, for it is interleaved with some of the typical representatives of the Dhārwārs, such as indurated chloritic schists. Perhaps it may include both interbedded and intruded elements. The occurrence of southerly dips amongst the beds north of the band of volcanics, and of northerly dips amongst those south of it, might lead one to infer a synclinal structure, but this is not confirmed by any repetition of the beds on either side of the supposed synclinal axis. Moreover, the occurrence of masses of hæmatite on the north side of the volcanic rocks, similar to those observed along the northern faulted boundary of the Dharwars, suggests the existence of local faults indicating that the structure is complex.

Lithologically the "Dalma Trap" is sometimes compact, sometimes vesicular and amygdaloidal. At other times it exhibits a brecciated structure. It belongs to the class of rocks which petrologists classify under the name of "epidiorite," that is, a basic igneou rock which has undergone alteration through earth-movements subsequent to its consolidation, the main result of the alteration being the transformation of the mineral "augite" into the mineral "hornblende."

The Dalma Trap appears to represent one particular horizon corresponding with a period of exceptionally pronounced volcanic activity. It is not, however, the only volcanic rock associated with the Dhārwārs; all through the Dhārwār outcrop there are hornblendic rocks and presumed ash-beds which seem to be of volcanic origin.

At Bāngurda, six miles south-east by south of Barābhum, there is a basic igneous rock which forms a range of bare red hills. The colour is due to the weathering out and decomposition of magnetic iron, and the detritus from it is almost identical with one of the commonest varieties of laterite.

Degree of metamorphism of Dharwars.

The Dhārwār strata of Mānbhum, in spite of their great geological antiquity, are often but very slightly altered, much less so than in most other outcrops of these rocks in other parts of India; slaty cleavage is sometimes so feebly developed that the argillaceous varieties of the strata are merely in the condition of shales. It often happens, however, that the rocks are considerably metamorphosed, just as much as in other parts of India, and have become slaty, or even crystalline.

In places where the degree of metamorphism is not greatly pronounced, the finer sediments do not assume the form of slates, but merely consist of ordinary shales, some of the green-coloured varieties of which might be easily mistaken for Tālcher shales were it not for the quartz-veins which traverse them and which are not observed amongst the Gondwāna sediments

Auriferous veins.

The metamorphism is perhaps less pronounced in the eastern and southern portions of the Dhārwār band than in its northern and western parts; it is, however, very irregularly distributed. The quartz-veins, which cut through the Dhārwār sediments in all situations, are frequently auriferous.

Granitic intrusions are absent from the great spread of Dhārwār rocks which occupies the southernmost part of the district. Yet the intrusive granites observed in the middle belt of the district may be partly of later age than the Dhārwārs; only as the rocks with which they come into contact are either pre-Dhārwār gneisses, or else schists which may be of Dhārwār age but are metamorphosed beyond recognition, it is impossible, at present, to obtain undoubted evidence in this respect.

Dhārwār outliers near Mānbazar.

Close to the eastern edge of Mānbhum district there are some outliers of Dhārwārs surrounded by gneiss, but situated quite close to the main outcrop. They are observed principally in the neighbourhood of Mānbazar. They are affected by well-marked faults, the edges of the different formations being in some places in abrupt contact and in others only separated by ridges of pseudomorphic quartz or lodes of brown hæmatite. The rocks occurring in these detached areas are chiefly alternations of quartzites, potstones, and hornblendic rocks corresponding to the lowest zone of the Dhārwārs of this area.

Susunia hill.

In the middle belt of Mānbhum, the Dhārwārs are interfoliated to such an extent with older gneisses and perhaps with younger granites that it becomes difficult to separate them, and no accurate mapping of this area has yet been attempted. The most remarkable outlier of the Dhārwārs in this middle belt is that constituting Susunia hill, and which yields the so-called Burdwan paving stone. Susunia hill is about 15 miles south-south-west of Rāniganj; it rises abruptly to a height of 1,443 feet. It is chiefly formed of quartzites and felspathic quartzites, with occasional traces of mica. The beds dip generally 10° east of north at angles of 20° to 25°, but owing to some rolls and contortions, the azimuth varies to east, north-east, and north-west. The beds are traversed by three systems of joint planes which facilitate the quarrying of the stone to a very material extent.

Altered rocks perhaps referable to the Dharwars.

Other outcrops, probably also representing altered Dhārwārs, are observed up to the northernmost limit of the district. For instance, at Pāndua Hāt, a locality situated 13 miles west of Barākhar, midway between the Rāniganj and Jharia coalfields, there are mica schists succeeded to the north by thick and thin even-bedded grey, pale drab and brown quartzo-felspathic rocks with a dip of 10° to 15° to the north, which show but small signs of metamorphism, and probably represent a local outcrop of Dhārwār rocks.

Another series of rocks which possibly may represent metamorphosed Dhārwārs, are a succession of schists which are situated south of the eastern portion of the Jharia coalfield, and which are particularly clearly exposed in the Tasarkua river and in the Gowai river below its confluence with the Tasarkua. They include mica-schists and chloritic schists passing into potstones, some of which have been quarried for plate-making, but being generally distinctly schistose, and therefore too fissile, are much less suitable for the purpose than are the compact varieties which are common in the unaltered or slightly altered areas of the Dhārwārs. The mica schists of the Tasarkua and Gowai exposures frequently contain crystals of garnet, tourmaline and kyanite. All these rocks are profusely injected with veins of granite and pegmatite which no doubt account for their condition of metamorphism.

Alluvial gold. Alluvial gold washings occur at a number of localities throughout the Dhārwār area. The gold in the alluvium originates from the disintegration of the numerous auriferous quartz veins which intersect the Dhārwār slates, but do not contain the precious metal in sufficient proportion to repay the cost of mining.

The largest grains of alluvial gold so far recorded were obtained from the Gurum river never Dhadka, and were accompanied by minute flakes of platinum.

Magnetic sands. The same streams which contain alluvial gold that has accumulated in the sand owing to its heavy specific gravity, also contain accumulations of magnetic iron sand, whose accumulation is due to the same mechanical causes. The magnetite is derived from the disintegration of certain chlorite schists crowded with magnetite crystals which abound in certain parts of the Dhārwār outcrop.

Archæan Gneisses.

Distribution of Archæan gneisses. The northern belt of Mānbhum is not occupied exclusively by the Gondwāna rocks described in connection with the coalfields but also includes various ancient gneisses and schists occupying the interval between the Rāniganj and Jharia coalfields. They have received very little attention as compared with the rocks of the coal-basins, and, in all their characters they agree essentially with the crystalline rocks occupying so extensive an area throughout the middle belt of Mānbhum.

The Bengal gneiss. The rocks in the middle belt of Mānbhum consist partly of an older set of foliated gneisses and schists and partly of a newer set of intrusive granites. The older set which constitutes the geological group, known as the "Bengal Gneiss," includes mica-schists, chloritic schists, quartzites, felspathic quartzites, hornblende schists, biotite and hornblende granitic gneisses some of which are porphyritic. A great many of these rocks are older than the Dhārwārs; but amongst them are probably included foliated members of the Dhārwār series whose characters have become disguised by regional metamorphism. The granitic intrusions are probably newer than the Dhārwārs.

Except for local disturbances, the general trend of the gneiss throughout the middle belt of Mānbhum is east-west.

Strongly foliated biotite and hornblende gneisses constitute the Tundi hills at the north-west extremity of the area. They are traversed by numerous basic intrusions and runs of siliceous fault-rock.

Constitution of gneisses.

The region situated north-east of the Jharia coalfield and south-east of the Tundi hills includes a considerable variety of gneissose and schistose rocks, amongst which we may specially mention hornblendic schists, mica schists, and coarse porphyritic granitoid gneisses.

These porphyritic gneisses are also observed at the extreme north of the district where they occupy a zone which can be followed from north of Gobindpur, a town situated on the Grand Trunk Road, up to the foot of Parasnāth hill.

The area situated between the two great coalfields is traversed by numerous runs of quartz rock, no doubt representing the continuation of the faults that affect the areas occupied by the Gondwana rocks.

Pegmatite veins and basic dykes are abundant also in the gneissose country intervening between the two great coalfields

The analysis of the porphyritic gneiss indicates a granite with two felspars or "granitite," with biotite and no muscovite. The silica is low for a granite (67·60 per cent.), and the proportions of soda, lime, and iron indicate an approach to the rocks known as "diorite" Rocks of this type are very abundant amongst the oldest gneisses of the Indian peninsula, belonging to the type of the "Bengal Gneiss."

Composition of porphyritic gneiss.

Certain varieties of the gneiss contain garnets; such are the gneisses with or without hornblende which constitute most of the hills situated immediately south of the Rāniganj coalfield. Garnet-bearing rocks, described as altered intrusions, also occur along the Ijri valley south of the Jharia coalfield.

Garnet and pyroxene gneisses.

The pyroxene gneiss constituting the lofty Parasnāth hill on the borders of Mānbhum and Hazāribagh also contains garnets and recalls the "Nilgiri Gneiss" of Southern India.

Ancient intrusive rocks.

Perhaps the most striking crystalline rock in Mānbhum is the intrusive porphyritic granite or gneiss known as the "domegneiss" which is conspicuously developed in the middle belt of the

The "dome-gneiss."

district where it outcrops principally along two elongated areas of considerable size, the more northerly or rather more north-easterly of which commences in the country round Bero, a village situated 5 miles south of Pānchet hill, and extends from there in a west by south direction with a total length of 20 miles and an average breadth of 4 or 5 miles. The second zone commences abruptly near the village of Ladhurka, about 11 miles east-north-east of Purūlia; it is about 4 miles wide, and from thence to the banks of the Subarnarekha, about 40 miles of it extends without interruption. Beyond the Subarnarekha, too, it has been traced for many miles into the district of Rānchi.

Distribution of granitic intrusions.

In addition to these two main outcrops there are some smaller areas occupied by the same formation, and lithologically similar rocks also occur interbedded, probably as intrusive sills, with the ordinary gneissose rocks in many parts of the district.

The numerous pegmatite veins which are scattered through the gneiss area are no doubt connected with the same set of intrusions.

Constitution of "dome-gneiss".

The "dome-gneiss" is a coarsely granitic rock composed of quartz, muscovite-mica, and orthoclase felspar, the latter occurring both in the general matrix and as large porphyritic "amygdaloidal" crystals which communicate to the rock almost a conglomeratic appearance. The colour of the felspar is usually pink or grey, though it is occasionally of a brick-red colour as in the picturesque conical hills situated west of Bero, a village situated 5 miles south of the hill known as Pānchet hill which forms the south-west corner of the Rāniganj coalfield.

The rock has a tendency to weather into dome-like bosses and tors. It is from this tendency that it derives the name of "dome-gneiss". Especially remarkable in appearance are the steep conical hills formed by this rock near the village of Jhalda, 5 miles from the left bank of Subarnarekha, near the western border of the district.

Hornblende bearing varieties also occur, for instance, north of Bero hill and at Raghunāthpur.

Another set of hornblende-granite gneisses detached from the main outcrop occurs in the Sindurpur and Tilabani hills situated some 12 miles north-east of Purūliā, Tilābani hill also containing porphyritic granitic gneisses. The hornblende-granite gneiss weathers into huge masses which are sometimes 40 feet in diameter; these, when seen piled on one another as on the Sindurpur hills, produce a very striking effect.

The porphyritic structure, although very commonly developed is occasionally wanting. "Segregation veins" of coarser texture constituting the rock known as pegmatite occur throughout the large outcrops of the "dome-gneiss." They also extend beyond the boundaries of the dome-gneiss into the surrounding older schists and gneisses, when they are apt to become excessively coarse-grained. When traversing mica schists they become loaded with mica which crystallizes in gigantic crystals yielding the commercial mica which is supplied in large quantities by the mines in the neighbouring district of Hazāribāgh.

Pegmatite veins.

Exceptional rocks.

Many remarkable minerals are found in the areas occupied by the gneisses.

A remarkable vein of blue kyanite (silicate of alumina) and muscovite mica (silicate of alumina and potash), with an average thickness of two feet, has been followed for a distance of 6 miles, approximately 3 miles east and west of Sālbani, a village situated some 6 miles west-north-west of Barābhum. At some places the kyanite is associated with large masses of corundum (pure alumina) of a beautiful sapphire colour, but too much flawed and clouded to be cut as gems. Occasionally the minerals tourmaline (complex silico-borate of alumina and magnesia) and rutile (oxide of titanium) are also found associated with the kyanite The kyanite vein accompanies some coarse-grained quartz-tourmaline rocks and micaceous beds running east and west and situated one quarter of a mile north of the boundary of the Dhārwār beds.

Kyanite and corundum vein.

Close to Pānchet hill, just outside the south-western corner of the Rāniganj coalfield, the gneissose and schistose rocks are locally characterised by containing interbedded calcareous schists which have been largely quarried to supply lime for the manufacture of iron by the Bengal Iron Works Company. It is possible that these rocks represent metamorphosed Dhārwārs.

Calcareous schists.

Throughout the gneissose areas one observes occasionally runs of siliceous fault rock, and also basic intrusions, some of which are very ancient and perhaps of the age of the "Dalma Trap," while other less ancient ones belong to the same system as the basic dykes of Rājmahal age which are so numerous in the Gondwāna coalfields.

Fault-rock and dykes.

The older basic rocks, whether intrusive or not, have almost invariably been altered by regional metamorphism, and owing to the transformation of the original augite into hornblende (uralite) they are in the condition of "epidiorites." The only recorded exception is in the case of some intrusive rocks situated in the midst of the gneiss north-east of Susunia hill (a hill situated 15 miles south-south-west of Rāniganj, from which the so-called "Burdwan stone" is quarried), and in the case also of the great mass of gneissose rocks constituting the lofty Parasnath hill on the borders of Mānbhum and Hazāribagh. The intrusive basic rocks near Susunia hill are said to contain the variety of augite known as "diallage," and would appear to belong therefore to the class of rock defined by petrologists as "gabbro" which is characterised by the presence of this mineral. It contains a large proportion of the silicate of lime and alumina known as "anorthite," in consequence of which it approaches in composition to the rocks known to petrologists under the name of "anorthosite". The rock of Parasnāth hill is a garnet-bearing pyroxene-gneiss resembling the "Nilgiri Gneiss" of Southern India.

Epidiorites.

Anorthosite.

Pyroxene-gneiss of Parasnāth.

In addition to the basic intrusions, there are also intrusions of felspar porphyry, perhaps offshoots from the same original molten mass as the granites constituting the "dome-gneiss". Porphyries of this kind are met with, in particular 7 miles south-south-east of Rāniganj, along the Bānkura road, where their direction of strike is 35° north of east, oblique therefore to that of the gneiss which, in this neighbourhood, seldom departs from true east and west. The porphyries can be traced in a south-westerly direction for about 7 miles from the road.

Felspar porphyry.

Laterite and clay.

The easternmost border of Mānbhum touches the margin of the great spread of lateritic and alluvial formations which occupy the greater portion of the districts of Bānkura and Midnapore, where the laterite forms a deposit of several feet in thickness Laterite also occurs in thinner spreads, pretty generally distributed over Mānbhum. Four distinct varieties of this rock occur, which may be thus described:—

1. Pisolitic, sometimes concreted, but towards the surface generally in the form of loose gravel.

2. (*a*) Conglomeratic—contains both rounded and angular fragments of quartz.
   (*b*) Conglomerate passing into coarse grit.
3. Concretionary.
4. Compact, occurring in stratified beds.

The two latter varieties are those principally occurring along the eastern borders of the district where they are gradually encroached upon, mostly outside the boundary of the district, by recent alluvium.

At many places in Mānbhum there are thick deposits of clay, the most important of which is at the northern base of the Bāghmundi plateau, an elevated tract of gneissose rocks near the western border of the district; here the clay deposit sometimes attains a thickness of 60 feet.

Valuable minerals.

The principal mineral of economic importance is coal since the district includes portions of the two richest coalfields in India, that is the western portion of the Rāniganj coalfield, and nearly the whole of the Jharia coalfield.

The other mineral products which are worked remuneratively but on a much smaller scale, are iron, "potstone", building stones, and to a very small extent, alluvial gold.

Coal.

The coal-seams worked in this district belong partly to the Barākhar and partly to the Rāniganj subdivision, the great majority of collieries exploiting the former in both coalfields so far as Mānbhum district is concerned: the rich seams of Rāniganj coal are situated mostly in Burdwan district. The Jharia coalfield produces on an average some 4 or 5 millions of tons annually, and yields about half the total output of the coal in India.

Iron.

The iron-ores from the ironstone-shales of the Rāniganj coal-basin are smelted at the works of "Bengal Iron and Steel Company" at Barākhar, which yield an average produce of 40,000 tons of "pig iron".

Building stones.

The only stone at present largely quarried and used for building purposes is the coarse sandstone at Barākhar. It has been used for public buildings in Calcutta, as well as locally for the Barākhar bridge and the railway. It is of very unequal quality and texture, and has been proved to be incapable of sustaining great pressure. For all ordinary building purposes, however, it is very useful.

The quartzites and felspathic quartzites of Susunia hill have long been quarried and manufactured into flags, curbstones, etc., and are known in Calcutta as Burdwan paving stones.

A rock of similar character to that of Susunia occurs in the south part of the district, but is not nearly so accessible.

Limestone.

Limestone occurs, but apparently in small quantity, on the southern fault of the Rāniganj coalfield. Limestone occurs at the junction of the Dāmodar and Pānchet beds at the north-west corner of the base of Pānchet hill.

Occasionally in this district, a kind of calcareous tufa derived from former hot springs is found in crevices in the hills. It is commonly spoken of by the natives as *Asarhar* or giant's bones.

Lead.

Close to Dhekia, a village situated 2 miles east by south of Dhādka, at the south-east corner of the district, there is a load of argentiferous galena in a sandy mica schist belonging to the Dhārwār system.

CHAPTER II.

HISTORY.

Of the early history of the territory now included within the district of Mānbhum but little is known with any certainty; no written records of any considerable antiquity exist, there are no ancient inscriptions, and the light that might have been thrown on the subject by the traditions handed down in the families of the proprietors of the soil is obscured by their attempts to manufacture for themselves an origin outside the district, and to secure for themselves recognition as Rājputs. Reference will be made to these traditional family histories, but little of value from the point of view of scientific history is to be gathered from them. EARLY HISTORY.

The district name is apparently derived from one of the fiscal divisions within it, and is a mere artificial product of comparatively recent times, which cannot be taken as indicating any specially close connection in earlier times between the different estates within the district. Though, therefore, we may accept the derivation of Mānbhum suggested in the preceding chapter as equivalent to the "land of the Mal, Māle or Maler," this does not assist us very much, beyond showing that one of the most easterly estates or petty kingdoms derived its name from one of the branches of the Munda family. The typical aboriginal race within the district to this day is the Bhumij, and of his close connection, if not complete identification, with the Munda, there can be no doubt. The Mundas as Monedes and the Mále as Malli were known to Pliny and are described by him as being, along with the Sauri, in occupation of the inland country to the south of Palibothra (Patna). The Sauri are generally identified with the modern Savāras, who, though they no longer speak a dialect of Mundari, are undoubtedly Mundari by race. It is suggested that this name is derived from the Prakrit form of the Sanskrit '*sukara*' "a pig," a contemptuous name given by their Aryan neighbours on the north and west to the inhabitants of this area, just as the Hindus of later times gave the generic name of Kol or Kolhu, from the Sanskrit '*kola*,' also meaning "a pig," to the Munda, Ho, Bhumij, Orāon, Sonthal and other aboriginal races of these parts generally.

Whatever the degree of accuracy in these derivations, there can be little doubt that Mundari or Kolarian races occupied the wild area south of Bihar in Pliny's time. Bihar itself, the ancient kingdom of Magadha, was at one time under the dominion of the Cheros, another branch of the great Mundari race, and Buchanan suggests that the modern Kols, using the word as covering all the Mundari races, are descended from that portion of the original population of Magadha which rejected the religion of Buddha and the civilisation of the Aryan immigrants, and migrated south towards the great forest country of Central India and Chota Nāgpur.

Ptolemy's Geography throws little more light on the subject beyond that he groups with the Mandalai and Sutrarai (the Monedes and Sauri of Pliny), the Kokkonagai, a name which is perhaps traceable to Karkhota Naga, the country of the Nāgbansis, and surviving still in the name Nāgpur.

THE JAIN OR BUDDHISTIC ERA. In the 7th century of the Christian era, some more definite geographical material is available in the accounts of the travels by Hwen Thsang. These, as interpreted by Cunningham, show that between Orissa on the south, Magadha or Bihar on the north, Chāmpa (*query* Bhāgalpur and Burdwan) on the east, and Maheswâra (in Central India) on the west lay the kingdom of Kie-lo-na Su-fa-la-na or Kirana Suvārna, ordinarily identified with the Subarnarekha river, '*rekha*' and '*kirāna*' both meaning in Sanskrit a "ray," and the river in all probability getting its name from its auriferous sands. This, General Cunningham writes, must "have comprised all the petty hill states lying between Midnapore and Sirguja on the east and west and between the sources of the Dāmodar and Vartārini on the north and south." The capital of this kingdom is variously placed by Cunningham at or near Barābazar in Pargana Barābhum, and by Hewitt at Dalmi in the adjoining pargana of Pātkum where extensive ruins still exist. Mr. Beglar, who identifies the Chinese traveller's Kie-lo-na with Karanpur, a subdivision of Chota Nāgpur, places the capital at or near Sāfāran (Su-fa-la-na), about 10 miles north-west of Dālmi. Both these places are situated on the river Subarnarekha, so that whichever interpretation of the name used by the Chinese traveller is adopted, it would seem to be more or less certain that somewhere on this river, and probably in the part of the district just referred to, was situated the capital of a powerful kingdom. We are told that its king at that time was She-Shang-kia or Sasanka, famed as a great persecutor of Buddhists.

MR. BEGLAR'S THEORY. The remains at Dalmi and other places in the immediate neighbourhood are elsewhere described; at Dalmi the Brāhmanical element is most in evidence, but there are sufficient traces of Jain or Buddhistic influence to suggest the probability that a Jain or Buddhistic civilisation preceded the Brāhmanical. The Jain element is more prominently marked at some of the neighbouring places, and there are very considerable remains also in other parts of the district, in some places purely Jain, in others Brāhmanical, superimposed on or alongside early Jain remains. Mr. Beglar, who made a comprehensive study of these and similar remains from Tamluk to Patna and Gaya in 1862-63, propounds an interesting and fairly probable explanation of these numerous remains of an advanced civilisation in a part of the country so little known in later years, and which from its natural features could never have lent itself readily to any general state of civilisation in the early days from which those relics date. This theory is that there must have been regular routes between Tamluk (Tamralipta), a place of very early importance in the east, and Patna (Pataliputra), Gaya, Rājgir and Benares in the north and west. Among the routes which he traces, so far as this district is concerned, is that from Tamluk to Patna *viâ* Ghātāl, Bishunpur, Chātna (in Bānkura), Raghunāthpur, Telkupi, Jharia, Rajauli (Gāya) and Rajgir. At or near all these places as well as others on the route are ruins; at Telkupi in Mānbhum the Dāmodar crossing is marked by very extensive ruins, mainly Brāhmanical but partly Jain; similar ruins exist near Pālganj where the Barākhar river would be crossed. According to tradition the temples at Telkupi are ascribed to merchants and not to Rājas or holy men, and the inference is that a large trading settlement sprung up at this point where the Dāmodar river would present, at any rate in the rainy season, a very considerable obstacle to the travellers and merchants. Another great route passing through this district would be a more direct road to Benares; marking the line of this are the extensive remains, Jain and Brāhmanical, at Pākbira, Buddhpur and other places on the Kāsai river near Mānbazar; it would pass further on through Barābazar and still further west strike the Subarnarekha river at or near Dalmi; Sāfāran and Suisa on the same bank of the river, another Dalmi and other adjoining places on the west bank, all contain traces of early Jain and Brāhmanical civilisation, and Dalmi would certainly appear to have been a very considerable town. Further west the route would pass Rānchi and Palāmau where also there are remains Cross roads connecting the main Benares and Gayā routes explain the large collection of remains in the neighbourhood of Pākbira and Buddhpur; from this point to Pālganj the route is marked by ruins at Balarāmpur and Charra near Purūlia, at Pāra, at Chechāongarh and various neighbouring villages on the Dāmodar, and at Kātras. Another route which Mr. Beglar has omitted, *i.e.*, from Dalmi to Pālganj, would after crossing the Ajodhya range pass Borām on the Kāsai river where also there are extensive remains of about the same period as those at Dalmi. An intervening place on this route, Arsha Karandihi, also contains ruins which have not been examined. This route would, like the other, cross the Dāmodar near Chechāongarh and find its way *via* Kātras to Pālganj.

Mr. Beglar justifies his theory in the following paragraph which is deserving of quotation *in extenso*.

"It appears to me quite a mistake to imagine that districts like Mānbhum, Palāmau, the Sonthal Parganas, Jhārkhand, &c., could ever have been extensively cultivated and peopled densely like the plains of Magadha or the valleys of the Jamuna and the Ganges; the occurrence of ruins among the wilds of Chutia Nāgpur can only be due to the cities having from some generally intelligible natural cause sprung up at points along a great road; and by no means to the whole district having been in a flourishing condition. The contrast between the profusion of remains scattered broadcast in the fertile and known densely-peopled plains of Magadha and the isolated remains in the wilder districts is too great to be explained away by any amount of imaginary dilapidations and destruction from any causes; indeed, so far as destruction goes, built remains, in the civilised tracts, are generally in a far more advanced stage of decay (even when they have not absolutely disappeared as structures, leaving only the materials as witnesses) than those in the wilder places."*

COL. DALTON'S THEORY.

It would be difficult to find a more reasonable interpretation than this theory gives of the hints we get as to the ancient history of this area from such archæological evidence as exists. Nor is the theory inconsistent with the inference to be drawn from ethnological sources. It is true that in one place Mr. Beglar seems to assume that the Kolarian races only found their way into the district after the period of Brāhmanical civilisation, a position which would not have been accepted by Colonel Dalton nor probably by later experts; it is not, however, necessary to assume an invasion to account for the extermination by the Kolarian races of the early civilisation, which was confined, as we have seen, to particular centres. Colonel Dalton's theory is a perfectly reasonable one, *i.e.*, that the scattered colonies, which he accounts for as resulting from a peaceable extension of Brāhmanical missions among the unsubdued Dasyas, gradually assumed a more aggressive

* Archæological Survey of India Reports, Vol. VIII, page 51.

attitude which drove the non-Aryan races living round about them into open revolt, and probably, after severe struggles, ended in a more or less complete extirpation of the Aryans, and the partial or complete destruction of their forts and cities and temples. The history of these races in more recent times gives more than one illustration of their capacity for living for years in apparent peace with their neighbours, and suddenly rising and attempting to overwhelm them. It is not difficult to suppose that the Aryan centres of civilisation contained the prototype of the modern moneylender, or that the absorption of the cultivated land by these, and the enslaving of the actual cultivator went on in those early days, and that when the cup was full, or his eyes were opened to what was happening, the Bhumij of those days rose and destroyed his oppressor, just as the Sonthal did in 1854.

Reference is made elsewhere to a peculiar people bearing the name of Sārak (variously spelt) of whom the district still contains a considerable number. These people are obviously Jain by origin, and their own traditions as well as those of their neighbours, the Bhumij, make them the descendants of a race which was in the district when the Bhumij arrived; their ancestors are also credited with building the temples at Pāra, Charra, Borām and other places in these pre-Bhumij days. They are now, and are credited with having always been, a peaceable race living on the best of the terms with the Bhumij. To these and perhaps their local converts Colonel Dalton would ascribe the Jain remains. He places them in the district as far back as 500 or 600 years before Christ, identifying the colossal image now worshipped at Pākbira under the name of Bhiram as Vir, the 24th Tirthancara whom Professor Wilson represents as having "adopted an ascetic life and traversed the country occupied by the Bajra Bhūmi and the Sudhi Bhūmi who abused and beat him and shot at him with arrows and barked at him with dogs, of which small annoyances he took no notice." The Bajra or terrible Bhūmi are, according to Colonel Dalton, the Bhumij. He suggests, therefore, that it is not improbable that the shrines referred to mark the course taken in his travels by the great Saint "Vira" and were erected in his honour by the people whom his teaching had converted, or, it may be—and this is more consistent with local tradition on which, however, no great weight can be placed—that he merely visited places at which Jains were already established, within sight of the sacred mount Samaye where 250 years earlier the Jina Paswa or Parasnāth had obtained Nirvāna.

Combining Colonel Dalton's and Mr. Beglar's theories we should get a long period of peaceful occupation of various centres by the Jaīns or Sāraks left undisturbed by the Bhumij settlers whose advent must have been some time before Vir's travels. The Sāraks must have been superseded some time before the 7th century by Brāhmans and their followers; such of them as survived or resisted conversion migrating to places away from the existing civilised centres where they remained unmolested by their Bhumij neighbours. The 10th century, judging by such of the buildings as it is possible to date with any accuracy, saw the Brāhmans at their prime, and some time between that and the 16th century the Bhumij, possibly assisted by fresh migrations from the west and north, must have risen and destroyed them root and branch. The destruction of the Hindu temples is ordinarily ascribed to Muhammadans, but, so far as this area is concerned, there is no trace, not even in tradition, of any invasion. Mr. Beglar draws a similar inference from two inscriptions found by him at Gondwâna *en route* from Barābazar to Chaibāsa, the earlier of which, though not interpretable, dates from the 6th or 7th century and the later to the 15th or 16th; the latter records the name of "Lakshmana first Banjara" which, read with the evidence of earlier use of the route to be inferred from the other inscription, suggests a period of 500 years or more during which trade along this route was stopped, and considering the reputation of the Bhumij in later years, it is hardly surprising that if the existing civilisation was forcibly uprooted, it would be long before the country would be even comparatively safe for the ordinary traveller.

History in the strict sense is certainly non-existent for the whole of this period; there are no remains which can be positively ascribed to any date between the 10th or 11th century and the 16th century, when Muhammadan influence on architecture begins to be evident; the local zamindars' geneological trees give regular lines of succession throughout the period, but, as already stated, no reliance can be placed on them and probably all that can be said with any certainty is that they had their origin as reigning families, whether from outside or local stock, during this period.

MUHAMMADAN RULE.

To the Muhammadan historians the whole of modern Chota Nāgpur and the adjoining hill states was known by the name of Jhārkhand; it was a disturbed frontier country, the barbarous Hindu inhabitants whereof required special military precautions to keep them in check. Perhaps the earliest historical reference to any part of the district is to be found in the Bramānda section of the Bhāvishyat Purāna, compiled in the 15th or 16th century

A. D., where it is stated that "Varâhabhumi is in one direction contiguous to Tungabhumi, and in another to the Sekhara mountain; and it comprises Varâbhumi, Sâmantabhumi, and Mânbhumi. This country is overspread with impenetrable forests of *sâl* and other trees. On the borders of Varâbhumi runs the Darikesi river. In the same district are numerous mountains, containing mines of copper, iron and tin The men are mostly Râjputs, robbers by profession, irreligious and savage. They eat snakes and all sorts of flesh, drink spirituous liquors, and live chiefly by plunder or the chase. As to the women, they are, in garb, manners and appearance, more like Râkshasis than human beings. The only objects of veneration in these countries are rude village divinities."

The area described is still identifiable with a portion of the Châtna thana in Bânkura and parganas Barâbhum and Mânbhum in this district, Tungabhum corresponding with the Raipur thana of the former district, while Sekhara is identifiable with Parasnâth or more probably the Pânchet hill. Sekhar is a name formerly borne by all holders of the Pânchet Râj, and the name Sekharbhum survives as the regular name of a portion of the estate and is commonly used in many parts of the district for the estate as a whole.

History can hardly be said to begin even with the period of Muhammadan influence in Bengal. We know that Akbar about 1585 sent a force to subdue the Râja of Kokrah, or Chota Nâgpur proper, a country celebrated for its diamonds. In the Ain-i-Akbari Chai Châmpa part of Hazâribagh district is shown as assessed to revenue as a pargana of Subah Bihar. To the north Birbhum and to the east Bishnupur were already under Muhammadan influence by this time, and in 1589 or 1590 Râja Mân Singh marched from Bhâgalpur through the western hills to Burdwan *en route* to reconquer Orissa, and again a couple of years later he sent his Bihar troops by what is described as the western road, called the Jhârkhand route, to Midnapore. In the latter journey, at any rate, he can hardly have failed to pass through a part of the present district of Mânbhum, and archæological evidence place about this time the building of the Pânchet fort as well as repairs to some of the older temples in that neighbourhood, *e.g.*, those at Pâra and Telkupi.

PANCHET ESTATE.

Some 30 years later (1632 or 1633) we get the first specific reference to Pânchet in the Pâdishâhnâma where it is stated that "Bir Nârâyan, Zamindar of Pânchet, a country attached to Subah Bihar, was a commander of 300 horse and died in the sixth year." Not till 25 years later, however, is there any record of liability to tribute or revenue, but in the improved Jama Tumari of Sultan Singh, as settled in 1658, Pānchet is shown as liable to a 'Peshkush' or fixed tribute. Yet just about this very time so little was known about this part of the country that we read that after Shuja's defeat by Aurangzeb at Kajwa near Allahabad in 1659, his pursuers Prince Mohammed and Mir Jumla with some difficulty got information of a route from Patna to Bengal other than the ordinary one *viâ* the Ganges. This alternative route is described as "the route of Sherghotty which is situated in the mountains of Jhārkhand ; it was circuitous, narrow and steep and little used on account of the difficulties it presented and the savage manners of the mountaineers."

In later records references to Pānchet are more numerous ; the Peshkush was gradually increased, implying a greater degree of control from Murshidābad, and it is possible that the abandonment of the Pānchet fort about 1700, in regard to which there is no very definite tradition, and certainly no internal evidence, to show that it was taken by force, was a mere withdrawal of the zamindar to a less easily accessible portion of his territory to avoid such direct pressure as, for example, was exercised on other Hindu zamindars by Murshid Khan in the early part of the eighteenth century when we read that he deprived them of everything but "Nankar, Bankar and Jalkar" and in many instances even of their liberty, and appointed Muhammadan Amils to collect the revenues of their estates. It is said that the zamindars of Bīrbhum and Bishnupur were the only exceptions the former (Asadullah) because of his reputation for religion and charity, and the latter "owing to the nature of his country which was full of woods and adjoining the mountains of Jhārkhand whither, upon any invasion of his district, he retired to places inaccessible to the pursuers and annoyed them severely on their retreat."* What was true of Bishnupur must have been even more true of Pānchet and of the zamindaris to the south and west. Of these, at any rate by name, there is not a single mention in any history of Muhammadan times, nor is there the slightest trace either in local tradition, in place names, or in archæological remains, of any sort of Muhammadan occupation, forcible or peaceful. What the exact position of these other estates was during this period it is impossible to state ; Bārābhum, if the identification with "Varābhum" is correct, certainly had a much earlier separate existence, and so also Mānbhum, but of the others we know nothing.

* Stewart's History of Bengal.

The territory comprised in the present district of Mānbhum was acquired by the British with the grant of the Dewāni of Bengal, Bihar, and Orissa in 1765. Even as late as this, however, our knowledge of the district hardly extends beyond the Zamindari Rāj of Pānchet, to which Jhalda was described a few years later as a recent annexation. The zamindaris of Barābhum and Mānbhum appear to have been among the kingdoms of the Chuars, and nominally attached to Midnapore. Pātkum and Baghmundi in the south-west were, when we first hear of them, included in Rāmgarh, as also were in all probability Nāwagarh, Kātras, Jharia, and Tundi in the north-west. Pāndra, the remaining estate in the north, was apparently under the dominion of the neighbouring zamindar of Bīrbhum. EARLY ENGLISH ADMINISTRATION.

Of portions of the district, at any rate, it may safely be said that the annexation was not effected without much trouble and military expeditions. Mānbhum and Barābhum, which were included in the Jungle or Western Mahals of Midnapore, were along with the others the object of an expedition led by Lieutenant Fergusson, acting under orders from Mr. Graham, Resident or Collector at Midnapore, who spent from January 1767 to January of the succeeding year in these Western Mahals, and further operations under other officers were necessary for several months longer. Jagan Nath Dhal of Ghātsila or Dhalbhum was the chief obstacle to the establishment of order, but both the Bārabhum and Mānbhum Rājas gave trouble, though eventually they agreed to pay respectively Rs. 441-5-9 and Rs. 316-2 as revenue or tribute. The settlement was, however, far from complete, and December 1769 witnessed a great outbreak of the Chuārs inhabiting the hills between Barābhum and Ghātsila, and five companies of sepoys divided into two parties under Captain Forbes and Lieutenant Nun respectively had to be sent to restore order; Subla Singh described as the Jaigīrdar of Kailāpal was one of the principal insurgents, and though special orders were given for his arrest and summary execution as an example to the rest, he was not on this occasion at any rate captured. In January 1770 Lieutenant Nun was supposed to have restored peace in Barābhum, but almost immediately afterwards he and his force were surprised among the hills and suffered considerable loss, and re-inforcements had to be sent from Midnapore and a more or less permanent military post established at Barābhum.

The records of later years are full of accounts of similar outbreaks and their suppression; thus in January 1771 Lieutenant

Goodyear was engaged against various rebels, among them the Chuār sardār Samganjin (Sham Ganjan) of Dhādki (Dhādka), Subla Singh of Kailāpal, and a third the Dubraj or eldest son of the Barābhum Rāja. As a base for his expedition he was building a fort some 3 miles from Kailāpal, and 8 from Dhādka. The place selected was one where the Chuārs used to assemble to commit their robberies and divide their plunder "which made him think it the more convenient to annoy them," and was strongly fortified with a palisade of trunks of trees from 10 to 22 inches in circumference and 12 feet in height. Dhādka was, however, too strong to be attacked from the Kailāpal side, and it was only with the aid of levies from the Mān Rāja (Mānbhum), Ghātsila Rāja and others, and by keeping the Barā Rāja (Barābhum) occupied with levies from Pānchet, that he was eventually able to reduce Sham Ganjan to terms and to march with considerable difficulty through the Dhādka pass. Peace was thus once more restored, and though the outbreak of the Dhalbhum Rāja in 1773 to some extent affected the neighbouring area in Mānbhum there was a period of comparative peace in Barābhum for several years. A detachment of sepoys remained at Barābhum, and during the rains of 1773 Mānbhum was held by a small military force under Lieutenant James Dunn.

The history of the remainder of the district during the earlier years of British rule seems to have followed a more peaceful and less interesting course. Pānchet was joined with Bishnupur and Birbhum under a single Supervisor or Collector, and the correspondence which survives is mainly taken up with revenue matters, though there are constant references to trouble with Chuārs to the west and south. In 1772 there was difficulty in obtaining a farmer for Pānchet, "none of the farmers offering to renew their leases apprehending a decrease of revenue, as there had been a wholesale desertion of the land by the ryots in consequence of the oppression of the superior farmers." Farmers were eventually obtained, apparently owing to the exertions of one Ram Kanta Biswas who was accordingly appointed Dewan.

During the next ten years Pánchet with Jhaldā was given a separate Collector. In 1782 we hear of the making of the military road still known in the district as the old Benares Road and cutting right through the heart of Pānchet Proper. Raghunāthpur on this road, within a few miles of the Pānchet zamindar's residence at Kāshipur, was, if not actually the head-quarters of the Pānchet district, a place of some importance. In November of the same year there were disturbances in Jhalda and Tamār; the zamindar of Pānchet is described as exposed to daily depredations from the petty estates of Jhalda, and at the same time the zamindars of Nāwagarh and Jharia had taken to plundering and the latter to withholding his rents. The immediate result was the deputation of Major Crawford with an armed force to Jhalda to quell the disturbances and take charge of the collections. By July of 1783 this officer had restored Jharia to tranquillity and was prepared to proceed with the revenue settlement of Jhalda; at the same time he recommended that the inhabitants of this area and also of parts of Rāmgarh on the west and Pānchet on the east should be disarmed.

About the same time the troubles with the Chuārs of the south of the district broke out once more, and military measures had again to be taken to restore order. The Jaigīrdar of Kailāpal was once again to the fore, and this small tract of difficult country had apparently become a regular place of refuge for the Chuārs of the surrounding country. The disturbances lasted all through the cold weather of 1783-84, and it was not till May 1784 that order was once more restored. At the same time there were outbreaks in the northern estates of the district which were apparently a place of refuge for the dacoits and others who gave such trouble to the Bīrbhum authorities.

In 1789 and 1790 there was once more trouble in Jhalda and the adjoining estates of Tamar in Rāmgarh. Pānchet, and with it apparently most of the district except perhaps the south-eastern estates, was at this time under the Collector of Rāmgarh. In 1792 depredations in Pātkum were treated as a sufficient reason for suspending the demand due from the zamindar of Nāgpur, and the inference to be drawn is that Pātkum was at that time a dependency of the Chota Nāgpur Rāja. Disturbed conditions seem to have continued here and in Tamar off and on during the next three years, and the Permanent Settlement of this area was not finally completed till 1795.

Meantime the Pānchet Zamindar had already fallen into arrears and his estate was in 1795 put up to sale and purchased by one Nilambar Mitra. The zamindar complained that the default and consequent sale was due to collusion between his Dewan and the Collectorate Staff, and prayed for the cancellation of the sale. No attention being paid to this prayer the zamindar defied the authorities and refused to allow the auction purchaser any footing in the estate. He was loyally supported by his tenantry and the various attempts on the part of the Collector to farm portions of the estate and to manage other portions khās were continually thwarted. By 1798 the whole area was practically in a state of insurrection and the trouble of the local authorities was enormously increased by a fresh outbreak of the Chuārs in Parganas Raipur, Ambikānagar, and Supur adjoining Mānbhum and Barābhum on the east. Durjan Singh, their chief leader, was captured by the military force sent to suppress this outbreak in 1798 but was again released as, when he was put on trial, no one dared to appear against him. The trouble consequently began again, and as the Chuārs lived in remote and inaccessible places, they were difficult to get at; they constantly made raids when they were least expected, and when troops were sent out against them, disappeared into their fastnesses, only to reappear and commit fresh depredations as soon as the troops were withdrawn.

So far as Pānchet was concerned an end was put to the disturbances by a complete climb down on the part of the Government; the zamindar was restored to his estate and the sale cancelled. At the same time the supervision of this area was transferred once more from the Collector of Rāmgarh to the Collector of Birbhum with a view apparently to closer control.

In the south-west of the district there was also trouble at this time. The zamindar of Pātkum was a minor, the succession was disputed between him and his brother, and his uncle to whom the management had been made over by Government was inclined to give trouble; Bāghmundi had been confiscated, apparently in consequence of the participation of the zamindar in the disturbances in Pātkum and Tamār a year or two earlier. A portion of the estate was subsequently restored to him probably in pursuance of the policy forced on Government in the case of Pānchet by the strong objection of the local aborigine to the rule of any one but his hereditary chief.

Barābhum in 1800.

Some interesting details of the state of affairs in the south-east of the district Barābhum and neighbouring parganas in the early days of British rule are given in a report of Mr. Henry Strachey, the Magistrate of Midnapore in 1800. At the time he wrote the estate was in the throes of a disputed succession between two minor sons of Raghunāth Nārāyan, with whom the Permanent Settlement was concluded, and who died early in 1798. Pending settlement of the dispute by the civil courts Government had assumed the management, but for their own ends the various sardār paiks, the talukdars of Barābhum, and the ancestors of the present ghātwāl sardārs had taken sides, and were engaged in ravaging one another's and the Rāja's territory. Neither the regular police nor the military detachments stationed at Barābazar, or from time to time sent to quell the disturbances, were of any avail against the large forces of the sardārs, particularly those of Lal Singh of Satarakhāni; the climate was unhealthy, the area full of impassable hill and jungle in which the sardārs and their paiks or Chuars took refuge whenever pressed. "Perfect tranquillity," according to Mr. Strachey, "had almost never been known in Barābhum and the zamindar had never had complete control over the different descriptions of persons residing within his estate" and depredations had been constantly committed by one sardār or other on his neighbour sardārs, on the zamindar himself, or on the neighbouring zamindars. As a sample of what these dreaded sardārs were, he describes one of them, Lal Singh, in these terms:—

"Lal Singh appears to be the most powerful of these sardārs. A short account of him and of his conduct during the late disturbances will serve to convey an idea of the others.

"Lal Singh and his ancestors have long possessed lands in the zamindari of Barābhum, and have paid with punctuality their revenue of 240 rupees yearly to the zamindar. Lal Singh resides at Sāuri, a place described to me as an almost inaccessible mountain about 5 or 6 Crose from Barābhum, the residence of the zamindar, and above 90 miles from hence. A stone quarry near his house yields him a revenue of about 1,000 rupees yearly, and the produce of his lands may amount to another thousand rupees. Every year he levies a small contribution from almost every village in the zamindari. In case of refusal or the least delay in the payment of sookmudi, so the contribution is called, the village is infallibly plundered.

"Lal Singh possesses large tracts of land in other zamindaris, some of them at a great distance from his own residence. These lands he has seized within these few years, and maintains himself in the possession of them by threats of laying waste the zamindari in which they are situated. The zamindar of Pānchet has found it his interest to grant him several villages in his estate, and he accordingly maintains quiet possession of them, treats his ryots well, and affords them effectual protection.

"A few years ago he took possession of ten villages belonging to Jagannath Dhal, zamindar of Ghātsila. This produced a war between them, and, after a long struggle, and much slaughter on both sides, he was forced to yield to the superior power of the zamindar, retire to his own domains, and relinquish the lands he had occupied in Ghātsila.

"The two minor zamindars and their adherents have respectively used every endeavour to engage this powerful sardār to support the pretensions of one against the other, and it appears that as soon as the eldest succeeded in gaining him over to his interest, the younger accused his brother of joining the Chuārs. The elder brother, probably to avoid this imputation, left the zamindari, came into Midnapore, and has resided here ever since.

"This event occurred above a year ago. Most of the other sardārs in the zamindari at the same time attached themselves to the younger brother, and all parties proceeded to open hostilities, that is to say, to murder each other, to plunder, lay waste, and burn the property in dispute, to depopulate the country as far as lay in their power, and to commit every species of outrage and enormity. During this general scene of havoc and disorder the Serberacar being robbed and stripped of all he had, and his house being entirely plundered by Lal Singh and other sardārs escaped to Midnapore. At the same time twenty Sebundies who were stationed there by the Magistrate likewise retired precipitately.

"At this period disturbances had broken out owing to other causes entirely unconnected with the dissensions of Barābhum in many other parts of the jungles in Raipur, Phulkusma, Dompara, and in the Rāni's estate contiguous to Midnapore.

"A considerable military force being at length sent to Barābhum hostilities ceased between the contending parties, and they retired to their strongholds, from whence they have since occasionally sallied out, and plundered indiscriminately every part of the estate.

"Before the arrival of the troops, Lal Singh, with what avowed object I cannot discover, had in conjunction with other sardārs plundered the greater part of the town of Barābhum, or other village (since there is not a single brick house in the whole zamindari) and prevailed on above 100 paiks of the place to join him and take up their residence at Sāuri; 50 of these paiks afterwards joined Kishen Pator, another powerful sardār of the other party. The rest remain with Lal Singh, so that all became Chuars and still remain so."

Mr. Strachey's report deals with the question of restoring order; his proposals involved the pardoning of these sardārs for all past offences and making them responsible as police for the maintenance of order in their respective tenures and the estate generally. Further reference to these measures, which were actually adopted, will be made in dealing with the police tenures of the district in a later chapter. Mr. Strachey succeeded in restoring a state of comparative peace, without recourse to further military measures, and the settlement of the question of succession in favour of the elder son Ganga Gobinda by the courts, a few years later, removed the immediate excuse for dissension and disorder, and the peace was not seriously broken in this area till some 30 years later.

The records of succeeding years show that so far as administration of revenue went, things had to a certain extent settled down, though the Pānchet zamindar, taking advantage no doubt of his successful opposition in 1798, was constantly in arrears and from time to time proposals were put forward for the sale of the whole or portions of the estate. For revenue purposes the Collector of Bīrbhum exercised jurisdiction over the whole area now included within the district, but by Regulation XVIII of 1805 the Jungle Mahals (23 Parganas and Mahals in all, including the wilder portions of Burdwan and the present district of Bānkura) were constituted into a separate magisterial charge of which the headquarters was at Bānkura.

During the 25 years succeeding the formation of the Jungle Mahals district the area included therein was brought under much closer control. There were small military establishments at Jhalda and Raghunāthpur on the Calcutta-Benares Road and these with the police organisation were sufficient to reduce the district to a state of comparative order. The police system was, except in Pānchet, that provided for in the Regulation of 1805; the zamindars themselves were the police Darogas, and they provided and were responsible for the subordinate rural police. In Pānchet, where the area was too big for the zamindar to exercise a close enough control, the system was supplemented by a thana system, the cost of which was provided by the zamindar; under the Darogas in charge of the thanas worked the rural police, consisting of the Digwars and their subordinates in all the more northerly portions, and the considerable body of Ghatwals in the south and west. Mr. Dent writing in 1833 remarked that, with regard to police, "the rules in Regulation XVIII of 1805 seem well adapted to these Jungle Mahals and where the Rāja and his Dewan have been duly qualified they have fully answered in practice and crimes of violence and blood had greatly decreased.'

In 1832, however, the peace of the district was somewhat rudely disturbed by the outbreak known to this day as "Gangā Nārāyan hangāma" which followed almost immediately upon the Kol rising, which disturbed the peace of Singhbhum, Rānchi and Palāmau in the preceding year. From participating in this the Bhumij Kol of this district had almost entirely abstained except in Pātkum, where a small disturbance in January 1832 was not GANGĀ NĀRĀYAN'S REBELLION.

put down by the Magistrate until a military force had been called in. The people of this country, besides being very closely allied with those of Tamār, one of the chief centres of the disturbance in Rānchi, had special grievances of their own in the fact that there had been a general enhancement of rents of all inferior holders without regard to the rights of the parties or the usage of the country by the Sazāwal appointed by Government in the Court of Wards to manage the estate during the long minority of the Rāja. On the outbreak being suppressed the Rāja being then of age was put in possession, and in the later troubles he gave material assistance to the Government forces.

It was in Barābhum, the adjoining estate, that the disturbances of 1832 commenced; the causes were complex and will be referred to later. The origin of the disturbance, however, lay in a disputed succession to the Rāj. In the previous century Rāja Belak Narayan died leaving two sons, Raghunath and Lachman Singh; the latter, though the younger by birth, was the son of the elder or Pát Rāni and as such claimed to succeed. His claim was, however, rejected and he was driven out by a military force and shortly afterwards, as he continued to make efforts to wrest the estate from his brother, he was apprehended and later died in Midnapore Jail. On Raghunath's death in 1798 an exactly similar dispute arose between his sons Gangā Gobinda and Mādhab Singh which was decided after lengthy litigation in favour of the former, as the eldest son born in wedlock, by the Sadar Dewāni Adalat. Mādhab Singh settled his differences with his brother and became his Dewān, but unfortunately for himself, put himself into direct opposition to Gangā Nārāyan Singh, son of his uncle Lachman, who had maintained his father's feud against the other branch of the family. Mādhab deprived Gangā Nārāyan of Pancha-Sardāri, the largest of the *ghātwali tarafs* which had been held by Lachman after being driven out of Barābazar, and prior to his arrest and death in Jail. As Dewan Mādhab appears to have made himself thoroughly unpopular by imposing additional taxes or rents on the holders of the different Ghats and a general house-tax or '*ghartaki*' throughout the estate; over and above this he went extensively into the moneylending business; his charges were particularly usurious and apparently he made full use of the courts, and also of his own position in the estate, to exact the uttermost farthing from his debtors. The odium in which he was held resulted in his murder on the 2nd April 1832 by Gangā Nārāyan Singh who came upon him with a large force of Ghātwals from Pancha Sardāri and Satrakhāni while he was checking his store of grain in an outlying village. Mādhab was seized and carried off a few miles to a small hill near Bāmni and there deliberately murdered by Gangā Nārāyan himself; the latter however, though he struck the first blow, insisted on every ghātwal present shooting an arrow into the body, thinking thereby to ensure their continued co-operation and their not betraying him, all being equally implicated in the murder. With a large body of ghātwals thus attached to his cause Gangā Nārāyan Singh proceeded to lay the whole country under contribution and on the 1st of May marched on Barābazar; the Munsiff's cutchery was attacked and the Bazar plundered, and the zamindar was obliged to concede all Gangā Nārāyan's demands including *taraf* Pancha Sardāri as his *khorposh* or subsistence grant, in order to escape being attacked in his own palace. On the following day Gangā Nārāyan once more advanced on Barābazar and burnt down the Munsiff's and Salt Daroga's cutcheries and the police thana. On the 14th he attacked, with a force of three thousand Chuārs, the troops who were with the Magistrate Mr. Russell; the latter tried to reason with the insurgents, but as an essential condition was the surrender of the murderers of Mādhab Singh, the negotiations failed. On the 4th, 5th and 6th June the troops were attacked on their march to Bāmni and again on their retirement from that place to Barābazar with such effect that the whole of the Government force had to retire on Bānkura, leaving Barābhum in the undisturbed possession of Gangā Nārāyan. A lull then followed, but as soon as the rice crop had been planted out in August, Gangā Nārāyan once more assembled his followers and proceeded to plunder the estates of Akro, Ambikānagar, Raipur, Shāmsundarpur and Phulkusma, to the east of Barābhum, and now part of Bānkura district. The Bhumij of these areas as well as of Sildah (now in Midnapore) and Kailāpal for the most part joined the insurgents and the whole country side was in a general state of disturbance, or, as it was then described, of *Chuāri*, until the end of November when the 34th regiment of Native Infantry arrived at Raipur. Gangā Nārāyan had already retired through Dhalbhum, where he forced on the Rāja one of his nominees as ghātwal of Dompāra, to Dhādka and later to Baridih. From these places expeditions were made towards Gokulnagar and Puncha, and operations would probably have extended further north into the Pānchet country but for the arrival of Mr. Braddon and Lieutenant Trimmer with a force of sepoys and Barkandazes, who succeeded in repelling an attack made on them by Gangā Nārāyan at

Chākultor, a few miles south of Purūlia. Mr. Braddon's force, proceeded then to re-occupy Barābazar; a thana was established at Balarāmpur and the intervening country held in force and further incursions northwards prevented. In November Mr. Dent assumed charge at Chākultor and offered a free pardon to all concerned in the disturbance except Gangā Nārāyan himself and some ten of the leading Sardārs. This offer having no result, Mr. Dent proceeded to make simultaneous attacks on the night of the 16th November on Bāndhdih, Gangā Nārāyan's head-quarters, and on Bārudih and Bhāoni, those of two other leaders, all of which were successful. During the following month elaborate military operations were undertaken, small detachments being sent out in every direction through the hilly country to break up and destroy or secure the surrender of the now disorganised forces of Gangā Nārāyan. The leader had by this time retired into Singhbhum with some of his followers, and there he met his death in attempting to establish among the Kols his reputation as a great military leader by attacking a strong post of the Thakur of Kharsāwan. With the death or rather the flight of Gangā Nārāyan the disturbances in this district came to an end; order was quickly restored and the active services of the troops dispensed with.

CAUSES AND RESULTS OF THE OUTBREAK.

Mr. Dent in his report to Government, on which the account just given is largely based, dealt in considerable detail with the various causes, which, though not directly accounting for this outbreak, made it possible for Gangā Nārāyan to enlist so readily the services of a large body of men, and to spread confusion over so extensive an area. Dissatisfaction with the administration of the law of debtor and creditor appears to have been rife at this time in Barābhum, and the sale of ancestral holdings for debt was particularly objected to as something entirely opposed to the custom of the aboriginal tenantry. Nor were indebtedness and its consequences confined to the tenantry, but we are told that almost all the zamindars, the members of their families holding maintenance or other grants, the Sardār Ghātwals, and the bigger intermediate holders generally were in embarrassed circumstances. General improvidence seems to have been the order of the day, and much of the land had already at this time passed more or less permanently to money-lending outsiders. The rule of inheritance by primogeniture kept the large estates nominally intact; in practice the necessity of providing for members of the family by maintenance grants imposed a continually increasing burden on the zamindar, and continually decreased his cash resources, putting him more and more at the mercy of the money-lender. To all these people, therefore, Gangā Nārāyan's outbreak came as welcome opportunity of getting back some of their own; the memory of the Pānchet zamindar's successful objection to his estate being sold still remained, and there seems to have been a general idea that if success attended the outbreak there would be a general wiping off of burdensome debts. The state of things disclosed was not unlike that already found in Chota Nāgpur Proper, and the recommendation already made in consequence thereof, *i.e.*, "to exclude the area from the operation of the general regulations and form it into a separate jurisdiction superintended by the Political Agent for the South-West Frontier as Commissioner acting under the special rules which might from time to time be prescribed for the said area by the Government and aided by one or more assistants as might be requisite for the due administration of the tracts placed under his authority", was now given effect to, and embodied in Regulation XIII of 1833. By this the district of the Jungle Mahals was broken up; the estates of Senpahāri, Shergarh and Bishnupur were transferred to Burdwan and a new district called Mānbhum with its headquarters at Mānbazar constituted, including, besides the present area of the district, the estates of Supur, Raipur, Ambikānagar, Simlāpal, Bhelāidiha, Phulkusma, Shāmsundarpur and Dhālbhum. In 1838 the headquarters was removed to Purūlia, described then as lying "in the centre of the jungles." Prior to the mutiny the only further changes were the transfer of Dhālbhum to Singhbhum and the change in titles of the chief officers, the Principal Assistant at Purūlia becoming the Deputy Commissioner, and the Agent to the Governor-General for the South-West Frontier the Commissioner of Chota Nāgpur, by Act XX of 1854.

MUTINY OF 1857.

During the mutiny the attitude of the local garrison which consisted of 64 sepoys of the Rāmgarh battalion and 12 Sowars was such that the Deputy Commissioner was obliged to abandon the place for a time, retiring *viâ* Raghunāthpur on Rānīganj The garrison proceeded to loot the Treasury and release the prisoners in the jail and then marched off without apparently creating any serious disturbance, either in Purūlia itself or *en route*, to join their fellows at Rānchi. Most of the respectable residents left the town at the first sign of an outbreak, and in the absence of the sepoys and also of any constituted authority the jail birds and badmashes, led, it is said, by a member of the Pānchet family, committed various outrages in the town and on the roads towards Raghunāthpur; the court-house was burnt down and the old records destroyed. Captain Oakes, the Deputy Commissioner, had on his retirement called on the then Rāja of Pānchet, Nilmoni Singh, for assistance which, however, he did not give. Consequenlty, on his return less than a month later with reinforcements from Rānīganj, his first act was to arrest the Rāja and send him in custody to Calcutta, where he was not released until March 1859. Beyond a certain amount of anxiety due to the disturbed state of the adjoining districts there was little further of interest or importance in the mutiny history of Mānbhum. The Sonthals of the district were reported by Captain Oakes to be in a state of great excitement, but no actual outbreak occurred; the zamindar or Jaypur was indeed attacked by some of them, but he was able to beat them off and reduce them to order without assistance from outside.

Writing in April 1858 Colonel Dalton, the Commissioner, remarked that Chota Nāgpur was full of "tribes whose predatory habits were notorious long ago and whom recent disturbances have shown that they have not forgotten their hereditary renown". He believed that they were "not impelled by feelings hostile to the British Government but they cannot resist the temptation of following any chief who will lead them on plundering expeditions." The comparative freedom from trouble during this period in Mānbhum may perhaps therefore be ascribed to the prompt arrest of the Rāja of Pānchet and the absence of any other suitable leader; it is worthy of notice, at any rate, that the trouble among the Sonthals was due to local causes entirely, and at no time were their energies directed against any but the local zamindars.

From the mutiny onwards the history of the district differs little from that of other districts in British India; the records show a steady advance in more systematic and more closely organised and supervised administration, and the general peace of the district has not been broken. Agrarian troubles threatened in 1869 and 1870 in the north of the district where the Tundi zamindar and his Sonthal tenants were at variance, but the difficulty was smoothed over by an informal settlement arranged by Colonel Dalton as Commissioner, which was renewed 10 years later by Mr. Risley and again at the beginning of the present century.

LATER HISTORY.

The history of the disputes between the ghātwals of Barābhum and Messrs. Watson and Company will be referred to in a later chapter; the so-called compromise of 1884 arranged by Mr. Risley removed for a time the acuteness of the ill-feeling, which the ghātwāls bore towards the Company and its European managers, and which for a time threatened to culminate in serious disturbances of the peace. The proneness of the Bhumij population of this area to revert to their old "Chuāri" habits has been displayed on the occasion of every famine and period of scarcity in the regularly recurring outbreaks of dacoity, but nothing in the shape of organised opposition to constituted authority has been noticeable. The latent possibilities of such organisation among the Sonthals, who within the last 20 years have become a very considerable part of the district population, were just suggested in 1907, when after a bad harvest prices rose to what would, ten years earlier, have been treated as indicative of famine conditions. On that occasion a decision was come to by the Sonthals, assembled for their annual hunt on the Bāghmundi hills, that rice should be obtainable at 10 seers per rupee, and as a result of that decision and the refusal of the merchants to supply at that rate, several of the "Hāts" were systematically looted within a few days, and there was every prospect of this being repeated. Prompt police measures, and a rapid rush by the Deputy Commissioner and the Superintendent of Police through the country affected brought the Sonthals very quickly to a sense of the folly and futility of their action, and the trouble promptly ceased.

FORMATION OF THE DISTRICT. The only matter calling for further mention is the formation of the district as at present constituted. When it was first established in 1833 under Regulation XIII of that year, it included the estate of Dhālbhum, now attached to Singhbhum, besides a large part of the present district of Bānkura, and Shergarh, now a part of Burdwan. In 1845 the estate of Dhālbum was transferred to Singhbhum, and in the following year, owing to a press of criminal cases, the fiscal divisions of Shergharh, Chaurāsi, Mahisara, Cheliāma, Chātna, Nalichānda, Bankhandi, Bārpāra, and portions of Banchās and Pāra were placed under the criminal jurisdiction of Bānkura district, though remaining a part of Mānbhum for revenue purposes. At this time the nominal area of the district was no less than 7,896 square miles comprised in 31 zamindaries. In 1871 Shergarh with part of Pāndra (east of the Barākar river) was transferred to Burdwan, and Chātna and Mahisara to Bānkura, while the criminal jurisdiction of the remainder was retransferred to Mānbhum, the civil, criminal and revenue jurisdiction being made coterminous. A further change in the jurisdiction of the district was made by the Government orders of the 27th September 1879, by which parganas Supur, Raipur, Ambikānagar, Simlāpal, Bhelāidiha, Phulkusma and Shāmsundarpur, comprising Raipur, Khātra and Simlāpal thānas were transferred to Bānkura district, thus reducing

Mānbhum to its present limits. This final change in jurisdiction originated in a representation made by Messrs. Gisborne & Co., who held a considerable portion of these parganas, and with some reason complained of the inconvenience and hardship to people having to go to Purūlia and Rānchi from these areas, the distances being great, and also of the delay in disposal of cases in Mānbhum which, they said, was under-officered, while work in Bānkura was light.

Since 1879 no changes have taken place in the jurisdiction of Mānbhum, though in 1904 it was seriously contemplated to cut off the whole of the northern subdivision, and form it with Rānīganj into a separate district, which would have contained within its boundaries the greater part of the existing coalfields of Bengal. Other counsels, however, prevailed, and the main objections to the then existing arrangements were met by the removal of the headquarters of the Rānīganj subdivision to Asansol, and more recently of the Gobindpur subdivision to Dhānbaid, both of which places are more centrally and conveniently situated with reference to the actual coalfield areas.

Archæological remains. Reference has already been made to the more important of the numerous archæological remains in connection with their bearing on the history of the district, and a more detailed description will be found against each place of interest in the concluding chapter of this volume.

CHAPTER III.

THE PEOPLE.

AT the conclusion of the Revenue survey of 1864-67 the population of Mânbhum, including 1,404 square miles subsequently transferred to Bânkura and Burdwan, was estimated at 694,498, giving a density per square mile of 126 persons; this figure was based on an enumeration of the houses, allowing an average of 4½ persons per house. Two years later, in 1869, a preliminary census was held, but the results were even then admitted to be inaccurate and may be rejected. In 1872 the attempt to carry out a simultaneous enumeration through the agency of the inhabitants themselves was abandoned, and a gradual enumeration was made by a salaried agency. The population was then returned as 915,570 for an area of 4,914 square miles and 820,821 for the district as at present constituted. In 1881 the first regular simultaneous census took place and disclosed a population of 1,058,228 for an area of 4,147 square miles, comprising 3 towns, 6,144 villages and 178,494 occupied houses; the average density of population per square mile was thus 225, a very large increase on the approximate figures of earlier enumerations. The large increase of 237,707, or nearly 29 per cent. in 9 years, must be treated as to a large extent due to the inaccuracy of the earlier enumeration, though part, possibly as much as half, may be ascribed correctly to normal growth of population, added to the gradual opening out of the country which then, as till a much later date, was the least difficult of access of any of the Chota Nagpur districts and was more especially open to immigration from the already densely-populated districts of Bengal proper. GROWTH OF POPULATION.

The census of 1891 disclosed a further increase of 135,100 or 12·8 per cent. Purūlia had by this time been connected up by railway with Asansol and had developed into a fairly important trading centre; the urban population of Jhalda and Raghunāthpur had also increased considerably, but comparing the figures for the different rural areas it is obvious that the main causes of increase were natural and common to the whole district.

Census of 1901. In the succeeding 10 years the increase amounted to only 108,036, the total population being returned in 1901 as 1,301,364 persons. The percentage of increase was 9·1, but an examination of the thana figures shows that over 44 per cent. of the total increase is accounted for by the two thanas of Jharia and Topchānchi which contain the bulk of the collieries, most of which were opened out for the first time during the last few years of the decade. Excluding these areas, the increase over the rest of the district was only 5·6 per cent., a very considerably diminished rate as compared with that of the previous decade, which may be accounted for by the fact that there were short crops in 1891, 1892, 1895 and 1896, the last of which years was followed by a year of acute scarcity. Apart from the direct and indirect effects of scarcity on the fecundity of the people, emigration from and through this district to the tea districts, which was considerable throughout the decade, reached very large figures in 1896 and 1897. During the 5 years ending 1900 nearly 40,000 persons were registered at Purulia under the provisions of Act I of 1882, and the number of emigrants not so registered is estimated at about the same. These figures, however, include a large number of coolies recruited in the Central Provinces, Rānchi and other districts, and probably not more than half in all were actually residents of Mānbhum. Over and above this, however, there was considerable emigration to the adjoining coalfield of Rāniganj and by way of set-off in the later years of the decade immigration to the Jharia coalfield from Hazāribagh and the Sonthal Parganas. The number of immigrants is, however, far short of the number of emigrants, and the excess of persons born in Mānbhum and living elsewhere over persons born elsewhere but living in Mānbhum was returned at the last census as nearly 74,000.

Migration. In spite, therefore, of the attraction of the coalfields the district had lost by migration. The number of female immigrants was slightly greater than 1891, and there were about 14,000 more male immigrants, chiefly from Hāzaribagh, Bihar and the United Provinces, who had for the most part come to work in the mines. The increase in the number of emigrants was even larger, the excess over the figures of 1891 being some 5,500 in the case of males and nearly 12,000 in the case of females. It is interesting to note that more than half the emigrants (136,000 in all) were enumerated in Assam; of the remainder one-third were found in Burdwan, while another third were accounted for in the adjoining districts of Bānkura, Hāzaribagh and the Sonthal Parganas.

No great number go from Mānbhum to the dockyards or mills of Calcutta, and Assam is evidently preferred to the coalfields of Burdwan; further reference to the emigration to the tea gardens will be found in a later chapter.

GENERAL CHARACTERISTICS. Density of population.

The district supports 314 persons per square mile as compared with 181 per square mile for the whole Chota Nāgpur Division. The density of population is nearly twice that of Hāzaribagh and Rānchi, rather more than twice that of Singhbhum, and just 2½ times that of Palamau. It varies very much in different parts of the district, but generally speaking, if the northernmost thana, Tundi, be excluded, it is greatest in the north, and gradually decreases as one approaches the southern boundary. Topchānchi which includes a considerable part of the Jharia coalfield returns as many as 447 persons per square mile ; Jharia adjoining it has 380, and Nirsa which includes a portion of the Rāniganj coalfield has 370, while Gobindpur which immediately adjoins the Jharia coalfield on the north returns 300. The remaining thana in the northern subdivision, Tundi, is a purely rural area and is the least densely populated thana in the district, the number of persons per square mile being only 203. Immediately south of the coalfield area and of the Dāmodar river are Chās with 427 per square mile and Raghunāthpur with 400. The latter thana contains a small coalfield area, but the main reason for the density of population in both thanas is, perhaps, the fact that they contain much more comparatively level ground than any other part of the district and offered in the past attractions in the way of comparatively easy cultivation to immigrants from other parts of the district and from Hāzaribagh on the west and Bankura on the east. The census figures, however, show that the tendency to increase of population in these areas had practically disappeared before the last decade ; an indication, perhaps, that the limits of easy cultivation have been reached. In the centre of the district there is less variation in density, the average being about 330 for the thanas Purulia, Mānbazar, Gaurāndi and Pāra. South and west of this area there is a considerable drop, the density being greatest, 260 in Jhalda and least in Baghmundi 231, the other two thanas, Barābhum and Chāndil returning 233 and 250, respectively.

Excluding the colliery tracts Purūlia, Mānbazar and Chāndil are the areas in which there was the greatest increase in the decade ending in 1901 ; in the case of the two latter the population has practically doubled itself in the last 30 years.

The lowest rate of increase in recent years has been in Pāra, Chās, Gaurāndi and Jhalda, from all of which areas the labour force of the coalfield is recruited.

Towns and villages.

The only places recognised as towns are the three Municipal towns of Purūlia, Jhalda and Raghunāthpur, which have a population of 17, 291, 4,877 and 4,171 respectively. The remainder of the population is contained in 5,521 villages, most of which are very small, over 92 per cent. of the rural population living in villages containing less than 500 inhabitants, while the average number of residents in each village is only 231. The number of villages containing between one and two thousand inhabitants was in 1901 sixty-three; fourteen contained from 2 to 4 thousand, and only one, excluding the Municipal towns, over 4,000.

Language.

The prevailing vernacular of the district is the western dialect of Bengali, known as *Rārhi boli*, which is used by 72 per cent. of the inhabitants. Along the western border this merges into the Magāhi form of Hindi, variants of which are locally known as Kurmāli, Khotta or Khottāhi, or even Khotta Bangāla. Including these dialects, which are spoken by over 40,000 people mainly in the north and west of the district, as Hindi, Hindi is the language used by nearly 163,000 or 12½ per cent. of the population. Of non-Aryan languages the most prevalent is Sonthali, spoken by 182,000 persons or nearly 14 per cent. of the population. Other Mundari or Kolarian languages are represented by 3,770 persons who speak Kurmāli, 2,340 Bhumij, 2,229 Kora, 1,888 Mundāri and 1,169 Mahli. No great reliance can, however, be placed on these figures as the distinction between the different dialects is not, as a rule, very marked, and the enumerators as a class were not likely to have shown any great discrimination. The small number of persons speaking Bhumij, barely 2 per cent. of the whole Bhumij population, is perhaps partly accounted for by the fact that the Bhumij of eastern Barābhum, at any rate, and probably of a larger area, profess Bengali as their mother tongue, though they speak freely with their Sonthal neighbours in so-called Sonthali, which a closer examination by an expert would probably show to be a survival of their own original dialect. To a large extent the members of the aboriginal tribes are polyglot, speaking Bengali or Hindi, usually the former, in addition to their own dialect, even where, as in the case of the Sonthals, they are a sufficiently numerous community to force a knowledge of their own language on their neighbours, and on the courts and offices with whom they come into contact. The aspirations of the upper grades of Bhumij to take position as Rājputs, and the general spread of Hindu religious ideas among them no doubt account largely for the extent to which they have given up their own language for Bengali; the census figures show that in the case of the Sonthals a similar tendency is not as yet very marked

The census figures distinguish between Hindus, Animists, Musalmāns, Christians and others. For Mānbhum, according to the figures compiled for the census tables, 87 per cent. of the population are Hindus, 7·9 per cent. Animists, and 4·8 per cent. Muhammadans, while Christians and others number together barely 3,000, or less than ½ per cent. of the district population. **Religion.**

As Mr. Gait* points out, the dividing line between Hinduism and Animism is uncertain. Animism is defined as "the belief in the existence of souls or spirits, of which only the powerful, those on which man feels himself dependent, and before which he stands in awe, acquire the rank of divine beings, and become objects of worship. These spirits are conceived as moving freely through earth and air, and either of their own accord, or because conjured by some spell, and thus under compulsion, appear to men (Spiritism). But they may also take up their abode, either temporarily or permanently, in some object, whether living or lifeless, it matters not; and this object, as endowed with higher power, is then worshipped, or employed to protect individuals and communities (Fetishism)". But Hinduism does not, like Christianity and Islam, demand of its votaries the rejection of all other religious beliefs as a social organisation. The great points, on which the Brāhmans insist, are the recognition of their own supremacy, and the existence of certain Hindu gods, and the observance of certain restrictions in the matter of food and drink and social practices. Subject to these limitations, there is nothing to prevent the neophytes admitted from a non-Hindu race from worshipping their own peculiar gods or devils in their own way and with the aid of their own priests. Consequently it is almost impossible to say where the exact line dividing Hinduism from Animism lies, and in a district like Mānbhum, with a large aboriginal population, a considerable part of which has been subjected to Hinduising influences for several generations, this is particularly the case. **Hindus and Animists.**

Judged by the outward and visible signs of Hinduism in the shape of regular temples and places of worship, it would be inferred that the Hinduism of a large part of the population is not much more than a veneer. At the same time races like the Bāuri, the Kurmi and the Bhumij have adopted in varying degrees the observance of the regular Hindu festivals, Hindu customs and ceremonies in regard to births, deaths and marriages,

* Census of India, 1901, Vol. VI, Part I, pages, 151, 398.

and though the Bhumij, at any rate, retain a very large leaven of their purely tribal customs in matters of religion, they are sufficiently Hinduised to be classed as Hindus rather than Animists. The same cannot be said for the Southals, though the census figures show that half of these have been classed as Hindus and half as Animists.

The Sun God and other local deities.

Among all the aboriginal and Hinduised aboriginal races of the district the sun holds a very high place in their primitive beliefs; the Bhumij and Mundas worship him under the name "Singbonga" with offerings of fowls and country liquor, and the most binding form of oath amongst them begins with the formula "the Sun God is in the sky." Equally prominent among both Mundas and Southals is the reverence for the great mountain or Marang Buru, to whom a buffalo is the appropriate form of sacrifice. Among other objects of nature the *karam* tree (*Adina cordifolia*) is especially sacred, and a special festival is held in its honour at the time of the harvest home, a branch of a tree being brought in from the forest by the young men and women of the village to the accompaniment of singing and dancing and beating of tomtoms. In the village it is stuck in the ground, and decorated with flowers and lights and forms the centre of a night of great merriment In the morning it is thrown into the nearest stream and the spirit of evil is believed to be removed with it.

Grāmya devata.

The worship of a *Grāmay devata* is almost universal, and among the Southals Marang Buru, already referred to as the spirit of the mountain, is the principal. In every village where the tribe, which originally cleared it, still remains, there is sacred grove, *Jāhira* or *Sarna*, a small patch of virgin jungle preserved from the axe as a refuge and local habitation for one or more sylvan deities. Their worship is conducted, ordinarily without the assistance of any regular Brāhman or priest, by the head of the village; a handful of rice is deposited in three places in the grove and the sacrificial goat is made to eat this, after which its head is severed at one blow; the head is the perquisite of the Lāya or priest, if there is one, and the body is shared by the members of his family.

Witchcraft.

A belief in witchcraft and the evil eye is universal; cases of murder of persons suspected of being witches are far from uncommon. The murderer is, it may be noted, almost invariably a member of the family to which the witch belongs. Cases of human sacrifice are very rare, but hook swinging is still occasionally practised, though, as a rule, the hooks are merely inserted in the fleshy part of the back, and the devotee or victim swung with his weight taken by a cloth bound round his chest, and not by the ropes attached to the hooks.

Festivals. There are no special places of pilgrimage within the district, though the ancient temples of Tolkupi and Budhpur are the scenes of small melas on the occasion of the Chaitra Sankrānti and other festivals.

Muhammadans. Of the Musalmān population more than half were returned as Shaikhs and the remainder, except for some 2,000 odd Pathāns, as Jolāhas. Nearly one-fifth of the whole population is to be found in Purūlia thana, and Chās and Jhalda in the Sadar subdivision return over 6,000 and 4,000 respectively. The proportion Musalmāns bear to the general population is more marked in the Dhānbaid subdivision, where in Gobindpur thana they represent nearly one-sixth, and are also numerous in Topchānchi, Jharia and Nirsa. Very few among them hold any sort of position, and their general poverty and obscurity is marked by the fact that, except in Purūlia, Chās, Gobindpur and a few other places, there are no regular mosques. Enquiries recently made elicited the fact that there was not a single recognized Maulvi in the district.

Christians. The Christian population, though small, had almost doubled itself in the decade ending 1901. Towards this result the largely increased number of Europeans brought into the district by the opening out of the colliery area and extension of the railway system contributed very materially.

The native Christian population is most numerous in the Purūlia, Jhalda and Tundi thanas. In the two former, as well as in Bāghmundi thana, the main proselytizing agency is the German Evangelical Lutheran (Gossner's) Mission, an important branch of which has its headquarters at Purūlia with small outlying posts in charge of native pastors at Sirkabad, Ilu and Tunturi. The Mission has been working since 1864 and the progress made in proselytizing has not been very marked; the majority of the converts come from the purely aboriginal castes and the lowest strata of Hindu society. One of the most useful branches of their work is the management of the Purūlia Leper Asylum, to which reference is made elsewhere.

The established Church of England is represented at Purūlia now by a few converts as well as the resident European population. From 1903 till 1907 there was a resident clergyman, a member of the S. P. G. Mission whose headquarters are at Rānchi, but he has now moved to Adra where a large railway settlement has sprung up in the course of the last few years and a handsome church is now under erection. A church has recently been built near Jharia for the common use of Protestant Christians, whether Church of England or non-conformist, but there is at present no resident pastor. The Dublin Mission is represented by a chaplain at Dhânbāid, another large railway centre, and funds are now being raised for the construction of a church there.

In the extreme north of the district at Pokhuria in thana Tundi is the headquarters of a branch of the Free Church of Scotland Mission to the Sonthals.

CASTES AND TRIBES.

The marginal table shows the strength of the different castes, tribes or races which number over 25,000. As will be seen, aboriginal races largely predominate, the Kurmis, Sonthals, Bhumij and Bāuri alone accounting for half the total population.

Caste	Number	Caste	Number
Kurmi	... 241,006	Ahir and Goālā	... 37,885
Sonthal	... 194,730	Bhuiyā	... 36,703
Bhumij	... 109,016	Rajwār	... 32,166
Bāuri	... 99,096	Kalu	... 29,816
Brāhman	... 57,025	Kāmār and Lohār	... 29,569
Kumhār	... 38,877		

Kurmis.

The Kurmis are fairly well distributed throughout the district, but are proportionately most numerous in the southern and central parts: in Jhalda they make up one-third of the whole population, and in Purūlia and Barābhum more than one quarter. In the north of the district there is a small intermixture of the Bihar Kurmi, who keeps himself for the most apart from the local man, to whom he considers himself superior as coming from the west. The distinction first drawn by Dr. Grierson between the Bihar and the Chota Nāgpur Kurmis, which is now generally accepted, is exemplified in this district by the fact that marked traces of the characteristic Kolarian village system remain, the Mahato or village headman of the Kurmis corresponding exactly with the Mānjhi of the Sonthals, the Sardār of the Bhumij and the Munda of the Horaces. The Hinduisation of the Kurmis is much more complete than that of either the Bhumij or the Sonthal; they abstain from both beef and pork, though they still eat fowls, and in consequence are not reckoned among the castes from whose hands a Brāhman may take water. Their characteristic festivals, the "Karam" described in an earlier paragraph, is, however, essentially animistic, and typical of an aboriginal tribe. Sir H. H. Risley considers that they may perhaps be a Hinduised branch of the Sonthals. "The latter", he writes, "who are more particular about what they eat or rather about whom they will eat with than is commonly supposed, will eat cooked rice with the Kurmis, and according to the tradition regard them as elder brothers of their own. However this may be, the totemism of the Kurmis of western Bengal stamps them as of Dravidian descent and clearly distinguishes them from the Kurmi of Bihar and the United Provinces. They show signs of a leaning towards orthodox Hinduism and employ Brāhmans for the worship of Hindu gods, but not in the propitiation of rural or family deities or in their marriage ceremonies." They are almost entirely an agricultural caste, but in this district, at any rate, they fall far short of their namesakes in Bihar both in energy and skill in matters connected with agriculture.

Like the Kurmis the Sonthals are well distributed throughout the district; in Tundi, which immediately adjoins the Sonthal Parganas, they form nearly half of the population, and in Barābhum and Mānbazar, in the extreme south and east of the district, more than one quarter. The high rate of increase among this people, as shown by the census figures, is partly accounted for by their well-known fecundity, but there must have been also a considerable influx from outside, more especially in the coalfield area, where the Sonthal is usually considered as the best miner, and considerable trouble is taken by mine managers to attract and retain them. There can, however, be no question that a large part of the present population springs from families that have been established in the district for four generations or more, and it is perhaps open to doubt whether their establishment in this district was not earlier in date than in the Sonthal Parganas. For a detailed description of the Sonthals, their traditions, their septs and their religious and other customs reference may be made to the account given by Sir H. H. Risley in Appendix VIII to his recent work "The People of India," and to the account of the Sonthals of Bankurā printed as an Appendix to Chapter III in O'Malley's Gazetteer of the Bānkura District. In this district, as elsewhere, their primary occupation is cultivation; their special genius is the opening out of new cultivation in hilly or jungle area. They are for the most part a law-abiding race, and beyond an occasional disturbance arising out of a land dispute with their neighbours of other castes or tribes, practically no serious or even petty crime is reported from Sonthal communities. They are universally considered as good tenants, requiring, however, to be tactfully treated. Unfortunately for themselves they are improvident and peculiarly liable to fall into the toils of the money-lenders with usually disastrous results to themselves. They are also good workers and many go to the mines for employment; there they earn money quickly, much of which they spend in drink; once they have accumulated some small savings they return to villages and live at home until these are exhausted, when they return to work once more. Sonthals.

Bhumij. The Bhumij or Bhumij Kols are generally considered to be the characteristic and autochthonous race of the Mânbhum district. As a matter of fact they are strictly speaking confined to the part of the district lying west and south of the Kâsai river, thanas Chândil, Purūlia and Barâbhum, accounting each for some 25,000, and Mânbazar and Bâghmundi for 10,000 each out of the total of 109,000. The history, tradition and customs of this tribe are dealt with at great length in Colonel Dalton's Ethnology of Bengal, and a good deal has been written about them by later writers on linguistic and ethnological subjects. Though a certain difference of opinion remains as to their exact position as regards the allied Kolarian tribes, there can be no doubt that they are closely allied to, if not identical with, the Mundas. In his earlier work (Tribes and Castes of Bengal) Sir H. H. Risley doubted whether they ever had a distinct language of their own, and was inclined to believe that they were nothing more than a branch of the Mundas, who had spread to the eastward, mingled with the Hindus, and thus for the most part severed their connection with the parent tribe. His view is based largely on the fact that the Bhumij of south-west Mânbhum, *i.e.*, the western part of Pargana Chāndil, and Parganas Mâtha and Bâghmundi, call themselves Mundas or rather Muras, and practically in all respects correspond with their Munda neighbours in south-east Rânchi with whom they intermarry. The language used by the Bhumij in this area is closely akin, if not identical with Mundâri, whereas further east and north Bengali is the ordinary language of the Bhumij, though, as has already been stated, the Bhumij of the south-east are largely bilingual and can speak what they call Sonthali, but which may well be a survival of their own particular dialect of Mundari. The identification of the western Bhumij or Mura with the Munda of Rānchi is not, however, complete. The Bhumij uses the word Mura as a title in these parts, instead of the word Sardâr ordinarily used by the eastern Bhumij, but in the same villages may be found both Bhumij and Munda admittedly distinct and local tradition makes the Bhumij the original inhabitant. On the Ajodhya hill, for instance, Bhumij and Munda live side by side; the burial stones of the former are at Ajodhya on the hill itself while those of the Mundas are at Tunturi, a village in the plains below, and the Mundas admit that the Bhumij were the earlier settlers. As far as language is concerned, not only the Bhumij and Munda but also the Sonthals, of whom there is a still more recent settlement in the same village, profess to use identically the same.

In any case, however, there can be no question that in this western tract the Bhumij has retained the tribal religion and customs as well as the language to a very much greater extent than the Bhumij of the eastern and northern tracts. There Hinduising tendencies have been at work for several generations. Writing in 1833 Mr. Dent remarked that the Bhumij of Barābhum speak Bengali and were adopting Hindu customs. Sir H. H. Risley speaks of the Bhumij of western Bengal as a typical example of a whole section of a tribe becoming gradually converted to Hinduism, and transformed into a full-blown caste without abandoning their tribal designation. "Here," he remarks, "a pure Dravidian race have lost their original language and speak only Bengali (but *vide supra*); they worship Hindu gods in addition to their own (the tendency being to delegate the tribal gods to the women) and the more advanced among them employ Brāhmans as family priests. They still retain totemistic exogamous divisions closely resembling those of the Mundas and Sonthals. But they are beginning to forget the totems which the names of the subdivisions denote, and the names themselves will probably soon be abandoned for more aristocratic designations. The tribe will then have become a caste in the full sense of the word, and will go on stripping itself of all customs likely to betray its true descent." Hinduisation has, perhaps, not greatly improved the original Bhumij; he is, it is true, no longer the wild marauder of the seventeenth and early eighteenth century, but to this day the tribe provides innumerable recruits to the gangs of petty burglars and dacoits of the south and east part of the district. He is at the best a poor cultivator, displaying the minimum of skill and energy and is notorious as a bad tenant. To the improvidence of the Sonthal he has added the litigiousness of the Bengali, with the result that he has generally fallen a very easy prey as well to the alien zamindar and mahajan as to the petty local moneylender.

Bāuris. Last of the four great aboriginal or semi-aboriginal castes is the Bāuri, and as might be expected they are found in largest numbers in the areas immediately adjoining what is called by Mr. W. B. Oldham the Bāuri land of Burdwan and Bānkura. Nearly one-third of the whole number are accounted for in thāna Raghunāthpur alone, and the bulk of the remainder in thānas Purūlia, Gaurāndi, Pāra and Mānbazar in the Sadar and Nirsā in the Dhānbāid subdivision. In the mining thanas Jharia and Topchānchi there is also a considerable number, a large percentage of whom are recent immigrants to the collieries. The Bāuris hold a very low place in the social scale, their Hinduism is described by Sir H. H. Risley as of the slenderest kind, and their favourite objects of worship are Manasa and Bhādu, whom they share with the Bāgdis, Mān Singh, Barpahāri, Dharmarāj and Kudrasini. Barpahāri is merely another name for the great mountain (Marang Buru) of the Sonthals, and is propitiated with offerings of fowls. Their priests are usually men of their own caste, termed Lāya or Degharia, and frequently holding land rent-free or at a nominal rent (*lāyāli*) as remuneration for their services. Agricultural labour and pālki-bearing are the traditional occupations of the caste, and the former is still their main occupation, though they take fairly readily to most forms of manual labour including mining. In Mānbazar (as also in Bānkura) a considerable number of them hold more or less substantial tenures as hereditary ghātwals, a fact which lends support to the theory that here and in adjoining portions of Bānkura the Bāuris represent the real aboriginal inhabitant.

Brāhmans. Of the purely Hindu castes which return more than 25,000 it is perhaps unnecessary to say more than that they differ to no great extent from their fellow castemen in other districts. Brāhmans, though fairly numerous, are not very evenly distributed; Purūlia, Chās and Raghunāthpur return the highest actual numbers as well as the highest percentage on the total population. The area roughly represents the heart of the ancient Pānchet estate whose zamindars appear to have been specially lavish in their grants of land to the Brāhmans. These for the most part were immigrants from the eastern districts, but in Chās there is a considerable admixture of the typical Bihar or Tirhutia Brāhman, who apparently migrated here about a century ago, and are now, thanks chiefly to successful money-lending, the holders, as tenure-holders or tenants, of a very considerable part of the country. Over the remainder of the district they are spread but thinly for the most part in scattered small colonies, and their numbers are barely sufficient to provide an adult priest for every two or three villages. A good many of these, as has already been noticed, are Brāhmans of more or less degraded orders, administering to the Hinduistic tendencies of the semi-aboriginal castes.

Kāmārs and Lohārs. Kāmārs and Lohārs who number nearly 30,000, though classsed as Hindus by religion and Aryan by race, include almost certainly considerable drafts from aboriginal or semi-aboriginal castes, Munda, Bāuri and Bāgdi in particular, who have adopted the caste occupation, and have been to a certain extent absorbed in the caste.

Bhuiyas are most numerous in the Dhānbaid subdivision, and to some extent take there the position occupied by the Bhumij in the south of the district. The distinction between Bhuiyas by tribe and Bhuiyas by title—Bhuiya by itself meaning simply "connected with the land,"—is not an easy one to draw, as Sir H. H. Risley has pointed out, and it is difficult to say how far those who have been enumerated as Bhuiya represent members of an homogeneous race or caste. It is noticeable that the Ghātwars or Ghātwals have disappeared from the census tables as a separate caste, Ghātwal being essentially a title assumed by a Bhuiya of somewhat superior position to distinguish himself from a mere Bhuiya field-labourer. Colonel Dalton considered the Bhuiyas, including those of northern Mānbhum, to be Dravidian rather than Kolarian in origin, and he remarks on their more or less pronounced negritic type. He believed that most of the proprietors of estates in this district as well as in Hazāribagh, round the Parasnāth hill, were Bhuiyas, and this theory is perhaps supported by the survival of the name "Tikait" as the title of the eldest son of the reigning zamindars among them, a title used also in Bonai by the eldest sons of Rājas, and in Gaya assumed by the richer members of the Ghātwar community. No very careful study has been made in recent years of the religious beliefs and customs of the Bhuiyas of this district, and it can only be said that they are generally much more Hinduised than even the Bhumij in the south. Bhuiyas.

The Kolarian race is represented in Mānbhum mainly by the Bhumij, but there were enumerated besides in 1901 some 22,000 Koras, over 9,000 Mahlis and nearly 4,000 Mundas, and the same number of Kharias, besides a few Turis and Birhors. Other Kolarian tribes.

Koras are found fairly evenly distributed through the district, their numbers being proportionately greatest in Purūlia thāna; they are essentially a tribe or caste of earth-workers. It is noted by Sir H. H. Risley that outside Mānbhum there are sub-castes whose names preserve the memory of their original settlements in Mānbhum and Dhalbhum; within Mānbbum no sub-castes appear to have been formed and the caste is still more or less in the tribal stage. In matters of religion they affect to be orthodox Hindus, calling themselves Sāktas or Vaishnavas as the case may be. Manasa, the heavenly patroness of snakes, and Bhādu, the virgin daughter of the Pānchet house, are said to be their favourite deities. The cult of the latter is more or less peculiar to this caste and the Bāgdis. The story is that Bhādu was the favourite daughter of the former Rāja of Pānchet and that she died a virgin for the good of the people. Her festival is Kora celebrated on the last day of Bhadra, when the Koras and Bāgdis carry her effigy in procession, and the whole population, men women and children, take part in songs and wild dances in her honour.

The Koras of Mānbhum rarely employ Brāhmans, but a member of the caste styled Lāya or Nāya acts as the priest. In social status and occupation there is little to distinguish Koras from the Bāuris; the tendency to abstain from beef is probably more pronounced than when Sir H. H. Risley wrote; they are for the most part earth-workers, field-labourers and petty cultivators, with here and there a few substantial agriculturists. As earth-workers they are conspicuous for their objection to carrying earth on their heads, carrying it instead in triangular baskets slung on a shoulder-yoke (*bangh-*).

The census figures return over 2,000 Koras as speaking the Kora dialect, which in all essential points corresponds to Mundari.

Mahlis. The Mahlis are described as a caste of labourers, palanquin bearers and workers in bamboo, more or less closely connected with the Sonthals, a dialect of whose language a considerable number of them still employ. Their religion is described by Sir H. H. Risley as a mixture of half forgotten animism and Hinduism imperfectly understood. Manasa, the snake goddess, and Barpahāri, identical with Marang Buru of the Sonthals, are the favourite deities. Their primary occupation is basket-making and bamboo-working generally, but many of them are now petty cultivators or landless day-labourers.

Mundas and Kharias. Of the Mundas and Kharias, whose main habitat is in other districts, no detailed description is required here. The Mundas, as has already been stated, are mainly confined to the south-western corner of the district bordering on Tamār in Rānchi; the Kharias are found in largest number in Barābhum, their settlements being scattered along the Dalma range; they have now lost, if the census figures are to be trusted, their distinctive language, though nearly half their number are still shown as animists. As a caste, they are classed as cultivators, but outside the hill villages they are for the most part mere day-labourers, and from an administrative point of view, they have an unenviable reputation as professional thieves and burglars.

Of other castes the following deserve some mention as being more or less peculiar to the district or for other reasons.

Malliks. Malliks, treated for census purposes as a sub-caste of Māl, form a community numbering just over 7,000 found only in Mānbhum, and confined here to the Jharia, Nirsā and Raghunāthpur thānas. Locally they are treated as a separate caste, and quite distinct from the Bāgdis who use the word Mallik as title. The zamindari of Pandrā (in thāna Nirsā) belonged formerly, according to tradition, to Malliks, who were defeated and driven out by a member of the Tundi family. Mr. Gait suggests that they probably belong to the Māl Pahāria stock found in the adjoining area of the Sonthal Parganas. He gives the following account of them based on information supplied by the Sub-divisional Officer.

"They call themselves Deobansi Malliks as distinguished from another group called Rājbansi Mallik with which they repudiate all connection. The whole caste has the same totem Patrishi, the Indian Paradise fly-catcher. The only bar on marriage is that a man may not espouse his first cousin or any nearer relation. Divorce, polygamy, and widow-marriage are allowed. The former is effected by publicly tearing a leaf in two. Marriage is both infant and adult. The binding part of the ceremony consists of the placing of an iron bangle on the left wrist of the bride. They profess to be Hindus, but their religion is of a very low order. They specially worship Māhāmai, Kāli, Manasa, and five Devatas called Thuiha, Baghut, Monongiri, Babiāri and Māya. The offerings to these deities are usually fowls, sheep and goats. They perform the ceremonies themselves, but once in five years, when they worship the sun (Bhagawān), a degraded Brāhman is called in, and he also assists at marriages and funeral ceremonies. The dead are usually burnt. They are cultivators and day-labourers. They eat pork and fowls, but abstain from beef and vermin. They will take cooked food from Bhuiyās, but not from Doms or Hāris."

Pahira. The Pahiras, numbering 977, are a small tribe found only on the Dalma range in Pargana Barābhum. They are apparently the same as the Pahāria of earlier censuses. They were grouped by Mr. V. Ball with the Kharias found in the same *locale* and apparently they are of Kolarian race, though it is stated thay have abandoned their original Munda language in favour of Bengali. Neither their dialect nor their special customs, if any, have apparently been studied, living as they do in most out-of-the-way and inaccessible places.

Sārāks. To the Sārāks reference has already been made in an earlier chapter as the remnant of an archaic community, whose connection with the district must date back to the very earliest times. Though a considerable number are found in the adjoining districts, Mānbhum is essentially the main habitation of this caste, the census figures showing 10,496 out of a total of 17,385 as resident therein. The following account of this interesting caste is taken from Mr. Gait's census report.

"The word Sārāk is doubtless derived from Srāvaka, the Sanskrit word for 'a hearer.' Amongst the Jains the term is used to indicate the laymen or persons who engaged in secular pursuits, as distinguished from the Yātis, the monks or ascetics, and it still survives as the name of a group which is rapidly becoming a regular caste of the usual type (Saraogi). The Buddhists used the same word to designate the second class of monks, who mainly occupied the monasteries; the highest class or Arhans usually lived solitary lives as hermits, while the great majority of the Bhikshus, or lowest class of monks, led a vagrant life of mendicancy, only resorting to the monasteries in times of difficulty or distress. The origin of the caste is ascribed in the Brahma Vaivartta Puran to the union of a Jolāha man with a woman of the Kuvinda or weaver caste. This, however, merely shows that at the time when this Puran was composed, or when the passage was interpolated, the Sārāks had already taken to weaving as a means of livelihood. Mr. Risley says that the Sārāks of Mānbhum, though now Hindus, retain traditions of having formerly been Jains.

"It is now reported from Mānbhum and Rānchi that they claim formerly to have been Agarwāls who venerated Parasnāth and inhabited the country on the bank of the river Saraju which flows into the Ganges near Ghāzipur, in the United Provinces, where they lived by trade and money-lending. They cannot explain why they left their original home, but in Mānbhum they say that they first settled near Dhalbhum in the estate of a certain Mān Rāja. They subsequently moved in a body to Pānchet in consequence of an outrage contemplated by Mān Rāja on a girl belonging to their caste. In Rānchi it is believed that their first settlement was at Ogra near Puri, whence they subsequently migrated to Chota Nāgpur. In Burdwan and Birbhum there is a tradition that they originally came from Gujarāt, but in the former district the popular belief is that they were brought thither as sculptors and masons for the construction of stone temples and houses, the remains of which are still visible on the bank of the Barākhar. They themselves say that their ancestors were traders and revered Parasnāth, but at the present time in Birbhum, Bānkura, and Mānbhum, they call themselves Hindus. The Sārāks of this part of the country are served by Brāhmans, who in some parts are, and in others are not, held to be degraded by acting as their priests. In Mānbhum it is said that they were not served by Brāhmans of any kind until they were provided with a priest by a former Rāja of Pānchet, as a reward for a service rendered to him by a Sārāk, who concealed him when his country was invaded by the Bargis, *i.e.* the Mārhattas. There are seven Gotras or exogamous groups, Adi or Adya Deb, Dharma Deb, Rishi Deb, Sandilya, Kashyapa, Ananta and Bharadvaja. In Birbhum Goutam and Vyāsa are also given as the names of *gotras*,* and in Rānchi Bātsava is added. They are also divided into four *thāks* or sub-castes based on locality, viz:—

(1) Pānchkotia or inhabitants of the Pānchet estate in Mānbhum.
(2) Nadipāria, or Sārāks residing on the right bank of the Dāmodar in Mānbhum.
(3) Birbhumia, or residents of Birbhum, and
(4) Tamāria, or residents of Pargana Tamār in Rānchi.

"There is a fifth sub-caste based on occupation, viz., the Sāraki Tāntis or Tānti Sārāks of the Bishnupur subdivision of Bānkura, who live by weaving and are held to be degraded. The latter again have four subdivisions Asvini Tānti, Pātra, Uttarkuli and Mandarāni. In the Sonthal Parganas the sub-castes are Phul Sāraki, Sikharia, Kandala and Sāraki Tānti.

"Except for the few traditions mentioned above, the names of some of their *gotras* and the extreme tenderness for animal life mentioned by Mr. Risley, which not only makes them strict vegetarians, but even leads them to eschew altogether the use of the word 'cut', there is little to distinguish the Sārāks of West Bengal, Mānbhum, and Rānchi from the ordinary Hindus amongst whom they live In Rānchi the Sārāks specially venerate Syām Chānd whose worship is performed by a Brāhman. All fines imposed for caste offences are set aside for the worship of the godling."

The Sārāks in this district are mostly found in thanas Raghunāthpur and Pāra; writing of a visit paid to Jhapra near Pāra in 1863, Colonel Dalton mentions that it was their pride that no member of their community had been convicted of any heinous crime, and it is probable that they could justly make the same boast now; they are essentially a quiet and law-abiding community, living in peace among themselves and with their neighbours.

The old village communal system of the Kolarian races still survives to a very large extent in Mānbhum, though the intrusion of non-aboriginal elements and the substitution of outsiders for the head of the tribe or family as the rent collectors or *ijārādārs* of the village, and the importation of Brāhmans as priests, where the Hinduising tendencies are more marked, all tend to disintegration. In most villages, however, there is still a recognised headman, even if he is no longer also the *ijārādār*; **Village officials.**

and the Mānjhi among the Sonthals, the Sardār among the eastern, or Mura among the western Bhumij, the Mahato or Des-mandal among the Kurmis, and to a certain extent the *ijārādār* in mixed communities, is referred to in all village disputes, and takes a leading position in all social and religious ceremonies. If not also the holder of the village lease, and the latter, *i.e.*, the *ijārādār*, is non-resident, the tribal headman is usually his representative, and may cultivate for him the '*mān*' or *khas* lands, ordinarily attached to the post of *ijārādār*. For groups of villages among the Sonthals there is occasionally a superior official, the Parganait, to whom reference is made on questions of importance and who presides at the annual hunt and the tribal assembly which follows. In many villages the headman is also the priest, but frequently there is a separate priest, Lāya or Nāya whose post is hereditary, and who is remunerated partly by a share of offerings made to the Grāmya Devatā, and partly by a special grant of land, held rent-free or on a quit rent (*Lāyāli*). *Goraits*, who help the tahsildars of the bigger landholders to collect rents in *khas* villages, are found occasionally, but ordinarily this work is done by non-resident peons or *Naydis*, usually upcountry men, in the personal service of the zamindar.

VILLAGE SOCIAL LIFE.

General appearance of the village.

As has already been stated, the vast majority of the villages are small, villages containing 150 to 200 houses being, with a few exceptions, confined to the areas which are in fairly close touch with the railways and the industrial centres; elsewhere the average village contains from 25 to 100 houses, and in the wilder portions of the district collections of a half a dozen or a dozen scattered huts frequently represent the nucleus of a recently formed village. In style there is a general homogeneity, the general arrangements being, as a rule, similar, and the houses, though those of certain castes can usually be distinguished, differing but little in size and manner of construction. The earliest settler naturally places his house near the land he proposes to cultivate, and usually therefore on some ridge, or near the crest of a slope above and not far from the spot which he has selected or is likely to select later for a *bāndh*. Other houses follow, unculturable land, or land not likely to be brought under cultivation without great expenditure of labour, being selected as sites, and the result in course of time is a long straggling village often confined to a single row of houses or a single street known as the *sadar kuli* with occasionally other rows or detached houses on lanes striking off from the main street at various angles according to the nature and lie of the ground. In the earlier stages the houses are well away from one another, each having a considerable yard or compound; later, as suitable ground for extension becomes more limited, builders have to be content with more contracted sites and smaller enclosures. The street or streets which are rather below the level of the houses usually serve in the rainy season as drains to carry off the surface water, besides being the means of communication from house to house and to the cultivated fields. It would, however, be a mistake to assume from this that the villages generally are dirty and insanitary; on the contrary the average small village compares very favourably in this respect with villages in Bihar and Bengal, though certain castes, among which may be mentioned the Bāuris, the Haris and the Doms, are here, as elsewhere, conspicuous for their dirty habits. Much, if not most, of the household rubbish is burnt from time to time and utilised as manure for the *bāri* or cultivated plots nearest the houses, and ordinarily the drainage from the houses is limited to the rain water; in the rains the village street is necessarily at times a watercourse, but the soil being gravelly and the slope, as a rule, considerable, it quickly dries, and the condition of the village street of more level districts, a foot or more deep in mud for several months at a time, is, though not uncommon in the larger villages, by no means universal.

The absence of trees in the individual compounds as compared with the typical Bengal village described by the Rev. Lal Bihary Dey*, is another distinguishing feature. An occasional jaman (*Eugenia jambolana*) may be noticed, and perhaps a solitary pipal (*ficus religiosa*) or banyan (*ficus bengalensis*) or a fine mango at some point along the village street, usually near the house of the village headman, alongside which an open space is usually reserved as the *akhara* or village meeting place. In villages where the immigrant element prevails, the usual fruit trees of the Bengal compound, plum, mango, guava, lime, papaya and plantain are more common, but the position of the villages on high land and the poverty of the soil do not tend to any great luxuriousness of growth, and a Mānbhum village can seldom be described as a bower of foliage. Round about Mānbazar in the east of the district the *kul* or plum tree is cultivated wherever space permits for rearing lac, but as the trees are regularly pollarded, their presence adds little to the general picturesqueness. Immdiately outside the village are usually one or more groups of trees, in most villages of aboriginals, of *sāl* trees, or at any rate a single tree, a *karam*, or *bar*, which represent the grove, *Sarna* or *Jāhira* sacred to the village deity, *Grāmya*

---

* Bengal Peasant Life, MacMillan & Co., London, 1902.

Devatā. Older and larger villages may boast a group of mango trees, under which the local market or *hāt*, if there happens to be one, is held, and the village cattle, when not out in the jungles, take shelter during the heat of the day.

The smaller villages, as a rule, contain no shop of any sort, the wants of the villagers, such as are not supplied from their own fields or the jungles, being obtained weekly from the nearest or most convenient *hāt*. The bigger villages may contain one or more shops supplying salt, tobacco and various oddments of pedlar's wares, but it is only in those of considerable size that the grain and cloth dealers and general merchants congregate.

Dwellings. The ordinary house for a family, neither poor nor very rich, consists of three different mud-walled and thatched buildings, one of which is the sleeping apartment (*sobār ghar*), one a kitchen (*rānnā ghar*), and one a cattle-shed (*goāl ghar*), arranged on three sides of a quadrangle; on the fourth or open side is the *bāri* or *bāstu*, *i.e.*, an open plot of high level land on which are grown various *bhadoi* and *rabi* crops and vegetables for the consumption of the family. Behind one of the three huts is another plot of open land usually enclosed by mud-walls, which is the *khāmār bāri* or place for threshing corn and storing fodder and manure.

The "sleeping apartment," the main building, is, according to the means of the owner, 9 cubits × 6 cubits, or 12 cubits × 7 cubits, or 15 cubits × 8 cubits, or 21 cubits × 10 cubits in floor area, with a verandah (*pinrā*) on the side facing the quadrangle, varying from 2 cubits to 5 cubits in width. These dimensions are more or less fixed by custom and seldom deviated from. The building may be either of one, two or three rooms according to size, but the most common type contains one room only. The floor is generally of mud raised about 1½ to 3 feet. The walls vary from 5 to 9 cubits in height and from 1 cubit to 2 cubits in width at the base, according to the size of the building.

The roof is of thatch varying from about 3 to 9 inches in thickness resting on a framing of ballas (*sāl* poles), and brushwood, or split bamboos (the latter are used only by the well-to do), supported on a rough timber framing of beams (*sāngā*), king posts (*mūri khūntā*), ridge (*mūdān*), and hips (*konāch* or *kānr*). Well-to-do people often put a flat mud terrace, a layer of mud on a layer of jungle-wood planks, or bamboos closely packed, resting on cross-beams fixed on the walls, between the thatch and the floor, chiefly for protection against fire. A building provided with a terrace roof of this kind is known as *māt-kōthā*.

This building as a rule has its back wall against the village street, as all the valuables, including, in some cases, stocks of paddy are kept in it, and its situation, as well as its use as a sleeping chamber, makes it the safest against thieves and burglars. Each compartment or room has a single door, ordinarily a rough wood frame with wattle and dab panelling, which swings on two vertical wooden pivots, fitting into holes in a thick plank (*kādā pātā*) which is placed on the top of the door opening and in a small piece of wood fixed in the floor below. Those who can afford to do so use ordinary wooden door frames, with rough plank and batten shutters in two leaves, fixed on to the frames with rough hinges, all locally made by village artisans. Windows or other openings are rather the exception than the rule, but circular holes or apertures not bigger than 9 inches in diameter are sometimes left in the walls for light and air at a height of 6 feet or so from the floor. The verandah is of simple construction, the floor raised about a foot above the outside ground level and the roof supported by a row of wooden posts (*khuntā*) along which runs the post plate (*pārh*).

The kitchen building is constructed in similar style but more cheaply both as regards walling and roofing. On one side of this room is the cooking place (*chulā*), and on the other the *dhenki* or paddy husking mill or lever. In some cases the latter has its place in the verandah of the building where there is one, and the space inside is then used as an additional sleeping apartment.

The cattle shed has seldom any verandah, and a stout wooden post-and-bar fencing is generally substituted for the wall on the quadrangle side of the building. In many cases the walls on the other three sides are only about 4 feet high, and the roof rests on posts and post plates. It is divided according to requirements by wooden fencing into compartments, one for cows and bullocks, another for buffaloes, and a third, if necessary, for goats and sheep. Geese and fowls are ordinarily kept in the verandahs or kitchen and occasionally in special sheds constructed for the purpose. For pigeons, which many householders keep, a pigeon-cot (*tang*) is usually provided, consisting of a number of earthen pots placed on a platform supported on posts fixed in the centre of the quadrangle, and covered by some kind of roof as a protection against the weather.

The poorest class of cultivator and the landless labourer has to be content with a single building. In this and its verandah he and his family cook their food and sleep and generally live such part of their lives as is not spent in the open; his yard is small and he has no *khāmār* and, more often than not, no *bāri* or at most a minute plot. In the case of more substantial cultivators the number of buildings constituting the house is larger, and there is separate accommodation for the master of the house and for the wife and children. As the family grows up an additional quadrangle arranged on similar lines may be added, connected with the original house by a narrow passage. In all such big tenements, provision is made for the storage of grain in the shape of *morāis* (capacity 100 to 500 maunds) or *hāmārs* (500 to 1,500 maunds). These are erected in the middle of the quadrangle and rest on platforms of planks or *ballas* and bamboos, supported on rough stone or brick pillars, about 18 inches above ground, so as to admit of free ventilation and to protect the grain from flooding during the rains. In shape both are similar and present the appearance of an inverted *frustrum* of a cone, surmounted by a thatched roof. The *morāi* has an outer casing, and to extract the grain it is necessary to remove the roof, while the *hāmār* is of fine wattle plastered with mud and supported by *balla* and bamboo posts, with a trap door above the level of the stored grain, or two trap doors at different heights according to the size. Poorer people who can store only small quantities of grains do so in spherical shaped bundles of straw and straw ropes known as *kunchuri* or *purā* with capacities varying from 2 to 10 maunds each. These are kept on stone slabs, or wooden supports inside the sleeping apartments or kitchen, if anybody sleeps there, if the bundles do not contain more than 3 maunds, or in the verandahs if they are heavier. Still smaller quantities are stored in the large earthen pots used for fetching water (*kalsi*) or boiling rice (*hānri*) arranged in rows inside huts.

Furniture. By way of furniture, a cultivator, whose house consists of three buildings as described above, has the following:—

The *khāt* or bedstead consisting of a framework of thin *sāl* wood poles or thick bamboos, on four legs, cross-woven with string, commonly made from the jungle grass *bābui. Khāts* of different sizes are provided for the various members of the family to sleep on, and in the day time they are used for various purposes, among others for spreading out grain to dry. The full-sized *khāt* is ordinarily 3½ cubits in length and 2 to 2½ cubits in width, and ¾ to 1½ cubits in height. They are never made long enough to enable the sleeper to stretch himself at full length inside the framing, the superstition being that if this should be the sleeper will shortly die.

Machuli.—Stools, a foot to eighteen inches square, of similar construction to the *khāt*. Of these there may be two or more in a house for the use of the family and of visitors.

Chauki.—Low wooden stools about 18″ to 2′ square. One or more are kept in every house and are used for the same purpose as *machulis* and occasionally for bathing.

Pinrā.—Rectangular pieces of wood about an inch in thickness of various sizes, used for sitting on during meals.

Khāts and *machulis* are sometimes very neatly made with dressed *sāl* wood frames on turned legs with the rope-work artistically woven with string of coloured jute or hemp in fancy patterns. Clothes and bedding are, when not in use, kept on a rope or bamboo or wooden pole stretched from wall to wall, or on wooden pegs projecting from the walls. Shelves of various lengths of wood or plastered dab wattle, resting on pegs driven into the walls, are placed rather above a man's height from the floor for keeping cooking pots and cooked food. Oil, *ghi* (clarified butter), *murhi* (fried rice), *chinra* (dry parched rice), *gur* (molasses), etc., are kept in earthen pots or jars suspended from the roof in string loops, sometimes very artistically made of coloured strings. Valuable things (such as silver ornaments, cash, documents, rent receipts, etc.) are kept inside earthen pots imbedded in a wall, or buried in the floor in places known to the head of the family only. Wooden and tin boxes are gradually coming into use amongst well-to-do people chiefly for keeping clothes and valuables.

Earthen pots of various sizes are used for cooking purposes but there are generally also an iron *karāi* (a semi-spherical pan with two loop handles) used for boiling milk and frying purposes; and a *loki* (a shallow brass pot) specially used for cooking for guests, who for caste reasons require their food separately cooked.

Other utensils in daily domestic use, of which there may be one or several in a house according to the circumstances of the owner, are:—

1. *Garayā* or *Gharā* (water-pot of brass cast or wrought).
2. *Thālā* or *Thāli* (circular dinner plates of various sizes with more or less raised edges).
3. *Ghati* (small sized pots for drinking water).
4. *Galās*, *i.e.*, glass (tumblers for drinking water).
5. *Bāti* or cup, ranging from one holding an ounce or two to large bowls holding a gallon or more.

Nos. 2 to 5 are mostly of bellmetal, but small sized brass cups are also used. Stone pots, dishes and bowls of different sizes and varieties manufactured at the quarries in Pātkum are also used.

Dress. The ordinary apparel of the cultivating classes consists of the following made in local looms for the most part from imported cotton yarn. (1) *Kācha*—5 to 7 cubits in length and about 1 cubit wide. This is passed between the legs and under a piece of string round the loins; over this the *kāchā* is wrapped once or twice, according to its length, so as to leave a piece about 18 inches in length to hang loosely downwards from the loins. (2) *Gāmcha*—This is about 5 cubits in length by 2 cubits in width, worn in various ways; when working in the field or walking long distances in sun and rain half of it is tied on the head, turban fashion, leaving the other half to hang down to cover the back and sides. It is also worn over the *kācha* and loosely turned round the waist and tied in a knot or else loosely wrapped round the body. (3) *Dhuti*—The ordinary *dhuti* a longer piece (7 to 8 cubits) of about the same width as a *gāmchā* reserved as a rule for use on special and festival occasions. (4) *Gelāp*—This is a two-fold wrapper of about 5 cubits in length and 3 in width, sewn to that size from stuff especially made for the purpose, and used as a wrapper in the winter season, both when going out or sleeping. (5) *Bādha*—Wooden sandals used only in the rainy season when going about and not when working in the fields.

The umbrella (*chhātā*) of common use is made of split bamboo ribs and shaft with covering of fine bamboo mat. Imported or country-made umbrellas of European fashion are now generally used by well-to-do cultivators. The *ghong* is a covering for the head and back in one, woven out of leaves of a creeper of that name which grows in the hills. The portion for the head tapers to a point and rests on the head hat like, the remainder spreads round to cover the arms and back down to a little below the waist. The lower edge is semi-circular. It is used mostly by women, especially when working in the fields during the rains, and by ploughmen.

Female swear the *thenti* which is a stout piece of cotton cloth with a border on the two long sides, and varying from 5 cubits by 1½ cubits for young girls to 10 cubits by 2 cubits for grown-up women. This is turned and tied round the waist, forming a kind of skirt, and the remaining length passed over the shoulder, so as to cover most of the upper part of the body and, when necessary or desired, the head. The ordinary *thenti* is plain but coloured cloth is not infrequently used, and the borders worked in various patterns; the portion at one end, which is thrown over the left shoulder, called the *anchla*, is also occasionally worked in some fancy pattern.

Younger girls are clothed in pieces of cloth, plain or striped, just large enough to go comfortably round the waist and to hang down to the ankles; these are called *putli* or *pharāni*. Similar but rather larger pieces of cloth called *nahanga* are used in the same manner by very old women.

European cotton-clothes, coats, shirts, vests, etc., are gradually coming into use amongst those who have opportunities of frequent intercourse with advanced people living in centres of trade and industry and near railway stations.

Bedding. The ordinary bedding consists of a mat made of palm or date palm leaves and split bamboo. *Kāntha* made of old and useless clothes sewn quilt fashion, sometimes with coloured thread, form the best mattresses in most houses, and these are also used by old women as wrappers during winter. Country-made blankets and *durries* (Satranja) are also fairly common. Straw is abundantly used in winter for sleeping on, either on a *khāt* or on the floor. Pillows for the head are generally made by placing bundles of straw underneath the mat, *kāntha* or blanket. Ordinary pillows made of silk cotton, stuffed inside a cotton-cloth casing, are also occasionally used.

Village Festivals. Apart from the usual ceremonies in connection with births, deaths and marriages, which vary according to the race, religion and caste of the villagers, the main feature of village social life is the observance of the various festivals of which almost every month has its own particular one. The following account of the most important of these, other than the regular Hindu festivals recognised and observed by the strictly orthodox, has been furnished by Rai Nanda Gopal Banerji Bahadur; the festivals described represent for the most part semi-Hinduised survivals of what were originally the non-Hindu festivals of the different animistic tribes, or else regular Hindu festivals to which various aboriginal forms and ceremonies have been tacked on.

Bysakh.—*Sārul* is observed on the last day of the month of *Bysakh* (April-May). The *Lāya* or village priest offers flowers and sacrifices a cock, or less frequently, a goat or sheep, in the *grāmya thān*, *i.e.*, the seat for the presiding deity of the village. The Sonthals and Bhumij offers various kinds of jungle edibles to the deity and brew *hānriā* or rice-beer and spend the night in dancing, men and women together, to the accompaniment of the *mādal.* The Kurmis abstain from both drink and dance and merely decorate the entrance to their houses, and do not work on that day. If there is any death or birth in the village, the festival is postponed for a more auspicious day. This festival is obviously a survival of the *baha bonga* or flower festival of the Hos and the *sārul* of the Mundas described by Col. Dalton, though these are held slightly earlier in the year. They mark the bursting of the trees into new leaf and blossom, and the beginning of spring.

Joistha.—The *Rohini* festival is observed on the 13th day of the month of *Joistha* (May-June). Pujas are offered to Manasa, the deity presiding over snakes, and a band of cow-dung is smeared around every house and enclosure wall. The young men and boys go about the village dancing, rubbing mud and throwing dust at each other.

Ashar.—The last day of the month of *Ashar* (June-July) is devoted to the *Jāntal Parab* or *Ashari Grām Puja* (the *baihar horo nawai* of the Sonthals) when the first fruits of the new crops are offered to the presiding deity of the village. A goat is sacrificed by the Lāya at the *grāmyā thān* and the meat distributed to all families, cultivators abstaining from work in the fields for the day.

Sraban.—Manasa is again propitiated on the last day of *Sraban* (July-August) with offerings of goats, geese or pigeons.

Bhadra.—In *Bhadra* (August-September), on the 11th day of the bright half of the month, are celebrated the *Karam* and *Ind* Pujas. A branch of the *karam* tree is planted in the *akhra* (meeting place) and offerings are made by a Brāhman who gets some rice or paddy and pice from every family as his fees. The day as well as the preceding night are spent in fasting but in the evening every one meets at the *akhra* and dancing round the *karam* occupies the night. Next day Indra, the special deity who presides over the rains, is propitiated with the sacrifice of a goat, branches or twigs are planted in the paddy fields, the transplantation of which ought by this time to be complete, and the *chhātā* (umbrella) ceremony is then gone through. For this a big *sāl* pole topped with an umbrella, with bamboo ribs and shaft covered with white cloth, and ornamented with flower frills and tassels, has been previously prepared and pivoted on a framework of vertical *sāl* posts fixed in the ground, with ropes arranged for hauling the umbrella on its long shaft into an upright position. On the arrival of the zamindar on horseback or in a *pālki* preceded by a horseman, the umbrella is rapidly run up and the zamindar and his cortege make the circuit of the pole seven times amid the shouts and applause of the crowd, which then disperses. A similar festival is observed in some localities under the more descriptive name of *Chhātā Parab* on the last day of the same month. Both the *Ind* and the *Chhātā* festivals are closely connected with what may be called the semi-feudal zamindari system of the district, and the celebrations take place only at present or past headquarters of one or other of the local Rājas, and by way of imitation, of one or two wealthy Kurmi land-holders. These festivals mark the completion of the trans-plantation of the lower land rice, and the beginning of the harvest of the early *gora* rice. The *karam* festival referred to in an earlier part of the chapter is, however, more generally celebrated by Sonthals and other aboriginals in this district later in the year, at the end of *Aswin*, when the reaping of the main rice crop begins.

Aswin.—The *Jita Parab* takes place on the 8th day of the dark phase of the moon in *Aswin* (September-October). This is observed for the benefit of children by females who are mothers, and widowers with children. The green end of a sugarcane, a branch of a fig tree and a small bundle of green paddy plants are fixed in the place selected for the purpose in the village. Those who observe the ceremony fast the whole day and night, and *puja* is offered to Bhagabati Durga. At night there is the usual dancing and merry-making.

Kartik (*October-November*).—The *Garayā puja* is observed on the 15th day of the dark phase of the moon in *Kartik*. The usual *Kāli puja* drinking and dancing begin in the evening and the drums are kept going all night "to keep the cattle awake." Pujas are offered inside the cattle-shed the next morning for the propitiation of the goddess Bhagabati Durga and a she-goat is generally sacrificed. The following day, *i.e.*, the second day of the light half of the month is the *Kārā Khūnta.* On this occasion the horns of the buffaloes (both male and female) and of the cows and bullocks are smeared with oil and vermilion and various devices daubed on their bodies. In the afternoon selected buffaloes and bullocks are tied with strong ropes to different posts close to each other along the main street of the village. These are then frightened and scared by constant drumming and the display of red cloth, blankets and even bear and tiger skins, till they break their ropes and bolt away.

Aghan (*November-December*).—The succeeding month *Aghan* or *Agrahayan* is not marked by any special festival of the type just described.

Paus (*December-January*).—In *Paus* the *Tusu Parab* is observed by unmarried girls throughout the month. Small cowdung balls are prepared, and stored in an earthen pot, which is painted outside with a solution of pounded rice. Paddy is sprinkled over the balls, and *pujas* offered to the goddess of wealth with flowers of mustard and radish every morning before anything is eaten. Hymns are also sung invoking the goddess and calling on her to provide wealth and good husbands. On the last day of the month the girls bathe, set fire to the cowdung balls and join in the general *Pitha* or cake festival. This is celebrated by the whole village bathing very early in the morning, preferably in some large river, and on their return eating cakes prepared a day or two before of pounded new rice, and stuffed with a paste of cocoanut or cocoanut and *gur*.

Magh (*January-February*).—On the succeeding day, the first of *Magh*, held to be specially auspicious, all cultivators take an early bath and, having tied the yoke to the plough with a new piece of rope, go out to one of their fields and take the plough two and-a-half times round it. They then return home and take their breakfast and then turn out in bands and go about merry-making, cock-fighting, singing, dancing, etc.

Phalgun (*February-March*).—In *Phalgun* the orthodox Hindu festival, the Holi or Phāgua, is celebrated by all classes alike and takes the place of any special local festival.

Choitra (*March-April*).—In *Choitra*, on the last day of the month and also of the Bengali year, is celebrated the *Bhokta* or *Charak* hook-swinging festival, referred to earlier in this chapter. This, though essentially a festival in honour of the Hindu Mahādeva and organised by a Brāhman priest, is most popular with some of the aboriginal and semi-aboriginal castes, and the devotees are almost invariably drawn from among these classes, the higher castes and orthodox Hindus being content to look on.

Besides or as alternatives to some of the above, the Sonthals and Mundas observe the ordinary festivals peculiar to those tribes; no attempt need be made here to describe these as they differ in no important particulars from the same festivals as observed in the districts of the Sonthal Parganas and of Rānchi, and are fully described in the volumes of this series dealing with those districts.

Pastimes. Apart from the dancing, singing and too often drinking which, as will be seen, usually form a leading feature of the numerous religious or semi-religious festivals that follow one another at frequent intervals throughout the year, and constitute the chief amusements of the people, the most characteristic pastime is hunting. From their earliest years all aborigines use bow and arrow partly as a pastime and partly, when this is still possible, as a means of obtaining food. Besides the annual regular hunt or *Hānkwa* (*lo bir sendra*) of the Sonthals for which they gather in large numbers from all parts of the district south of the Dāmodar at Ajodhya on the Bāghmundi range of hills, and in the north of the district on the slopes of Parasnāth, smaller hunts are frequent in the wilder areas, and almost everywhere the boys pursue with great zeal any jackal, fox or hare that may be sighted near the village with their dogs, their bows and arrows, and sticks and stones. Arrow shooting matches are not uncommon, and form an essential part of the *Binda Parab* of the Bhumij and of the *Akhan Jatra* which corresponds to the *Pitha Parab* or cake festival as observed by the Kurmis. Over a great part of the district, and more especially in the south and east, cock-fighting is a very favourite amusement; this usually takes place on market days after the main business of the day is over, and takes the form either of individual matches or more rarely regular inter-village matches, over which great enthusiasm is displayed. The cocks are specially bred and trained for the purpose, and rough pieces of iron, three inches or more in length, with an edge hammered and ground till it is of knife-like sharpness, are attached to the spurs. The contests are usually fought to the finish and the beaten bird goes as the prize to the owner of the winner. Among the Bhumij in the west a kind of hookey (*Phuni khel* or *Phudi inganu*) is played with considerable zest in the month of January, large numbers taking part in the game which is played with any ordinary sticks and a ball of raw hide stuffed with cloth. The object of the game is to drive the ball over the opponent's goal line (there is no actual goal) which is usually formed by some natural boundary. Other games are marbles, and one resembling 'tipcat', and in the south of the district 'pegtops' are occasionally seen.

CHAPTER IV.

PUBLIC HEALTH.

GENERAL CONDITIONS.

MĀNBHUM enjoys the reputation among both Europeans and Indians of being a particularly healthy district; considerations of temperature indeed make Rānchi and Hazāribagh preferable to Europeans as places of residence but Purūlia is still, in spite of the accessibility of Rānchi, a favourite health resort among certain sections of the Indian population. The fact that the whole country is undulating and towns and villages are usually built on comparatively high lands, ensures a certain amount, at any rate, of natural drainage, and with it a relative immunity from the ordinary diseases, which account for the bulk of the mortality elsewhere. Statistics of mortality fully bear out the popular reputation, the mean ratio of deaths per mille of population, for the quinquennial period ending 1907 being returned at 25·37 only, as compared with the provincial average of 35·53, the only districts boasting a lower mortality rate being Singhbhum with 21·25 and Sambalpur with 24·29.

But the Sanitary Commissioner's figures show that there has been a gradually falling off in late years in the comparative immunity of the district from fever, the ratio of deaths from that cause having gone up from 15·73 for the ten years ending 1902 to 19·74 for the succeeding five years, and the district has also earned of late an unenviable reputation for severe epidemics of cholera and small-pox. These epidemics usually mark the hot weather months, April to June, recurring from time to time in the case of cholera in August and September. Ordinary fever is most prevalent at the seasons of excessive variations of temperature which mark the months of March and early April, and again the end of the rains, September and October, which is also the most favourable period for malarial fevers. The hot weather proper is usually, apart from epidemics of cholera and small-pox, a healthy period, as also are the cold weather months except for the old and for persons of otherwise impaired vitality. All three Municipal towns compare favourably with the rest of the district in point of view of mortality, and in contrast to the mufassal area the figures for the five years ending 1908 show a considerable improvement on those for the decennial period ending 1902; in Purūlia the ratio of deaths decreased from 23·13 to 20·89, in Raghunāthpur from 26·85 to 20·88 and in Jhalda from 22·55 to 17·96, the corresponding figures for the district as a whole being 22·45 for the earlier period and 28·13 for the later.

The present system of collecting statistics of births and deaths both in urban and rural areas was introduced in 1892; compulsory registration is in force in the towns and parents, guardians or the persons directly concerned are required to report births and deaths to the town police. In rural circles each village chaukidar is required to report at the time of the weekly parade at the police stations all births and deaths which have occurred in his village, or the portion of the village in his charge, during the preceding week. In the towns the statistics so collected are checked not only by the police but also by the vaccination staff working under the direct control of the Civil Surgeon; in rural areas the chaukidar's reports are from time to time verified by a superior police officer. The area of a thana or police circle is ordinarily, however, considerable and the amount of control which can be exercised over the chaukidars is necessarily small; the reporting staff is moreover illiterate and ordinarily of no very high level of intelligence, and not given to displaying any inordinate amount of energy over this or any other branch of their work. It follows that registration and classification of diseases are much less accurate in rural areas than in the towns where the general level of intelligence is higher, and the supervision closer. The chief defects in vital registration are the omission to report still-births, births of females, and births in outlying hamlets and among the lowest castes. Deaths are more carefully recorded but the causes of death, except perhaps cholera and small-pox, are hopelessly confused, the bulk being classified under the general head of fever. Vital Statistics.

The returns from 1892 to 1908 show that since 1895 the birth rate has generally been above 30 per mille, the average for the ten years ending 1902 being 32·78, and for the five years ending 1908 it was as much as 39·11. The lowest ratio recorded was 25·91 per mille in 1895; in more recent years the lowest reached was 31·47 in 1908. The highest rate recorded was 44·51 per mille in the year just preceding, and this extraordinary drop in the birth rate, though to some extent due to incomplete registration, can only be fully accounted for as the result of two successive years of short crops and high prices with resulting reduced vitality, and the very considerable emigration of women as well Births.

as men during the period of scarcity. As is usually the case elsewhere the ratio of births is lowest in the towns, Purūlia showing for the five years ending 1908 an average of just over 20 per mille, and in the preceding ten years only 18·33. For the same periods in the town of Raghunāthpur the ratio of births fell from over 29 to 23 per mille, and in Jhalda from over 27 to 25·65. The highest ratios of births were generally in the areas in which the aboriginal element, more especially the Sonthals whose fecundity is proverbial, is strongest; the lowest rate is curiously enough found in Jharia, where a large part of the enumerated population is a floating population of mining coolies, and apart from the fact that the women naturally make for their own homes, if possible, before confinement, the registration both of births and deaths is necessarily more difficult and more inaccurate than elsewhere.

Deaths. The death-rate during the same periods was lowest in 1898 when it fell as low as 16·43, a figure partially accounted for by the large amount of emigration in the preceding year; 1899 and 1900 were also years of low mortality, the ratios being just over 20 and 21 respectively. Since then there has been a fairly steady rise culminating in the high figure of 41·78 per mille in 1908, when cholera alone accounted for nearly 10 per mille, and the mortality from fever exceeded the ordinary average of deaths from all causes, the predisposing cause being undoubtedly the low vitality resultant on two years of comparative scarcity and high prices. This is clearly shown by the figures showing age at death; of 54,375 deaths 8,949 or 16·46 per cent. were of infants, 6,940 or 12·76 per cent. of children between 1 and 5 years of age, and 6,515 or 11·98 per cent. of persons of 60 years and upwards; over 41 per cent. of the deaths in all being children of tender years or the extremely old.

Infantile Mortality. Infantile mortality even in ordinary years is high though on the whole Manbhum compares very favourably with many districts in the province. In 1906 something less than 16 per cent. and in the following year slightly over 16 per cent. of children born in the district died within 12 months of their birth, as contrasted with over 20 per cent. in 1908: another 10 to 15 per cent. die between the ages of one and five. More male infants die than females and the feverish and early cold weather months, September to December, are especially fatal. In the rural areas, given normal conditions, there is no reason why infant mortality should be specially high, the climate being ordinarily dry and the villages naturally drained. Conditions in the larger villages and towns and in the coal field areas, where large numbers of coolies live more or less crowded into a very small space with inadequate sanitary arrangements, are not conducive to child life.

DISEASES. The great bulk of the mortality is reported as due to fever, the ignorant chaukidar for the most part being incapable of distinguishing more than three specific causes of death (other than death by misadventure); cholera he knows, small-pox he knows, all others he treats as due to fever.

FEVER. The average mortality from fever for the five years ending 1908 was 19·74 per mille as compared with 15·73 per mille for the ten years ending 1902; in the urban areas the variation was in the way of decreased ratios; Purūlia showing a small improvement from 8·44 to 7·83, Jhalda rather more from 13·91 to 10·82 and Raghunāthpur a very marked decrease from 17·98 (more than the district average) to 11·82 per mille. Major S. Anderson, I.M.S., Civil Surgeon of the District, writes, "in the rural areas there has been a marked increase in the death-rate, the ratios having gone up from 14·39 to 27·19 during the quinquennial period ending 1908. The year 1908 records the largest number of deaths, almost double that of 1904, as previously noted, the ratio of deaths for the district from this cause, having gone up from 15·73 for the ten years ending 1902 to 19·74 for the succeeding five years. The increase is noticeable in all the thanas of the district. Thanas Para, Chāndil, Barābazar (Bandwân side), Topchānchi, Tundi and Jharia persistently recorded an annual increase in the death-rate. From this it would appear that the most malarious portions of the district are the forest country at the foot of the hills, and especially the rice-growing tracts.

"The figures shown under head 'Fever' practically represent the residue of deaths from all causes after abstracting a certain number of deaths from small-pox, dysentery, &c., owing to sheer ignorance on the part of the registering agents. Further I am of opinion that a large percentage of the cases of this disease are imported. Mānbhum possessing a dry climate and being within easy reach of Calcutta, is resorted to, every year, by a large number of health-seekers and patients suffering from malaria, enlarged spleen and phthisis.

"The meteorological data also bear some relation with the prevalence of malaria, as it has been noticed that a heavy rainfall together with high level sub-soil water, occurring mainly at the foot of hills—as in Topchānchi, and at Dalma in the Barābazar thana—favours malaria. The water here forms pools quickly, which remain for a long period, and so allow of multiplication of the mosquitoes carrying the fever.

"*Seasonal prevalence.*—Apart from epidemics of cholera and small-pox, which occur from April to June, 'fever' due to various causes is most prevalent in March and early April and again in September and October at the end of the rains. In February and March a form of 'Influenza' prevails, mainly a catarrh attended with slight fever and frontal headache.

"Simple fever mainly due to heat occurs during the dry hot months of April, May and June; this when more severe causes syncope (failure of heart), difficulty in breathing or acting upon the thermal regulating centres produces the so-called 'Siriasis' of Manson.

"True malaria occurs from August to October, but 'relapses' may occur at any time."

Cholera. Cholera is endemic in this district, the average death-rate during the five years ending 1908 being 2·91 per mille, as compared with an average of 1·58 in the preceding 10 years. The latter figure may be taken as representing the normal death-rate, as the second period includes 1908 in which the death-rate from cholera reached the exceptional figure 9·27 per mille, the maximum recorded for the district for any year for which statistics have been compiled. In this year the enormous number of 12,075 deaths were recorded, and even this figure probably falls far short of the actuals as the coal field area in Jharia and Topchânchi thanas was for some time reduced to a state of panic, and neither colliery managers nor chaukidars furnished complete information. When the epidemic started work was being carried on at high pressure all through the field, owing to the exceptionally high prices obtainable for all qualities of coal; the disease spread rapidly through the field and panic-stricken coolies hurrying away from the infected collieries spread the disease into all parts of the district. In March the epidemic started and in May it reached its height; in June there was some abatement and it died rapidly away shortly after the rains broke. The primary causes were undoubtedly the absence of proper sanitary arrangements for the large population collected together in the comparatively small area covered by the coal-field, the exceptionally dry cold weather following on an early cessation of the rains, and the consequent drying up or pollution of the ordinary sources of water-supply.

It is not very easy to specify any definite part of the year as the cholera season, but taking the statistics for a number of years the months March to July would appear to be those in which a serious outbreak is most usual, though occasionally, as in 1907, the disease starts as early as January and reaches its height in

February. Generally speaking, the last four months of the year are comparatively free.

It is worthy of note that during the outbreak of April-June 1908 a large number of persons both European and Indian in and near Jharia submitted to inoculation at the hands of Professor Haffkine, with excellent results.

Small-pox appears every year but is rarely either epidemic or widespread; it was only in 1902 that the death-rate rose over 1 per mille, the incidence being greatest in the months of April and May. For the five subsequent years the average incidence was somewhat less than 2 per 10,000, as compared with rather more than 3 per 10,000 for the preceding decennial period. Small-pox.

Dysentery, diarrhœa and other forms of bowel complaints are credited with barely two deaths per 10,000, but as has already been pointed out the general tendency is to report all deaths, where the disease is accompanied by fever, as due to "fevers." No great reliance can therefore be placed on these figures, though it may perhaps be asserted with some degree of confidence that the climate is not, as a rule, provocative of this class of diseases, and in respect thereof the district is among the healthiest in the Province. Bowel complaints.

From the ravages of plague the district has been singularly immune; the disease indeed appeared at Jharia in the cold weather of 1906-07 and for some months there were sporadic cases, but the prompt measures taken by the Local Committee which included the burning down of part of the Jharia bazar where the disease had started, and a vigorous campaign of rat-killing throughout the adjoining colliery area apparently prevented the disease from getting a hold. The number of reported deaths was only nine and there has been no recrudescence in the area then affected. In the following year there were two isolated cases, both imported from Mirzapur at Balarāmpur, and in 1909 one death occurred at Purulia, the victim having brought the disease from Calcutta. Plague.

The infirmities of blindness and leprosy are very common, the number of blind persons and lepers per 10,000 head of population being in 1901 something over 35 and 30 respectively, as contrasted with only 18 and 9½, the figures for the province as a whole. No special reasons are assignable for these high figures, though in the case of leprosy the number is swelled by the inclusion of a good many from the neighbouring districts of Burdwan, Bānkura and Bīrbhum, which with Mānbhum appears to be a special focus of this disease, brought together in the local asylum, of which an account will be found at the end of that Infirmities.

chapter. The majority of the persons afflicted belong to the lowest classes.

Vaccination. Vaccination is compulsory only in Municipal areas, but on the whole it does not appear to be regarded with any great disfavour by the people generally; the ordinary attitude is one of more or less passive indifference, and it is only occasionally and in limited areas that active objection is taken. In 1908-09 57,593 persons or 44 per mille of the population were successfully vaccinated, and the average annual number in the previous five years was 47,984 representing 36 per mille. The district was formerly the great centre of inoculation for the whole of the Chota Nāgpur Division, and though the practice has now practically died out the following account taken from the Report on the subject by the Inspector-General of Civil Hospitals in 1869-70 and reproduced in Hunter's Statistical Account may be of interest. "Most of the inoculators (called *tikaits*, from *tika*, a mark) were Brāhmans, and the District was divided between them, so that each inoculator had a circle within which he had an exclusive right, recognized both by other *tikaits* and by the inhabitants, to carry on his profession. Besides this they practised in the neighbouring districts of Lohārdaga and Singhbhum, and to a limited extent in Hazāribagh. As a rule each family of *tikaits* held some land which had been granted to them by zamindars for their services, but depended chiefly on inoculation for a living. The average fee charged was four annas for a male child, and two annas for a female; but the expenses for the religious ceremonies attending the event, and the present usually made to the inoculator on the thirteenth day after the operation, made the outlay so great that it was regarded as an expense to be incurred only once in a lifetime. The instrument used was a small iron screw about two inches long, sharp at one end to prick the skin, and flattened at the other to apply the small-pox matter, which was carried in the shell of a fresh-water mussel."

SANITATION. In 1873 the Sanitary Commissioner reported that "in the district at large, sanitation, even in the most ordinary sense of the word, is not attended to, except in the larger villages, such as Raghunāthpur, Jhalda, Mānbazar, etc. Where municipalities exist, conservancy is looked after, and a certain amount of care and cleanliness is observed. European and native ideas differ widely in matters of household sanitation. The dwellings of the natives are constructed without the least regard to light and ventilation; and generally, heaps of bones, broken pottery, animal ordure, straw saturated with offensive liquids, dried and rotten leaves, etc., are found around them." To a great extent this description remains true to the facts, though it is perhaps unfair to describe the smaller villages as generally insanitary, the natural conditions ordinarily obviating the necessity of any elaborate sanitary arrangements, and the habits, at any rate, of the superior aboriginal races, *e.g.*, the Sonthals, being for the most part rather more cleanly than might be inferred from this description. Of the larger villages, with few exceptions, the description is much nearer to the facts, and outside the municipal towns and the Jharia coal field, to which reference will be made later, there is an entire absence of any methodical sanitary arrangements.

In Purulia. Purulia was described in the same report as having generally excellent sanitary arrangements; its population was then under 6,000, which had by 1901 grown to over 17,000. Even now, however, few parts of the town are congested, and the natural drainage (most of the main roads have pukka roadside drains) is sufficient to keep the town fairly clean, though the eventual necessity for a regular drainage system is realised, and a scheme is now under preparation. The conservancy arrangements, usual in municipal areas, are in existence and, besides the road-cleaning and scavenging establishment, a large body of sweepers are maintained for private latrines. There are numerous good wells in the town, the municipality maintaining some nine, and the Sahibbândh, elsewhere referred to, is a practically never-failing source of good drinking water, special precautions being taken to prevent its pollution by surface drainage and when necessary, by persons or cattle bathing therein. Besides the Sahibbândh there are a few other fairly clean tanks; the chief obstacle, however, to good sanitation is the large number of smaller tanks, a few of them public property but the bulk private, which are to be found in all parts of the town and which are more or less permanently polluted by surface drainage, sullage or other sources of pollution. The task of filling up or draining many of these is one which has to be faced sooner or later, but in its present financial condition the municipality can do but little.

In the villages. Beyond short lengths of roadside drains, the provision of a few municipal wells, and of a small conservancy and scavenging staff neither the Jhalda nor Raghunâthpur Municipalities have been in a position to provide very much in the way of improved sanitation; strictly speaking, however, they are not towns but merely large villages, and as such conditions are certainly very much better than in some of the rural villages, with rather smaller population, but almost as important as centres of trade. In these, as for example Balarâmpur, Châṇdil, Mânbazar, Châs and

Cheliâma all in the Sadar subdivision, of which all but the last named are centres of the lac industry, the sanitary condition leaves much to be desired; attempts are made from time to time with varying success to regulate the nuisance arising from the waste-water from the lac factories, and occasionally the local shop-keepers combine for a time to employ one or more sweepers to keep the main street comparatively clean ; generally speaking, however, no special attention is paid to sanitation beyond the provision of an occasional well by some public-spirited shop-keeper or merchant or by the District Board. The latter body, it may be noticed, has now on its books 21 wells besides 8 tanks, and provision is annually made for some 8 or 10 new wells in different parts of the district. Dhânbâid which has recently become the head-quarters of the subdivision and shows signs of rapidly growing into a considerable town, has taken early steps to regulate itself ; a strong local committee has been formed with the Subdivisional Officer as President and about one thousand rupees, raised by subscription locally, is spent annually on a conservancy staff. A similar committee is mooted for Katrâs, and it is proposed eventually to convert these into regular Union Committees.

In the coal fields. Sanitation in the coal field area is a problem which has given infinite trouble during the past five years, and is far from being solved yet. Prior to 1906 when plague broke out at Jharia and there was a general scare, practically nothing was done ; coolies were indifferently housed, or left to arrange for themselves, here and there only attempts were made to provide comparatively pure drinking water, and conservancy arrangements were conspicuous by their absence. The outbreak of plague resulted in the formation of a special Sanitary Committee consisting of representatives of several of the leading firms interested and of the local zamindar, the Civil Surgeon of the district, the local Medical Officer of the Indian Mining Association and the Subdivisional Officer with the Deputy Commissioner as President. The suppression of the plague outbreak and the warding off of any possible recurrence were the primary objects of this Committee and with the active co-operation of the Raja's Manager a good deal was done to clean out the Augean stable existing in the shape of the crowded and filthy Jharia bazar. A staff of Inspectors with gangs of coolies was organised, which, besides directing the rat-catching operations, were to take steps to clean up specially insanitary *bastis* or collections of coolies' huts. At the same time most of the larger collieries employed a more adequate staff of sweepers for the conservancy of their own particular collieries, and a more enlightened policy began to be adopted in the matter of provision of regular cooly lines and the supply of drinking water. With the departure of plague and in the absence of any law or recognised rules which could be enforced, the energies of the Committee and their staff very soon ceased to have any great effect, and on the smaller collieries and in the villages adjoining or in the midst of the colliery area, where the authority of the Committee, or of individual colliery managers of more enlightened views or greater public spirit, did not extend, conditions rapidly reverted to what they had formerly been. The recurring cholera epidemics of 1906 and 1907 stimulated to renewed efforts on the part of a few managers, and in the matter of cooly lines the good example set was of considerable effect; little attention was, however, paid to the water-supply question outside a very limited circle, and the result was the disastrous epidemic of 1908, which, besides causing enormous mortality, practically brought the working of the mines to a standstill for nearly three months at a time when every extra ton of coal raised meant a record profit. The immediate result was the expenditure of very large sums by most of the leading concerns on more or less elaborate arrangements for improving the water-supply of their respective collieries; two or three had already, before the outbreak, installed Jewel filter systems, and these proving generally satisfactory, were quickly introduced elsewhere, in some cases on a very large scale. The housing of coolies also received renewed attention, the medical and conservancy staff on many collieries was strengthened, and here and there some effort was made to clean out and reserve tanks, and to provide surface drainage in the cooly lines. It was generally felt, however, that the solution of the problem did not and could not lie with individual colliery managers, or in individual schemes; insanitary conditions in adjoining villages and in the numerous smaller collieries, where the efforts towards improved sanitation were neither vigorous nor sustained, remained a constant source of danger to the better managed properties in their neighbourhood; moreover in many cases private arrangements for proper water-supply by means of Jewel filters or otherwise were rendered difficult by the absence of a sufficient supply of pit or other water which might be filtered and rendered potable. A general scheme to supply the whole coal field was mooted, and was gone into with some care; *primâ facie* such a scheme is desirable and ultimately necessary but the problems involved, both engineering and financial, are of considerable complication, and up to date no scheme has been worked out in sufficient detail to enable a proper examination of the possibilities and difficulties to be made.

Necessity for legislation.

Another lesson brought home by the 1908 epidemic following as it did on serious, though less severe, outbreaks in the two preceding years was the necessity for legislation enabling the enforcement of ordinary sanitary and conservancy rules. The interests engaged in the coal industry are many, and to some extent conflicting, and till recently any general public spirit over-riding individual and temporary interests has been conspicuous by its absence. Concerted action was to a certain extent possible where collieries belonged to the Indian Mining Association, but there were and are many which do not. Moreover the number of small concerns with very small capital, and of others whose working capital is inadequate owing to the inflated sums paid to promoters when the mines were first opened or taken over from their previous owners during the height of the boom, is considerable; any heavy expenditure on water supply and sanitation, the return from which is only at the best prospective, can hardly be expected, and the result is that danger spots remain alongside and in the midst of areas where the most enlightened and wealthier collieries have sunk large sums in improving conditions. A similar state of things exists in regard to many of the villages in the neighbourhood of collieries, originally small agricultural villages, now largely crowded out by extra population connected with the mines; here too power to compel the reservation of tanks and wells, to control the manner and place of disposal of the dead, to clear out congested areas and to enforce comparative cleanliness within the village site is an urgent desideratum.

Various proposals have been made from time to time and have been rejected as unsuitable or impossible. The proposal to form the whole area into a municipality was one of the earliest, but the Act was obviously unsuitable for an area so large; the limitations of the Epidemic Diseases Act rendered a second proposal to promulgate rules under that Act of little value, as such rules could only have been enforced for the short period of six months. Great things were expected of the new provisions in regard to Union Committees embodied in the Local Self-Government Amendment Act of 1908 and it was hoped that it would be possible to form two or three Union Committees under the Act with sufficient powers to enforce the sanitary rules already propounded. Unfortunately it proved that the provisions of the Act in regard to finance put such Committees out of the question, and this proposal like the others had to be abandoned. The solution of the problem has still to be found; it is generally thought to lie in some amendment of the Indian Mines Act, extending the definition of "mine" to include not merely the actual workings as at present but also the colliery premises, including the cooly lines generally, and in order to meet the difficulty in regard to outside villages, the addition of a suitable definition of a mining settlement, which should include them. These changes with due provisions for suitable committees with powers to enforce rules and a staff to inspect and report on sanitary conditions will, it is hoped and anticipated, meet a great part, at any rate, of the present difficulties of the situation. A general water-supply scheme to supply pure water pumped from the bed of the Dâmodar river, throughout the coal field has so far failed to materialise, and in the present depressed condition of the coal industry it is hardly likely that any such scheme, even though feasible from an engineering point of view, could be financed. Meantime the Sanitation Committee already referred continues to exist and maintains a small staff whose main business it is to give early information of any outbreak of epidemic disease, and to form a nucleus for the larger staff which would be necessary to deal with any really serious outbreak. The provision of improved cooly lines continues, experience showing that the labour force now looks upon weather-proof huts or "dhowras," as they are locally called, as more or less essential; when not provided the coolies will not stay. Some attempt is also made in most of the larger collieries to provide comparatively pure drinking water, but even now there is much to be desired in this respect, and instances are not infrequent where a couple of wells, without any arrangement for distribution through the lines or workings, are the only provision for a labour force of upwards of a thousand. Tanks and old quarries filled with water must in such cases be used and also the pit water, and all these are more often than not polluted, so that the possibility of a recurrence of serious outbreaks of cholera is a constant one. Nowhere as yet in the coal field is latrine accommodation provided and the resulting evils must necessarily grow more acute as the area becomes more and more congested. Altogether though in the last few years there has been a considerable improvement, the absence of method and system in matters of sanitation in the Jharia coal field presents a far from pleasant picture, and considerations of common humanity as well as the interests of the industry call for early and concerted action.

Medical Institutions. There are eight public dispensaries situated at Purūlia, Jhalda, Raghunāthpur, Chās and Barābazar in the Sadar subdivision and at Dhânbâid, Topchānchi and Gobindpur in the Dhānbāid sub-division. Private dispensaries supervised by the Civil Surgeon, are also maintained at Jharia and Pândra by the proprietors of those estates. The zamindar of Nāwagarh also keeps up a small private dispensary and the majority of the larger collieries have their own arrangements for the medical relief of their labour force. At Pokhuria medical relief is provided in ordinary cases by Revd. Dr. Campbell of the United Free Church of Scotland Mission to the Sonthals, and occasional visits are paid by one of the medical missionaries from other stations in the Sonthal Parganas or Monghyr.

In-patients are received at (1) the Purūlia dispensary which has 26 beds for men and 8 for women; (2) the Jhalda dispensary with 2 beds for men and 2 for women; (3) the Barābazar dispensary with 4 beds; (4) the Jharia dispensary with 5 beds; (5) the Purūlia infectious diseases' hospital with 8 beds for men and 8 for women, and the new dispensary at Dhanbaid, when complete, will have accommodation for 6 male and 4 female in-patients.

The oldest dispensaries are those at Purūlia, established in August 1866, and at Pândra, established by the liberality of Râni Hingan Kumāri in December 1872. The most important of the medical institutions is at present the dispensary at Purūlia; it is maintained by the municipality with the help of a contribution from the District Board, private subscriptions, and a small endowment fund, devoted to the maintenance of a trained *Dhai*. From time to time improvements have been made from funds obtained from various private donors, and a new operation ward is shortly to be constructed and other improvements made, the bulk of the money required having been subscribed by the two leading zamindars of the district, Jyoti Lal Prosad Singh Deo of Kāshipur and Rāja Durga Prosad Singh of Jharia.

The new dispensary at Dhanbaid promises, when complete, to be a model institution; besides the main dispensary building there will be separate wards for males and females providing accommodation for 16 patients in all, an infectious diseases' ward with 2 beds, a moribund ward with 4 beds, besides a fully equipped operation room built on the most approved principles, and suitable quarters for the dispensary staff. The dispensary is managed by the District Board which contributes Rs. 500 annually towards its upkeep; there is a subscription list amounting to some Rs. 2,675 per annum, a large part of which is contributed by the various colliery companies, and Government, besides meeting the charges on account of the Assistant Surgeon's salary and allowances, contributes Rs. 545 annually. The dispensary has been open as an outdoor dispensary since July 1908, and the remaining buildings are now practically complete.

Dispensaries are maintained by the East Indian Railway Company at Dhanbaid and by the Bengal-Nāgpur Railway at Adra, at both of which places there are resident medical officers.

Indigenous system of medicine.

The European system of medicine and surgery has steadily gained popularity, and at Purūlia, Dhānbāid, Jharia and a few places within the district there are medical practitioners with Calcutta or other qualifications, whose practice is considerable and is for the most part conducted on European lines. Outside, however, the immediate radius of the dispensaries European drugs are not commonly used, and the majority of the people consult Indian doctors, either Muhammadan Hakims or the Vaidyas who practise the Hindu system of medicine. In the remoter areas the village *ojha* or the barber is consulted, and the treatment consists in many cases of incantations, charms or the performance of *pujas* varied with the use of a few comparatively simple herbal remedies, the knowledge of which in particular diseases has been handed down from father to son. More or less complete starvation and abstinence from drink is ordinarily prescribed in fever cases: in other diseases the remedies range from comparatively harmless and occasionally suitable drugs such as opium, camphor, nutmeg, myrabolam, aloes, lime-juice, salt, vinegar, assafœtidā to various nauseating compounds including such materials as animal urine.

Leper Asylum.

The Leper Asylum at Purūlia was started on a small scale in 1886-87 by the Rev. Heinrich Uffmann of the German Evangelistic Mission in connection with the Mission to Lepers in India and the East. It was removed to its present site, about two miles west of the public offices and entirely separated from the town and its outskirts by a broad strip of cultivation, some four years later, and in the years succeeding has grown into a small town of itself, neatly laid out in a large *sāl* plantation with well-built brick houses accommodating each some 12 persons, each house being 50 feet from its neighbour on either side. Down the centre runs a wall which separates the male wards from the female, and along it at intervals are the offices, the shop, the hospital and in a central position the church. For doubtful cases there are separate observation wards, and half a mile or more away and nearer the town is a large building and compound forming a home for the untainted children of the lepers. Both here and in the Asylum itself are schools, including for untainted children a Technical School where carpentry, mason-work and other useful crafts are taught. In the main Asylum there are now 22 wards for men and 18 for women, of which all save 3 (two male and one female, built at Government expense) have been provided by the supporters of the Mission and other friends.

The average population is from 600 to 700, the actual number in May 1910 being 629, inclusive of 41 cases under observation and 50 children in the "Untainted Children's Home." The popularity of the Asylum is such that the majority of cases find their way there willingly, and the number of lepers sent there by the Magistrate under the Act is, as a rule, very small. A large majority of the inmates are, however, such as could legally be sent there, and in consideration of this fact and the useful work done by the Asylum, it receives an annual grant of Rs. 12,000 from Government.

The Asylum is now the largest of its kind in India; as already stated it is situated pleasantly and in a healthy situation. Numerous wells have been sunk, and cisterns and bathing platforms provided and both houses and compound are kept scrupulously clean by the lepers themselves, each separate house having one of it inmates responsible as house-master or mistress as the case may be. Those who are able to do so are encouraged to keep up their own small patches of garden, and recently advantage has been taken of the Land Improvement Loans Act to build a tank and bring some of the extensive waste land beyond the Asylum under cultivation.

One of the features of the place is the shop where small luxuries can be purchased, each adult male getting a cash allowance of 5¾ annas and each adult female 4 annas per week besides a daily allowance of uncooked rice; the making of their small purchases and the cooking of their own food add undoubtedly to the pleasure of their lives and to the popularity of the Asylum, and make cases of evasion rare, though the opportunity is always present, the Asylum being open on every side and in no sense of the word a prison.

From the outset the working of the Asylum has been in the hands of the German Evangelical Mission, and to the Rev. H. Uffmann, who initiated the work, and the late Rev. F. Hahn and the Rev. P. Wagner (now in charge) especial credit is due for its thoroughly efficient organisation and management.

CHAPTER V.

AGRICULTURE.

THE surface of the district consists generally of a succession of rolling uplands with intervening hollows, along which the drainage runs off to join the larger streams. The soil is naturally an infertile laterite of, as a rule, no great depth, and the general tendency is towards continual detrition, the process being continued till the underlying rock or heavier gravel is exposed, wherever the higher lands are denuded of vegetation and nothing done to bring them under cultivation, before the disappearance of such vegetable loam as had formed there in the days when the forest or vegetation remained. Similarly, the more level spaces between the ridges and undulations require constant protection, if they are to retain the soil that has been washed down from the higher slopes, as every heavy shower tends to wash the soil down, first into the smaller streams and finally into the larger rivers. The first essential, therefore, from the cultivator's point of view, is to break up this constant surface drainage and stop the consequent detrition, and the result is to be seen at the present day in the conversion of the slopes and hollows, wherever practicable, into terraces of different levels, these again being cut up into smaller patches each with its protecting embankment, varying in height from a few inches to several feet. The rainfall is thus retained on each particular terrace and field, and cultivation of a wet rice-crop made possible. The power of retaining moisture varies, largely, of course, with the nature and depth of the soil, and percolation from one terrace to another is more or less slow or rapid; the lower, however, the level, the more the field benefits by the moisture percolating from those above it, and except where the nature of the soil and the absence of proper drainage is such that they become water-logged, the lowest levels ordinarily furnish the best and most secure rice lands. **GENERAL CONDITIONS.**

A system of cultivation, such as is described above, is suitable mainly for rice, and rice is the main crop of the district. Land on the ridges, where there is a sufficiency of soil, is cultivated without the preliminary process of levelling with a crop of early (*gora*) rice sown broadcast, or with *kodo*, or one of the pulses *urid* and *mung*, known locally as *biri*, in the early rains, May to October, and with various oil-seeds in the cold season. High lands near the village sites, which are within reach of such manure as is available, are cultivated in the autumn with maize, *kodo* and *biri*, and in the spring such lands may also yield a crop as oil-seeds, or occasionally of wheat or barley.

The extent of cultivation varies with the predominance of particular characteristics. South of the Dāmodar in the northern half of the Sadar sub-division, an area of some 1,500 square miles, the undulation of the country is comparatively slight, and except along the eastern and western borders where much scrub jungle still remains, cultivation is fairly close, and the eye is met, as one tops each ridge, with the view of a large expanse of terraced rice fields, dotted with numerous small tanks and here and there clumps of trees, marking the village sites. In places, more especially in thana Raghunāthpur and the eastern portion of thana Chās, the ridges are comparatively low and the intervening hollows so extensive that the terracing is barely noticeable except to a close observer, and the impression obtained is rather that of a stretch of ordinary Bihar or Eastern Bengal rice fields; such favoured tracts are, however, rare.

South of Purūlia itself and a line drawn east and west, practically coinciding with the Bānkura and Rānchi roads, conditions are less favourable, bare uncultivated stretches of high land are more in evidence, the country is more broken up as it falls rapidly away to the Kāsai river. Towards the west the rugged Ajodhya range rises abruptly from the plain south of, and at no great distance from, the Kāsai. To the east the country is better clothed with vegetation, but scrub jungle and bare high lands are more in evidence than cultivation. South of this again is an area of fairly close cultivation stretching towards the hilly range which, with the Subarnarekha below it on the south, divides the district from Singhbhum. As the hills are approached cultivation becomes scattered, giving way as one advances further to stretches of scrub jungle and when the foot hills are reached to traces of the great forests which once clothed this range.

INFLUENCE OF RAINFALL.

The second main condition on which the nature and extent of the agriculture depend is the climate and, more especially, the rainfall. As will be seen from the account just given of the physical conditions which prevail in the district of Mānbhum, rainfall is necessarily a matter of prime importance. Without adequate rain in due season, both preparation of the soil and sowing of the crop is impossible, the soil itself not being naturally one that can retain moisture for any considerable length of time. The normal annual rainfall of the district is 53 inches of which nearly 44 represent the ordinary fall in the months of June, July, August and September; 3 inches may be expected in October and November, less than $1\frac{1}{2}$ inches in the three succeeding months, and somewhat under 5 inches in the months of March, April and May. The ideal distribution for the cultivator who relies mainly on his winter rice crop, is a sufficiency of showers in early May to enable him to get his fields dug over and ploughed. He then requires fairly heavy rain at the end of May in order to prepare his seed beds, sow his seedlings and have sufficient moisture to keep the young plants green till the regular rains commence. This should be between the 15th and 20th of June, and to be really useful the fall during the latter half of June should measure some 8 to 10 inches. While he is going on with the preparation of his fields, which includes several ploughings, the repairing and strengthening of the *ails* and embankments and other preliminary preparations, his seedlings are growing rapidly and by the second week of July he should be able to begin transplantation, and with fairly regular but not too heavy rain throughout July and in the earlier part of August, he should complete this in fields of all levels by the middle of that month. Thereafter, all that is required is sufficiently heavy rain at intervals to keep the young crop almost continuously standing in a few inches of water. About the second week of September, it is usual to run off the surface water with the idea of encouraging the formation of the grain but in doing so the cultivator incurs a considerable risk and this practice makes a heavy fall of rain at the end of September an absolute necessity. Given this, however, and some 3 or 4 inches in the first fortnight of October his crop, even if no further rain is received, should be a bumper one.

It will thus be seen that it is not merely the quantity of rainfall which is important, but also the timeliness or otherwise of the different falls. If, for instance, the May rains fail, the preparation of the fields, the sowing of the seeds in the seed beds and their subsequent transplantation are all delayed, and the crop ultimately suffers in a greater or less degree, even though the rains in the latter months are timely and adequate. Again, when after suitable rains in May the June rains are delayed, the cultivator will have his time cut out to keep his seedlings alive; in extreme cases he may have to begin over again, when the rains do come, by sowing fresh seed at the time when he ought to be transplanting, with the result that by the time the fields are planted out the best part of the rainy season will have gone by and his chances of getting anything more than a poor crop will be very small. Again, when all conditions have been favourable down to the middle of September, the absence of rain during the succeeding three weeks or a month will mean probably the entire loss of his crop on the higher level fields, and at the most a 50 per cent. crop on those on the lowest level, unless by irrigation he is able to make up for the deficiency in the necessary moisture. For the *bhādoi* crops an early cessation of the rains does not so much matter, but the earlier rains must be ample. For Indian corn, though ample rainfall is necessary, ample sunshine is almost equally important as without it the grain will neither fill out nor ripen. For the *rabi* crops the September rains are all important, as without them the fields will not contain sufficient moisture to germinate the seed, and to ensure a full crop periodical showers from December to February are also necessary.

Irrigation. The dependence of the crop on rainfall is thus such as to make it very necessary that the cultivator should be prepared to supplement deficient rainfall by irrigation. Unfortunately, the nature of the country lends itself to one system only, viz., that of irrigation from *ahars* and *bāndhs* themselves dependent for their supply of water on the rainfall. In other districts, as for example in Gaya, it is possible to feed the *ahars* by channels or *pains* taking off from the different streams which depend for their water not on local rainfall but on the rainfall of the hilly regions where they have their source. In this district all the larger rivers, and most of the smaller streams, run a very rapid course along beds which are usually very much below the general level of the surrounding country and, in order to utilize their water for irrigation purposes, it would ordinarily be necessary to construct channels of great length and through very difficult country at an expense which would be prohibitive.

The *bāndhs* of this district of which there are, as a rule, several in every cultivated village, are simply embankments thrown across a favourable dip in the general level of the ground. In some cases the embankment is a comparatively high one across a deep valley, but ordinarily any existing natural depression is made use of by raising a low bank on one or more of its sides. In a few cases as much as 100 acres of land may be irrigable from such a *bāndh*, but in the vast majority the area irrigated is from 5 to 10 acres only. Such *bāndhs* are constructed practically wherever it is possible to catch a certain amount of surface drainage and at the same time to terrace a few rice fields below them. The irrigation is effected ordinarily by percolation; only in exceptional cases is the *bāndh* cut or the water drawn off by a pipe or other outlet, as for instance, when water is required to preserve the seedlings or, towards the end of the season, to make up for the deficiency of the rainfall. For cold weather crops such *bāndhs* are ordinarily useless, as in a dry year the majority retain little water after December. When land is first brought under cultivation, the cultivator naturally tackles first the land in the lowest part of a dip and the *bāndh* constructed is usually some way down the slope and, consequently, gets a large amount of surface drainage and is so much the more useful for irrigation purposes. As cultivation extends, the lower *bāndhs* are themselves converted into rice fields except where they have been excavated to any great depth, and the new *bāndhs* constructed higher up get proportionately less water and at the same time have to serve a larger area. The general result, in areas where practically the whole of the easily available land has already been brought under cultivation, and this applies to a large part of the district, is that the *bāndhs* are of comparatively little value as a safeguard against failure of the crops and in a year of very deficient rainfall, being themselves dependent on the rainfall for their water, they can hardly be classed even as protective works.

Irrigation from wells is practically unknown; only masonry wells, sunk to considerable depth, would be suitable in a soil composed so largely of gravel and disintegrated rock, and construction of such wells, the cost of which can never be accurately estimated in advance owing to the possibility of meeting hard rock, is only within reach of the exceptionally prosperous cultivator; they are rarely met with therefore outside the village site. Kutcha wells are occasionally sunk a few feet in the beds of *bāndhs*, or in low level rice fields, but this is done ordinarily in order to supply drinking water for men and cattle, when other sources have failed, and not for irrigation. WELLS.

Beyond multiplying the number of *bāndhs* and enlarging and deepening existing bāndhs, extension of irrigation is hardly possible except at prohibitive cost. Various schemes for irrigation dams and channels were considered in connection with the enquiries made by the Irrigation Commission of 1901-03, and a few of these were examined in greater detail in 1907 by an Executive Engineer specially deputed for the purpose. EXTENSION OF IRRIGATION.

Of these, only one project was of any size or importance, viz., the proposal to throw a dam across the Sāldaha Jhor some five miles south of Jhalda near the village Lagām. Here the stream passes between two hills in a valley about a mile wide, and the Executive Engineer considered that at a cost of about Rs. 60,000 it would be possible to form a reservoir of sufficient size to irrigate an area of some two to three thousand acres in some half dozen villages. No detailed plans and estimates have yet been prepared and it is, perhaps, doubtful whether the scheme is really at all practicable and it is certainly doubtful whether the return in the shape of additional rents, if the local Zemindar undertook the cost of construction, would anything like recoup him or, should Government construct the reservoir, whether a water-rate, such as the tenants could pay, would give an adequate return on the outlay. The stream being a comparatively small hill stream with only a small drainage area, it seems unlikely that sufficient water would be stored in the years in which water is most necessary, *i.e.*, the years in which the rains absolutely fail.

The District Famine Programme provides for the construction or improvement of *bāndhs* in a large number of villages. Such *bāndhs* make cultivation possible, and they reduce the chances of entire failure of the crop in years of badly distributed rainfall, though, as already explained, in a year of deficient rainfall they are liable to fail as sources of irrigation just when they are most needed. Still a degree of protection is better than none at all, and, in the absence of any workable scheme to ensure complete protection, it seems desirable that the construction and improvement of *bāndhs* should be encouraged in every possible way.

SOILS. The prevailing characteristic of the soil is hard ferruginous gravel with a thin overspread layer of vegetable mould, where protected by jungle growth or otherwise from detrition. The system of cultivation as well as the rapid denudation of the jungle, prevents any great addition being made to the alluvium, and for its phosphates and nitrates the cultivated area has to depend mainly either on rotation of crops which is barely practised at all except on the high lands, or on such manure as the cattle which graze unrestrained after the rice harvest provide, or the mud dug out periodically from the dried up *bāndhs* and tanks. Except on the high lands adjoining the homesteads and on lands selected for sugarcane, regular manuring with cattle dung is rarely gone in for, and the increasing difficulty of getting wood tends to make the cultivator trench more and more on the available supply of cattle dung as a substitute for firewood.

Scientific classification. Mr. Mukherji in his note on the soils of this district classifies them as follows :—

I. Clay or *chita*—

(*a*) *Gobra chita* is of a blackish colour, very hard when dry and impossible to plough till softened by much rain. It is retentive of moisture. Rice, oilseeds, gram and cotton are grown on this land.

(b) *Dudhi chita* is of white or reddish colour. It is an impermeable clay mixed with limestone nodules. It is sticky when wet but very hard when dry. Grows no crops.

(c) *Dhaba chita* or *karna* is also very similar to the above in physical character and agricultural value. It is a source of lime.

II. Loamy soil—

(a) *Dorasa* is found near the hills and on the tops of ridges.

(b) *Pali* is soil formed by rain washings from higher situations and consists of detritus of decomposed rocks and vegetable matter. When the proportion of clay predominates it is called *pali bāli* (clay loam), and when on the other hand the proportion of sand predominates it is called *bāli pali.* The silt deposited by the Subarnarekha river on its banks, grows good crops of jute.

III. Sandy soil is known as *bāli.* It is commonly found in river beds and used for growing melons and other cucurbitaceous vegetables.

IV. A number of inferior soils unfit for cultivation are distinguished by their colour, etc, *e g., sāda māti* (white), *kāla māti* (black), *lal māti* (red), *kankar māti* (calcareous), or *pāthar māti* (gravelly), etc.

This classification illustrates fairly clearly the general poverty of the soil, but for practical purposes the ordinary cultivator merely differentiates soils by position. Thus, there are the three classes of rice land, *bahal*, the lowest or the most benefited by percolation from a *bāndh* and most retentive of moisture, *kānāli*, somewhat higher, and less favourably situated in respect of moisture, and *baid*, the high terraces surrounding the *bahāl* or *kānāli*, and dependent entirely on the rainfall, much of which percolates rapidly on to the lower level fields. Popular classification.

High lands are known by the general term '*dānga*' or towards the west '*tānr*'; when cultivated they retain these names, or are called occasionally '*gorā*'; such lands give at the best a scanty outturn, and ordinarily they are cultivated only once in four or five years. The land immediately adjoining the homesteads is variously known as *bāstu, ud-bāstu* or *bāstu bāri;* it benefits by getting more of the available manure, and it is on this that the superior autumn and winter crops are grown.

Extension of cultivation. Some indication of the extent to which the area brought under cultivation has increased during the last 20 years is to be gathered from the latest Settlement Reports of the Tundi, Mātha and Kailāpal estates, to which reference has been made in an earlier chapter. The first named is characteristic of the hilly area in the extreme north, Mātha of the country immediately south and west of the Bāghmundi range, and Kailāpal of the wilder portion of the country bordering on the Dalmā range in the extreme south. In Tundi in 1904 it was found that the area terraced for rice had increased in 20 years by nearly 80 per cent.; in Mātha by 15 per cent., and in Kailāpal by 43 per cent. In the central and more advanced parts of the district the increase cannot have come up to even an average of these figures, but it would not be unsafe to estimate the extension of cultivation in the district as a whole during the last twenty-five years as approximating to 20 or 25 per cent. Cultivation is still extending in all parts of the district, though it is only in the areas still bordered by jungles that any rapid or considerable extension is now possible. The wasteful method known as "jhuming" is no longer very prevalent, but the destruction of jungle in order to bring under cultivation areas which are unlikely to remain culturable more than a few years at the outside, is common almost everywhere that any jungle remains. In the more closely cultivated areas extension is gradual, but in any favourable year new plots adjoining the existing cultivation are terraced and planted out with rice seedlings on the off-chance of getting some return, and here and there new *bāndhs* are excavated and new fields made below them, for the most part by tenants whose credit with the money-lender is considerable, or by the money-lender himself, such work involving a considerable outlay in cash, if the work is to be immediately productive.

PRINCIPAL CROPS. EXTENT OF CULTIVATIONS. According to the accepted Agricultural Statistics of the district, 59 per cent. of the district area was under cultivation in 1908-09, 7 per cent. consisted of current fallows and culturable waste, and the remaining 34 per cent. was not available for cultivation. This classification, which is not based on any detailed survey, can hardly be treated as more than an approximate one, and is probably only accurate, even approximately, so far as the percentage under cultivation goes. In Pargana Barābhum, which has recently been surveyed, and the area of which is rather less than one-sixth of the whole district, the figures prepared by the Survey Deparment show the percentage under cultivation as 48, current fallow and culturable waste 17½ per cent. and unculturable area 34½ per cent. Of the cultivated area included in the above figures, a considerable portion consists of high lands cropped only once in three or four years, and the average area under cultivation in any one year is barely 35 per cent.

In the other surveyed areas, which are of comparatively small extent and include a larger share of hill and jungle, the percentage under cultivation is 32 per cent. and 17 per cent., respectively, in the Kailāpal and Mātha estates. Allowing for closer cultivation in the more level and open parts of the district, it would probably be safe to assume that not more than 45 to 50 per cent. of the total area is under regular cultivation, and another 10 per cent. of high lands cultivated once in three years.

For statistical purposes the crops grown are divided into the three main divisions, *bhādoi, aghani* and *rabi*, according to the time of harvest; the *bhādoi*, the early or autumn crop reaped in the months of Bhādra, Aswin and Kartik, (September, October, November), includes *gora* and *bhadoi* rice, *marua*, *kodo*, maize and various less important millets; *aghani* is the winter crop including winter rice reaped in December (Aghan), sugar-cane cut in January and early February, and certain varieties of oil-seeds; the *rabi* crop harvested in the spring includes such cold weather crops as gram, wheat, barley and various pulses and oil-seeds. The distribution of the normal acreage under these crops cannot, in the absence of detailed survey figures for the whole district, be given with any degree of accuracy but on the basis of the figures recently made available for Pargana Barābhum it may be accepted that approximately 50 per cent. of the cultivated area is under *bhādoi* crops, 46 per cent. under *aghani* and 8 per cent. *rabi*, the twice cropped area being about 4 per cent. Even these figures must be accepted with caution, as those for *bhādoi* crops are swelled by the large area under rice which is reaped in November, and which is strictly speaking somewhere between a *bhādoi* and an *aghani* crop.

Rice is shown in the District Statistics as grown on an area Ric of 1,428 square miles, and in Barābhum the area under this crop represents no less than 73 per cent. of the net cultivated area in any one year; it is, therefore, without question the most important crop. No distinction is made locally between *bhādoi* and *aghani* rice, and the only true bhādoi rice is that known as *gora*, sown broadcast on high lands in May or early June and reaped in August and September. This, except in the portion of the district bordering on the Rānchi district, is a small crop and represents at the outside a very small percentage of the whole. The figures on which the estimate for *bhādoi* crops just given is based are swelled by the inclusion of all rice reaped earlier than December, that is to say, the whole of the rice crop grown on the *baid* lands, most of which in this district is transplanted and, except that it ripens rather earlier, differs in no respect from the winter rice reaped on the lower lands in December and January. Locally, the only distinctions drawn are between *gora* rice and other rice, the latter being sub-divided into *baidhān* (grown on *baid* lands) and *barhān* grown on *kanāli* or *bahāl* lands; the terms *bhādoi* and *aghani* as well as *aus* and *aman* are never used locally. Were the so-called *bhādoi* rice a variety sown broadcast and reaped not later than October, there would be some advantage in having the distinction drawn: as the facts are the differentiation is purely on paper and serves no really useful purpose: on the contrary it is probably misleading, because the impression obtained by any one familiar with conditions, *e.g.*, in Bihar where the *bhādoi* rice is a true *bhādoi* crop, from the assertion that the area under *bhādoi* rice in Mānbhum exceeds that under *aghani* rice would naturally be that, in a year in which the September rains failed after favourable conditions in previous months, at least half the rice crop was assured, which would, as a matter of fact, be far from justified by the facts. It should, therefore, be borne in mind that the bulk of Mānbhum *bhādoi* rice is, at any rate, a very late *bhādoi* crop, and likely to be adversely affected by conditions adverse to the later winter crop.

As already stated the area under *gora* rice is small, and, except towards the western border where the example of the Kol cultivators in Rānchi has perhaps had some effect, it is not a crop which the Mānbhum tenant ordinarily goes in for, preferring, when he does cultivate high lands at this season, to sow *kodo*, *gondli* or *urid*; a liberal estimate of the area cropped would be 5 per cent. of the whole area under rice, or about 70 square miles. The following are the chief varieties grown:—*charka*, *kala*, *sindurtupi*, *alsanga*, *bheriya*, *prosād-bhog*, *rudni*, *kaya*, *nela*, *himri*, *kalesh*, *aus*, *hengri*, *bhasa*, *bahāli*, *kanhua*, and *lowa*. In the north of the district where *gora dhan* is not grown at all its place is taken to a certain extent by the *Sāthi dhan*, so-called as ripening in 60 days, and remarkable on account of the fact that the grain ripens within the sheath and is, consequently, not exposed to the ravages of certain insect pests which attack other forms of early ripening rice.

The main rice crop grown on terraced lands and for the most part transplanted, may be taken as made up of 60 per cent. *bhādoi* or early ripening and 35 per cent. *āghani* or late ripening, the former being grown on an area of 858 square miles, and the latter on an area of 500 square miles. The former includes the whole of that grown on the highest or *baid* lands; that grown on the second class or *kānāli* lands is partly *bhādoi* and partly *aghani*, while the entire crop on the best lands (*bahāl*) is classed as *aghani*. The list and description given below of the chief varieties of rice grown on the different classes of land has been supplied by Rev. Dr. Campbell, whose experience of agricultural conditions in the northern part of the district extends over some 35 years. The list only professes to be accurate for the Dhānbāid Sub-division, but may be taken as approximately accurate for the rest of the district also.

I. *Sāthi.*—This variety of *Dhan* is grown on high lands, generally the highest portion of *baid* lands, but not extensively. A peculiarity of this variety is that the grain ripens within the sheath, and is therefore not exposed to the ravages of a certain fly pest, which renders early ripening *dhan* unproductive.

II. *High land Dhan locally known as Baid Dhan.*—Of this there are many varieties, the most important and most largely cultivated are:—

(1) *Badras.* Awnless, grain of a light brown colour, rice white. Ripens from 7th to 15th Kartik, and, in good soil and under good climatic conditions, yields from 50 to 60 fold. (2) *Jauae Laru.* Awnless, grain light straw coloured, rice white, grain medium size. (3) *Moifal.* Awnless, grain light coloured, narrow; rice white. Withstands drought well and is therefore cultivated in the higher *Baid* lands. (4) *Askuji.* Awnless, ripens from 7th to 15th Kartik; grain smallish and light coloured. (5) *Koya.* Fully awned, grain medium size, light coloured, ripens early. (6) *Dulngi.* Grain small, very dark coloured, rice white. If grown on sandy soils the grain is dark coloured, if on clayey soils it is light coloured. The grain is awnless.

III. *Dhan grown on second class lands, known locally as Kānāli.*—The most important varieties are:—

(1) *Kolom-Kāthi.* Awnless, grain long and narrow, light straw coloured, rice white. (2) *Ajan.* Awn on terminal grain of spike, grain large, light coloured, rice white. (3) *Pormai Sal.* Awned, grain very dark, often almost black, rice white. Emits a perfume when in process of being cooked. (4) *Kāli Kāsi Phul.* Awnless, grain dark coloured, often as if it had been smoked, rice white. Is also grown on *bahal* lands. (5) *Māloti.* Awnless,

grain small, darkish tinge, rice white. (6) *Kola Kandhi.* Awnless, grain small, light coloured, rice white, drought resisting. (7) *Bena Phul.* Awnless, grain medium size, light coloured, rice white. (8) *Kāsi Phul.* Awnless, grain small, straw coloured, rice white. (9) *Rāi Mundi.* Awned, grain small, light coloured, rice white.

IV. *Dhan grown on first class lands, known locally as bahāl.*—The most important are :—

(1) *Dhusri.* Awnless grain dark coloured and small, rice, white. Ripens early. (2) *Mânik Kolma.* Awnless, grain darkish coloured and small, rice white (3) *Kumra Sal.* Awnless, grain light coloured, short and thick, rice white. (4) *Kumhar Sal.* Awnless, grain straw coloured, short and dumpy, rice white. (5) *Getul.* Awnless, grain straw coloured, medium size, rice white. (6) *Sal Mungar.* Sparsely awned, grain a dark straw colour, medium size, rice white. (7) *Nari Kolma.* Awnless, grain small, light coloured, rice white. (8) *Jhuler.* Awnless, grain light coloured and small, rice white. Ripens late (9) *Bāsmati.* Sparsely awned, grain very small and straw coloured, rice very fine and clean. Emits a very pleasant perfume when being cooked. (10) *Bāg Panjar.* Has a few awns on each spike, grain very dark coloured, medium size, rice white, spikes of great length. This variety is grown in very moist situations. (11) *Pormāe Sal.* Awned, grain very dark coloured, often almost black, rice white. Emits a pleasant perfume when being cooked. (12) *Medi.* Awnless, grain short and thick, very dark coloured, has the appearance of having been smoked, the husked rice has streaks of colour lengthwise. (13) *Hemchā Rānge.* Awnless, grain bright brown colour and small, rice white. Ripens early. (14) *Kâmin Kajol.* Awnless, grain darkish coloured, small, rice white Ripens early. (15) *Sita Sal.* Awnless, grain light coloured, very small, rice very fine and white. (16) *Boro Kolma.* Upper grains in spike awned, grain darkish coloured and small, rice white. (17) *Bāli Chur.* Awnless, grain tinged brown, very small, rice white. (18) *Chini Sankar.* Awnless, grain darkish coloured and very small, rice white. (19) *Chandon Sal.* Awnless, grain dark coloured, small and narrow, rice white. (20) *Kari Bānki.* Awned, grain very dark coloured, rice white. Emits a pleasant perfume when being cooked. (21) *Ram Sal.* Awnless, grain light straw coloured, medium size, rice white. (22) *Narhi Kolma.* Awnless, grain lightish coloured, rice when husked has a reddish tinge. Grain does not readily become detached from the straw. (23) *Chachi Mohul.* Awnless, grain deep brown colour, medium size, rice white. Ripens early.

Grain is readily detached from straw, and is therefore reaped before it is fully ripe. (24) *Dudhi Kolma*. Awnless, grain light coloured, rice white. (25) *Sāheb Sal*. Awnless, grain light coloured, rice white. (26) *Lidhi Kolma*. Awned, grain light coloured, medium size, rice white. (27) *Sāgar Kolma*. Awnless. grain dark straw colour, long and narrow, rice white.

Next in importance to rice as a food crop is maize, occupying in Barābhum about 9 per cent. of the cultivated area, and in the district as a whole 172 square miles. This crop is cultivated on an extensive scale in the extreme north and south of the district only, elsewhere it is confined to small patches near the homesteads, every Sonthal and, generally, every aboriginal cultivator growing a small quantity for home consumption only. As compared with Bihar it is noticeable that the crop is a poor one, very little trouble being taken with the preparation of the soil or its subsequent tillage and weeding in the early stages of the crop's growth. Maize.

Other autumn crops are *gondli*, *bājra*, *marua*, *kodo*, *mung* and *urid* grown for the most part on roughly prepared high lands, cropped as a rule not oftener than once in two or three years. These with the winter crops, wheat and barley, gram, *rahar*, *khesari*, *kurthi*, *masuri* and various peas and beans, make up the miscellaneous food crops of the district and, according to the district statistics, are cultivated on 245 square miles, of which barely one quarter represents the area under the spring food crops. The unpopularity of such crops is due to several causes, one being the difficulty of arranging for the irrigation necessary for the superior crops, such as wheat and barley, and another the practice of allowing the village cattle to wander at will once the rice crop is reaped. If a second crop were raised on the moisture-retaining rice lands (a possibility which the local Agricultural Association is at present endeavouring to demonstrate), this practice would require modification unless the fields were fenced, which is out of the question on the ground of expense, except for very small areas. The conservatism of the local cultivator in this respect is not likely to be overcome until increasing pressure of population on the soil or higher rents compel him to make some endeavour to get more out of the land than the single, and at present in a normal year more than satisfying, rice crop. Other crops.

Of non-food crops oil-seeds, grown both as a winter and a spring crop, are the most important. Rape and mustard cover some 52 square miles, *til* or gingelly 16 square miles and others, of which the most common is *surguja*, some 40 square miles.

Sugar-cane is but sparsely cultivated, the area under this crop being barely 32 square miles; with few exceptions the quality of cane is inferior, and the outturn of *rab* or *gur* small. Cotton is a very small crop covering 16 square miles, and tobacco is grown in minute patches only, for purely local consumption, the total area under this crop in the whole district being estimated at less than 6 square miles.

Miscellaneous crops occupy a very small area. Potatoes and other vegetables are grown in small quantities only, in and near Purūlia and Jharia; the various varieties of sweet potatoes, *alu*, *suthni*, etc., are barely grown at all. Of productive mango gardens there are few, and fruits are represented almost entirely by the products of the jungles.

Outturn of crops. The conditions under which crop-cutting experiments are ordinarily conducted, and the large amount of personal error which is possible, make it difficult to attach any great weight to the statistics compiled therefrom; this is particularly so in the case of rice which in a district like Mānbhum is cultivated in small plots, each of which in the same area may differ more or less considerably in productivity by reason of its particular position in respect of the main source of moisture. From *bahāl* lands 30 maunds of paddy per acre would probably represent a fair average crop in a normal year, though outturns of 50 or even 60 maunds are by no means uncommon; for *kanāli* lands the average is from 20 to 25 maunds, though as much as 30 or 35 maunds are occasionally obtained. For *baid* lands it is almost impossible to state an average: 25 maunds would be an exceptional crop obtainable in a good year from specially favoured plots: 15 maunds is probably nearer the normal, and in many fields, cultivated more or less speculatively on the chance of getting a small return, 10 maunds would probably represent a fair outturn. For other crops the available statistics are of little value.

Improvements in cultivation. It is perhaps doubtful whether the last 20 years have witnessed any marked improvements in methods of cultivation, and the attempts made of recent years by the local Agricultural Association to introduce good or new varieties of seed have, so far, borne little fruit. As elsewhere noticed there is not yet any great pressure of population on the soil, and in normal years the ordinary cultivator can garner in a rice crop more than sufficient for his needs without any great expenditure of effort, and, so long as this is the case, it is unlikely that the intensely conservative and not too energetic cultivator of this district will change his ways. The exertions of the Agricultural Association have so far been mainly directed to the introduction of a superior variety of Central Provinces *aus* paddy, and the encouragement of the sowing of a second crop of gram or *khesāri* on suitable rice lands. The former has proved almost uniformly a failure, owing to blight or other causes; the latter is being persisted in and in course of time may, by force of example and the demonstration of what is possible, have good results, but at present the outlook is not very hopeful.

The cattle are generally small and of poor quality, the main cause of which is no doubt the entire absence of good grazing, outside the hill areas, for more than half the year. An additional reason is the insufficient attention paid to reservation of bulls for breeding purposes, numbers of undersized, ill-fed and barely mature bulls being regularly found with every herd. A few superior bulls are available here and there, and in the north and west some inter-breeding with Hazāribagh stock is done, with good results. Buffaloes compare favourably on the whole with the cattle, and in many parts of the district they are extensively used both in carts and for ploughing. Sheep are of a very inferior kind, undersized for the most part and yielding a poor fleece. Horses are scarce, except in the stables of a few of the larger zemindars, and country ponies are not very numerous. The pig and the goat are the most flourishing of the domestic animals. There is a Veterinary Dispensary at Purūlia, in charge of a Veterinary Assistant, established in 1905, and also an Itinerant Veterinary Assistant with head-quarters at Dhanbaid. Three thousand one hundred and sixty-five animals were treated by these two officers during 1909-10, and 272 inoculated with rinderpest serum. Cattle.

CHAPTER VI.

NATURAL CALAMITIES.

LIABILITY TO FAMINE.

The extent to which Mānbhum as a whole is dependent on a single crop, *i.e.*, the rice crop, and that again on the amount and the distribution of the rainfall, has been referred to in the preceding chapter, and it will not, therefore, be a matter of surprise to find that the district is classed as one liable, throughout its whole extent, to famine, though for reasons now to be explained it does not fortunately rank with those districts in which a failure of the crops involves 'intense' famine. The primary reason for comparative immunity is the extent to which in hard times jungle products afford a source of food supply, which, though neither specially nutritious nor specially conducive to good health, yet suffices to keep the poorest classes of people alive for several weeks, if not months, at a time. In Dr. Campbell's account of the botany of the district, reproduced in earlier chapter, it is mentioned that there are no less than 90 species of plants which minister to the necessities of the people by providing food of a sort during scarcity or famine. Of those the most important is the mahua, both as a flower and as a fruit. Even in ordinary years and in spite of the large demand for export for distillation and other purposes, the flowers of the mahua tree form a considerable part of the ordinary diet of the villagers, wherever the trees survive, during the months of April, May and June. Other important jungle products used by the poorest classes in ordinary years and resorted to by all classes in times of distress are the seeds of the *sāl* tree, the fruit of the banyan and *pipal*, wild yams, the *bhela* (fruit of the Semecarpus anacardium), the *piar* (Buchanania latifolia), and the *bair* (Zizyphus jujuba), besides innumerable others whether seeds, fruits or roots. The value of such products of the jungles as a safeguard was, perhaps, hardly realised prior to the famine of 1897, and of course there is now a danger of over-estimation, as not only has the population increased but the jungles have very considerably decreased in area since then, but even now it is probably well within the truth to say that intense famine is improbable, if not impossible, in the wilder parts of the district.

Another most valuable jungle product, though not an edible one, is lac which provides a considerable cash income to very many of the smaller cultivators not only in the more outlying villages, where the wild *palas* and *kusum* are available for the culture of the lac-producing insect without any great capital expenditure, but also to those in the more settled areas, who are sufficiently enterprising to grow the common, *kul* or plum tree (Zizyphus jujuba) for the purpose. Nor is the benefit confined to the cultivator, a considerable amount of labour is required for the collection of the crop and its transport to the markets, and at the centres where manufacture is carried on, both skilled and unskilled labour command good rates of pay.

The opening out of the vast mineral resources of the district has, even since the last famine of 1897, made a very large difference in the condition of the labouring classes and their liability to be seriously affected by any shortage of the crops. According to the census of 1901, 4 per cent. of the whole population or 53,500 in all consisted of landless labourers and their dependents, and in the same year an average of 31,196 coolies found employment in the mines: by 1908 this number had increased to 72,000 and even this figure does not by any means represent the number of coolies for whom work is available, or who are actually employed at the seasons when there is least demand for agricultural labour. Moreover the demand for above and below ground labour in the mines themselves represents only a part of the additional demand for labour due to the activity of the coal trade; new colliery sidings are constantly being built, roads are being extended, the upkeep of existing lines of rail and road, the handling of trucks at the transfer and assembling stations, the unloading and distribution of the enormous requirements of the coal field in the shape of grain, oil, cloth, etc., besides machinery and other colliery stores, all call for a constantly necessary labour supply. It follows therefore that for the classes accustomed to manual labour, or ready, if driven by stress of scarcity, to take to it, there is now an ample field locally where the able-bodied can not only support themselves but also, the rates of wages being high, send home supplies to the weakly or incapable members of their families.

To these advantages is now added a fairly comprehensive railway and road system by means of which almost all parts of the district are within comparatively easy reach of outside sources of food supply, and the liability, which existed in 1874, of particular areas being left for days or weeks at a time with absolutely inadequate supplies or even no supplies at all in the local markets, is a thing of the past. Mānbazar in the east, the Bandwān outpost of Barābhum thana in the extreme south-east, portions of Bāghmundi and Chās thanas in the west and of Tundi and Topchānchi in the north are the least well protected areas in this respect, and further protection in the shape of improved communications is still desirable, but even in these areas no real danger of an absolute failure of food supplies exists, and as a set off against their disadvantages in this respect, they are for the most part the portions of the district in which supplementary sources of food supply in the shape of jungle products are available in greatest abundance.

Further light on the subject of the present liability of the district to famine is to be found in the histories of earlier recorded famines and of the conditions of later years, when in spite of comparative failures of the rice crop this district escaped the famine or scarcity which affected other districts less favourably circumstanced.

Famine of 1770.

Of the great famine of 1769-70 there are no detailed records to show the extent to which this district suffered; we know, however, that Birbhum in which, so far as the district was under British control, the area of the present district of Mānbhum was for the most part included, suffered extremely, and the description given of the state of that district in 1771 "many hundreds of villages are entirely depopulated, and even in the large towns not a fourth of the houses are inhabited" probably applied to the northern part of Mānbhum with equal accuracy. In Birbhum district as then constituted there had been close on 6,000 villages under cultivation in 1765; three years after the famine there were little more than 4,500. So far as we know now this famine was due to the failure of a single crop, the rice crop of December 1769, following on a comparatively short crop the year before; its intensity was due to the failure being wide-spread, extending over the greater part of Bengal and Bihar, and to the entire absence of easy communications.

Famine of 1866.

Nearly a hundred years passed before any scarcity resulting in serious famine occurred, though in the intervening period there were years of short crops and presumably considerable distress; partial droughts affecting particular areas only have been numerous, and in 1851 there was a more or less general drought and failure of the rice crop, but not such as to result in famine. The immediate cause of the famine of 1865 was the excessive rain in the earlier part of the monsoon period which hampered agricultural operations and ruined the *bhādoi* crop, followed by a sudden and early cessation which spoilt the prospects of the main winter crop. There were besides predisposing causes; the harvests of 1863 and 1864 had been below the average, and the cyclone of the latter year, though it did not reach the Mânbhum district, led to exportation to an unusual extent, and stocks of grain were consequently already depleted, or at any rate unusually low at the time the new crop should have come into the market.

So early as the end of October 1865, a petition was presented to the Deputy Commissioner, praying that exports might be stopped and the price of the rice fixed; and in November he issued a notice to the zamindars recommending them to use their influence to check the export of rice. The outturn of the winter crop all over the district was estimated to have been between one-third and one-half of a full crop; but in a considerable tract towards the south-east the yield did not exceed one-fourth. On the 15th of March 1866, the District Superintendent of Police reported a great increase of robberies and dacoities, particularly in the southern and eastern parts of the district. "That these were largely due to scarcity was proved by the fact that the property stolen consisted of nothing but eatables, any valuables in the houses broken into being left as useless. Unhusked rice was selling at 18 or 20 seers for the rupee, husked rice at 8 and 7 seers, and it was reported that not only the very poor but even the more respectable natives had been forced to eat mahua and the like; numbers of the people were said to be actually starving, and subsisting on grass or anything they could get." In the middle of May the Deputy Commissioner called a meeting to devise measures for the relief of the distress, and asked the Commissioner of the Division to cause subscriptions to be raised in other districts, and to apply for a grant of money from Government. Colonel Dalton, however, while approving of the meeting, considered that there was no occasion for relief by distribution of food. Prices, he observed, were lower in Mânbhum than in other districts of the Division; and the robberies, cited in evidence of the distress, were committed for the most part by the landless low castes of semi-Hinduized aborigines, who gain but a precarious livelihood in ordinary years. This class, Colonel Dalton was of opinion, could best be dealt with by encouraging them to emigrate, and by establishing relief works for their employment. A letter from the Commissioner of Burdwan, reporting that the villages of Midnapore bordering on Mânbhum were threatened by armed gangs of Sonthals belonging to the latter district, had previously been forwarded to the Commissioner of Chota Nāgpur, who replied that although some Bāuris (not Sonthals) had committed numerous grain robberies, no disturbance had taken place with which the ordinary police were unable to cope, and that the inhabitants of both Mānbhum and Singhbhum were bearing up very well against the difficulties. Both at this time and later in the year, the Deputy Commissioner replied to Colonel Dalton's argument, that there could be no distress with rice selling at 14 seers to the rupee, by pointing out that in the interior of the district all transactions were carried on by barter, and that the recorded market price was therefore no criterion of the supply of grain. Even dealings by barter in open market were now uncommon, and in Raipur (now included in Bānkura district) there were no transactions in the markets, and no rates of price could be reported. Money, in fact, was so little used, that the copper coins received at the Treasury from Calcutta never passed into circulation at all. During May grain robberies increased more particularly in the south-east of the district and even the Commissioner was at last satisfied that some relief measures were necessary. Relief works were opened by the District Committee in the most distressed portion of the district, *i.e.*, the eastern thanas, and in June, when a grant of Rs. 2,000 was received from Government, depôts for gratuitous relief were started in the south of the district. Up to the 5th of June, employment had been provided for 1,000 persons daily, and gratuitous relief for 450. Distress, however, continued to increase all along the south of the District; the price of rice rose in Barābhum from 11 to 9 seers for the rupee, and grain robberies were occurring at the rate of four every night. The Relief Committee, therefore, applied for a further grant from Government, and the Deputy Commissioner reported that the ghātwali or rural police were wholly dependent on the produce of their lands, and that an outbreak might be expected unless their subsistence was provided for. In the meantime, a depôt for gratuitous relief was opened at Purūlia and placed under the charge of Mr. Onasch, a Lutheran missionary, as Secretary to the Relief Committee. With the opening of the grain depôts in the south of the district there was a marked decrease in the number of gang robberies, but distress now began to spread towards the north, and on the 25th of June a sudden rise in the price of rice from eleven to seven and-a-half seers for the rupee was reported from Gobindpur. At this time Mr. Onasch, visiting the south-eastern portion of the District, found the people living on the seeds of the *sāl* tree, on the chaff of rice, on oil-cake, and other less nutritious substances. Deaths from starvation had occurred in many places; the money paid as wages remained unused; no rice was to be bought; land which was ordinarily cultivated had been left fallow for want of seed; and in some villages the recruiters for emigration had aggravated the distress by taking away the men, and leaving the women and children destitute. Payment in grain instead of money was now commenced wherever such an arrangement was possible, arrangements being made to import grain from Calcutta. The Board of Revenue sent up 5,000 maunds of rice in the beginning of July, but a large amount of it was damaged in consequence of the absence of any facilities for storing at the Barākar station. Only a few carts could be procured, floods in the Dāmodar cut off communications, the roads were impassable from heavy rain, with the result that it was nearly 2½ months before the last of this consignment actually reached Purūlia. In fact, as the Famine Commissioners remarked, the isolation of Mānbhum, when once the rains had set in, was nearly as complete as that of Orissa itself. All through August, distress and mortality continued to increase, and at the end of that month rice was selling in Purūlia at the rate of from four to four and-a-half seers per rupee. Further south the state of things was worse, only three and-a-half seers being procurable for the rupee, and the people had eaten much of the early rice crop in the field before it attained maturity. The prospects of the later crop were good, but only one-third of the usual area had been sown, stocks in the district were exhausted, and the Deputy Commissioner urged the necessity of importing more rice from Calcutta. But the worst was now over, and though no more grain was actually sent from Calcutta it was reported on the 11th of September that distress was decreasing, although deaths were still very numerous in the south-east of the district. During that month ten new centres were opened by the Committee, but by this time the prospects of the late crop were secured, and the early rice which was now in the market began to reduce the rates. Thus, in Purūlia, rice was selling at 16 seers for the rupee; and on the 31st of October an order was passed that every man should be sent from gratuitous relief to the relief works as soon as he was capable of labour. On the 3rd of November rice was selling at 20 seers for the rupee, and distress rapidly decreasing. As the main crop was coming in, the Deputy Commissioner issued a notification to the landowners, pointing out to them the importance of leaving the crop of 1866 in the hands of the peasantry and not sweeping it away by distraint for arrears of rent. The landowners were also requested to explain to their tenants that a grain merchant has no right of distraint, except under the decree of a Court, and that cultivators were not bound to repay advances out of the crop of the current year. On the 14th of November a further grant of Rs. 8,000 was received from the Calcutta Relief Committee, and on the 16th the District Committee began closing all depôts where the number of applicants fell below 50. By the end of November, depôts were being rapidly closed all over the district. But the Deputy Commissioner anticipated that distress would continue for some months in the wilder tracts, where, owing to the absence of tanks and means of irrigation, nearly two-thirds of the crop of 1865 had been lost; while for want of seed little more than one-third of the available land had been sown in 1866. In those tracts, therefore, about twenty relief centres were kept open till the middle of December.

The total daily average number of persons relieved in each month in Mānbhum is reported by the Famine Commissioners as follows:—June, 322; July, 1,303; August, 2,924; September, 5,824; October, 9,950; November, 4,252; December, 1,988. Daily average from June to December, 3,794. Besides this, four depôts for the distribution of relief were opened and supplied by private persons at Pāndra, Jharia, Kātras, and Barākhar, where large numbers were fed. The total sum expended on relief amounted to Rs. 76,360 of which Rs. 43,346 was granted by the Board of Revenue, Rs. 28,200 including grain to the value of Rs. 5,000 by the Calcutta Central Relief Committee, and Rs. 4,814 was raised by private subscriptions. To this has to be added Rs. 25,346 being the cost of grain supplied from Calcutta by the Board of Revenue. The total cost of famine operations was, therefore, rather more than one lac of rupees. The report of the Famine Commissioners describes the distress in Mānbhum District as having been "severe" over an area of 2,318 square miles, and "intense" in a smaller area of 1,500 square miles, the total area included in the district as then constituted being 5,400. These areas are, however, only approximate. The famine was most severe in the Fiscal Divisions of Barābhum, Mānbhum and Raipur, in the south and south-east of the district; and diminished in intensity north of a line drawn from east to west almost through the civil station of Purūlia.

Of the mortality directly or indirectly due to this famine there have been various estimates; the figures finally accepted by the Commissioners were based on a detailed enquiry made in particular areas by the Deputy Commissioner, and inferences drawn from the census figures of 1872. According to this out of an estimated population of just under a million in 1865 no less than one-fifth perished either of starvation or disease, a percentage that can only have been possible if as was stated at the time the deaths in Barābhum and other severely affected parts amounted to one-fourth or even one-third of the population.

The circumstances preceding the famine of 1874 were not Famine of unlike those preceding the one just described; the year 1872 was not altogether a favourable one; in parts of the district, especially in the eastern Pargana of Mānbhum, the main rice crop was almost a total failure, and for the whole district the estimated outturn was only five-eighths of a full crop; as a small set off against this the rabi crop was almost uniformly good. In 1873 conditions were even more adverse; the rains were late in commencing, only 2·21 inches falling in June as compared with the normal fall of 8¾ inches; in July the fall was excessive, amounting to no less than 20½ inches as compared with 12½ normal, and over a large part of the district the rains almost entirely ceased in the month of August, the September fall at Purūlia being only 3 inches and the October fall a barely measurable quantity as compared with 7 inches and 4½ inches for the two months in normal years. The result was a crop estimated at only half the normal for the district as a whole, varying from four to six annas in the centre to nine or ten annas in the more favoured parts in the west. The outturn generally was slightly better than in 1865, but on the other hand the succeeding rabi crop was a smaller one, the area under cultivation being reduced to a minimum by the absence of moisture and of water in the reservoirs due to the early cessation of the rains. As in the earlier famine year there was at first a considerable drain on the district resources in the shape of export to other distressed regions; the local stocks must, however, have been considerable as the price of rice rose only from 15½ seers in January to 13 seers in April when Government importations had already begun to arrive, and it was not till March that distress began to make itself shown among the beggars and those who in ordinary times subsist on private charity. During April the ripening of the *mahua* harvest prevented a further increase of distress, the *mahua* blossoms affording cheap food to the poorer classes. To quote the Deputy Commissioner's words, "had it not been for this very timely supply of food, great distress, if not actual starvation, would ere this have taken place." In addition to the *mahua* harvest the spring crop of lac came in at this time, and as the lac market was favourable to sellers, this was also a material aid to the people, lac exchanging locally at the rate of one seer of the dye for three seers of rice. Meantime relief works had already been started on a small scale in February; in March the average daily attendance had risen to over 3,000 and in April the numbers mounted up rapidly, the average attendance for that month being over 10,000. By the time May came the area affected had greatly increased and included parts of the district till then comparatively well off. In the areas in which mahua trees were few in number cases of distress were numerous and on the increase, and the circle of distress generally had widened, so as to include the smaller cultivators as well as the mendicant and labouring classes. Even the south of the district, where the harvest had been better than elsewhere, had now begun to feel the pinch, prices then having levelled up owing to continued exportation. Thus by the middle of May the numbers on relief works had mounted up to nearly 14,000 besides nearly 6,000 receiving gratuitous relief, either in doles of dry grain or at the famine kitchens. The numbers on relief works reached their highest in the following month during which an average of over 14,000 were so relieved; but with the opening of the rains there was a rapid fall to slightly over 8,000: in August the relief works ceased to attract more than 800 a day and in September they were closed entirely. The departure of the able bodied, however, to ordinary field labour did not for some time relieve the district authorities of the necessity of feeding their dependants, and the number gratuitously relieved mounted up rapidly till it exceeded 20,000 in the middle of July, and nearly 22,000 in the early part of August and between that date and the first week of October between 13,000 and 9,000 were relieved daily. By that time the *bhādoi* crops were coming into the market, the prospects of the rice crop were more or less assured, and the price of rice, which owing to the large importations had never been higher than 13 seers for the rupee (in July), was steadily falling and the necessity for continuing further relief operations had gone. With the advent of the first of the new crop in the market prices quickly fell in November and December to 22 and 24 seers which had been about the average rates during the year 1872, and any cause for further anxiety had entirely passed away.

The largest number of people in receipt of relief at any one time, *i. e.*, rather more 28,000 in July, represents less than 3 per cent. of the district population, and the average number relieved during the 7 months, in which operations were in full swing, was less than 2 per cent. The total cash expenditure was Rs. 2,67,641, besides 8,830 tons of grain, the cost of which to Government it is almost impossible to estimate but which cannot have been less than 8 lakhs of rupees. The actual cost of relief measures was thus over 12½ lakhs of rupees as compared with three-quarters of a lakh expended in 1866. Of this amount, however, Rs. 99,000 represents loans made in cash, and approximately Rs. 5,30,000 advances in grain or 6¼ lakhs in all of which 4¾ lakhs were subsequently recovered. The net famine expenditure was, therefore, about 7¾ lakhs.

As the Famine Commissioners of 1880 remarked of Bengal general the immunity from mortality due to starvation was dearly purchased, and the means employed were entirely disproportioned to the end. At the same time it is hardly possible to endorse the view in the case of Mānbhum that the policy of importation of grain was a mistaken one. Communications had not improved materially since 1866, Barākhar was still the nearest railway station and cut off from the greater part of the district by the river Dāmodar, and it is conceivable that had exceptional steps not been taken to import grain in large quantities before the rains began, the experience of 1866 might well have been repeated in the remoter parts of the district. On the whole the measures taken, though possibly exceeding what was really necessary, were on sound lines.

Rainfall in 1892 was deficient and badly distributed and in consequence the outturn of both the autumn and winter crops was poor, viz., 12 and 10 annas respectively. In the previous year also there had been below the average and prices had generally risen. The district was, however, just then being opened out by railways, the mining industry was also beginning to develop, and in consequence the demand for labour was considerable. Though, therefore, there were some distress in places the year can hardly be classed as one of anything more than partial scarcity, and nothing in the way of relief measures was necessary. *Scarcity in 1892.*

The next and most recent year of famine was 1897 and, as in the two previous cases, the cause lay in a succession of bad seasons rather than in a single failure of the crops. In 1895-96 the district rainfall was only 35·77 inches as compared with a normal fall of 53·27 inches, and though the *bhadoi* crop was an average one, the winter crop amounted to only five-eighths of the normal. The succeeding spring crop was rather better, average thirteen-sixteenths, but this is at the best a very small crop in Mānbhum. The result was that prices had begun to rise as early as the beginning of 1896, and by September had risen to 14 seers at Purūlia and 11 at Gobindpur. The rainfall of 1896-97 was only slightly heavier than that of the previous year, and its distribution could hardly have been worse. In the Sadar Subdivision only 1½ inches were received in May after an *Famine of 1897.*

absolutely dry April with the result that preparation of fields and the sowing of the seed beds were seriously delayed. The next two months conditions were more or less normal, but in August only 9½ inches fell as compared with a normal of nearly 14, and the September fall was less than half the normal. In the Gobindpur (Dhânbâid) Subdivision conditions were rather more favourable in May and June, but in the two succeeding months the rainfall was in marked defect. The fall in September was over 7 inches but most of this fell in the early part of the month; in both Subdivisions October was absolutely rainless. The result was that the outturn of *bhādoi* crops was only half the normal, and of winter rice even less, 7 annas for the district as a whole, and in parts of the district no more than 4 annas. The very early cessation of the monsoon was not compensated for, as in parts of Bihar, by favourable cold weather rains and the consequence was that the rabi crop of 1897 was almost an entire failure, the outturn being estimated at 3½ annas only. To add to the misfortunes of the District the *mahua* crop, which is largely consumed by the lower classes, was seriously damaged by untimely rain in March 1897. By January of that year it was evident that severe distress, if not actual famine, was probable, and preliminary arrangements for the organisation of relief measures had been put in hand. Prices had by this time risen to 10 seers at Purūlia and 9 at Gobindpur, and gratuitous relief to beggars and wanderers was necessary. By the third week of February gratuitous relief was being administered to nearly 4,500 persons and the test works opened in Gobindpur, Tundi, Châs and Jhalda earlier in the month were being attended by another 3,000. During March and April the area treated as affected gradually widened until it included the whole district, except thanas Mānbazar and Barâbazar in the east and south, and at the end of that month though the numbers of relief works had only increased to 4,000, those on gratuitous relief had mounted up rapidly to over 12,000. The price of rice had risen to 8½ seers per rupee in April, and by the end of May only 7⅝ seers were obtainable at Gobindpur and slightly more at Purūlia, and at this level or slightly lower prices remained during the two succeeding months, reaching as high as 7 seers per rupee at Gobindpur towards the end of the latter month. During May and June the numbers on relief works increased but slightly, the ordinary field work of the season being then in full swing and stricter scrutiny of the applicants for gratuitous relief had brought down the numbers so relieved to a little over 7,000. From then onwards there was a rapid increase, the average attendance on relief works in July being 8,508, and in August 10,759, the figures for the last week of that month being as high as 16,388. An attempt was then made, as in other districts of the division, to summarily close down all forms of relief other than kitchens, granting two weeks gratuitous relief to each worker and to the recipients of grain doles. The attempt was, however, premature as the early *bhādoi* crop, consisting of *gora* or *sāthi* rice, maize, *marua*, etc., is a comparatively small crop, and the main rice harvest, even that part of it which is classed as *bhādoi*, does not begin till November. Both works and gratuitous relief centres were, therefore, opened again after a few days interval under the Commissioner's orders and the numbers on relief works had again risen to over 13,000 by the end of September, at which time over 3,000 persons were still in receipt of gratuitous relief. Prices were, however, by this time steadily falling and the prospects of the new crops assured, and at the end of October, though 9,000 persons were still on the works and 2,000 in receipt of other forms of relief, the operations were finally closed.

The total area affected was 3,373 square miles in extent with a population of 991,000; the average number under relief during the six months, when the distress was at its worst, was 14,162 representing 14 per mille of the population: the largest number relieved at any one time, *i.e.*, the last week of August was 23,696, or rather less than 2½ per cent. The total expenditure incurred from public funds was Rs. 2,80,177, besides Rs. 42,093 and 40,052 (partly from public funds and partly from the Charitable Relief Fund) paid out in advances under the Land Improvement and Agriculturists' Loans Acts respectively. From the Charitable Relief fund also Rs. 31,500 was expended in advances and gifts for seed to cultivators, some Rs. 10,000 in valedictory doles to the relief workers and recipients of gratuitous relief, and the remainder on general relief.

One of the most interesting features of these operations was the successful organization for the relief of weavers in the north of the district by Dr. A. Campbell of the Free Church of Scotland Mission at Pokhuria where, apart from other forms of relief, there were at one time between 1,300 and 1,400 persons engaged in spinning and some 200 others in weaving. The cost of these operations was shown at Rs. 5,462, viz., Rs. 2,220 spent in materials and Rs. 3,242 paid in wages, the estimated value of the cloth received being Rs. 2,395. Dr. Campbell's services as an Honorary Circle Officer can hardly be spoken of too highly. His charge extended over what the Commissioner in his report states to have been the only part of the division where general distress in anything approaching an acute form of famine can be said to have existed, and the same officer remarked that "from the point of view of relief administration Dr. Campbell's arduous and unostentatious work in Pokhuria was a performance of the highest merit, and will long be held in grateful memory by the people of the neighbourhood." Dr. Campbell's services were acknowledged by the bestowal on him of the Kaisar-i-Hind medal, and those of the District Engineer, Babu Nanda Gopal Banerji, on whose shoulders fell the whole of the organisation of the relief works, by the grant of the title of Rai Bahadur.

Mortality due to actual starvation was successfully avoided but the extremity of distress was marked by a very high death rate, the rate for the months, June to September being 15½ per mille as compared with 9½, the average for the corresponding period of the five preceding years. This excessive rate was due largely to a severe epidemic of fever, but that the general health of the district considerably deteriorated is shown by the fact that 66 per cent. of persons admitted to the jails during the months April to October 1897, were classed as in bad or indifferent health as compared with only 24 per cent. in the previous year. Other indications of the extent of the distress were the large increase in dacoities and burglaries, from 9 and 426 respectively in 1896 to 34 and 1,179 in 1897, and in the increase of registered emigrants from 1,073 in 1896 to 4,776 in 1897.

In contrast to previous famines nothing was done to import or encourage the importation of grain from outside, or from one part of the district to another; exports practically ceased in 1897, in which year, instead of an excess of exports over imports amounting to over 80,000 maunds in 1895 and 5,000 maunds in 1896, there was an excess of imports of nearly 209,000 maunds, a fact which at once proves that the deficit in the district was considerable, and that private trade was quite able to make it good. Communications had, of course, greatly improved since 1874 but it may well be borne in mind that neither the Grand Chord of the East Indian Railway nor the Purūlia-Ranchi branch of the Bengal-Nāgpur Railway were even projected till a much later date.

Distress in 1903. Since 1897 there were comparatively short crops in 1904-05, 1906-07 and 1907-08 and in the last year the situation was one which gave rise to considerable anxiety, owing to the previously unparalleled prices to which food-grains rose almost generally throughout the district, and more particularly in the parts more remote from the railway. As early as October 1907 the price of rice had risen to 7 seers per rupee, and though there was a slight recovery when the new crop came in, the improvement was only temporary and prices ranged between 7 and 7½ seers at Purūlia, rising at times as high as 4½ and 5 seers at more remote markets, until the new crop began to come into the market in September and October. In spite, however, of these obviously adverse conditions only one of the various signs, which are treated as famine warnings, *i.e.*, increase in crime, was noticeable in marked degree, and even this was practically confined to the southern and eastern parts of the district where the Bhumij population have not yet outgrown their earlier reputation as "chuārs" and apparently still prefer thieving to hard work, when the opportunity is given, or the necessity for one or the other is forced on them by hard times. Nowhere in the district at any period of the year was there any marked increase in the number of beggars, or of obviously underfed wanderers. The year was, it is true, one of excessive mortality, but the immediate cause, *i.e.*, a severe epidemic of cholera, cannot be ascribed as due to insufficient or improper food, as it originated in the coal fields where wages and food supplies were ample; the primary cause was the inadequacy of the water supply and absence of sanitary arrangements for the enormous population employed in the coal industry, which was then at the height of the boom. The ability of the people to resist famine was due to the causes already enumerated in the early part of this chapter, the large demand for labour in the coal fields and elsewhere, the enormous sums made out of the lac crop, and the ability of a considerable part of the population to carry on for some time on *mahua* and various edible jungle products in lieu of or in addition to a scanty dole of rice or other staple foods. Additional causes were the considerable sums made by the cultivators by the sale of their surplus rice in the previous year, the fact that their credit was far from exhausted, and finally the very considerable demand for field labour throughout the district for the excavation of new *bāndhs*, clearing out of old *bāndhs* and making of new fields for rice cultivation, the two first of which operations were facilitated by the exceptional drought, which had resulted in an exceptionally low subsoil water level, while capitalists, whether money-lenders or cultivators with savings or substantial credit, were specially encouraged to bring new land under rice cultivation by the prospects of high profits in the event of a continuance of the prices that had ruled in the preceding years. To persons on more or less fixed income whether from service or rents the year was undoubtedly a hard one, and numbers of small cultivators must have ended it in heavy debt, if not with absolutely exhausted credit, and not a few were obliged to alienate permanently a part, at any rate, of their holdings. Rupees 32,000 was distributed in loans, Rs. 20,000 under the Land Improvement Loans Act and Rs. 12,000 under the Agriculturists' Loans Act mainly in the north of the district during the first six months of 1908, but beyond this no direct or indirect famine expenditure was incurred.

General conclusions. The general conclusion to be drawn from the histories of scarcities given in the preceding paragraphs is that Mānbhum, though dependent mainly on a single crop, *i.e.*, the late or winter rice crop, is no longer liable to the extremes of famine, which the absence or difficulty of communications made possible 35 and 40 years ago; that the outturn of rice even in a year of partial failure, *e.g.*, from 75 per cent. to 80 per cent. of a normal crop, still leaves a considerable margin over what is required for a year's consumption, and that in consequence a single year's failure not preceded by a partial failure in the year previous, is hardly likely to result in anything more than distress among the smaller cultivators and persons on small fixed incomes, and that even when the crop is a more or less complete failure in such a year, the other sources of subsistence available and the large local demand for labour will considerably reduce the numbers of those for whom, in less favoured districts, relief works would be necessary.

Floods, earthquakes, locusts. Floods are practically speaking an impossibility in Mānbhum, no earthquake has within the memory of man done any serious damages, though that of June 1897 was felt, and more recently smaller shocks in May and August 1909. Visitations from locusts have been very rare and the damage done small. In short, except in respect of liability to famine, the district may be classed as a specially favoured one.

CHAPTER VII.

RENTS, WAGES AND PRICES.

No regular settlement of rents has yet been carried out in the district as a whole, and accurate information of the actual incidence of rent per acre of the different classes of cultivated land is difficult to obtain, owing to the fact that land is ordinarily measured in terms of *muris*, *powas*, *rekhs*, *kats*, etc., which represent either fractional shares in villages and not specific areas of land, or else the area which can be sown with a specific quantity of the seed, usually rice, which will necessarily vary not only with the quality of the soil but also the idiosyncrasies or customs of particular villages. For purposes of assessment of rent lands are usually divided into rice or *dhānkhet* and upland. *Dhānkhet* is again sub-divided into *bahāl*, *kānāli* and *baid*, the distinction between which has been given in the preceding chapter. These again may be further distinguished into three or even more classes, but this is a comparatively rare refinement. Uplands are classified into *gora* (or *tāur*) and *bāstu*. Cash rents.

In the extreme north of the district in some 52 villages tenanted by Sonthals in the Tundi estate the rates of rents adopted as the basis for a resettlement conducted by the district authorities in 1906-07 were as follows :—*Bahāi* Rs. 6, *kānāli* Rs. 4-8, *baid* Rs. 3 per acre but, as a matter of fact, the total assessment only worked out to something less than Rs. 2 per acre all round, as considerable concessions had to be made in order to keep the enhancement in the case of individuals and of villages below the limit of 100 per cent. fixed by the Board of Revenue; the uplands were in the case of this area left unassessed, and rice fields newly prepared since the previous settlement were assessed only at half rates.

In the small temporarily settled estates of Mātha and Kailāpal the rates adopted in the last settlement (1900) were for *bahāl* Rs. 3-6 and Rs. 2-10 per acre, for *kānāli* Rs. 2-4 and Rs. 1-14 and for *baid* Rs. 1-14 and Rs. 1-8, respectively. In the case of

Kailāpal *bāstu* was assessed at 12 annas and *gora* at 3 annas, but the assessment was subsequently cancelled. Both these estates lie in the least developed part of the district and the rates in comparison with those adopted for Tundi are apparently very low. They are, however, not very different from the rates generally prevalent over the southern half of the district.

Thus in Barābhum and Pātkum where in 1884 a survey was made of the ghātwali tenures, the rates adopted in the compromise as the basis of settlement of the excess lands with the ghātwals holding them were Rs. 3 for *bahāl*, Rs. 2 4 for *kānāli* and also for sugarcane land, Re. 1-8 for *baid*, and annas twelve for cultivated *dāngu* per acre respectively. Except, however, in one *taraf* or tenure, that of Dhādka, settlements were not actually effected at these rates.

In the large area within the Zamindāri of Barābhum which is held in patni by the Midnapore Zamindāri Company, the standard rates shown in the agreements taken from their tenants are for *bahāl* Rs. 4-8, *kānāli* Rs. 3, *baid* Rs. 2-4, *ikkhu* (sugarcane) Rs. 2-4, *udbāstu bārī* (cultivated land near the homestead) Rs. 3, *gora* annas 12, besides various rents for trees, etc. These rates, however, represent what the Company would like to enforce, and are very much in excess of what they are actually able to collect. Thus to quote a typical instance, when the total calculated at the rates shown in the kabuliyat, worked out to Rs. 16-2, the actual rent agreed upon was Rs. 7-4, the difference being described as a temporary remission. In another where the rent for rice lands at these rates amounts to Rs 31-10, and for *gora* to Rs. 5-14, the amounts shown as the demand in the collection books are only Rs. 11 and Re. 1-8 respectively. It follows, therefore, that the actual rates in force in this area are from one-third to one-half only of the nominal rates shown in the tenants' agreements.

Further north, however, and more particularly within the Pānchet Estate, where sub-infeudation of the proprietary right is of old standing and in a large majority of the villages the immediate receivers of the rents are outsider *ijārādārs* whose interest it must always be to screw rents up as much as possible during their limited tenure of the post, the general rates are much higher and frequently range from as much as Rs. 7-8, Rs. 5-10, Rs. 3-12 for the different classes of rice lands to Re. 1-8 or Re. 1-14 for uplands and attempts are occasionally made through the courts to obtain rents at double these rates.

In general terms, therefore, it may be said that the average rates for rice lands vary from Rs. 7-8 to Re. 1-8 per acre according to quality and position, and for other lands from Rs. 3 to annas 12 per acre.

This statement, however, is at the best a general one, the fact remaining that in very many villages in the district lands are still held on what are practically quit rents averaging not more than 8 annas to a rupee on the total area now under cultivation. Elsewhere, on the other hand, where the aboriginal settler has been ousted or is in process of being ousted, new settlers hold at what are practically competition rents, and which represent more accurately the present productive value of the land. It is obvious that a new tenant inducted on lands already terraced and levelled for rice cultivation can afford to pay a higher rent than his predecessor who has been ousted after undergoing all the labour and expense of preparing the fields. The general tendency, however, is for the old settler strenuously to resist all attempts to enhance the rent which he and his ancestors have paid for generations, even when his holding has undoubtedly extended far beyond the original area settled or assessed to rent; the landlord, as a rule, finds it difficult to prove excess cultivation, and even to rebut the pleas regularly set up of non-enhanceability, and in consequence generelly fails in enhancement suits; when he is unscrupulous he more often than not has recourse to underhand and roundabout methods of ousting the refractory tenant from the whole or a part of the tenancy, a course for which the absence of any survey records and of any description of lands in documents by metes and bounds, the ordinary description being by a name only, gives special facilities. **Prevalence of customary or quit rents.**

The arrangements customary in regard to lands brought under cultivation under leases for that specific purpose vary in different parts of the district, but ordinarily the holder of a *nayābādi* or *ahriat* tenure, terms which correspond fairly closely to *korkar* and *khandit* of other districts of the Chota Nāgpur Division, gets a permanent deduction of six annas in the rupee on the rent fixed, which becomes payable only after the land has actually been prepared for cultivation, for which a period is ordinarily fixed. In other cases the arrangements may be for a progressive rent, the full rent, in this case also six annas in the rupee less than the rent calculated at the ordinary rates, being reached in 5 or 7 years. **Nāyābādi settlements.**

The above applies, however, to comparatively modern settlement of specific areas. The old and original '*nayābādi*' settlement was almost invariably one of a village or portion of a village specified in terms of *poyas*, *i.e.*, quarters, or of *rekhs*, each *rekh* being the sixteenth part of a village. The settlements so made were of the nature of *jangalburi* or clearing leases, the applicant being given permission to clear and bring under cultivation any land within the boundaries of the village, or the share of it agreed upon. Nominally, therefore, the tenant's rights extend over the whole village or a specific fraction of it, both cultivated and waste, subject to payment of either a fixed quit rent, or of rents at fixed rates calculated on the area under cultivation. In practice, however, the landlord or farmer assumes, wherever he can, superior rights over all lands not actually under cultivation, and endeavours to lease out the lands still waste with other cultivators when the descendants of the original settlers do not meet his terms. The assumption that the *rekh* represents a fraction of the cultivation, and not of the whole village, was, it may be noted, followed in the ghātwali compromise of 1884, and the example then set by Government (against its own and the ghātwal's interests) has naturally been widely followed. Another variation of this class of settlement usually met with in the north of the district in the case of settlements of ancient date is when the tenant is given permission to bring under cultivation of land as much land as will require a certain quantity of seed grain, from which comes the use of *kāt* and *muri* both of which words mean a maund or thereabouts of grain, as a measure of area. The opportunities for dissension between the modern landlord and his tenant, where areas are so vaguely expressed and settlements made in such haphazard fashion, are sufficiently obvious and require no special description.

Produce rents. Produce rents are not very common except in the case of small areas let out to the poorer class of cultivating labourers, not infrequently also the real tenant holds under his mortgagee on *bhāg*, when he has got so involved as to be obliged to convert his simple mortgage into an usufructuary mortgage Ordinarily, in the case of such *bhāg* settlements, the produce is divided half and half, but where the landlord provides seed and cattle for ploughing, the tenant receives one-third only. In these cases the tenant is really a mere servant, known as *krishan ardhiar* or *aidhar* and his third share of the crop represents his wages for cultivating his master's land.

It is not uncommon for a part of the rent to be paid in kind, usually only a small quantity of rice or other grain required for the consumption of the landlord's family; this is more especially the case where the landlord has little or no *khās* land on which to grow his own grain. In some cases this demand is, perhaps, a true rent, but in the majority of cases in which it is claimed through the courts it is treated as *ābwāb*.

Besides rent and cesses, the latter of which are not infrequently demanded and paid at more than the legal rate of six pies per rupee, there are other customary demands of the nature of *ābwāb* or predial conditions. *Abwāb.*

Among these the commonest are *shyāma ghi*, representing the money value of a goat and a certain quantity of *ghi* due annually to the Zamindar at the time of the Durga festival. *Shyāma chaul* is similar, rice being substituted for *ghi*; a certain quantity of straw is also occasionally demanded. The following actual instance from a Brahmottar village in Pargana Barābhum may be quoted, as illustrating these and other *ābwāb*. Here, for what is described as Re. 1 worth of rice land, the tenant is expected to pay:—

in cash—		
Rent	...	... 1 rupee
Batta	...	... 1 anna
Cess	...	... 1 „
in kind—		
Rice	...	... ½ seer
Dhān	...	... 3 seers
Straw	...	... 80 bundles
Ghi	...	... ¼ seer

besides furnishing 4 days' labour per annum with a plough (*hāl-bet*), and one day with a spade (*kodāl-bet*) in the landlord's own cultivation, and one day's *ghar-chhauni*, *i.e.*, assisting to repair the landlord's thatched roofs.

Bet-begāri or the system under which the tenant has to do a certain number of days' work on the Zamindar's own cultivation still survives, as the instance above quoted shows, but the extent to which the landlords are able to enforce their demands for assistance in cultivating their *khās* lands is now largely limited, and, except in the more out-of-the-way tracts, little attempt is actually made now to enforce such demands, cultivation of the *khās* lands being done for the most by *bhāgis* or *sājas*, *i.e.*, labourers or undertenants paid by a share of the produce.

Other demands, which do not appear in the rent papers, are the customary dues of the collecting staff, and what are known as *māngan* or "occasional benevolences," namely payments in cash and kind made to the Zamindar on the occasion of births, deaths and marriages in his family, or on his paying a persona visit to a particular village, or to help him with the expenses of some big civil suit.

Bāstu rent. Where the old customary rents continue, and even in some places also where, for one reason or another, these have given place to rents based on the present condition and productive powers of the soil, it is not usual to assess to rent any but the rice lands, and such other lands as are planted with sugarcane or other special crops. For the high land round his hut, and for other high lands from which in one year out of four or five a scanty crop of *kodo*, *kurthi*, or some inferior oilseed is obtained, the tenant ordinarily pays no specific rent. In lieu thereof in Barābhum pargana it is customary for the tenant to pay a regular *bāstu*, or homestead rent. The rates at which this rent or tax was assessed in 1884 were

	Rs.	A.	P.
For every cultivating family ...	1	1	0
" " non " " ...	0	8	6
" " widow	0	4	0

and these rates have continued to the present day, except in areas which came under the influence of Messrs. Watson and Company and their successors in interest, who have succeeded in many villages in getting the tenants to agree to pay double these rates, on condition of being freed from the obligation of growing indigo.

When a *bāstu* rent in cash is not charged, it is not unusual to find the rent of the high lands represented by a demand for a fixed quantity of grain or other produce, *e.g.*, in one instance noticed the demand was 80 heads of maize, and one cartload of manure.

Miscellaneous. A rent or cess is also not infrequently charged for the privilege of rearing lac on *palās*, *kusum* or *bair* trees and of collecting the flower and fruit of the *mahua*. Tenants ordinarily claim the right to take such jungle produce as they require for their own use free of charge, but in some estates at any rate they are unable to resist the landlord's demand for a jungle cess, known variously as *jangalkar*, *bankar* or *kathikar*. For bamboos cut from the jungles *bānskar* is charged, and even the privilege of grazing cattle in the jungle does not invariably escape assessment. The liability to pay such demands is, however, constantly in dispute, and it is probable that most of them are of comparatively recent origin, the landlords having taken advantage of the indefiniteness of the customary rights claimed by the tenants, to force on them these demands now that the increasing population and the denuded jungles have made all ordinary jungle products an easily marketable commodity. In the case of lac the imposition is undoubtedly of recent origin; no objection is ordinarily taken where trees or specific patches of jungle are leased out for the express purpose of rearing lac, except where the tenants are strong enough to assert their claim to all rights in the jungle and waste lands. The attempt, however, to assess trees standing on a tenant's holding, or reared by him thereon, is a gradually growing cause of friction between landlord and tenant.

For some years past there has been a steady rise in the wages paid for labour, among the chief causes for which must be placed the development of the mining industry and the improvement of communications by road and rail. Another accelerating cause in recent years is the increased activity in the lac industry, the high prices obtainable for the raw product in 1908 and the two years preceding having enormously stimulated production, as well as encouraged the opening of new factories. In the case of skilled labour the increase is not very marked in the last ten years as the rise had already taken place prior to that period; still expert masons and carpenters now get from 10 annas to 12 annas or even one rupee per diem; superior blacksmiths, who already got 12 annas in 1900, now earn from 12 annas to one rupee. In the same period the daily wages of a common mason and carpenter have risen from a maximum of six annas to eight annas and those of a common carpenter to as much as ten annas; and the common blacksmith, who could earn only 8 annas per diem in 1900, now demands and receives from 8 to 10 annas. The price of unskilled labour, so far as paid in cash, that is to say, in the towns and industrial centres, has risen more appreciably; the daily wage of a cooly varies now from 3 to as much as 5 annas as compared with only 2½ annas in 1900; women and boys, who then got only 1½ annas a day, now get from 2 to 2½ and 2 to 3 annas respectively. In the villages wages are almost entirely paid in grain, two to three seers of rice or some cheaper grain being the ordinary field-labourer's daily wage; this at the rates at which the cultivator realises on his surplus crop may be taken as equivalent to 2 to 2½ annas, though to the cooly who has to purchase in small quantities it means a good deal more. Ploughmen earn rather more, 2½ to 3 annas in cash or its equivalent, and cartmen from 3½ to 4 annas. *Ghārāmis* both in town and country can earn from 3 to 5 annas per diem. Much of the field labour in the case of larger holdings is done by quasi-sub-

WAGES.

tenants khown as *krishan*, *ardhiar*, or *aidhar*, who do the ploughing, sowing, transplanting and weeding of the crop and get usually one-third of it as their remuneration. Harvesting is largely left to women *kāmins* usually also paid in kind out of the standing crop, one edge of the field, known as *chhincha*, usually where the crop is poorest, being left them as their perquisite.

The fact that the demand for labour in the coal fields within and just outside the district is constant and considerable, and that the possible advantages of Assam as a field for surplus labour are well known in every part of the district, probably accounts for the comparatively liberal treatment of the ordinary field labourer including the *aidhar* just mentioned, and for the small extent to which, in this district, as compared with some of its neighbours, the labourer or *kamiya* is a mere bond slave. Every zamindar and indeed every holder of any considerable extent of land has his *kamiyas*, but it is ordinarily only those of the purely money-lending classes or the petty foreign *thikādar* or *ijārādar* type, who are in the strict sense bond-slaves, that is to say, persons more or less permanently bound to work for a particular master in consideration of an advance or advances of money; such persons are housed, clothed and fed, and not too well, by their master, and their wages are set off against the loan, the chances of paying off which are usually but small. Obviously, in a district like Mānbhum this system, formerly very common if not almost universal, must tend to die out, as the over-driven *kamiya* will sooner or later find an opportunity of clearing out with his family to the mines or Assam, leaving his creditor in the lurch. The system of large advances in order to attract labour is, it may be noted, common in the lac factories, and recourse is frequently had to the courts to enforce the contracts under the provisions of Act XIII of 1859; this system is not in itself objectionable, but where, as is often the case, the factories do not provide continuous labour, being closed for several months in the year, and regular payment of the advance while the cooly is earning high wages is not insisted on, it very quickly assumes most of the objectionable features of the *kamiya* system, with the added terror of the criminal law as a means of enforcing the contract.

Village labourers. The blacksmith and the carpenter in the villages, who make and repair the agricultural implements, household utensils, etc. of the ordinary cultivating families, are ordinarily remunerated by a regular annual allowance of grain per family or householder. The blacksmith supplies his own coal; his remuneration is 20 seers of *dhan* a year per plough, and a *binra* or sheaf, yielding 2½ to 3 seers when threshed. For every adult resident he gets also 1 seer of grain per annum for sharpening sickles and another seer for affixing the share to a new plough. The Dhobi or washerman, when one is employed, gets cash at the rate of 1¼ anna per score of articles washed. The other village officials or servants, *i.e.*, the barber, the Kumhar or potter, the Goāla, Chamar and Dom are usually paid in cash or kind, as their services are required. The barber gets special gratuities either in grain or cash on the occasion of any birth in a family, the fee for a boy being invariably double that for a girl.

Supply of labour. The following remarks regarding the supply of labour in Mānbhum are quoted from Mr. Foley's Report on Labour in Bengal (1906)—

"Besides the emigration to tea, a certain number, but not apparently a very large number, emigrate every year to Calcutta where they work mostly as scavengers throughout the year, returning for some six weeks in June to transplant their paddy. Others go to the Sundarbans. Lac-rearing gives occupation to many others. The district is not congested, the people are fairly well off, and the Jharia coal-fields in the north and the Rānīganj coal-fields across the Dāmodar form the natural outlet for all the labour available in the district. The Kurmi, Sonthal and Bhumij are the most numerous castes in the district, but there are also 99,000 Bāuris. The labour is not suitable for mills and, for the same reason stated in the case of Hazāribāgh and Rānchi, not to be recommended for handling goods. Only a few castes seem to have taken to mining, and thus there is a scarcity of coal cutters in the Jharia mines, though there is no scarcity of surface labourers. It would appear that recruits for the coal mines, especially from the south of the district, are increasing but only gradually. The people should apparently be encouraged to take advantage of the high rates they can make in the mines. There is no reason why they should migrate to any other industry, and from the opinion given me by the Manager of the Pānchet Encumbered Estate, increased migration to any other industry would be looked on as objectionable of the Zemindars."

Since the above was written the demand for labour in the coal-fields has greatly increased, and with rates of wages generally high throughout the district there is but little inducement for labour to migrate, and the Assam Labour Committee of 1906 fully realised that the days were numbered in which Mānbhum could be looked upon as a favourable field of recruitment for Assam.

Prices.

The average prices (in seers and chittacks per rupee) of common rice, wheat, maize and salt during the last fortnight of March, for the 15 years ending in 1910, are given in the margin.

YEAR.	Common rice.	Wheat.	Gram.	Maize.	Salt.
	Sr. Ch.	Sr. Ch.	Sr. Ch.	Sr. Ch.	Sr. Ch.
1896-1900...	14 10	10 9	18 6	16 4	9 13
1901-1905...	13 11	11 12	14 1	22 8	10 8
1906-1910...	10 11	9 3	10 11	14 0	16 8

Excluding salt, the fall in the price of which is due to successive reductions in the import duty thereon, the prices of all food-staples have risen; in the case of rice which is the ordinary food-grain produced within the district, and consumed by the bulk of the inhabitants, the average price for the more recent quinquennium was more than 25 per cent. in excess of what it was in the five years which closed the last century; maize, which is much less important but grown and consumed in considerable quantities in the wilder portions of the district, had increased in price by over 12 per cent. Special causes, however, affected prices generally to an unusual extent in the years 1907 and 1908, *i.e.*, the general shortage of the rice crop in the Province of Eastern Bengal in the former year and the local scarcity in the succeeding year, and in the last year of the period prices considerably improved, the year ending with rice selling at 14 seers per rupee and maize at 20 seers.

Within the year the course of prices varies in normal years mainly with the time of the harvest. Maize is cheapest in September and October, and rice in December and January when the main crop has been reaped; with a full harvest they remain fairly steady with a tendency to a slight rise till April and May. By this time the bulk of the local maize crop has been consumed and prices harden rapidly till the new crop is harvested in September. In the case of rice, the rise throughout May, June and July is fairly continuous, August as a rule marking the highest limits. Then, if the prospects of the early crop and of maize are good, and conditions are hopeful for the main winter rice crop, there is a steady fall with perhaps a sudden and considerable drop in November, when it is quite certain that the crop is to be an average or a bumper one. Variations of price in the more remote markets are greater, as a rule, than those at the main centres and near the railways, where the retail prices are more or less regulated by the big traders, who watch the course of prices in the outside world as well as locally.

The maximum price of rice in the famine of 1866 at Purūlia was 4 seers for the rupee at the end of August; in 1874 the price never went above 13 seers in July; between October 1896 and September 1897, ten seers was obtainable at Gobindpur for the rupee during two fortnights only (the 1st in October and the 2nd in December) and from May to September less than eight seers, the maximum price seven seers being reached in the early part of July. At Purūlia prices did not fall below 10 seers till March, and below 8 seers till the end of May and the maximum price was $7\frac{5}{16}$ seers in the latter half of July. With these figures may be compared those for 1907-08, during which the average price of rice was $7\frac{1}{2}$ seers for the rupee, the maximum variation being from 8 seers, for short periods only in November 1907 and the following January, and again in September 1908, and 7 seers at which it remained steady throughout July during which month, in the more remote markets, *e.g.*, Mânbazar and Bandwân, prices as high as 6 and even 5 seers per rupee were reported.

MATERIAL CONDITION OF THE PEOPLE.

No more striking illustration of the improvement that has taken place in the material condition of the people generally can be given than the manner in which, without assistance from Government, they were able to tide over nearly two years of high prices in 1907 and 1908; high prices, of course, if coincident with good crops, mean considerable direct benefit to the cultivator but in the latter year, at any rate, it was only the fortunate few who could have had any appreciable margin over the amount required for home consumption by which they could have profited financially. Moreover, it must be remembered that rice is in this district the ordinary staple consumed, and cheaper grains are not produced in anything like sufficient quantity to take the place of rice converted into cash. Though, therefore, it must be accepted that the high prices they obtained for their surplus in 1907, must have gone some way to securing the position of the cultivating classes throughout the ensuing period of short crops and famine prices, some other cause must be found for the smaller cultivators' and landless labourers' ability to hold out without some form of relief from outside. For the latter, as has already been shown, there was an ample field for employment at rates on which they could live comparatively well even at famine prices; in the case of the small cultivators, it was most probably the high prices obtained for lac in the previous years which made resistance possible, inasmuch as they were thereby saved from exhausting their credit. Moreover, the continuance of high prices over a considerable number of years had, in itself, improved their credit by increasing the selling value of their holdings, more especially in the more congested areas where additional land could not readily or cheaply be brought under rice cultivation. At the end of the period of high prices there can be no doubt that the smaller cultivators, and many also of the bigger men, had come practically to the end of their resources, and the records of the registration offices show that during the period an abnormal number of usufructuary mortgages and sales of occupancy and fixed rent holdings and portions thereof were executed, and arrears of rent mounted up in almost all estates. Since then, however, there have been two full rice harvests, and credit must have been fully restored, while stocks of grains are largely held, wherever the necessity for raising cash by an immediate sale was not necessary. At the time of writing, therefore, the general condition of the cultivating classes is probably better than it has been at any time during the past ten years.

Of the condition of labourers it is unnecessary to say very much; in the villages there is ample employment at the customary rates, and, as has been shown in an earlier part of this chapter, there is an ample field for them in the coal and other industries within the district.

Landlords. The condition of the smaller landholders, who have considerable cultivation of their own, besides rent collections from tenants, is similar to that of the cultivators in general. Their expenses are larger, they have as a rule more non-earning members of the family to maintain, but on the other hand their income is larger. Many of them, however, show a tendency to ape the bigger landholders in the matter of expensive marriages, feasts to Brāhmans and other ceremonies, with disastrous results to themselves. With very few exceptions the larger landholders, including most of the Zamindars or so-called Rājas of the district, are more or less heavily involved in debt. The causes are mainly and primarily their own or their predecessors' gross extravagances, and the resultant permanent alienation of considerable portions of their estates to money-lenders and others, and the necessity of providing for the maintenance of near and remote relatives, either by cash allowances or grants of land. In many cases it is the aping of a Rājput status which has been their ruin, improvement in status being mainly effected by marriages —necessarily expensive—into families of rather higher status in local or popular opinion than their own. Another cause in recent years has been the general rise in the standard of living, the fashion being largely set by the comparatively few big Zamindars, whose income has been doubled or even quadrupled by the fact of their being the owners of the mineral rights in the coalfields. Further reference to this state of things will be found in the paragraph dealing with Encumbered Estates in Chapter X.

Increasing improvidence.

Though, as above stated, the condition of the mass of the people is generally better now than it has been for years past, there are not wanting signs that the tendency is for expenditure to increase more rapidly than income. The improvidence of most of the aboriginal and semi-aboriginal races is almost proverbial, and the absence of any wish to provide for the morrow, or even of any idea of the desirability of making such provision, is everywhere conspicuous. The considerable earnings of the cooly classes are very largely spent in drinking and feasting, and the higher their wages the fewer days in the week or month will they, as a general rule, work. Similarly among the cultivating classes, though the drinking habit is less noticeable, (and even among the classes from whom a large part of the labouring population is drawn, it is largely confined to the consumption of home-made rice-beer (*nāndia* or *pachwai*) on the occasion of the regular festivals), there is little, if any, tendency displayed towards saving. Larger sums are spent on clothing and improved utensils, more expensive and more numerous ornaments are purchased, and also larger supplies of the articles of food and household use for which the cultivator has at all times to go to the nearest market, but the bulk of the extra proceeds of his crops go in more expensive show and *tamāsha* on the occasion of the various social ceremonies; the aping of superior social status is not confined to the Zamindars or bigger tenure-holders; among the Bhumij, especially, the claim to the dignity of Rajput extends much lower, and the holder of a few bighas more than his neighbours now not infrequently sets up to be a Rājput. Generally, wherever the tendency is towards Hinduisātion of a particular tribe or race, increased means stimulates the movement, and the extra earnings of the family are rapidly used up in the imitation of Hindu customs of early marriages and large dowries, expensive *srādh* ceremonies and the like, and a nucleus of debt to the *mahājan* remains even after a succession of good years. Even the high prices obtainable for rice have not as yet stimulated, in any great degree, extension of cultivation beyond what the requirements of an increasing family necessitate, and hardly anywhere within the district are serious efforts made to improve the yield from existing fields, and, as has been remarked in a previous chapter, any marked improvement in the system of agriculture whether in the matter of improving on the present yield, or in trying new or additional crops, can hardly be expected until it is forced on the cultivator by his sheer necessity.

Indebtedness.

Indebtedness is more or less general, but the amounts are probably not, as a rule, excessive in proportion to the real value of the holdings, and in the majority of cases not more than could be cleared off without much difficulty or effort in a year of good crops, if the cultivator cared or were pressed to do so. The effects of the introduction of the Chota Nāgpur Tenancy Act which prohibits sales, and limits mortgages of lands held by occupancy tenants, will undoubtedly affect their credit, and will probably operate to their ultimate advantage by limiting their capacity for extravagance. It should certainly lead to greater advantage being taken by him of the Land Improvement and Agriculturist's Loans Act, very little use has been made of which in the past, except in years of scarcity ; it may also stimulate the opening of Co-operative Banks, which at present only exist among two small Christian communities at Purūlia and Pokhuria.

CHAPTER VIII.

OCCUPATIONS, MANUFACTURES AND TRADE.

THE statistics obtained at the census of 1901 show that 67·1 per cent. of the total population of Mānbhum are supported by agriculture, a figure considerably below the average for the Division. The agricultural population in all numbers 873,500 of whom 46 per cent., including some 1,300 rent-receivers, 347,000 rent-payers and 53,500 agricultural labourers, are actual workers. The industrial population accounts for 11·7 per cent. of the total, and of these rather more than half are actual workers, and include 16,000 miners, 9,800 cotton-weavers, 6,600 basket-makers and 4,400 workers in iron and steel; oil-pressers, rice-pounders, and workers in brass and bellmetal and in gold are also fairly numerous. Commerce and the professions support a very small number, only three per thousand of the population being engaged in trade, and 2·3 per cent. dependent on the professions for their livelihood; of the latter nearly half are actual workers and include some 1,500 priests, 2,700 religious mendicants, 400 teachers, 150 lawyers and 1,000 members of the medical profession of whom more than half are ordinary unqualified midwives; 118,000 persons are employed as earth-workers and general labourers and, with their dependants, make up nearly 15 per cent. of the whole population; numerically important also are the herdsmen and others engaged in breeding, keeping and tending cattle, who number over 33,000. OCCUPATIONS.

The predominance of agriculture in one form or another among the occupations of the district is as marked as it is elsewhere in Bengal, and excluding the landless labourer class there are few trades or professions, a considerable percentage of whose members are not also supported by agriculture. Of the more important manufactures and industries of the district and of its trade generally, a brief account is given in the succeeding paragraphs. MANUFACTURES AND INDUSTRIES.

The coal industry is naturally the most prominent feature of the trade and commerce of this district, and Mānbhum now ranks COAL.

even ahead of Burdwan as producing the largest amount of coal of any district in India, though, as a competitor of Burdwan, it entered the field comparatively recently. The present limits of the district still include a portion of the Rāniganj field, but its fame as a coal-producing area is now practically identified with the Jharia field, of which, as well as of the industry generally, a more detailed description will be found in the succeeding chapter. In 1891, apart from the older mines of the Rāniganj field, only two mines were being worked in the district with an output of 78,000 tons, but with the opening of the Dāmūdar branch of the East Indian Railway in 1894 development became rapid; in 1903 there were 141 collieries at work, 115 in the Jharia and 26 in the Rāniganj field, with outputs of 2,746,000 and 246,000 tons respectively, and by 1908 the total number of mines working had risen to 281 and the total output to 7,062,000 tons. In 1900 the mines gave employment to 27,000 persons, a figure which had risen to 72,000 in 1908. The latest year (1909) for which figures are available show a considerable fall both in outturn, which dropped to 6,326,000 tons, and in the labour force employed (59,000 persons), due to the general depression in trade. The bulk of the miners employed are Bāuris and Sonthals, both local and immigrant, but of recent years there has been a tendency to import labour from upcountry (Peshwāris and others) on an increasing scale. For above-ground labour the field of selection is wider, and representatives of all the ordinary labouring castes and local aboriginal tribes are to be found. Wages of Re. 1 or even more per diem can easily be earned by a man, and as most of his family can find employment on proportionately remunerative terms above or below ground, there is everything to make the cooly prosperous. Few, however, of them can be induced to work more than five days in the week, and large numbers of them only work for a few weeks at a time and go off home to spend their earnings. There is also a considerable exodus on the occasion of the various important village festivals, and during the cultivating seasons. All these causes of course go to reduce the average number actually employed and an average of 70,000 for the year probably means an actual labour force varying from a lakh or even 120,000 to as few as 40 or 50,000, according to the season.

FACTORIES. Iron and Steel. Pottery. The factory industries, so numerous and important in the coal-field area in the neighbouring district of Burdwan, have still to be developed in Mānbhum. The Barākhar Iron and Steel Works, which is just outside the district, draws a large part of its raw material in the shape of ore from Malti, Dudhapāni, Chandil and other places in this district, and most of its coke from Jharia, but any description of the works belongs more properly to the Burdwan volume. Altogether 10,000 tons of ore valued at nearly Rs. 51,000 were drawn from their various quarries in this district by this company in 1909, and a considerable labour force was employed. Iron is smelted on a small scale at a few places in the district, but the outturn is very small and only a very few families, mostly of Kols, are employed in this industry.

There are two brick, tile and pottery factories, both situated with the Rāniganj coalfield in pargana Pāndra. Of these the Brick and Tile Syndicate's factory at Gurtalbāri is of some years standing and employs from 250 to 300 persons; the Kumārdubi Fire-brick and Pottery Works have recently been started and employ some 150 persons only. The only other factory worked under the Factories Act is the Barakar Coal Company's Engineering Works at Kumārdubi where 300 persons are employed, the work done being mainly such as is required for the replacement and repairs of parts of machinery used in the company's various collieries.

The most important industry in the district after coal is the collection and manufacture of lac. The extent of the trade in this article in one form or another is shown by the large exports. No accurate figures are unfortunately obtainable, as separate statistics were not compiled by the Railway Companies till 1909, in which year the total export of lac in the form of stick-lac, *i.e.*, not manufactured, and in the various manufactured forms was 200,311 maunds, valued at Rs. 40 to 50 lakhs. Lac

The number of people engaged in the collection of raw lac cannot be estimated as almost every small cultivator in the greater part of the district has at least a few trees on which he rears lac, and there are now also several large firms who arrange with the actual producers for more systematic cultivation; among these may be mentioned Messrs. Schröder Smidt & Co., who have leased the right to rear lac in the Mahta Protected Forests for five years at an annual rental of Rs. 400, and Messrs. Shaw Wallace & Co. who combine a lac business with coal-mining in their properties in the north-west of the district. In 1909 there were 118 regular lac factories in the district employing an average of nearly 6,000 persons. Jhalda is the most important centre of manufacture, but there are numerous factories also at Purulia and Balarāmpur, and a few at Chāndil, Chās, Mānbazar, Tulin and Gobindpur. The manufacturing industry is almost entirely in the hands of Armenian and Mirzapur firms; the rates of wages given are high, an adult male being able to earn from five annas to eight annas per diem, and skilled workers, both male and female, even more. The most important markets for the raw article are Mānbazar, Balarāmpur and Jhalda, but in almost every weekly *hât* throughout the district lac is brought in and sold to the agents of the manufacturers and exporters during the season.

The raw lac is a resinous incrustation produced round the bodies of colonies of the lac insect (*Tacchardia lacca*) after it has fastened on the twigs of various trees, of which the most important as lac producers in this district are the Kusum (*Schleichera trijuga*), the Palās (*Butea frondosa*) and the Bair or Kul (*Zizyphus jujuba*). The production of the lac of commerce commences with the birth and swarming of the larvæ which occurs twice or occasionally three times in the year, viz., in July, December and January. The larvæ emerge from the dead bodies of the female and crawl away in quest of fresh feeding grounds covering the adjoining branches and twigs till the latter look red and literally alive. In this stage they have numerous enemies and the vast majority perish; the more fortunate are wafted by the breeze or carried by the bees, birds or squirrels or by their own exertions to new situations. There the larvæ become fixed, their legs no longer required fall off, and a resinous excretion begins to form round their bodies, and in course of time, by the aggregation of many, the twigs become more or less completely and thickly encrusted. Two and a half months after swarming the insects are produced, the females have no power to locomotion and remain in the cells, the males emerge winged and fly and flutter away visiting and impregnating the females. Shortly afterwards, the bodies of the females become greatly enlarged, assume a bright red colour and in the due course develop viviparous larvæ. The mother then dies, the body becomes the resting place of her numerous offspring (about 1,000 in number) which at their appointed time escape by swarming, and thus twice or sometimes thrice in the year the strange cycle of life is repeated.

The system of propagation or cultivation ordinarily followed consists in lopping off a few twigs of well-formed lac shortly before the expected date of swarming, and tying these in convenient portions on fresh trees or fresh boughs of the same tree. In the case of the Bair, and to a certain extent also Kusum, it is the practice now to regularly pollard the tree so as to encourage vigorous growth of new branches and twigs on which to propagate the lac; in the case of Kusum the seed in the shape of an old branch, well encrusted, is applied to the fresh tree or branch in the month of Māgh (January-February); a bundle of seed twigs, a foot or so in diameter and costing about five rupees, suffices for four trees. The principal crop in the case of Kusum is gathered in Kartik (October-November), but a smaller crop called 'Jethua' is also cut in Chait (March-April). The encrusted branches are removed entirely and the lac scraped off; the produce of an average tree weighs about 30 seers, including a comparatively small amount of wood and bark; the quality depends on the brightness of the colour and the thickness of the incrustation, which is often as much as one inch, completely encircling the twig.*

Palāsi and Kul lac are reckoned inferior to Kusum, and of the two Kul is of slightly better quality but involves more cost in cultivation. The method of application is much the same. The principal crop is in Baisākh (April-May) when the twigs are lopped off and the lac removed with a sickle, the twigs in the case of Kul being first soaked in water to facilitate this operation. Palāsi lac reaches the market as a rule with a larger percentage of wood, and indeed much of it still attached to the twigs, and the price is in consequence lower. A second crop is taken from the Palās, on which a part of the earlier crop is usually left as seed, in Kartick (October-November) and is known as 'Chuchia' when it is cut and sold as seed. 'Chuchia' or seed lac is not left on the Kul, for which seed from the Palas is ordinarily used. The yield from a Kul tree of average size may be taken as 20 to 25 seers, and from the Palās slightly less. The risks attending the cultivation of lac generally are considerable. Excessive heat in March or August is said to be fatal to the seed; fog or mist is supposed to damage it, and cloudy weather accompanied by thunder and lightning to injure or even destroy the crop. In May 1908 the comparative poorness of the outturn was ascribed to excessive heat which had literally melted the incrustations on the branches, but a more probable explanation of the shortage was the large prices obtainable in the previous year, which led to an insufficient quantity being reserved for seed.

The price obtainable by the cultivator varies between very extreme limits according to the quality of the lac, its comparative purity from foreign matter in the shape of bark and wood, and the market for the manufactured article. In the specially favourable season of 1907 Kusumi lac fetched as much as Rs. 70 per maund in the local market, Palāsi Rs. 50 and Kuli Rs. 70, the demand for Europe and America being at that time enormous; in the two succeeding years prices dropped and the average did not exceed Rs. 25, Rs. 20 and Rs. 25 per maund for the three varieties respectively. At Rs. 20 per maund it is calculated

* The Commercial Products of India. Sir George Watt, London, 1908.

that the cultivator can make a profit of Rs. 7 per tree with a produce of Rs. 20 seers per tree and seed lac selling at Rs. 5 per bundle, and allowing for payment for assistance in applying the seed, watching the trees and gathering and preparing the crop for the market; where all this is done by members of the cultivator's family the actual cash profits will of course be considerably higher. Even with lac selling at Rs. 10 per maund, the profit per tree is still considerable, though the margin is not large where hired labour has to be prepared and seed to be purchased.

The process of manufacture followed in most of the factories is as follows: the raw lac is first crushed on a flat stone, and as much as possible of the woody material removed; the crushed lac (*būili*) is then made over to the *ghasandārs* (literally those who rub) who put it in earthen jars called *athālis* in which they wash and rub it between the palms of their hands or trample it with their feet. More of the foreign matter is thus removed and also the colouring matter, the water being constantly changed until it comes away comparatively free of dirt and colour. The lac itself is in the course of this process converted into what is known as seed lac, and is divided out into large and small grains, called respectively *chauri* and *mulāma*. The washing process is done either with or without *saji māti*, *i.e.*, impure carbonate of soda, the use of which gets rid of a larger percentage of the dye or colouring matter, and results in a more valuable quality of lac. After the washing and separation of the grains these are spread out and exposed to the rays of the sun to dry; over-exposure results in blackening of the lac and consequent reduction in value. When dried, the grains are winnowed to get rid of dust and dirt. A certain quantity of powdered yellow arsenic is mixed with them, the object being apparently to improve the colour; resin is also added partly as a cheap form of adulteration and partly because it makes the melting point of the shellac lower, and therefore makes it more suitable for certain purposes. Thus prepared the lac is made over to the regular shellac manufacturers (*kārikars*) who are mostly skilled workers from Mirzapur. They proceed to stuff the grain into long cylinder-shaped bags; one end of the bag is then attached to a *chorki* or wheel, not unlike a spinning wheel, placed close to a long open fire, and the other is held by the *kārikar*. The wheel is revolved and the surface of the bag gradually heated all round, and as the *kārikar* from time to time gives his end of the bag a complete twist round, the melted lac gradually exudes on the surface. In this state the lac, known as *pak*, is removed with a piece of flat iron and dropped either into a vessel of hot water or on to tiles kept wet and clean alongside the fire. The next stage is the conversion of the lumps of cooked lac into sheet or shellac; the lump, still hot, is taken by another workman and spread smoothly round a cylinder of wood or iron, or the stalk of a plantain the smoothing out is done with a ribbon of palm leaf stretched between the hands and is continued till the lac is a smooth sheet about one-eighth of an inch in thickness. The sheet is then opened out by a *belua* or opener and removed from the cylinder and trimmed into rectangular form, when another assistant carrying it in front of the fire seizes it with his hands, toes and even his teeth and spreading his arms and legs and straightening himself out stretches it to three or four times its original size and to the thinness of paper. It is then laid on a mat or cloth and allowed to cool gradually. The sheets thus prepared are carefully examined, all pieces of darker colour or containing impurities broken off and put away separately, and the remainder, broken into pieces two or three inches square of uniform clear golden colour, is ready for the market as first class shellac. The other forms in which lac is put on the market are as garnet, button or refuse. For garnet lac, which as its name implies is a rich red colour and is in demand where colour is not a disadvantage, the palāsi lac is largely used as well as the rejections at the different stages of the manufacture of shellac. The manufacture differs only in the fact that the process is complete at the cylinder stage, no further stretching being necessary. For button lac the molten material is not stretched at all but is simply allowed to drop off from the bag in which it is cooked on to a smooth clean surface, where it forms round pieces about 3 or 4 inches in diameter.

The bags used in the process above described contain a considerable residue of lac of which part is extracted by boiling with *saji* and made into cakes called *pasheba* which sell at somewhat less than half the rates obtainable for shellac and which are used mainly in the local manufacture of lac ornaments, bangles, toys, etc., and common sealing wax, and also by cabinet makers for covering up cracks in wood.

For lac dye there is now practically no demand, and no attempt is made to recover it from the water used for washing the raw lac in the earlier stages of manufacture. This water is allowed to run to waste and incidentally its disposal is a constant source of trouble in the factories within the municipal towns and larger villages, as it contains a large amount of both animal and vegetable refuse and has a most objectionable odour. The system now being enforced on manufacturers so far as possible is to run off the water to some distance from inhabited areas in pucka drains, and then to allow it to spread out over level fields; the earth saturated with the refuse water forms a valuable manure and cultivators regularly dig it out and put it on their fields, not infrequently paying small sums to be allowed to do so.

The finer qualities of manufactured lac, shellac, garnet and button are exported direct for the most part to Calcutta; no attempt has yet been made to convert any part of it locally into varnish, though in the mahua tree, which is usually abundant in this district in the very areas from which the raw lac is drawn, there is ample material for the distillation of a cheap spirit suitable for use in conjunction with lac in the manufacture of varnish.

Silk and Tasar weaving. Tasar silk weaving is still carried on at a few centres of which Raghunāthpur (3 miles west of Adra station on the Bengal-Nagpur Railway) is the most important; Singhbazar near Purūlia and Lohāgarh, 15 miles south-east of the same place, each contains a few looms; the total number of families engaged in the industry is about 150, and in 1907-08 there were reported to be 95 looms. The estimates of outturn are only approximate and range from 32,000 yards in 1905-06 to 20,000 in 1907-08. Raghunāthpur appears to have been the chief centre of the manufacture in earlier days, but the industry has declined, since, it is said, the forests from which the cocoons were locally obtained have disappeared, and it is necessary now to go to a distance for these; the cost of the raw material is thereby enhanced, and as the profits of manufacture are reduced, many of the weaving families have had to take to other occupations. The quality of cloth produced at Raghunāthpur is good and there is a small local demand for it for *dhutis*, *saris*, *chadars*, napkins and *pagris*, but the bulk of the outturn finds its way to Burdwan and Calcutta. Attempts were made for several years to teach improved methods of manufacture and to adopt the fly-shuttle loom; the innate conservatism of the leading weavers was not, however, to be overcome, and neither in the methods of winding the cocoon nor in the method of weaving has any material improvement been effected.

Tasar rearing is still carried on fairly extensively in a small area near Kenda about half-way between Purūlia and Mānbazar; the rearers are chiefly Kurmis but Sonthals, Bhumij and others also go in for it. The Asan (*Terminalia tomentosa*), Sidha (*Lagerstrœmia parviflora*) and Dhau (*Anogeissus latifolia*) are the trees ordinarily used for rearing *dābas* and the Asan only for *buguis*.

Cotton weaving. Cotton weaving other than as a home industry, *i.e.*, production on a small scale for merely local consumption, has almost disappeared; there are now no great weaving centres or large colonies of weavers, but in almost every village a few weavers will be found who prepare the coarse country cloth used by the poorer population for the ordinary articles of clothing; the cloth produced is coarse but strong and durable and is preferred to the more showy but less durable Manchester goods which are available in any quantity at every bazar and *hāt* throughout the district. Formerly locally grown cotton was used, and in the wilder areas the aboriginal races still grow their small patches of cotton, but generally speaking the bulk of the cotton used is imported. Attempts have been made to introduce the fly-shuttle loom at Raghunāthpur where cotton as well as Tasar weavers are fairly numerous, but these have not been successful. At Pokhuria in the north of the district Dr. Campbell has been more successful, weaving is taught in a regular school and various improved looms are in use. The object of this school is primarily to teach the Sonthal to be entirely independent of the outsider and to have in every Sonthal village a few Sonthal weavers able to supply the local requirements; no attempt is therefore made to teach anything but ordinary coarse work.

Iron ware and cutlery.

The ordinary iron utensils required for domestic use are made locally throughout the district; the ordinary village blacksmith works in a very primitive method and the produce of his hearth and anvil has no pretensions to being fine work; the raw material is usually supplied by his customers and he makes it up to order to the best of his ability. In Purūlia, Jhalda, Tanāsi and one or two other places, however, theer are more skilled workers, and the two former places have a considerable reputation for the manufacture of agriculturla implements, cutlery and firearms.

The reputation of Jhalda for guns hardly compares with that of Monghyr and the outturn is now very limited, two or three per annum only; the industry was, however, at one time a flourishing one, and the gun-makers of both Jhalda and Tanāsi were suspected in 1857 of supplying matchlocks and other weapons to the discontented Sonthals and others who gave trouble in the neighbourhood of Jaipur and Gola. The manufacturers have not, however, lost their skill and can effect passable repairs of weapons of European manufacture and also turn out weapons which are a fair imitation, so far as appearance goes, of the cheaper products of Birmingham. Their methods differ in no material respect from those followed by the gun makers of Monghyr which are described in detail by Mr. E. R. Watson in his Monograph on Iron and Steel work in Bengal (1907). Sword-sticks (*gupti*) are also manufactured in considerable numbers, as well as similar walking sticks of various patterns without the concealed weapon. The bulk of the outturn of the smithies consists, however, of ordinary household and agricultural implements of somewhat superior workmanship to those produced by the regular blacksmith of the smaller villages. The technical schools at Jhalda and Tanāsi referred to elsewhere are in connection with the superior blacksmiths' shops, and boys mainly of the regular blacksmith or Lohar castes are taught the various stages in the working up of the rough material into ploughshares, *kodālis*, axes and the smaller cutting instruments in ordinary use. According to Mr. J. G. Cumming,* the workers at Jhalda are capable of doing much better work than he found them doing, and only require an extended market for their manufactures. It is doubtful, however, whether without a capitalist behind them there is much possibility of their obtaining this.

Stone-carving. The only survival of the art of stone-carving, which to judge by the many relics of ancient skill to be found in the ruined temples scattered about the district, must at one time have had skilled exponents, is the small industry carried on at Dalmi and one or two other places in the south of the district, where the local pot or soap-stone is quarried on a small scale, and plates and other vessels manufactured from it. The number of people employed is small, a few dozen families in all and among these only a few individuals are skilled workmen. The blocks of stone are roughly dressed with a hammer and chisel, and then put on a rough lathe on which they are turned to the desired shape, and finally polished by hand. Occasionally somewhat more elaborate work is undertaken in the shape of idols, and it is stated that a few years ago some of the pot-stone masons were employed to do the carving for a new temple at Chirkunda. For such work, however, it is more usual to import skilled labour from Calcutta, Puri or elsewhere.

Gold-washing. Gold-washing is an industry which still survives at a few places along the Subarnarekha river in the fiscal division of Patkum. The methods followed are primitive and the results are very small, a hard day's work being well rewarded if the outturn in gold dust is worth four or five annas.

---

* Review of the Industrial position and prospects in Bengal in 1908.

Other industries. Other industries call for no special description; workers in brass and bellmetal at Purūlia supply the ordinary local requirements in the way of vessels for household use, and gold and silversmiths, usually immigrants from the Bihar districts, manufacture the usual ornaments; the local pottery is of the most ordinary description, and neither wood-turning nor wood-carving approaches anything in the shape of fine art. Basket-making is carried on for the most part by Doms and Hāris of whom a few may be found in most villages. Rope is made in the villages nearer the jungles from various jungle grasses and fibres; aloe fibre is also used, but the commonest material for ordinary purposes is rice straw.

TRADE. Coal is of course the most important article of export, followed closely in point of value by lac; a long way behind these both in quantity and value come rice, paddy, gram and various pulses, in all of which, however, a comparison of the figures for the last two quinquennial periods (ending March 1905 and 1910 respectively) there is a tendency to decline, due largely no doubt to the rapidly increasing industrial population of the coalfield area, and the diminishing area available there for cultivation. The extent of the lac trade has already been referred to; its financial importance to the district may be inferred from the fact that, taking the lowest computation, the value of lac exported in 1909 was approximately 40 to 50 lakhs of rupees as compared with 150 lakhs for coal and 3 lakhs for all kinds of food-grains. The chief imports are food-grains, namely, rice and pulses, sugar, refined and unrefined, salt, English and Indian cotton piece-goods, and Indian cotton-twist, tobacco, and kerosine oil. The bulk of the exports go to Calcutta, though coal in large quantities goes to Bombay, the United Provinces and other Provinces, and a considerable quantity of raw lac to Mirzapur. Bihar and Burdwan take the bulk of the exports of rice, and Rānchi and Singhbhum the various pulses. Of the imports the bulk of the rice comes from Burdwan, Bankura, Singhbhum and Sambalpur, and of gram and pulses from the Bihâr districts and Rânchi. Burdwan and Bihar share in providing most of the raw sugar and tobacco; oil-seeds come principally from districts of Bihar and other districts of Chota Nāgpur; raw lac in considerable quantity comes from Rānchi and Singhbhum and the bulk of the remainder of the imports come direct from Calcutta. The chief centres of trade are the towns of Purūlia and Jhalda, Dhānbāid, Jharia, Kátras and Chirkunda in the north of the district, Balarāmpur and Chāndil in the south, all on the line of railway, and Mānbazar and Barabāzar in the east and south-east,

The Dhānbāid subdivision is particularly well served by railways, the Purūlia subdivision not so well, but the Asansol-Sini line intersects it from north-east to south-west almost centrally, and the western half is again intersected since 1908 by the Purulia-Rānchi line; the Kharagpur-Gomoh branch cuts across the north-eastern corner and connects up the rest of the area with both Calcutta and the coalfield. Communications by road are on the whole good; passable fair-weather roads connect all parts of the district with one or more railway stations, and the main routes are metalled with either stone or gravel. The one existing drawback which hampers trade at all times and periodically stops through communication in the rains is the large number of unbridged rivers and streams. Outside the places mentioned there are comparatively few permanent markets, and the bulk of the ordinary trade of the district is carried on by means of the weekly *hāts*, many of which are held at places more or less intermediate between the distributing centres and the rural areas which they serve. In the wilder parts of the district pack-bullocks are regularly used as the only suitable means of conveyance, and the travelling purveyor of Manchester cloth and other village requirements or luxuries is no uncommon sight. For the purchase of the products of the rural areas agents are sent out from the chief centres to the *hāts* and villages and much of the produce, more particularly such articles as grain, oilseeds, hides, etc., for export, are thus bought locally; lac and other forest produce is usually brought in to the larger *hāts* and to the places of manufacture. Inter-district traffic by road with the southern and western portion of Rānchi is considerable, Chāndil being the main distributing and collecting centre, and a great part of the produce of the south-eastern corner of the district finds its way to various stations on the Bengal-Nāgpur Railway in the Singhbhum district. In the west Jhalda, which is now connected by a good road with Gola, does a large amount of trade with the south-eastern portion of Hazāribāgh; in the extreme north there is a considerable inter-district traffic betweeen Tundi and the Sonthal Parganas, gram and straw from which as well as timber from Pālganj in Hazāribāgh find their way in large quantities to the coalfield by road.

Weights and measures.

The extension of the coal industry and the opening out of the district generally, which has resulted from it, has naturally led to the standardization of weights in the district. In the larger markets and generally at most places within reach of the railway the only weight in use is the standard seer of 80 tolas. In the more out-of-the-way parts, a seer varies from as little as 60 to as much as 112 tolas in Mānbazar. south-eastern Barābhum, Baghmundi and elsewhere. Actual transactions, when dealing retail, are usually by measurer bowls supposed to hold ¼ seer (*powa*) or a seer (*pailā*) being used to measure grain.

The standard cubit for all ordinary purposes is one of 18 inches ; smaller units are the *anguli* or thumb-breadth, the *mushtis* of 4 *angulis*=three inches, and the bigha equal to three *mushtis*. Five *hāths* in length by four *hāths* in breadth makes a chittak of 45 square feet land measure, 16 chittaks equal 1 katha, and 20 kathas one bigha. Divisions of time are but vaguely recognised by the rural population, a *ghari* is about 24 minutes, a *ghanta* approximately an hour, and a *prahar* three hours. *Duprahar* represents midday. Other times of day are usually marked by reference to this or to sunrise or sunset or to the regular meals.

CHAPTER IX.

THE COALFIELDS OF MĀNBHUM.

Early discoveries. THE first Englishman to discover the existence of coal in Bengal was probably Mr. Suetonious Grant Heatly who, in 1774, was the Collector of Chotā Nāgpur and Palāmau. In that year he and a Mr. John Sumner obtained from Warren Hastings a license empowering them to work coal mines in "Pachete and Birbhum." A Mr. Redferne subsequently joined the firm which, as Sumner, Heatly and Redferne, applied for and obtained the exclusive right for a period of 18 years to work and sell coal in Bengal and its dependencies. In addition to paying a Government royalty of one-fifth of the value of all the coal raised by them, they also agreed to supply Government with ten thousand maunds of coal a year for a period of five years. Under this agreement the firm in 1775 announced the arrival of 2,500 maunds or 91⅓ tons of Pachete coal and asked that it should be taken over. This appears to be the first occasion on which Bengal coal in any large quantity was brought into the market. The coal, however, was not taken over until 1777 when, upon a second application from the firm, the Commissary of Stores was directed to examine and report upon it.

In 1777, about the same time, Farquhar and Motte asked permission "to bore cannon and to cast shot and shell in the district of Jherria, lying between the rivers Dammuda and Barakar." They gave as their reason for the selection of that locality that it "abounds in iron ore and is contiguous to the coal mine of Messrs. Sumner and Heatly." Unfortunately the coal Heatly produced was reported as being much inferior to that of England. In fact the Commissary of Stores, as the result of a series of experiments, came to the conclusion that it was only half as good as English coal, and it was returned to the firm. This circumstance, together with the indifference of Lord Cornwallis to measures calculated to develop the internal resources or promote the external commerce of India, led to the neglect and apathy that characterised the first few years of coal mining in India. Mr. Heatly was afterwards transferred, and it is doubtful whether any more of the coal was actually brought into the market. The mines first worked by him are said to have been six in number, three of which were at Aituria, Chinakuri, and Damulia, and the others further west near the Barākar. In his Wild Sports in the East (1808), Williamson alludes to Indian coal, but says that the Company "finds it easier to send coal from England, as ballast, to their arsenals abroad, where quantities are occasionally used in fusing metals for casting ordnances." But none of the early European travellers in India make any mention of coal, prior to the first decade of the 19th century. This is abundantly exemplified by the silence of Milburn (Or. Comm., 1813) and of Macpherson (Hist. Europ. Comm. Ind., 1812), two authors who were certain to have had chapters on Indian coal and India's requirements in coal had these been questions of public importance at the time in which they wrote.

In 1808 the Indian Directors of the East India Company actually complained of the heavy charges involved by the indents for coal made by their Indian representatives, and they accordingly recommended an enquiry whether charcoal could not be substituted; and if not, they further recommended the transference of the ordnance works to England. The Earl of Minto, who was at the time Governor-General of India, directed that Indian coal should be submitted to actual tests by the military authorities in India, and further experiments were accordingly made by Colonel Hardwicke. His report, however, which is dated May 19th, 1809, was again very unfavourable, and the subject of coal for a time dropped out of notice. But in 1814 the Marquis of Hastings once more urged on the Military Board the desirability of ascertaining beyond doubt "whether the coal of India was of a quality calculated for the purpose of the forge." He also announced that a fully qualified person would be appointed to examine the mines, who would be furnished with the necessary apparatus to make borings and who would for experimental purposes procure a supply of coal from such a depth as to ensure that it would represent the average quality. Previous experiments where thus discredited owing to the coal used having been obtained from the surface and therefore much deteriorated.

By this time apparently coal was being regularly conveyed by boat down the Dāmodar river to Calcutta, and we hear of a Calcutta merchant having commenced to use Bengal coal notwithstanding the unfavourable reports published by the Military Board.

Mr. Rupert Jones' enquiry.

The expert deputed by Government was a Mr. Rupert Jones who was sent from England on purpose to examine the Bengal coalfields, and his report (written in 1815) will be found in the

Asiatik Researches (1833, XVIII, 163-70). Mr. Jones rediscovered Mr. Heatly's workings and also found the seam at Rānīganj, which later in 1815 or 1816, he began to work on his own account. His report was on the whole favourable and showed that Bengal coal might very well be used for many of the purposes for which English coal was being imported. But he did not himself realise the full value of his investigations. He foretold increased prosperity to Calcutta through the coal he had discovered being a better and more economical fuel for burning the Sylhet limestone than the firewood then in use, but apparently he knew little of the great revolution steam was destined to effect, nor of the imperative necessity of an abundant and cheap supply of coal for commercial and industrial prosperity.*

Early developments in Mānbhum. The Rānīganj field.

The history of Mr. Jones' undertaking at Rānīganj belongs to the Burdwan district, but barely 10 years after Messrs. Alexander and Company took over his workings and started the first regularly constituted Indian mine under European supervision and worked by European capital in 1820, Mr. Homfray of Messrs. Jessop and Company opened the Chānch and Luchibad mines at the other end of the Rānīganj field west of the Barākhar river and within the present limits of this district. In 1837 these mines with others passed into the hands of Messrs. Gilmore, Homfray and Company, and six years later in 1843 this firm and that of Carr, Tagore and Company, who had acquired the Rānīganj mine in the Burdwan district, combined to form the Bengal Coal Company which still owns the most extensive coal properties in the Rānīganj field. Progress was, however, slow until the opening of the East Indian Railway as far as Rānīganj in 1854, and so far as mines in the Mānbhum portion of the Rānīganj field are concerned until its extension to Barākar in 1858. A return of production submitted in 1860 shows three collieries working within the present limits of the district, *i.e.*, Chānch, Luchibad and Domurkonda, with a total outturn of 4½ lakhs of maunds for 1858 and 3¼ for 1859. In 1861 Mr. Blanford of the Geological Survey saw quarries being worked at these three places and also at Hirākund, and in a few other places surface coal was being quarried on a small scale by natives; at Domurkonda development had gone to the extent of the installation of a steam engine of 10 horse-power. But with no outlet to the rail-head and to the consuming centres except by road or in the rains by the somewhat

* This and the preceding paragraphs are reproduced from the Burdwan Gazetteer. J. C. K. Peterson, 1910. Ed.

uncertain route of the Dāmodar river, which does not in this district or for some distance further east lend itself very readily to regular boat traffic, development was very slow, and as late as 1868, the report on the "Coal Resources and Production of India" states that a single mine with a yearly output of 1½ lakhs of maunds was being worked west of the Barākhar river. Though the East Indian Railway line was opened as far as Barākhar in 1858, it was not till 1870 that the road bridge over the Barākhar river was completed, and another 24 years elapsed before the Barākhar railway bridge and the Chānch branch, a purely colliery line connecting the collieries at Chānch, Luchibad, Domurkonda, etc., with the main line, were opened in 1894. Even as late as 1891 the only extensive workings in this part of the field were those of the Bengal and Barākhar Coal Companies at Laikdihi and Kumardubi respectively, and the total output in that year was only 77,000 tons. Though, therefore, coal mining within the district of Mānbhum in the Rāniganj field was initiated so many years before, it can only be said to have got its full opportunity of development almost at the same time as the Jharia field was brought into touch with the outside world by the opening of the Barākhar-Dhānbāid line in 1894.

The Jharia field.

It has already been mentioned that so far back as 1777 Farquhar and Motte had asked permission to bore cannon and cast shot and shell in the district of Jharia, which they describe as "abounding in iron ore and as contiguous to Sumner and Heatly's coal mines." The latter, however, were east of the Barākhar, and it is probable that Farquhar and Motte referred rather to the eastern part of the Rāniganj field which answers their description in other respects than to the Jharia field proper. Mr. Jones, in a paper written in 1817 and published 10 years later, referred to coal in the neighbourhood of Jharia or "Jarrigarh," but the map which accompanied it did not include the Jharia field. It was Major Sherwill, the officer in charge of the party which did the Revenue Survey of this part of the district in the years 1861 to 1863, who once more brought to notice the existence of coal in Jharia. An application had indeed been filed a few years earlier (1858) by Messrs. Borrodaile and Company for a mining lease of the whole Jharia estate which was then under Court of Wards management, but nothing came of this. Major Sherwill's information led to the deputation of Mr. Theodore Hughes of the Geological Survey, as soon as the topographical maps were ready, to make a proper examination of the mineral resources of this area, and his report was made public in the Memoirs of the Geological Survey of India in 1865

(Vol. V, Part III). An optimistic view of the quality and future of Jharia coal was not, however, taken by Mr. Oldham, the Superintendent of the Geological Survey, and no steps were taken to exploit it till 1890, when the East Indian Railway Company deputed Mr. T. H. Ward to make a definite report on the economic resources of the field. Mr. Ward's report was a most favourable one. He considered the Jharia coal superior to the general average of the raisings in Rānīganj field, and was sanguine that with good railway communications it would command the north-west market. The construction of a railway line from Barākhar to Kātras was sanctioned in April 1892 and taken in hand at once, and there was an immediate rush for settlements of coal lands in Jharia. The estate was just then about to be released from management, and the Court of Wards declined to undertake the responsibility of making any settlements with the result that the earliest mines to be opened were some near Kātras. The new line from Barākhar to Dhānbāid and Kātras was opened on the 20th May 1894, and a year later another line from Kusunda to Pathordi, and the whole length of the coalfield was thus brought into direct communication with the outer world, and the result was an immediate and rapid development of the industry. In 1894 the outturn from all mines in the district was only 128,686 tons; in 1895 it rose at once to 1,281,294 tons, the enormous increase being almost entirely from the Jharia field. In the two succeeding years there was a set-back, but from 1898 there was a steady rise in the outturn which first touched two million tons in 1901. In 1905 the outturn had swelled to nearly three million tons, and in 1906 to nearly four millons; in 1907 over 5,800,000 tons were raised, and in the following year no less than seven millions of tons. These figures are, by themselves, sufficient to show the extraordinary rapid development of the coal industry in the district; the Jharia field is of course the one which accounts for the bulk of the increase in outturn, but since 1894 there has been a very considerable expansion in the Rānīganj field also, and many new mines have been opened out, more especially along what is known as the Pāndra extension of the field and also south of the Dāmodar river, where the famous Deshargarh seams have been worked by the Equitable Coal Company at Chaurāsi since 1902. The entrance of the Bengal-Nāgpur Railway in the Jharia field in 1904 and the subsequent extension of various loops and small branches, besides innumerable sidings from both Railway systems, the doubling of the line from Barākhar to Dhanbaid, the opening of the section of the Grand Chord of the East Indian Railway from Dhanbaid to Gomoh in 1907, have all facilitated rapid development, and at the present time it may be said that every part of the field, including the extension on the west towards the Rāmgarh Bokaro field which almost immediately joins on to the Jharia field across the Hazāribagh border, has been brought into close touch with the railway and by means of it with the outside world. The tendency, however, which was manifest in 1907 and 1908 to open out new collieries in this part of the field, and also in the continuation of the main field south of the Dāmodar, has for the time being been checked. From two concerns representing some half a dozen mines, working in 1891 the number of collieries in the district has grown to 281 in 1908, 222 in the Jharia field and 59 in the Rāniganj field, producing $6\frac{1}{2}$ millions and 650,000 tons respectively, or more than double the output of the Burdwan mines in the same year and nearly seven-twelfths of the total output of British India. The value at the pit's mouth represented over 2 crores of rupees or nearly $1\frac{1}{2}$ millions sterling, and the number of work-people employed amounted to an average of 72,000 persons daily.

Geology of the Jharia field.

The geology of the Jharia field is thus described by Mr. Hughes. Two series are developed,—the lower the Tālcher, and the upper the Dāmodar,—comprising a total thickness of 6,800 feet of strata, and forming a trough or basin, the beds usually dipping at right angles away from the boundaries, at varying amounts towards a common centre of depression. A large and well-defined fault, possibly continuous and directly connected with the one that forms the southern boundary of the Rāniganj field, cuts off the whole of the beds to the south, throwing them several hundreds of feet. The Tālcher series is easily recognised by those peculiar mineral characters which serve so readily to distinguish it, where developed in neighbouring localities A "boulder-bed" occurs at the base, and above it are flaggy green shales and mammillated sand-stones, the former of which may be considered the distinctive rocks of the series. The Dāmodar series is characterised by its containing coal, by the mineral composition of its beds and by the nature of its flora. In subdividing it, I have followed the classification and nomenclature first introduced by the Geological Survey of India in the Report on the Rāniganj field:—(1) Barākhar group at the base, (2) Carbonaceous shales with iron-stones, and (3) Rāniganj group. In the present instance, however, there is no evidence of decided unconformity between any of the above three groups, and my divisions are based entirely upon lithological grounds. Even this test, however, almost fails with respect to the carbonaceous shales with ironstones, as they are not developed to such an extent in the Jharia district as in the Rānīganj field; and in many instances the ironstones are altogether wanting in the shales, so that they wholly loose their distinctive character. No formation higher than the two above mentioned occurs, and the Pānchet rocks (the next in order of succession above the Dāmodar), which possess such a splendid development at a distance of only eighteen miles to the east in the Rānīganj field, have been removed from this district, so that no vestige of them remains. This phenomenon is no doubt in great part due to the fact that the southern boundary has not been thrown to the same enormous extent as that of the Rānīganj field, although connected with it; and that, therefore, the Pānchets were less protected and more easily swept away by the denuding forces that acted against them. The metamorphic series, composed mainly of gneiss and constituting the bottom rocks of the country, is represented by a large inlier in the neighbourhood of Dumra, which must have been an island in the old Tālcher sea at the time when the sedimentary substances which formed that group were being deposited, and doubtless furnished some of the material which we now see piled up against its old shores. The most common varieties of rock are syenitic and porphyritic gneiss, but another very prevalent form is a binary compound of quartz and felspar. The last element is very subordinate, and as the grains of quartz are by no means sharply crystalline, this peculiarity when the rock is much weathered,—and it occurs near the boundary of the coal measures,—often at first leads one to the very natural supposition that it is an unaltered silicious sandstone.

With the exception, then, of the middle series, coal is found at all depths in the Dāmodar series, the larger seams generally being at the base, while those occurring at the top are smaller. The excellence of the coal in the Rāniganj group of the Rانīganj field is well known; but in the Jharia field, although there are many seams in the upper series superior to some in the Barākhars, the finest coal and the freest from ash occurs in the latter.

Mr. Ward traced out altogether 17 seams upwards of 5 feet in thickness within the Barākhar group. In the main central area these measures dip at an angle very moderate from a miner's point of view of 10° to the south, whilst on the flanks east and west the dips increase to 30° and 40°. In nearly every case the seams are overlain by a roof of sandstone. The seams numbering 14a, 15 and 17 contain first-class coal; their characteristic thicknesses are 7½, 25 and 10 feet respectively. No. 14, which is a very fair coal, is unfortunately spoilt over large areas by intrusions of trap. Mr. Ward estimated the net quantity of coal of No. 13 seam which he considered among the best, at 730 millions of tons, of which 159 million tons are at depths less than 800 feet.

In the Barākhar series eighteen well-defined seams are now recognised, of which, according to Sir T. Holland, the upper eight seams include enormous supplies of good coal; such seams as there are of the higher beds of the Dāmodar series have for the most part yielded poor coal. "The two classes of coal present a well-marked and constant difference in the amount of moisture they contain; the older, Barākhar coals, both in the Rānīganj field and in Jharia, contain on an average about 1 per cent. of moisture, whilst the average for the younger coal of the Rānīganj series is 3·8 per cent. in the lower seams, and nearly 7 per cent. in the upper seams. There is a corresponding, but less marked, difference in the proportion of volatile hydrocarbons, which form a larger percentage of the younger coals than of those at lower stages in the Dāmodar series." (Sir T. Holland.)

The results of certain assays of coal and coke made by Mr. E. P. Martin and Professor H. Louis of carefully procured samples from the Jharia and Rāniganj fields are thus summarised by Dr. Watt. Composition.

Coal.	Fixed Carbon.	Volatile matter.	Sulphur.	Ash.	Moisture.	Lb. of water evaporated by 1 lb. of coal.
Jharia field (12 samples).	60 5	22·0	0·55	16·49	1·0	12·71
Rāniganj (4 samples).	52·31	31·43	0·47	14·10	1·68	12·88

Coke.	Carbon.	Sulphur.	Phosphorus.	Ash.	Moisture.
Jharia coke (9 samples).	75·16	0·65	0·17	24·64	0·48

Commenting on these results, Sir T. Holland observes: "The beds in which the coal is now being mined in the Jharia field were long ago correlated by the Geological Survey with the

Barākhar series of the Rāniganj coalfield, and it is interesting to notice that the low percentage of moisture recorded by Saise in the coal of the Barākhar series in the Rānīganj field is characteristic also of the Barākhar coal in the Jharia field. In the case of the Barākhar coal from the Rānīganj field the moisture amounted on an average to 1·0 per cent., whilst in the case of these Jharia coals the average for moisture is 0·90 per cent."

Method of working. The methods of working are at the time of writing in a transition stage. Up till very lately the miner, helped by the nearness of the coal to the surface, the slight inclinations of the seams and the excellent sandstone roofs above the coal, had been able to do his work with little knowledge or experience of real mining such as is known in England. Now that the workings are at lower levels and the profitable work of pillar extraction is being carried out, scientific mining is a necessity.

There are three methods in which mining is carried on in this area, (*a*) the coal is quarried, (*b*) brought to the surface along an "incline", or (*c*) raised up a shaft. Although no less than 88 mines were classed as quarries in 1909, yet as a matter of fact these have passed beyond the quarry stage and are worked by inclines from the original quarries. Inclines are open cuttings leading from the surface to the coal measures always near the outcrop. Usually they are furnished with rails up which tubs of coal are hauled. Pit shafts are all circular and used to be made by hand. In this way a depth of 60 feet through moderately hard sandstone could be reached in a month. Now there is a growing tendency to use machine tools for this work. The completed shaft has an unlined jagged surface save on the rare occasion when it goes through alluvium or faulty ground, but the guide ropes prevent any danger to the cages from the rough rocks.

When the shaft or incline has reached the level where work on the coal is to start, two series of galleries at right angles to each other (one series along the dip of the seam) are driven right up to the boundary of the area to be worked. All the coal is thus extracted except the pillars formed by the spaces between the galleries. These pillars support the soil above the coal and thus protect the workings. This method alone was employed in this field up till a short time ago. It involved the temptation to make the galleries as wide and the pillars as small as possible. In addition, the coal on the pillars being easy to extract, the coolies who are paid by the amount produced, naturally "robbed" the pillars whatever orders were in force. The excellent sandstone roof and the absence of explosive gas hid for some time the danger of these methods. Here and there, however, nature asserted herself and the weight of the strata has crushed out the weak pillars so that large areas, if not the whole of the mine, have been irretrievably lost. Such a system with 12 feet galleries and 12 feet pillars yields 70 per cent. of the coal, but the remaining 30 per cent. cannot be touched.

At present the tendency is to cut the galleries so that the coal in the pillars also may be extracted. With a view to this the galleries are driven 40 feet to 60 feet apart throughout the area to be worked. Then small galleries are driven through the pillars themselves, leaving slight columns of coal to support the roof. In time these columns are removed, working from without inwards until only the one nearest the remaining pillars is left, the roof meanwhile being supported by timber. The area of this pillar is then left, and sooner or later the roof falls in. Proceeding from the outer boundary of the property, the pillars are all extracted till the whole area is worked out. By this method quite 90 per cent. of the coal can be extracted, but great care is needed to guard against any workers being under or close to the roof at its fall.

For removing the coal dynamite is the explosive most in use. Blasting powder is used in only a few mines, but in many collieries all the work is done with picks as the coal is easily worked.

Owing to the absence of explosive gas, naked lights are used for lighting. Small kerosine oil lamps have quite replaced the indigenous *chirāg* formerly in use, but they make the atmosphere unpleasant because there is seldom adequate ventilation. In only a few collieries has any attention been paid to ventilation, but when deeper levels are reached this must be systematically taken in hand.

The method of conveying the coal from the place of extraction to the railway waggons is still with one or two exceptions very primitive As the coal is cut it is gathered into wicker baskets and carried on the heads of the coolies (generally women) right up to the surface, where it is stacked or tumbled at once into the railway waggons. In some mines the coal is deposited in tubs at the mouth of the incline, and these are pushed by hand along rails to the railway siding. In others the tubs are filled in the workings and hauled up the inclines by steam power, four to eight at a time, or raised up shafts in cages. The rails often extend a considerable distance under ground, but there is always a long lead along which the coal has to be carried by coolies.

As indicated above, manual labour still bulks largely in the working of mines. Machinery is, however, coming more generally into use, and in 1908, 94 out of 222 mines in the Jharia field and 11 out of 59 in the Rāniganj series were classed as worked by steam. In a few collieries only has electricity begun to take the place of steam-power, principally for pumping or driving new galleries, and it is probable that when the present depression in the industry passes and the demand for labour once more largely exceeds the supply, as was the case in 1907 and 1908, one or other of the various systems of mechanical cutting will be substituted for hand labour.

Labour. As in England, 100 years ago, the miners are still essentially an agricultural class. Almost all of them are cultivators who are attracted to the mines by the high and constant wages and find there the means to satisfy their landlord and moneylender. As yet there are no hereditary miners. A large number of the colliers are aboriginals, and for underground work Sonthals, Mundas, Oraons and Kols are probably the best workers. Semi-aboriginals and among them Bāuris are largely employed both above and below ground, but almost all the local castes, which go in for any form of manual labour, are now represented in the mines. In a few collieries a number of Pathans and Peshwaris are employed and are said to be the best workmen; coolies from Bilāspur are also imported. Employment is not confined to the cooly himself, but practically every member of his family can get work of some sort. Underground work is usually paid for at a fixed price per tub of coal, ordinarily 5 annas equivalent to about 7½ annas per ton. This rate includes not only cutting but loading into the tubs, but the latter part of the work is done by the cutter's family or other members of his gang; the latter also push the tubs to the main gallery from which they are hauled up the incline. In ordinary circumstances a man can cut from 2 to 3 tub loads of coal in a working day of 8 hours, but one of the chief difficulties in colliery management is to get the coolies to do a full day's work, and even the most energetic will not work more than five days in the week while at the colliery, and will ordinarily go to their own homes for all festivals, as well as during the marriage and cultivating seasons. Surface labourers and others who are not paid by outturn can earn four to five annas per diem, women two to three annas, and boys and girls of 10 to 15 years almost as much. The gross earnings of a family may therefore be considerable. Unfortunately the desire to earn more than suffices to feed him well and enable him to get drunk fairly frequently is generally absent, and from the colliery manager's point of view the classes of coolies, who really work hard while on the colliery, as for example many of the Sonthals, are as trying as the rest because their periods of absence in their own villages, where they go when they have amassed sufficient to pay off the moneylender and redeem a field or two, are the longest. Sunday afternoon, after the morning distribution of pay, witnesses a considerable exodus, strings of coolies may be seen crossing the Grand Trunk Road making different short cuts to their villages in Tundi and the Sonthal Parganas; on other days small parties may be seen making their way back to the mines after spending their earnings or celebrating their local festivals or preparing their fields or sowing, transplanting or reaping their crops according to the season. Strikes are unknown and serious quarrels, when they do arise, are settled by the miners leaving the collieries for their homes. As a rule the supply of labour is less than the demand, hence the Managers, to keep what they have, must treat their workers well.

The methods of the workers are still more or less primitive; the average cooly prefers to fill his tub in the easiest and quickest way that suggests itself to him, quite irrespective of whether the results of his want of method may be fatal to himself or others. One of the most frequent causes of fatal accidents is the practice of what is called "robbing pillars," the miner surreptitiously hacking at the pillar and filling a few baskets on his way to his appointed place, where the same amount of effort will result in a very much smaller outturn in coal. Apart from this cause of accident, and accidents due to other forms of sheer carelessness on the part of the labourers above and below ground, accidents are few, though the death-rate figures for recent years show that there is a tendency to an increase in this respect. The most fruitful source of serious accidents in English mines, explosions of fire-damp, is almost unknown, and in very few mines has it been found necessary, as yet, to insist on the use of safety lamps. The only serious accidents of this kind that have occurred in this district were at the Laikdih and Chánch mines in 1907 and 1908 respectively; both of these are in the Rāniganj field and are among the oldest worked in the district.

The largest concerns now working in the district are the East Indian, the Eastern, and Gopālichak Coal Companies, the Indian Collieries Syndicate, the Lodna Colliery Company, the Rānīganj Coal Association, the Reliance, Sijua, Standard, Bengal, Bengal-Nāgpur, Equitable and Bhālgora Coal Companies, all of which employed a daily average of more than 1,000 labourers during 1908. The majority of the above are managed by European firms; the chief Indian firm owning or managing collieries is that of Messrs. Laik and Banerji, which was as a matter of fact one of the earliest in the field in Jharia.

Inspection.

The headquarters of the Department of Mines in India was removed from Calcutta to Dhānbāid on the 20th April 1909, and besides the Chief Inspector, one of the three Inspectors of Mines is resident there. The whole of the Jharia field is included in Inspection Circle No. I, and the Rānīganj portion with part of the field in the Burdwan district is in Circle No. II, the dividing line being one drawn from Adra at mile 175 of the Bengal-Nāgpur Railway to Gobindpur at mile 169 of the Grand Trunk Road. On the Chief Inspector and Inspectors rests the whole responsibility of seeing that the rules framed under the Mines Act are complied with; inspections in connection with sanitary and other arrangements are also made from time to time by the Deputy Commissioner, Subdivisional Officer, and Civil Surgeon.

CHAPTER X.

MEANS OF COMMUNICATION.

Development of means of communication.

TILL within comparatively recent times the district of Mānbhum was very badly served in the matter of means of communication both by road and rail, but the last 15 years has seen a very considerable development.

In 1854, so far as can now be ascertained, the only metalled road was the then new Grand Trunk Road, 43 miles of which, from the 149th mile at the Barākhar Bridge to the 192nd mile at the foot of Parasnāth hill, lie within the district. Mr. Ricketts writing in that year refers also to fair-weather tracks, between Sili on the Rānchi border, through Purūlia and on to Bānkura, and from Purūlia through Raghunāthpur to Rānīganj, the terminus of the East Indian Railway. A road from Gobindpur, on the Grand Trunk Road, to Rānchi *via* Mahoar, about 4 miles north-west of Chās, and Gola in Hazāribagh, was also under construction. The alignment of the old Benares Road, which was not, however, metalled, passed through the district, from a point near Gaurāndi about 6 miles from the Bānkura border and 18 miles from Bānkura, to the Hazāribagh border, some 4 miles west of Chās. The semaphore towers still remain on commanding positions along this road to mark its previous importance as the direct military route between Calcutta and the North-West Provinces.

Between 1854 and 1874 Purulia had been connected by good, bridged (except for the Dāmodar river) and metalled roads with Barākhar (46 miles) and Rānchi, the Mānbhum portion of the latter road ending at the Subarnarekha river 35 miles west of Purūlia. The Chaibāsa Road, 40 miles in length, had been almost completed, and a direct road to Bānkura, about 28 miles, was under construction. Altogether it was at that time reported that there were 500 miles of road in the district, which, however, included at that time several Parganas which were afterwards transferred to Burdwan and Bānkura districts; within the present limits of the district the mileage was probably not more than

350, of which 215 only were under the management of the District Road Committee.

Roads. The latest schedules of the District Board show a total road mileage of 1,168 maintained by the District Board, besides 88 miles maintained by the Public Works Department. The whole of the latter, which includes 43 miles of the Grand Trunk Road and 35 of the Purūlia-Rānchi Road are metalled. Of roads maintained by the District Board 123 miles are metalled. These include 42 miles of the Purūlia-Barākhar Road which is a Provincial road, and some 26 miles of roads in the Jharia coalfield, besides various short lengths of Railway Station approach roads, and portions of several of the main routes. There are besides some 30 miles of roads, classed as unmetalled, in which the wheel tracks, two and a half feet wide, on each side of a central gravelled strip, three feet wide, are metalled. Of other unmetalled roads all the more important are surfaced with gravel, and more or less completely drained. Except on the Purūlia-Barākhar Road, the rivers and rivulets crossed are generally unbridged, but within the last few years causeways have been constructed over the beds of the smaller streams, crossed by the more important roads. The Dāmodar, the Katri, and the Khudiya rivers in the north of the district, the Gowai and Ijri in the centre, and the Kāsai, Kumāri and Subarnarekha in the south of the district are the only streams which cause any serious interruption to traffic; the Kāsai which runs within 3 miles of Purūlia makes communication with the whole of the south-eastern portion of the district very difficult during the rainy season, and its broad sandy bed is a considerable obstacle to traffic even in dry weather.

Railways. The East Indian Chord line was completed to Barākhar in 1858, and for the next 31 years communication with Calcutta and the outside world generally was *viâ* Barākhar or Rāniganj. In 1885 the Bengal-Nāgpur Railway Company started the construction of the Bilāspur-Asansol branch connecting their main Nāgpur line with the East Indian system, and this branch was opened in 1889. The line crosses the Dāmodar six miles south of Asansol, and for a distance of 83 miles traverses the district in a south-westerly direction, connecting Purūlia with Asansol, on the East Indian Railway, and with Sini and Chakrādharpur on the Bengal-Nāgpur Railway.

In 1894 the East Indian Railway Company extended their system from Barākhar to Jharia and Kātras, so opening up the Jharia coalfield area. Nine years later, in February 1903, the Kharagpur-Gomoh section of the Bengal-Nāgpur line was opened to goods traffic as far as Bhojudih, and in the following year for goods and passenger traffic as far as Mulkera, the complete length to Gomoh not being ready till January 1907, this affording another outlet for the products of the coalfield. In February 1907 the Grand Chord of the East Indian Railway, which practically doubled the existing line through the coalfield and gave a direct outlet towards the North-West Provinces and Bombay, was opened. The most recent addition to the railway system is the Purūlia-Rānchi line on the 2′-6″ guage, which was opened in February 1908; 36 miles of this railway lie within the district of Mānbhum, and afford an outlet for the grain and jungle products of the western portion of the district.

The collieries are served by a network of loops, branches, and sidings taking off from the main lines of both the Bengal-Nāgpur and East Indian systems, and the inter-connection of the two systems at Gomoh, Kātrasgarh and Jharia makes it possible for the colliery proprietor to despatch his coal to any part of India by the most convenient route.

Further extensions of the railway system are in progress or contemplated. A direct line from Pradhānkhunta on the Grand Chord to Pathordih at the extreme south-eastern corner of the coalfield is under construction, the intention being to relieve the congestion of eastward bound traffic which at present has to pass through Dhānbāid. An extension of the Bengal-Nāgpur system from Khānudih in the extreme west of the Jharia field, through the Bokhāro-Rāmgarh field in the Hazāribāgh district, is at present under survey. **Extensions of the railway system.**

According to the figures supplied by the Agents of the Railway Companies, there are at present some 300 miles of open line within the district, of which 230 are available for both passenger and goods traffic, the balance consisting of special colliery branches. Connected with the Bengal-Nāgpur system there are some 75 colliery sidings, and with the East Indian system no less than 160 with a total length of over 70 miles, and these are constantly being added to.

There are no canals or navigable rivers in the district. In pre-railway days the Dāmodar river was utilised during the rains for the despatch of coal, timber and other local products in small country boats or rafts, but the currents are so rapid and the bed so liable to changes that navigation was at all times difficult and dangerous, and now that railways provide safer and easier means of transport, practically no attempt is made to utilise this river. **Rivers.**

Ferries.

The District Board maintain ferries over the larger rivers during the rains, but the streams rise and fall with such rapidity that regular use cannot be made of them and the income obtained is very small.

Staging and Inspection Bungalows.

There are dāk bungalows at Purulia and Tulin on the Purūlia-Rānchi Road maintained by Government, and on this and the Grand Trunk Road there are staging or inspection bungalows at approximately every 10th mile. Bungalows and rest-houses are maintained by the District Board at the majority of the police-stations and also at convenient distances along all the more important roads. These are ordinarily in charge of chaukidars, but at Bhāga (Jharia), Kātras, Jhalda and Bāghmundi there are Khansāmas in charge.

Postal communications.

There are altogether 56 post offices in the district, and 258 miles of postal communication. The number of postal articles delivered in 1908-09 was 628,530, while the value of money-orders paid was Rs. 8,69,073 and of those issued Rs. 27,55,189. The number of savings bank deposits in the same year was 5,690, the amount deposited being Rs. 1,77,876. There are 11 postal telegraphic offices from which 25,688 messages were despatched during the same year.

CHAPTER XI.

LAND REVENUE ADMINISTRATION.

FOR purposes of Land Revenue Administration the district, as now constituted, is divided into 26 major estates, 24 permanently and 2 temporarily settled, besides 4 minor estates, consisting of Government camping grounds, let out from year to year. The revenue-roll also includes as a separate unit the demand in the shape of "police contribution" from one of the major estates (Pānchet). Besides these there are 25 "Digwāri" estates, the holders of 14 of which pay a small *panchak*, or quit rent (Digwāri cess) to Government, the remainder paying Road and Public Works cesses only. The roll of the district also includes some 32 revenue-free properties, of which, however, only 27 include land within the present district boundaries. DIVISION INTO ESTATES.

Of the revenue-paying estates Pānchet is by far the largest both in extent and in respect of the revenue demand; it includes no less than 19 out of the 39 Parganas which make up the district area, covering in all 1,650 square miles in this district besides some 250 to 300 square miles in the adjoining districts of Burdwan, Bānkura and Rānchi, and paying a gross revenue of Rs. 55,794 on account of land and Rs. 1,754 by way of police contribution, or Rs. 57,548 in all. The remaining Parganas of the district constitute each, with two exceptions, single estates; the exceptions are Nāwagarh and Pāndra, each of which, for reasons to be detailed later, is subdivided into 4 shares or *kismats*, each constituting a separate estate. They range in size from the county-like Barābhum (according to the new survey records, 635 square miles) to the petty manor of Torang, barely 11 square miles in extent. Pātkum pays the highest amount in land revenue, *i.e.*, Rs. 3,165, after Pānchet, and Torāng the least, being assessed at Rs. 235 only. The total land revenue of the district is only Rs. 84,000, a sum which represents barely one anna per acre on the estimated area under cultivation. The reasons for this light assessment are to be found in the conditions existing when the Permanent Settlement was made, of which some indication has already been given in the second chapter of this volume.

Probable origin.

The generally accepted theory is that in the earliest times the greater part of Mānbhum district was occupied by Bhumij or Munda communities, each of which was under the authority of a village head, styled Munda. Groups of about twelve villages, called *parhas* were presided over by a divisional head or Mānki; and the Government of the country was carried on by those two grades of headmen in village or *parha* conclave. No one can say precisely at what date this system was changed; but it was the opinion of Colonel Dalton, that "soon after the election of Phani Mukuta Rai as Rāja of the table-land of Chota Nāgpur Proper, the *parha* chiefs of Mānbhum followed the lead of the highland chiefs, and elected Rājas of their own, all miraculously nurtured foundlings, and all now claiming to be Rājputs." Even in Colonel Dalton's time there remained only one (the zamindar of Bāghmundi) who had the good sense to acknowledge his Mundāri descent, but the conclusion that "all originally belonged to the races amidst which they dwelt is more or less forced on us by their position, their various fables of origin, and by the fact that intermarriages between the different families are or have been usual". Not all, however, were of Kolarian origin, one at least (Mānbhum) was probably a Bāgdi, and those of the north of the district almost certainly Bhuiyā. Of Pānchet, the conditions in which were somewhat different when the British took over the government, and which had a recognised position in the latter part of the Muhammadan era, perhaps all that need be said here is that, though probably the origin of the estate or of its nucleus and of the family was similar to the rest, its emergence from primitive or semi-primitive conditions must have been much earlier. It is in the southern and western estates, Barābhum, Pātkum and Bāghmundi that the clearest traces of their origin in the regular Mundāri system are still extant. Thus the Bāghmundi estate is to this day made of five groups of villages, one held *khas* by the zamindar, the other four by Mānkis on small rentals fixed in perpetuity. The small adjoining estate of Torang is an instance of a single *parha* being treated at the Permanent Settlement as an independent estate; its zamindar is still entitled 'Mānki'. In Barābhum the present arrangement of the grades of ghātwals provides an exact parallel to the regular Mundāri system; the lowest grade or *tabedars* are the *bhuinhars* or original tillers of the soil, the village *sardārs* the Mundas, and the *taraf sardārs* the Mankis, whose *tarafs* correspond with the *parhas* of the Mundari system. In Patkum a similar division into *tarafs* existed at one time throughout the estate, the quinquennial papers for 1202 Fasli (1797 A.D.) referring specifically to 12 such divisions, and of these at least two survive, one the shikmi tenure of Naro, the other being at present described as held on a *Murāri* tenure, and its holder as a 'Manda' or *Mura*.

Elsewhere traces of the Mundāri village system survive in various forms, though for the most part the grouping of villages into *parhas* or *tarafs* has disappeared; this in the area which came more directly under the influence of the Pānchet Rājas may well have been due to deliberate action taken to break up the local organisations as a source of possible opposition to their own authority, and to the substitution of a system of petty semi-military, semi-police chieftains drawn from their own entourage and more under their direct control; to this theory the survival of a large number of *jaigirs* usually consisting of one or two villages, and for the most part on the outskirts of the estate, lends support. North of Panchet and of the Damodar river there are even fewer traces of the typical Mundari organisation; and assuming that the chiefs are Bhuiyā rather than Bhumij in origin and that the original home of the Bhuiyās was in the southern parts of Chota Nāgpur and the states adjoining where they had to give place to the invading Kols, it may be inferred that they had already their recognised chiefs when they arrived in northern Mānbhum, and that the constant necessity of resisting pressure from outside, the powerful states of Pānchet, Bīrbhum and Bishnupur being their near neighbours, was sufficient to counteract any tendency to lessen the power of their chiefs by the formation of smaller groups based on a communal system. The local traditions that the Jharia, Kātras and Nāwagarh houses were offshoots from the powerful Pālganj house in Hazāribāgh, and Pāndra and Nagarkiāri from Tundi, and that Pāndra was previously a distinct "Mallik" state conquered by a scion of the Tundi house, suggest at any rate that the development of these estates was rather from a centre than to a centre (as was apparently the case in the south), a difference due to their chiefs being immigrants obliged from the first to hold their own under conditions adverse to any return to their original tribal conditions.

It is claimed on behalf of Pānchet that prior to the British accession all the northern estates and several of those on the west also acknowledged the suzerainty of the Panchet Rāja. This claim is not, however, borne out by any specific historical facts nor by internal evidence except perhaps in the case of Jhalda, which is described by Mr. Sheristadar Grant as "a recent Suzerainty of Pānchet.

territorial accession to Pānchet", but even in this case there was no such absorption into the conquering Rāj as to raise any question as to its suitability for separate settlement with its proprietor, and though the then Pānchet Rāja was, as the old correspondence shows, quite ready at any time to file protests and petitions to higher authorities in regard to the manner in which the permanent settlement of his estate was effected. no mention appears anywhere of any claim to have any one of these estates settled with him. At the most his suzerainty, if it existed at all, must have been a nominal one, and can never have extended to interference with the internal arrangements of any of these estates.

The Permanent Settlement.

The Permanent Settlement was, therefore, effected with the hereditary chieftains or headmen of the various existing states or "Rājs" under circumstances which made it difficult, if not impossible, in most cases to fix the revenue with any definite reference to the value or the assets of the estate. As already noticed, there is no evidence to show that any of these estates, excepting perhaps Pandra, paid any regular revenue to the Muhammadan rulers, and it is probable that it was only on very rare occasions, if at all, that any of them were induced or forced to pay something in the shape of tribute, and when the British succeeded to the Dewāni of Bengal, Bihar and Orissa there was very considerable difficulty for many years in enforcing the authority of the new Government on the chiefs of the estates, who are variously described as banditti, robbers or "chuārs" in such literature as survives of this period. Of the manner in which the Permanent Settlement, and the temporary settlements which preceded it, the destruction of the district records in the mutiny, as well as the fact that parts of the district were settled from Midnapore, others from Rāmgarh, and others again from Bīrbhum, renders it impossible to give any very accurate account except in the case of Pānchet which will be referred to later. The general inference to be drawn from such facts as are on record is that the settlement was less of the nature of a settlement of revenue with an ordinary zamindar than the fixing of a definite tribute to be paid by a number of semi-independent border chieftains.

Barābhum.

This conclusion is illustrated by the little that is definitely known about the early arrangements in Barābhum which, with Mānbazar, was one of original Jungle Mahals or Western Jungles of Chakla Midnapore and attached to Orissa. In 1778 the Jungle Mahals were described as divided into two thanas, thana Balarāmpur and thana Jaunpur, Barābhum being one of seven Parganas attached to the former thana. These are described as "governed each by a zamindar, who is dignified among his ryots with the title of Rāja. These zamindars are mere free-booters, who plunder their neighbours and one another; and their tenants are banditti, whom they chiefly employ in their outrages. These depredations keep the zamindars and their servants continually in arms; for, after the harvest is gathered, there is scarcely one of them who does not call his ryots to his standard either to defend his own property or attack his neighbour's." Reference has been made in an earlier chapter to the military operations of 1767 and 1768, as a result of which Mr. Graham, Collector or Resident at Midnapore, and his Assistant, Lieutenant Fergusson, first succeeded in bringing these people to some degree of subordination and stipulated with them for an annual revenue of Rs. 22,000, instead of Rs. 1,200 formerly paid by them, and some years later, *i.e.*, in 1776 Mr. Higginson, Resident of Burdwan, settled the Jungle Parganas of the two thanas for Rs. 17,846. Of this settlement Mr. Higginson reported to the Council of Revenue on the 23rd November 1776 that the *jama* was based on the *bandobast* of the last and preceding years, excusing even "the Rasad or increase, which by the old settlement with Mr. Beber * becomes due in the present Orissa year 1184. This amounts only to Rs. 515-10 gandas, and I have thought it prudent to deduct it in order to begin by showing an example to the zamindars that Government's intentions were not founded on any other plan than to establish a certain reasonable tribute from their frontier zamindars on condition of their living peaceably and becoming faithful subjects, and I have the pleasure to tell you that when I made known to them the above sentiment they were unanimously pleased and satisfied with the settlement and conditions to be observed which I had proposed to them, in so much so that I flatter myself, unless unforeseen revolution happened to change the face of affairs, I do not believe that there will, in future, be occasion for the assistance of a single sepoy in any of the fifteen zamindāris which I have settled."

Form of agreement, 1776.

The revenue fixed in 1776 in the case of Barābhum was Rs. 829-15-9 sikka, equivalent to Rs. 885, which is the exact amount of the present Government Revenue. The form of kabuliyat executed by the Barābhum and other zamindars of the Jungle Mahals in favour of Government was as follows:—

"Article 1st. That we will annually pay our revenue to Government agreeably to last year's jama by the established kistbandi to the Tahsildar who may be stationed at our thanas.

* Edward Beber, Collector or Resident at Midnapore, 1770-1773.

"Second. That we will bind ourselves by a separate muchalka to forfeit all rights or pretentions to be continued in our zamindāris if we oppose or interrupt the march of the English Company's troops which may pass through our zamindāris. We will on the contrary engage to furnish them with guides and the necessary saranjāmis or articles of provisions at the established rates and our ryots shall not in this case desert from their habitations.

"Third. That we do likewise bind ourselves not to plunder the frontier Parganas adjoining to our several zamindāris, and if any of our chuārs should contrary to our agreement and will commit any depredations we will deliver them up for punishment to the Tahsildar in order to be tried by the Faujdāri of Midnapore.

"Fourth. That we will regard our present agreement with the Chief of Burdwan on behalf of the English Company as permanent and valid whilst our several zamindāris are continued to ourselves on the present mokrara jama, and all matters of dispute, which may exist either betwixt ourselves or others, we do hereby bind ourselves and heirs solely and truly to submit to the decision of the established mofussil courts of Adawlat with a right of appeal to the Honourable Governor-General and Council of Calcutta.

"Fifth. That we further engage not to assist in any shape or hold correspondence with Jagannath Dhal or any of the rebellious zamindars or enemies of the English Government under penalty of being dismissed from our zamindāris."

In return for this Mr. Higginson gave to each an *amalnama* or "deed of possession and encouragement that on condition of his duly executing the above agreement the right and privileges of his zamindāri are confirmed by the English Company to himself and his heirs for ever on the present fixed jama without being subject to any increase, māthat, salāmi, nazarana, or expenses of any denomination." The settlement is described in the contemporary records as a *mokurrari* or fixed settlement, and the Board declared that their chief purpose therein was not "to effect an aggrandizement of the revenue, but the settlement of an easy peshkush or quit rent, as an acknowledgment merely of the Company's sovereignty."

From the form of agreement alone it would seem obvious that the arrangement with the Barābhum zamindar was essentially of the nature of an agreement with a semi-independent State and not the ordinary agreement with a zamindar held responsible for the collection of the Government Revenue. Of the reasons which led the authorities to convert this agreement into a regular permanent settlement of revenue (if this can be said to have been actually done) there is no existing record; but it is obvious that no attempt was made, or, if made, was successful, to get from the zamindar any detailed account of his assets, or else that it was considered that the terms of Mr. Higginson's settlement in 1776 precluded any interference with the jama then fixed. The "Daul bandobast" of the Decennial Settlement, which is extant, throws no light on the question, and the so-called quinquennial papers of 1197 (1790), which were furnished by the zamindar in this as in other estates regularly settled in order that in the event of default and a portion of an estate having to be sold, material for allocation of the revenue might be available, contains nothing but a list of 149 villages without any distribution of the revenue.

Meaning of "Zamindar".

In 1787 Mr. Serishtadar Grant distinguished between three uses of the word Zamindar, which was often "indiscriminately applied to express an independent Rāja or sovereign Hindu prince, one made tributary by conquest, treaty or convention, or merely an officer of Moghul Government employed in the collection of the revenues with certain assigned jurisdictions, rights and privileges appertaining to the office." The former class, he adds, are obviously not meant when speaking of "the several classes of zamindars and landholders who are held responsible for the revenues of Government. Of the second he adds: "We have only to boast in all the British territories immediately dependent on Fort William, of the tributary Rājas of Cooch Behar, Nāgpur, Rāmgarh and Palāmau with perhaps a few more very inconsiderable landholders in different situations near hills or jungles, the nature and extent of whose jurisdictions must ever be imperfectly ascertained, while the intrinsic value of dominion affords no temptation for an entire conquest beyond the desire of imposing the fresh yoke of civilization, so that it is alone the third class or official zamindars which are now in question."

Two years earlier, in 1789, Mr. Shore had expressed his agreement with the Collector of Nāgpur that the regulations should not extend to his district, on the ground that "the amount received from this Pargana being more in the nature of a tribute than a revenue proportioned to the produce of the soil, the apportioning the present jama on the villages will be attended with great disadvantage to the Company in case any of them should be hereafter sold at the assessed rate for a balance, because it is well-known the country yields more than is paid by the Rāja, consequently his villages must be much underrated to bring them within the sum he now pays."

It seems possible therefore, if not probable, that the Chief of Barābhum was treated as a zamindar of Mr. Grant's second class, *i.e.*, one made tributary by conquest, treaty or convention, without either full political or proprietary rights and yet not a mere official Revenue Collector, and that the Permanent Settlement, though nominally applied to his estate, was not applied in its full scope, though at the same time he was not allowed the political rights acceded to the more important tributaries.

Other Estates. Of Mānbhum, the other Jungle Mahal of Chakla Midnapore, now included in this district, the settlement was on similar lines, the revenue or tribute fixed by Lieutenant Fergusson in 1767-68 was Rs. 316-2 and Mr. Higginson assessed it at Rs. 1,702-1-6, at which amount it still remains. It is stated in connection with the former settlement that it was only the inclusion of the Aongabad Pargana that enabled the zamindar to pay anything for that Mānbhum had never had any *jama*. All trace of the separate existence of Aengabad has been lost. Of Pātkum it is related by Lieutenant Fergusson that the zamindar, as also the zamindar of Singhbhum, actually asked to be put on a footing with their neighbours in the western jungles, as they were constantly oppressed by a neighbour who made a practice and trade of plundering and carrying off their effects, but Pātkum was eventually settled at a later date from Rāmgarh as probably also were Bāghmundi, Torāng and Hesla. In the case of Pātkum there is some reason to believe that in the earlier days of British administration this estate was treated as an appanage of Chota Nāgpur, as the Rāja of Nāgpur gave on one occasion as an excuse for non-payment of his tribute or revenue the fact that disturbances in Pātkum and Tamār had interfered with his collections. Bāghmundi was in a state of disturbance very shortly after the Permanent Settlement and was for a time forefeited to Government and it was only a portion of the estate which was in July 1799 restored to the proprietor Anand Singh, a fact which perhaps accounts for the revenue being proportionately much higher than in the case of the other southern estates, though much of the estate is even now unproductive. Jhalda and the adjoining group of estates including Jaypur, Mukundapur, and Begunkodar apparently gave considerable trouble, and for several years from 1782 Jhalda was the headquarters of an armed force whose Commandant, Major Crawford, was entrusted with the duty of restoring order and making a proper settlement of the revenues. The result of this closer attention is apparent in the comparative incidence of the revenue, Jhalda with an area of only 82,000 acres being assessed at Rs. 2,787 as compared with Rs. 3,165 for Pātkum with more than double the area, or Barābhum with only Rs. 885 for five times the area. Major Crawford was also called in to restore order in Jharia and Nāwagarh, and both these estates as also Kâtras pay a proportionately heavy revenue in consequence. Little is, however, known of the history of the settlement in these estates or the others in the north of the district; Tundi was probably, and Pāndra certainly, a fief of the great Muhammadan Raj of Bīrbhum; it is described in the 'daul' of the Decennial Settlement as taluk Pāndra, Pargana Birbhum, and there is evidence that for some 60 years previous it had paid a rent or tribute of Rs. 300 to the Rājas of Bīrbhum. The revenue fixed in 1791 was practically the same sum, Rs. 301-14 sicca or Rs. 322, and the inference to be drawn is that its real assets were not known, or that it was treated as a quasi-ghâtwāli tenure, and assessed to a mere quit-rent only. The assets were actually stated within 4 years of the Decennial Settlement to be either Rs. 5,000 or Rs. 20,000 per annum, the holder putting them at the former figure and the claimants to two-thirds share in a suit for partition at the latter.

PĀNCHET. Muhammadan era.

The settlement of the Pānchet estate was conducted on more regular lines. It had already come within the Muhammadan sphere of influence as early as 1632-33, and the entry in the Pādishānāma (B. i., page 317) that "Bir Nārāyan, zamindar of Pānchet, a country attached to Subah Bihar, was under Shah Jehan, a commander of 300 horse," implies that a fixed peshkush was paid to Delhi, and this fact is definitely stated in the improved Jama Tumāri of Sultan Singh 30 years later. The subsequent revenue history is related by Mr. J. Grant in his report on the revenues of Bengal, where he describes the 'Zamindari Raj of Pānchet' as a jungly territory of 2,779 square miles, situated within the portion of country ceded to the Company, and differing very little in circumstances of financial history or internal management from the adjoining district of Bishnupur. From the year 1135 to 1150 of the Bengal era (1728-43 A. D.), Rāja Garur Nārāyan was subject to an annual tribute of Rs. 18,203 for the fiscal division of Pānchet and the kismat of Shergarh. In 1743 an additional charge of Rs. 3,323 was levied from the estate in the form of the âbwâb chaut Marhatta imposed by Ali Vardi Khan. In 1170 (1763) the sarf-i-sikka, or impost imposed by Kasim Ali to cover losses on the exchange of coins, swelled the net assessment to Rs. 23,544. Muhammad Reza Khan in 1766 raised the demand to Rs. 30,000, but only Rs. 5,969 was in fact collected during that year. In 1771

Fifth Report, Madras edition, 1866, page 464.

a *zor talab* or compulsory exaction of Rs. 1,44,954, including a *saranjāmi*, or deduction for collection charges of Rs. 17,302, was established, and the demand enforced by military authority. In the 'gross medium settlement' of 1777 with Rāja Raghunath Nārāyan 'the actual payment of Pānchet, with the recent territorial annexation of Jhalda,' is stated at Rs. 69,027. Yet the amins had discovered sources of revenue amounting in all to Rs. 1,54,423 including *palātika* or revenue chargeable on lands that had been deserted by cultivators. Finally, in 1783, the total assessment of same territory amounted to Rs. 76,532, charged with a deduction of about Rs. 57,000 for collection expenses. This, Mr. Grant points out, gives little more to the sovereign than the original tribute, and 'leaves a recoverable defalcation exceeding one lakh of rupees, if we take the *zor talab* or compulsory exaction of 1771 as the proper standard.'

Early British era. The early days of British rule were marked by a constant struggle between the authorities and the zamindar who was persistent in neglecting to pay the revenue demanded, and from time to time portions of the estate were made over, generally unsuccessfully, to farmers. Eventually the Decennial Settlement was concluded in 1791 with the proprietor, and 18 months later, in March 1793, was made permanent and the revenue fixed at Rs. 55,794, this amount being arrived at by detailed assessment of every village within the zamindāri, with the exception of the numerous rent-free grants, of which a list had been furnished by the zamindar as early as 1771. According to this list and the later one of rent-paying villages returned at the time of the Decennial Settlement, the whole estate consisted of 1,280 villages, of which 404 only were *māl* or rent paying, and 49 *khās khamar* or retained in the zamindar's hands. The remainder included 388 Brahmottars, 68 Debottars, 2 Bhatottars, 2 Mahattrans and 180 Jaigirs held on quit-rents and variously described as *moghuli*, *talabi* or *panchaki*; $57\frac{3}{4}$ villages were set aside as 'Digwāri' and over 200 villages were entirely rent-free; these latter form respectively the Digwāri and revenue-free properties now borne on the district roll and will be referred to in more detail in a later paragraph; similarly the quit-rent tenures which were not, as these were, excluded altogether from the estate as settled with the zamindar, will be dealt with under the head of subordinate tenures. The extent of these deductions from the area of the estate capable of paying a full rental no doubt accounts very largely for the low incidence of the revenue fixed, which works out at almost exactly half-an-anna to the acre on the total area of the estate. The revenue then assessed was made permanent in 1793, the estate being, however, at the same time made liable to a contribution of Rs. 1,754 per annum as contribution towards the upkeep of the police, a demand which continues to the present day.

TEMPORARILY SETTLED ESTATES. Māhtā.

The origin of the two temporarily-settled estates of Mātha and Kailāpal is wrapped in a certain amount of obscurity. Mātha is traditionally a part of Bāghmundi, and it presumably corresponds with the portion of that estate which was not restored to Anand Singh in 1799. According to tradition, the zamindar or Thākur of Mātha is a descendant of Bayar Singh, a robber whose name was once a terror in Western Bengal, and who is credited with having killed a police Daroga sent to arrest him. Other attempts to arrest him failed, and on his death his son Paban Singh succeeded in 1212 B. S (about 1805 A. D.) in getting himself recognised, with the assistance of the police, as zamindar of Mātha. Bayar Singh is said to have had a private arrangement with the zamindar of Bāghmundi to abstain from raiding the latter's estate in consideration of an annual payment of Rs. 35 in cash and 35 maunds of *dhān*, while he on his part agreed to pay Rs. 60 as tribute to the zamindar. From Paban Singh the zamindar proceeded to demand a larger tribute, and eventually a claim was submitted to the authorities, when the Rāja of Pānchet intervened and claimed Mātha as his subordinate tenure. Proofs were called for from all three but none were forthcoming, and eventually it was declared that Mātha was held on an invalid lākheraj title. Nothing more was done, however, till 1860 when Colonel Dalton reported the facts to Government, and recommended settlement with the holder at a sadar jama equal to one-third of the gross rental, of which he declared himself to be in receipt, in the absence of any correct data of the real assets. This arrangement was approved and accepted by the holder Anand Singh Thākur, and the estate was resumed and settled with him at a sadar jama of Rs. 135-8. In 1881 a survey and settlement of the estate was made and the revenue was fixed at Rs. 647-5-9 for a period of 15 years which expired in 1896. The fresh survey then made showed that the gross assets had in the 15 years increased from Rs. 1,942 to Rs. 3,464, and it was proposed to resettle with the holder at half the latter amount; the proprietor, however, refused settlement on these terms and an attempt was made, which was not successful, to settle direct with the tenure-holders; eventually in 1904 the gross jama arrived at originally was reduced from Rs. 3,464 to Rs 2,849, and the holder was allowed to take settlement at one-third rates with effect from the date of expiry of the previous settlement and for a term of 12 years expiring in 1916-17. The present revenue demand is, therefore, Rs. 949-15-3.

Kailāpāl. The other temporarily-settled estate of Kailāpāl is a small pargana intervening between Barābhum and Mānbhum in this district, and Silda and Shāmsundarpur of the Midnapore and Bānkura districts, respectively. The predecessors of the original proprietary family appear to have been prominent among the robber chiefs of the jungle mahāls of Chakla Midnapore, and as early as 1784 there are references to a zamindar of Kailāpāl having been taken prisoner by a force deputed to suppress disturbances in this area. Apparently he was let off, and we hear later of one Shab Lal Singh who lived in the hills south of the village Kailāpāl and spent his time making inroads on the neighbouring estates, and extorting blackmail for the cattle and other valuables he carried off. Attempts made to arrest him failed, but he was eventually offered a pardon, and on his coming in, terms were settled between him and the neighbouring zamindars, by which, in consideration of his sparing their villages, he was allowed a few villages in each of the neighbouring parganas. These were eventually resumed through the civil courts, but Shab Lal and his successor apparently lived in comparative peace with their neighbours until the rebellion of Gangā Nārāyan Singh when the then zamindar Bahādur Singh's two brothers joined the insurgents. Bahādur Singh was called on to deliver them up, and eventually did so, and as a reward for his services Mr. Harrington, Collector of the jungle mahāls, is said to have declared his estate, pargana Kailāpāl, to be a rent-free service tenure. How it escaped assessment when the other estates in this area were assessed is nowhere stated, but presumably, though not specifically exempted from revenue, it was not actually assessed as being an entirely wild and uncultivated area; even at the time of Gangā Nārāyan Singh's raid it is stated that there were only 5 villages in existence within the estate. The validity of Mr. Harrington's grant was not called in question till 1860 when the zamindar put in a petition complaining that he had already lost many of his villages and that his neighbours of Barābhum, Silda, etc., were bent on filching away more. He prayed, therefore, that he might be assessed to Government revenue and be protected by Government from further encroachments. Colonel Dalton then reported the facts, and recommended resumption and, as in the case of Mātha, settlement with the holder at a sadar jama equal to one-third of the declared gross rental. These proposals were accepted and the estate settled on a revenue of

Rs. 196. The subsequent history of the estate is similar to that of Mātha; the revenue was increased on survey in 1881 to Rs. 1,021, and a fresh survey was made in 1896-97 resulting in an increase in the rental from Rs. 3,066 to Rs. 5,393. Settlement at half the gross rental was offered to the proprietor, but it was only with considerable difficulty that he was eventually induced to accept it, and the new settlement at a revenue of Rs. 2,696 did not come into effect till 1901-02. The term fixed is 15 years. Prior to this settlement the estate had passed out of the hands of the original proprietary family, the present settlement holder, who is also zamindar of Simlāpāl in Bānkura district, having acquired it by purchase in the civil courts.

In the case of both these estates the forest areas were excluded from the last settlement, all the waste lands and forests excluding portions sufficient for the requirements of the villagers being formally declared as Protected Forests under the Act.

LATER HISTORY. The rule of primogeniture.

The subsequent history of the permanently settled estates of this district, which with a single exception have remained in the families of the original settlement holders and are still nominally undivided, has been largely influenced by two special circumstances, *i.e.*, the strict rule of succession by primogeniture and the policy of exemption from the ordinary sale laws. The former existed from before British rule, and was no doubt due to the circumstances attending the origin and early conditions of the estates themselves, which obviously called for a central and undivided authority, which would rapidly have disappeared had the estate been divided on the occasion of every death of a ruler. The existing custom was recognised from the outset of British rule, an attempt to prove divisibility in the case of the Pānchet estate was defeated and the right of the then head of the family to settlement of the whole estate was recognised in spite of objection at the Decennial Settlement; and Regulation X of 1800 definitely affirmed and confirmed what had been the existing practice. The only variations are to be found in the Nāwagarh and Pāndra estates in the north of the district, and these exceptions when carefully examined are more apparent than real. In Nāwagarh, which was treated at the Permanent Settlement as four *Kismats* (two of six annas each and two of two annas), the origin of the division is said to be that one Fateh Singh in the early 18th century having no son divided the estate during his lifetime between himself, his brother and his uncle. The last-named divided his share again between his two sons, since which there has been no further ubdivision, and indeed, through failure of heirs, the 1st and 2nd *Kismats*, *i. e.*, 12 annas of the estate, have since 1872 been held in one interest. The strict rule of succession by primogeniture is now followed in all the divisions of the estate, but the very fact of a division being possible in earlier years illustrates the somewhat different origin of the estates in this area, which are, if tradition is to be believed, all offshoots of Pâlganj and the result of a series of partitions, Pālganj being first divided into Pālganj and Kātras, and the latter at a later date into Jharia, Kātras and Nâwagarh. The case of Pândra is different; it was treated at the Decennial Settlement as one and undivided and settled with Jadunandan Singh; a suit was then, however, filed by his two brothers claiming that they were entitled each to a third share, and a decree was given accordingly in 1795, apparently in error or through collusion, as an examination of the evidence in a later suit (1885) showed conclusively that there had been no partition prior to 1791 (as claimed by these persons) and that the strict rule of primogeniture had always been followed. A further division of one of the third shares was made in 1819 when the widow of one of the original claimants, having no son, divided her share between the others; the three *kismats* thus became four, the first and third of which are held by the elder branch of the family and the second and fourth by the younger branch. The former follow the rule of primogeniture strictly, and the existence of this rule has been affirmed on more than one occasion by the courts; in the latter, bound as they are by the decision of 1795 which gave them the property, succession follows the ordinary Hindu Law, and there are now a number of shareholders, though there has been no recognised partition of the shares.

Exemption of Estates from sale for arrears and debt.

The policy of exempting the estates of this district from the ordinary Sale Laws arose, according to Mr. Ricketts, who made a tour of inspection of the South-West Frontier Agency in 1854, from an unauthorised extension of the applicability of certain Government Orders, dated 13th October 1834, substituting attachment and adjustment of accounts for sale in the case of the Ghatwals or Tikaits of Khârakdiha in Hazāribagh. These orders, however, gave authority to the Governor General's Agent to extend the same method of settling accounts to "all the old hereditary landholders in the jungle estates for generations", limiting the application to cases of urgent necessity. In Mânbhum, at any rate, they were constantly applied and probably only regularised an existing practice, as no cases of sale either for arrears of land revenue or for private debts appear to have been effected between 1800 and 1834, and there can be no question that the fear that the transfer of ancient estates to persons other than members of the old families might lead to disturbances, must have been a very present one in Mânbhum in view of the circumstances attending the sale of Pānchet to one Nilambar Mitra in 1795, which was the occasion for the general rising, described in an earlier chapter, which was only put an end to by the annulment of the sale. The practice, as Mr. Ricketts found it, was to attach and bring under direct management such estates as were likely to default or to be sold up in the civil court on decrees for debts, etc., and this procedure was definitely regularised by the passing of the Chota Nāgpur Encumbered Estates Act VI in 1875 and the issue of notifications in 1878 and 1879 prohibiting sales in execution of civil court decrees without the previous consent of the Commissioner. The necessity of obtaining previous sanction was done away by a notification of 1880, but it was still left open to the Commissioner to step in and stay the sale and, where circumstances required such a course, forbid it altogether. A further extension of the system has been made by the recent amending Act which gives the Deputy Commissioner power in certain circumstances to file *suo motu* an application for protection of any estate. At the same time it is more definitely laid down that the holder of an estate so exempted must belong to a family of political or social importance, or if this is not so, Government must be satisfied that it is desirable in the interests of the tenantry that the estate should be protected.

The Encumbered Estates Act.

The result has been that there have constantly been several estates under Government management; thus, when recommending in 1834 the application of the Khārakdiha orders for general application, the Agent stated that "the necessity was urgent in the case of five or six zamindars of the Mānbhum division particularly those of Jhalda, Mānbhum and Chātna who were so deeply involved in debt that nothing but the adoption of some plan, similar to the one now recommended, can possibly prevent the sale of every village in their estates." In 1854 Mr. Ricketts found no less than 9 zamindāris, 2 Shikmi Mahals (Mānki tenures), 1 Ghātwāli, and 5 rent-free holdings under attachment, and of the zamindāris one had been attached since 1837, another since 1839, and a third from 1842. Forty-two years later, in 1896, 11 estates were being administered under the Encumbered Estates Act, including the four largest in the district, *i.e.*, Pānchet, Barābhum, Pātkum and Mānbhum, and comprising nearly three-quarters of the district area; in 1909 there were 7 estates, *i.e.*, Mānbhum, Pātkum, Pāndra (all four *kismats*, held in two separate interests) and Torāng, one Shikmi zamindāri, Naro, one Mānkiāri tenure, Kalimāti, one Ghātwāli tenure, Tinsaya, and one Jaigir, Bharāmahal, covering in all rather more than one-fifth of the district area. The statistics of the district show that almost every major estate besides several Shikmi, Jaigir, Ghātwāli and other subordinate tenures have at one time or another been attached or brought under management as encumbered estates, and so protected from sale or dismemberment; the few major estates which have escaped have done so for special reasons, as, for example, the fact of their being managed by the Court of Wards for long periods, or in more recent years having received unexpected additions to their revenue through coal settlements.

The one unfortunate exception to the general rule which has preserved these estates to the original families is that of Jainagar, which was sold in execution of a civil court decree in 1866 and purchased by the Court of Wards on behalf of the zamindar of Jharia, then a minor. The reasons which led to the ordinary practice being departed from in this case are not now traceable, but according to local tradition the zamindar of Jainagar treated the various processes of the civil court preliminary to the sale with such contempt that he entirely alienated the sympathies of the then Deputy Commissioner. Another estate has suffered dismemberment by private sale, half of the Mukundapur estate having been sold to the zamindar of Jaypur by private treaty; no partition of the shares has, however, been made.

Revenue-free properties. Of Revenue-free properties there are 32 on the district roll, all lying within the ambit of the Pānchet zamindāri and having their origin in the rent-free grants already referred to. The majority of them are small, consisting of a village or at most two or three villages, but two are of considerable size, *i.e.*, one of 14½ villages, which constitute a Debottar grant to the family gods of the zamindar and are recorded in his name, the income therefrom being devoted to the maintenance of the various family deities, their shrines and priests; the other also a Debottar consisting of 57½ villages dedicated to the upkeep of the worship of Keshab Rai, a deity belonging to the Gurus or spiritual guides of the zamindars of Pānchet, who live at Bero in pargana Chaurāsi. Over and above this large revenue and rent-free grant, the Mahants of Bero have at various times received other villages both from the Pānchet zamindars and from others, and their property is now a considerable zamindāri in itself, within which, in imitation of other landholders, subordinate tenures of all kinds including even Patni Taluks have been created.

The position of the Digwāri estates, 25 in number (of which, however, two lie within parganas Shergarh and Mahishara, now belonging to Burdwan and Bānkurā, respectively) is somewhat difficult to define. All of them are within the ambit of the Pānchet estate and they correspond with the 57¾ villages which were declared as Digwāri and their assets excluded at the time of the Permanent Settlement, with the addition of two villages in parganas Mahāl, which are admitted as Digwāri though not reported as such by Lala Kanji, Tahsildar of Pānchet, who was examined in detail on the subject of police tenures in this estate in the year 1799. No revenue is, therefore, paid on account of any of these holdings, but the holders pay a cess variously known as 'Digwāri' or 'Road patrol' Cess direct to Government, amounting in all to Rs. 798, and varying from as much as Rs. 122 for four villages in Parganā Chaṛrā to Rs. 6-6-7 only for two villages in Domurkonda. A similar demand is levied from the zamindars of the Jharia, Kātras, Nāwāgarh, Nagarkiari and Pandra estates and the gross demand, Rs. 1,258, constitutes what is known as the Road Patrol Fund, administered by the Police Department. Strictly speaking, these Digwāri villages are neither estates nor revenue-free properties nor yet ordinary tenures, intermediate between the zamindar and the actual cultivator; the Digwārs are appointed by Government, and are liable to dismissal for non-performance of their duties, but ordinarily the succession goes from father to son. They are essentially, therefore, service tenures held directly under Government, and distinguished from others in the district by the fact that the villages assigned to them are definitely outside the Permanent Settlement though within the limits of the parganas settled as the Pānchet estate. Digwāri estates.

Subordinate tenures are in Mānbhum both numerous and of considerable variety; the following is a description of the more important classes. SUBORDINATE TENURES.

The *Shikmi Taluk* or *zamindāri* ranks first in local estimation, though only one tenure legally recognised as such now exists, *i.e.*, that of Naro in the zamindāri of Pātkum which is protected from liability in the event of the latter estate being sold for arrears of revenue by Regulation VIII of 1793, though its origin is undoubtedly development out of a "Mānki" or divisional headman's tenure under the Mundāri system rather than a mere transfer of a portion of the Pātkum estate by the zamindar, subject to payment of its share of the Government revenue. Attempts have been made to establish in the courts that the great ghātwāli tenures of the Barābhum estate are *Shikmi Taluks.*

shikmi zamindāris, but this claim was disallowed in a suit to which Bharat Singh, Taraf Sardar of Satrakhāni, the zamindar and Government were parties.

Patni taluks. *Patni Taluks* with their subordinate dar-patni and se-patni tenures, as defined in Regulation VIII of 1819, are, strictly speaking, confined to the Pānchet estate, to which the Regulation was not extended until some time after 1854, though many of the *taluks* date from a much earlier period. The system is not, however, confined to this estate. Small patnis exist in many of the others, and nearly half the estate of Barābhum was leased out in patni to Messrs. Watson & Co. (represented now by the Midnapore Zamindāri Company) in 1883. In such cases, however, if rents are not duly paid, the procedure prescribed in the Regulation is not followed, the zamindars realising the arrears under the ordinary rent laws. In Pānchet the number of patni taluks is very large, and some of them are of very considerable extent; altogether it is estimated that more than half the estate is held under patni leases, and nearly one quarter under other forms of permanent lease. The system undoubtedly spread from the adjoining estate of Burdwan, and was here, as there, a convenient method of raising funds to meet the zamindar's present and pressing necessities at the expense of his descendants. Since 1895, when the estate was last brought under management under the provisions of the Encumbered Estates Act, no fresh leases of this kind have been granted, and from time to time defaulting patnis have been bought in by the proprietor. It is obvious, however, that those which are most valuable by reason of their low patni rental and high *mufassil jama* are the least likely to come into the market, and the chances of materially increasing in this way the area under direct management are but small.

Mānkiari and Murāri. *Mānkiāri* and *Murāri* tenures have already been referred to as survivals of the old Mundāri Village System, under which each village had its "Munda" or "Mura" and each group or "parha" of 12 villages or so its 'Mānki' or divisional headman. The permanently settled estate Torāng, as well as the Shikmi tenure of Naro above described were probably both in origin 'parhas', and similar tenures, four in number, survive in the Bāghmundi estate, their holders being still known as 'Mānkis'. Their tenure is a heritable one, the succession being governed by primogeniture, and they pay to the zaminder a small quit-rent only. The *murāri* tenure as now existing is distinguished from *mānkiāri* in name only. The conditions are exactly the same, and though strictly speaking a 'Mūra' or 'Munda' should have only a single village, those now recognised in the Bāghmundi Pargana hold several villages; they are, however, for the most part subordinate still to the Mānkis, and not directly under the zamindar. In Pātkum there are also 'Muras' who hold single villages, but their exact status has still to be defined; the zamindar does not admit their claims which usually extend over the whole village including the jungles; and in a number of instances he has succeeded in getting the courts to hold that they are mere *ijārādars* and liable as such to ejectment and enhancement. Others still obstinately assert their rights or supposed rights, and the decision of the rival claims will be one of the most difficult problems of the settlement operations now in progress.

The commonest form of hereditary tenure at a low rent fixed in perpetuity is the *mukarrāri* or *mokrāri*; these are found in almost all estates and are most numerous perhaps in the Mānbhum and Bārabhum estates in the south-east; they vary in extent from several villages to a few acres of land; the latter, however, are more strictly raiyati holdings at fixed rents, and the term as properly applied usually covers the grant of a village or a specific share or portion thereof. The rent settled is usually a comparatively low one, the settlement being made on payment of a considerable *salāmi* or bonus, varying in amount from 10 to 15 years' purchase of the rental. *Dar-mokrāris* are created on similar terms by the larger mokrāridars. ***Mokrāri.***

The tenures known variously as *moghuli*, *panchaki*, or *talabi* Debottars, Brahmottars, etc., take rank among the hereditary tenures at a fixed rent not liable to enhancement, but except in respect of the quit-rents payable their nature is in every respect the same as the *lākhirāj* or rent free tenures bearing similar names. The origin of the qualifying names, *moghuli*, *panchaki*, and *talabi* is somewhat obscure, and it is difficult to make any distinction between the terms of the different tenures to which they are attached. *Panchaki* and *moghuli* quit-rents are invariably very small, and *talabi* usually so, though it is commonly said that *talabi* implies a more substantial rent. According to Professor Wilson (Glossary of Legal Terms) the term *panchaki* denotes lands originally rent-free but later subjected to a quit-rent and thence termed *panchaki lākhirāj*, and this description probably applies accurately to grants of this nature in Mānbhum. ***Panchaki Brahmottars, etc.***

According to the holders *moghuli* was the term used for the rent or quittance their predecessors had to pay to the Moghul Emperors, but this interpretation cannot be historically accurate; others say the word is a corruption of *mangali* signifying payments made as tokens of blessing by Brāhmans to kings and emperors in consideration of offices or lands granted them. *Talabi* means little more than rent-paying, and *betalabi* is the regular word used to distinguish rent-free grants of a similar nature. The large number of these tenures, which already existed in the Pānchet estate at the time of the Decennial Settlement, has already been noticed, and the explanation is no doubt to be found in the somewhat ambiguous position of the zamindar whose elevation to the dignity of Chattri Rajput necessitated the employment of many priests and Brāhmans, and the propitiation of various Hindu deities. Similarly in the other estates grants of this kind, usually absolutely rent-free, have been numerous in more recent times.

Ijāra. All the above are definitely tenures of a permanent nature and held in a fixed rate of rent and usually heritable and transferable; the *ijāra* which has now to be described is more complex and difficult to define, the term being applied not only to mere temporary lease-holders or collectors of rents but also to headmen of villages, who have held the post of *ijārādars* possibly for generations. Landlords claim that *ijārādars* are removeable at will or on the expiry of their lease, but in practice it is usual to find them holding without objection for years after their leases have expired, and resisting successfully efforts made to oust them. In many estates a distinction is made between *miādi*, that is, appointed for a term of years, and *bemiādi ijārādars*, but even in the case of the former the extensive rights claimed by the holders are seldom now admitted.

The common features of almost all *ijāras* are the fact that the *ijārādar* is supposed to collect the rents of the tenants on behalf of the landlord, and that as remuneration he gets either a percentage on the total demand, or else cultivates on a privileged rent or rent-free what are known as the *mān* or *khās* lands: occasionally he gets both cash and land. The regular *miādi ijārādar* is a mere *thikādar* with little interest in the village beyond the screwing out of the tenants the largest possible amount within the term of his lease, at the end of which the *ijāra* is ordinarily let out again to the highest bidder. In the *bemiādi ijāra* the *ijārādar* gets, until the landlord discovers them, and can force on him a larger demand, the benefit of all new lands assessed; he frequently claims and succeeds in asserting his sole right to make new settlements, and also himself to bring under cultivation without additional payment to the landlord extra lands, and ordinarily where there is jungle he takes to himself any profits there may be from it. In fact, he sets up to be what in many cases he no doubt originally was—the village headman of the Mundāri organisation, and though he may admit the landlord's right to raise the *ijāra jama* he resists any attempt at frequent or excessive enhancements, and as he has, as a rule, the whole village at his back, and the landlord no papers to show the previous extent of cultivation or the exact terms on which the *ijārādar* holds, he is more often than not successful. Such *ijārādars* are still common all through the north of the district, and almost universal where there are Sonthals; elsewhere many of the old headmen have been ousted by fair means or foul from the post and the *ijāra* made over to outsiders of the *miādi* type: this is especially the case when subinfeudation has been excessive as in the Pānchet estate, the petty *mokrāridar* or *darmokrāridar* naturally resenting the intervention of any privileged person between himself and his comparatively few tenants. At the same time many of the old *ijārādars* have themselves become *mokrāridars*, and their interests having ceased to be with the tenants against the common foe, the superior landlord, they have become themselves petty landlords instead of village headmen in their manner of dealing with the tenants. One of the most important results anticipated from a survey and settlement is from the point of view of the *ijārādars* and tenantry, the giving of a secure title to such headmen-*ijārādars* as survive, and from the point of view of the superior landlords the definition of the exact rights of *ijārādars* of all classes, and the simplification of the procedure for securing to the landlords a proper proportion of the additional profits of the villages.

Maintenance tenures. A very important class of tenures consists of the maintenance tenures or grants of land for the support of the younger members of a Rāja's or zamindar's family, known by the general name of *khorposh*. The necessity for these grants follows from the rule of succession by strict primogeniture, provision having to be made by the head of the family for his younger brothers as well as for more distant relations. The practice differs slightly in different estates, but generally speaking 2nd and 3rd sons are entitled by family custom to grants of land, while others may get either land or a cash allowance. These grants are, generally speaking, resumable on the death of the grantor or grantee, but in ordinary cases a new Rāja would not resume the *khorposh* grants of his father's younger brothers without making them fresh grants or providing for them in other ways. In Barābhum and Mānbhum the next younger brother of the reigning chief is called the Hikim; there is a special *khorposh* called the *Hikimāli* which passes on the death of one zamindar from the uncle to the next younger brother of the new chief. Similarly in many estates there are allotted villages which form the *khorposh* of the wife of the zamindar; these similarly pass on his death to the wife of his successor. Custom only requires that maintenance grants should be given to persons within a certain degree of consanguinity, and consequently, as the grantees become more and more distant from the ruling chief, the grants are proportionately reduced until eventually the heirs of a *khorposhdar* become little more than ordinary cultivating raiyats. It is not, however, uncommon in the case of distant relations for small grants at fixed rents (*mokrāri*) to be substituted for regular *khorposh*, and in some cases, through undue favouritism or for other reasons, members of now distant branches of the family are found in possession of comparatively large properties on patni or other secure permanent title.

Cultivating tenures. The distinction between superior tenures and the tenure of the ordinary cultivating tenant is not a very definite one. As already stated, there are many *mokrāri* tenures of small extent of which the holders should be classed as raiyats rather than as tenure-holders, and the same is the case with the *nayābādi*, *jangalburi*, *jalkar*, *jalsāsan*, and *ahriat* tenures, all of which are essentially and by origin raiyati or tenant holdings to which special conditions attach, though not infrequently the areas so held are in excess of what the grantee could possibly bring under cultivation without inducting other tenants.

The *nayābādi* tenure is self-explanatory; permission is given by the zamindar to bring new land under cultivation; the terms vary in different parts of the district, but the more usual are that the tenant should hold the whole area so settled on a small quit-rent for five or seven years, and that at the expiry of that period the area brought under cultivation should be assessed at the ordinary rates, and that ten-sixteenths of the rent so arrived at should be the rent payable by the tenant. Fresh terms would at the same time be arranged for the area, covered by the original lease, but not by that time brought under cultivation.

Jalkar and *jalsāsan* tenures may be distinct from or combined with a *nayābādi* lease, the essential condition on the tenant's side being that a tank or reservoir should be constructed, from which the land to be brought under cultivation, or other land already cultivated, can be irrigated. Usually the actual land on which the tank or reservoir is to be constructed, and a small area attached to it is given on a small quit-rent fixed in perpetuity, the remainder of the area taken up being on ordinary or else on *nayābādi* terms.

Ahriat tenures are practically identical with *nayābādi*, the name being derived from *ahra* an embankment, and having reference to the necessity for levelling, terracing, and embanking essential before land can be made suitable for rice cultivation.

A *jangalburi* tenure is, as its name implies, a clearing lease usually of a specific area of jungle; such tenures in this district are usually of ancient date, and are held on a fixed quit-rent; in some cases the rent is settled on similar terms to those usual in the case of *nayābādi* tenures.

Of ordinary cultivating tenants the vast majority have either by law or by custom settled occupancy rights, and of these again a comparatively small percentage are entitled under the Chota Nāgpur Tenancy Act (introduced into the district in December 1909) to the special rights of original settlers or descendants of original settlers (*khuntkatti*). Practically the only classes of tenants who are not customarily treated as occupancy raiyats are those who hold on produce rent, and who are in fact rather servants than tenants.

Rent-free grants for religious or charitable purposes.

Of rent-free grants for religious or charitable purposes those which were recognised as having been made prior to the Permanent Settlement were treated as revenue-free properties; the others of later creation are of a similar nature and similar also to those which bearing the same names are subject to a small quit-rent. The forms taken are either (1) *Debottar*, grants of land for the worship of idols, or of a particular idol; the holder for the time being is the mahant or priest attached to the worship of the idol in question, and he is in the position of a trustee; (2) *Brāhmottar*, lands given for the support of Brāhmans; large numbers of these grants were made by chiefs of aboriginal descent, who aspired to be pure Hindus, in order to induce Brāhmans to settle within their territories; (3) *Bhātottar* or grants for the support of Bhāts, who record genealogies; (4) *Vaishnavottar*, or grants for the support of the worshippers of Vishnu; (5) *Mahattran*, or lands granted for services by persons other than Brāhmans; (6) *Pirottar*, or lands given for the worship of Muhammadan saints. Of the last class there are very few examples in the district.

All these grants are of a permanent nature, and are heritable and transferable, though in certain cases the transfer is said to be limited by the requirement that the grant must not be diverted to purposes other than that for which it was created. There are, besides these, other rent-free tenures which are neither permanent nor transferable, but these are more strictly classed as service tenures.

SERVICE TENURES.

Of the service tenures of Mānbhum there are, according to Sir W. Hunter, ten classes, of which seven are major and three minor. A more distinctive division would be into police and zamindāri service tenures. Among the former he enumerates the Jaigir (confined to Pānchet), the Digwāri, the Naib Digwāri, the Sardar Ghātwāli, the Sadiyāli, the Ghātwāli, and the Tabedāri. To all of these the general term "Ghātwāli" tenures is ordinarily applied, and their importance is such, and their history and incidents so full of difficulty that to include any detailed account of them in the present chapter would make it inconveniently lengthy; for a full account, therefore, of these interesting tenures, the reader is referred to the appendix to this volume.

Pānchet Jaigirs.—The jaigirs of Pānchet were excluded from the general survey of ghātwāli tenures which was made in the years 1880-1883, as previously to that date it had been decided that their services were not worth retaining: their exact extent and area is not, therefore, known; 160 villages were shown in the village list of 1771 as jaigir, and within the present limits of the district there are 52 distinct recognised tenures of this class having lands in 99 villages, for which rent is paid to the Pānchet zamindar. Their chief features are that they are hereditary, impartible, and non-saleable for arrears of rent.

Digwārs.—The Digwārs of the parganas included in the Pānchet estate have already been described. Similar tenures are found in the Jharia, Pāndra, and Jhalda estates, the holders of which, however, are liable to the zamindar for small quit-rents. Begunkodar has, instead of Digwārs, Sardārs who are in no respect different from the Digwārs of the adjoining estate of Jhalda except in name, and in the Mānbhum estate the terms appear to be interchangeable. Ordinarily speaking, a Digwār has one or more whole villages as his tenure, and has a subordinate staff of Naib Digwārs, Sardārs, and Tabedars, with whose assistance he is supposed to police the whole pargana or estate, or in some cases some specific part of it; his powers are usually those of a head constable.

Sardār Ghātwāls.—Sardār Ghātwāls or *taraf* Sardārs are found in Barābhum and Pātkum only, where they may be said to take the place of the Digwārs of other parganas. Their tenures are of considerable extent, the four major *tarafs* of Barābhum including from 28 to 75 villages each. The majority of the villages are held directly by Sadiyāls or Sardārs who pay nothing more than a small quit-rent to the *taraf* Sardār, but each of the latter has several villages under his direct control. His police powers are those of a Sub-Inspector in the case of the larger *tarafs*, and of a head constable in the case of the others, and he is supposed to exercise control over the large force of subordinate ghātwāls within his *taraf*.

Sadiyāls.—The Sadiyāls are intermediate between the *taraf* Sardār and the village Ghātwāls; they are not mere rent collectors or assistants of the former, but in Barābhum at any rate are to the village sardār what in Munda areas the Mānki or head of a *parha* or group of villages is to the Munda or headman of a single village, and the *taraf* Sardār is himself only an overgrown Mānki or Sadiyāl.

Village Sardārs.—The Sardārs or village Sardārs are the ghātwāls proper of Sir W. Hunter's classification; in Pānchet and the other northern estates they are found subordinate to the Digwārs in Barābhum and Pātkum to the *taraf* Sardārs; in Kailāpal, Begunkodar, and for the most part in the Mānbhum estate independent. Their tenures consist either of a whole village or of a definite part of a village, and their jurisdiction in any case extends to the whole village, and is confined to it.

Tabedars.—Below them and directly under their control are the lowest grade of ghātwāls, *i.e.*, the Tabedars, of whom there may be from one or two to as many as twelve or even twenty in a village. As their name implies, their position is more or less of a menial one, and on their shoulders fall the whole or the bulk of the police duties actually required of the ghātwāli force. These include the manning of a number of police road posts, the patrolling of the roads, the going on rounds at night, the escorting of prisoners or of informants to the police station, or the courts. Many of them have considerable holdings for which they pay a nominal quit-rent to the village sardār, but in a large number of cases the land held is now barely adequate for their support, more especially where, as is often the case, it is let out to cultivating tenants on inadequate rents.

Ghātwāls of all grades are liable to dismissal and loss of their service lands for misconduct. On a vacancy occurring from death or other cause the son or next male heir is ordinarily appointed, and to this extent the posts and tenures are hereditary. The ghātwāl for the time being has no power to alienate any part of his tenure, and the approval of the Deputy Commissioner is required for any settlement of a permanent or semi-permanent nature; in regard to jungles and minerals the working rule is that the ghātwāl has the right to use but not to waste the resources of his holding or tenure; he may not use his tenure in such a way as to reduce its value to his successors.

Down to the year 1903 ghātwāli tenures were not saleable either for arrears of rent, or for any private debt, but in March of that year, section 5, paragraph 1 of Bengal Regulation XXIX of 1814 (a regulation for the settlement of certain mahals in the district of Bīrbhum, usually denominated ghātwāli mahals) was extended with some modification to Barābhum, and these tenures were thus made, in certain circumstances, saleable for arrears of rent and cesses. During the succeeding three years a number of tenures were thus allowed to go to sale, including one of the four great *tarafs*. Since then, however, the policy has been discouraged, and in no case has the Commissioner sanctioned a sale. Outside Barābhum, where the Regulation has not been extended, the ghātwāli tenures are still exempt from liability to sale.

Excluding the Pānchet jaigirs there were demarcated in 1883, at the time of the ghātwāli survey, no less than 590 tenures covering an area of 408 square miles and supporting a force of 1,974 ghātwāls of all classes, made up of 12 sardār ghātwāls, 40 digwārs, 23 naib digwārs, 11 sadiyāls, 504 village sardārs and 1,384 tabedars. Of the tenures no less than 498, and of the ghātwāls 1,606, were in the three estates of Barābhum, Mānbhum and Pātkum.

Minor service tenures. The three minor tenures are (1) *Goraiti*, a grant of land made to the village *gorait*, who is the messenger or peon of the landlord. It is his duty to assist in the collection of rent by summoning the tenants when required to attend on the tahsildar or at the tahsildar's or landlord's cutchery, and also to keep the landlord informed of what is going on in the village such as marriages, transfers of lands, cutting of trees, and any other of the numerous small matters which warrant the levy of a cess, or the demand for a *salāmi*, or a cash payment. The *gorait* is frequently a substantial tenant, and in lieu of a special grant of land he will often in such cases merely get a remission of part of his rent. (2) The *lāyāli* is a grant of land to the *Lāya* or village priest; it is to be found in most, if not all, aboriginal villages; the post is ordinarily a hereditary one, and the land passes from father to son. (3) *Chākran* grants are ordinarily petty grants to servants in the zamindar's employ, or to potters, barbers, smiths, washermen, and others who do menial service for the landlord. The grants are essentially conditional on the rendering of services and therefore resumable; in many cases, however, though the services have been dispensed with or are no longer demanded, no attempt has been made to resume.

APPENDIX.

A NOTE ON THE POLICE TENURES IN MĀNBHUM.

Police tenures in Mānbhum.

THE subject of police and quasi-police tenures in Mānbhum is one which bristles with problems, and the literature relating to these is voluminous, much of it hidden away in reports and office notes which are not easily get-at-able. The object of the present note is to collate so far as possible the main facts, and at the same time to state briefly the main theories and inferences based thereon as to the origin and nature of the different forms of tenure and the main differences between them. The importance of the subject will be evident from the fact that, exclusive of jaigirs, the holders of which are no longer treated as liable to render service to Government, though this was the case till comparatively recent times, there are in all 591 tenures of this kind scattered over 25 out of the 39 parganas which make up the district, and that these tenures covered in 1883, when they were surveyed in detail, an area of 785,192 standard bighas or 408 square miles, nearly one-tenth part of the district, and were held by no less than 1,974 ghātwāls, a term which is somewhat loosely applied to all classes of rural police, other than chaukidars, who do, or are supposed to do, any specific police duty.

Col. Dalton's account of their origin.

The continued existence of these various classes of police tenures and, to a certain limited extent only, their origin also, is due to the conditions prevailing in the district in the earliest days of British rule which largely influenced the arrangements made by the Government for the preservation of the peace and the maintenance of order. These conditions were described by Colonel Dalton, Commissioner of the Division, in a report to Government on the subject of the ghātwāli police of the Division, dated 9th December 1864, from which the following paragraphs are extracted.

"2. The Rājas of the Jungle Mahals of Chota Nāgpur and the adjoining Tributary Estates, were, under the ancient Government of India, neither officers appointed for the collection of the revenue nor land proprietors in the ordinary acceptation of the term. They were *Chiefs*, generally of the same race as the people they ruled, and who originally elected them to fill that position. Some of them indeed claim to be of alien blood, but those who do so can only found their pretensions on manifest tables.

"3. These Chiefs continued to exercise sovereign powers in their respective territories till the accession of the British Government. They were almost unknown to the former sovereigns of India, but according to their positions geographically, tribute to the rulers of Bengal, Bihar and Orissa was paid or exacted from them.

"4. For many years under our rule great difficulty was experienced in reducing them to any kind of subjection, and when this was effected, it was considered necessary to treat these countries as exceptional tracts for which a peculiar administration was required. The revenue was fixed low without much investigation in regard to assets, but as they contributed so little to the support of the estate and seemed to thrive best on the system of self-government to which they had been accustomed, it was determined, when police was organised in other parts of the British possessions, and other zamindars were relieved of the greater portion of their responsibilities in regard to crime by Regulation XXII of 1793, to throw on these Chiefs the entire duty and risk of maintaining order in their respective jurisdictions, and in addition to the amount of fixed rent demanded from them, they were required to execute engagements to provide for the safety of life and property, and rendering them personally responsible if, in the event of a felony being committed in their estates, they failed to arrest the criminal and cause the restoration of the stolen property. It was thus that the principal Chiefs, and in very large estates, the most important of their vassals, became hereditary Police Darogas, a position in which the Jungle Mahals' Chiefs were confirmed by the passing of Regulation XVIII of 1805.

"5. Previously, in the exercise of their sovereign rights, they had been assisted, first, by their great vassals, and secondly, by a large body of yeomanry, who, in lieu of the payments in cash or in kind contributed by others for the support of their Chief, rendered service in guarding the roads and passes and in military or honorific attendance on the Chief himself. The yeomanry we now recognize in the jaigīrdars, sardārs, ghātwāls, digwārs and tabedars, to be presently noticed in detail."

The general position, therefore, taken by Colonel Dalton and generally accepted since, is that prior to the British occupation the reigning Chiefs had already, for their own protection and support, both against their neighbours and against internal troubles, a number of quasi-retainers or feudal barons, holding considerable areas of land, either free of tribute or subject to a small tribute only, from the proceeds of which they were bound to maintain a large subordinate force of armed guardians of the peace. In the case of some of the estates these barons were almost, if not quite, the equals of the Chief in dignity and importance, and the latter was probably in the first instance one of them, to whom, as a matter of convenience and for better mutual protection, a more or less commanding position was given. Such were according to Colonel Dalton the sardār ghātwāls of the southern parganas, Barābhum, Mānbhum and Pātkum. Elsewhere, and more especially in the Pānchet estate, conditions were rather different. Pānchet was a congeries of many smaller estates or zamindaris, amalgamated probably by conquest, and all trace of the older rulers or Chiefs of those had disappeared long before history begins. Maintenance of order within the estate, and protection of the outlying parts against the incursions of neighbouring Chiefs, was as important as in the smaller zamindaris, and at the time British influence began to be exercised, we find an elaborate organization of digwārs, of whom each pargana had one or more, with a large force of subordinates whose duties were mainly, if not entirely, of a police nature, and besides these, a large number of jaigirdars, whose duties were apparently rather to render military assistance to the Rāja, and prevent incursions from outside.

It is possible, therefore, at the outset to draw a distinction between the police tenures of Pānchet and those of other parts of the district, and within Pānchet between the digwārs with their subordinates and the jaigirdars. A further distinction can then be drawn between the former and the digwārs and other ghātwāls of the northern parganas, leaving as a class by themselves the ghātwāli organization of the southern zamindaris.

From the outset the police arrangements in Pānchet were somewhat different to those adopted in other estates in Chota Nāgpur, though the agreement taken from the Rāja (Raghunāth Nārāyan Deo) with whom the Decennial Settlement was concluded, contained the same clauses in regard to the guarding of the roads, providing for the safety of travellers and bringing criminals to justice. For several years after the Permanent Settlement the zamindari continued in a state of great anarchy, the Rāja fell into arrears and the estate was sold, though the sale was eventually cancelled. When order was restored the Rāja was, like other zamindars vested with the control of his own

Early Police arrangement in Pānchet.

police, but curiously enough he was considered so poor that a sum of Rs. 1,600 was allowed him towards the expense of maintaining the necessary stations in his extensive jurisdiction. The arrangement was, however, unsatisfactory and very shortly afterwards he was relieved of the charge and the allowance withdrawn, and regular police stations, with establishment paid by and directly subordinate to the Government officials, were established at Chās and Raghunāthpur, and later at Purūlia. All control by the zamindar over the digwāri police was at the same time transferred to the authorities, and from that time on they became directly responsible to Government for the maintenance of order the reporting of crime and arrest of criminals within their several parganas.

Digwārs. According to Colonel Dalton's report the Rāja of Pānchet, when he exercised police powers, had the services of twenty-four sardār digwārs who were bound to maintain a force of 800 tabedars for the protection of the roads and passes, and this force was maintained from the whole proceeds of 573 villages excluded on this account from the settlement made with the zamindar and the gross assets of which were estimated in 1799 at Rs. 5,000 per annum. The existing force of digwāri police in the Pānchet parganas, now included within the district boundary, is made up of 28 digwārs, 16 naib or deputy digwārs, 2 sadiyāls, 24 sardārs and 163 tabedars, or 233 in all, for whose support 45 whole villages and portions of 8 others or 53 tenures in all are definitely assigned. These include 43½ out of the 57¾ villages specifically excluded from the Permanent Settlement as digwāri, and classed now as digwāri estates, 2 villages in Pargana Mahal also treated as such but not shown as liable to payment of 'road patrol cesses,' 2 whole villages and 2 quarter villages in Bankhandi held by digwārs which pay neither a quit-rent to the zamindar nor cess to Government, nor yet are recognized as 'Digwāri estates,' and another village, Ghātkul in pargana Chaurāsi, which has been definitely declared in a civil suit to be 'ghātwāli' and is held by a sardār who is not, as others are, subordinate to the digwārs of the pargana. The earliest reference to these digwāri estates or tenures is in a letter from Captain Crawford commanding in Birbhum in 1774 to Mr. Higginson, in which he says that "the full produce of these was given in consideration of their being a protection to the interior parganas and to provide that the chaukidars be ready for service in obedience to the orders of Government." He adds that with Government troops in the country their services might easily be dispensed with and the revenue considerably increased by assessing them to proper rents. Colonel Dalton remarks in this connection that the lands are for the most part in the open country and not in the vicinity of difficult and dangerous hill passes like the ghâtwâli villages elsewhere in Mânbhum. The inference to be drawn from this is that even at that date their services were mainly, if not entirely, those of internal police and not military. As to their relationship to Government and to the zamindar, there is and has been no dispute; the zamindar makes no claim on them; the bulk of the villages were excluded from the assets of the estate, and they are, therefore, essentially of the nature of the tenures referred to in section 8, clause 4 of Act I of 1793, and Government cannot at any time resume them or demand a proper assessment on dispensing with their services of the digwârs and the subordinates. As in other ghâtwâli tenures, the son ordinarily succeeds the father, but the digwâr is liable to dismissal, and there are now many tenures held by persons specifically appointed to the exclusion of the old families. The latter are in most cases so-called Chattris or Râjputs, but obviously of either Bhumij or Bhuiyâ origin. There are one or more digwârs holding digwâri tenures (four each in Bâgda and Pâra and three in Khâspol) for 17 out of the 19 parganas which make up the estate, the exceptions being the small parganas of Mârra and Jaytara, in each of which, however, there is a digwâr, supported partly by cash payment from the zamindar and partly by fees or *dasturi* levied from the villages; 11 parganas have one or more naib or deputy digwârs; the two sadiyâls who are supposed to represent the mohurrirs or tahsildars of the digwâr are found in a single pargana Charra; the sardârs in Charra, Palma, Ludhurka, Nalichânda, Domurkonda, Chaurâsi and Bankhandi, in which the digwâri tenure consists of several villages, and the sardârs hold specific villages under the digwârs, and control the subordinate tabedars. Tabedars are found in most of the parganas, but the system of remuneration differs; in a few cases they hold specific lands on quit-rents, payable to the sardâr or digwâr, and are themselves hereditary ghâtwâls; in the majority the digwârs pay a small cash or grain wage to their subordinate tabedars, or provide them with lands in lieu thereof, which, however, are not specifically reserved for the purpose, nor necessarily pass from one tabedar to his successor.

Digwârs of Mahal and Bankhandi.

According to Lalla Kanji, tahsildar of Chakla Pânchakot, who replied to certain questions "put by the Hazoor respecting the police" in 1799, the number of digwârs supported by the 57¾ villages excluded from the Permanent Settlement was 24, whereas at present there are 28, and there are tenures in 8 villages not included in the 57¾ recognised as digwāri. Of these additional holdings found, two are in pargana Mahal supporting 2 digwārs and four, also supporting 2 digwārs, in pargana Bankhandi; to the demarcation of these holdings during the survey of 1884 no objection was taken. That the list of 57¾ villages was not an exhaustive one will appear from Lalla Kanji's report itself, for he specifically refers to digwārs in pargana Bara and Mahal whose salaries were paid by the raiyats by subscription before the establishment of thanas, and also to digwārs in Mārra, Mahal, Chatra and Chagam, who held villages in jaigir. In pargana Mārra there is still a digwār who as a matter of fact is the holder of one of the recognised Pānchet jaigirs; in Jaytara there is also a digwār, whose only remuneration is what he can collect from the tenants of the villages in the pargana as *dasturi*. Bankhandi does not appear in this list and the theory is that it was not part of the original Pānchet estate but was attached to the zamindāri of Chatna and came to Pānchet as the dowry of a daughter married to the Pānchet zamindār at or just about the time of the Permanent Settlement. Whatever may be the facts as to the origin of these particular tenures, there is no dispute as to their antiquity and validity, and though the digwārs pay nothing in the shape of rent either to Government or to the zamindar, they are in all other respects exactly similar to the rest.

Ghātwals subordinate to the digwārs. According to Lalla Kanji, there were, besides digwārs, 'ghātwāls' who had charge of the jungles and places frequented by thieves and bad characters and "who take care of the travellers who travel by that road and watch the thieves and bad characters." According to him there were originally 36 ghāts, 23 of which were in charge of the digwārs themselves, and for the remaining 13 the Rāja maintained salaried men at an annual cost of Rs. 1,533. These were, however, dismissed when Government took over the police (*i.e.*, the thana police) and made the Rāja pay Rs 1,300 for the expenses of the thana. These ghātwals were evidently, therefore, not holders of tenures, and in no way corresponded with the hereditary tenure holders of other areas. They were in fact ghātwāls of the same kind as the bulk of the still remaining subordinates of the digwārs, that is to say, mere salaried subordinates with no special hereditary claim to lands held by way of remuneration, and in fact, in the majority of cases, mere recipients of a monthly wage.

Panchet Jaigirs. Of the jaigirs of Pānchet there is a very early mention in the list of the villages furnished by the zamindar in 1771, which shows 160 villages as jaigir; in Lalla Kanji's replies 167½ mauzas are referred to as held by jaigīrdars, but it is not quite clear whether these include or exclude the digwāri mauzas. According to the same authority, Mr. Higginson so arranged it that "the jaigīrdars should pay two-thirds of the rental to the zamindar and retain one-third as their own remuneration, and their duties were to assist the digwārs, if so required, to arrest thieves and turbulent men." The digwārs, he says, were responsible if there was any case of theft, but if there were many cases of rioting and theft both "digwārs and jaigīrdars used to investigate jointly, taking the assistance of the amlas of the Rāja, and any amount that was spent on this account by the digwārs and jaigīrdars was paid by the Rāja."

The records of the Permanent Settlement show that as a matter of fact each jaigīrdari village was assessed to a given revenue, the amount in all cases being the same as that shown in the older accounts as having been paid by the jaigīrdar to the zamindar. Two-thirds of the mufassil jama were treated as an asset in calculating the revenue payable by the zamindar, and the one-third retained by the jaigīrdar was not, and in consequence of this fact the Privy Council has definitely ruled that the services for which this share of the rent or revenue was allowed as compensation to the jaigīrdar were, whatever their nature and whatever were the antecedent facts, definitely made renderable to Government at the Permanent Settlement. That this was so, is also suggested by the fact that the jaigīrdars, or at any rate, some of them, obtained definite sanads signed by Mr. Higginson as Supervisor of Bīrbhum in 1774, a circumstance which appears to distinguish them from merely personal grants. Down to 1845 the jaigīrdars were treated as not very different from the digwārs, appointments and dismissals were made, and successions regulated as in the case of other ghātwāli tenures by the local officials. In that year, however, Colonel Ousley, the Agent to the Governor-General for the South-West Frontier, ruled that they were not police tenures and were liable to sale. The jaigīrdars, however, continued to assert that they were not liable to do personal service for the Rāja, and that they owed allegiance only to Government, but no further attempt was made to make regular use of their services, though, for a number of years afterwards, Government was regularly made a party in suits brought against jaigīrdars and not infrequently assisted the holder in defending them. In 1863 the High Court ruled in the case of Udai Chand Chakravarti that their duties differed little, if at all, from those required of all landholders by the terms of clause I, Regulation XX of 1817, namely, "to give information and assistance in the investigation of serious crimes, information as to thefts, notorious bad characters, and receivers of stolen property, to afford assistance in the apprehension of all persons for whose apprehension warrants have been issued by the Magistrate, and generally to co-operate with, assist, and support the police officers of Government in maintaining the peace, preventing, as far as possible, affrays and other criminal acts of violence, or apprehending the offenders under the rules and restrictions enacted and promulgated in the Regulations". From this view, however, the Privy Council dissented in the suit Rāja Nilmoni Singh Deo *versus* Bakranath Singh, Jaigīrdar of Taraf or Ghāt Dhekia in pargana Mahishara, disposed of on appeal in 1883 (I. L. R. IX Cal., pp. 187-208) and definitely ruled that the jaigirs of Pānchet are analogous to the ghātwāli tenures of Bīrbhum, that the jaigīrdars rendered services of a public and not a private kind, and that "the Permanent Settlement did not alter the nature of the jaigir or of the tenure upon which the lands were held, nor could it convert the services which were public into private services under the zamindar". The finding was therefore that the jaigirs were essentially police tenures, resumable neither by the zamindar nor by Government, and alienable neither at death nor by division, and but for the operation of Regulation XVIII of 1805 which removed Pānchet from the jurisdiction of Bīrbhum to that of the Jungle Mahals district, they would have been subject to Regulation XXIX of 1814 which related to the lands held by the class of persons denominated ghātwāls in the district of Bīrbhum. This ruling made it once and for all clear that the jaigīrdars' services were renderable to Government and that they owed no service to the zamindar, and their tenures could not be resumed by him. Government, however, held that "their services were of no special value, and though no formal relinquishment of Government right to the services of the jaigīrdars has been made, it has, since 1881, been taken as finally decided that Government would in future abstain absolutely from being a party to any litigation between the jaigīrdars and the zamindars." (Government order No. 560T., dated 23rd June 1881.)

The present position of the jaigīrdars is, therefore, a favoured one: no services are demanded from them, their tenures are not resumable, and it has been held that their very nature renders them impartible, and also nonsaleable for arrears of rent. The number of such jaigirs within the present limits of the district is 52, comprising the whole or portions of 99 villages. Kāsaipar contains the largest number, *i.e.*, 20, of which the jaigir of Mudāli comprises no less than 15 villages: Mahal contains 17, of which Bharamahal comprising 6 villages and portions of 11 others and Asansol with a one-third share of 16 villages are the largest. Bāgda contains 9 jaigirs and Pāra and Cheliāma three each, the jaigir in each case consisting of a single village. It is noticeable that the Kāsaipar jaigirs form almost a continuous line along the Barābhum and Bāghmundi borders, and the other pargana in which jaigirs are most numerous is also an outlying one, bordering on the Bhuiyā estates of the north Dāmodar area and of the Hazāribagh district. No specific details are forthcoming, but it is a fact that in some of the jaigirs (Sirkabad and Mudāli in pargana Kāsaipar) there are still tabedars, and there can be little doubt that originally a considerable force of subordinate ghātwāls was maintained by the Jaigīrdars, of whom those of Mudali, Bharamahal and Asansol hold positions not very different from those of the great taraf sardārs of Barābhum. The majority of the jaigirs are still, it is said, in the hands of the original families who claim, in most cases, to be Chattris or Rājputs, though their claims have probably as little foundation in fact as those of the zamindars.

The only other parganas in which ghātwals styled digwārs in possession of digwāri tenures are found are Jhalda and Begunkodar to the west of Pānchet, and Jharia and Pāndra in the north of the district. In the report of Munshi Nandji on the Ghātwāli Survey of 1880-83 it is stated that all these estates were in earlier days subordinate to Pānchet and we are left to infer that the origin of the digwāri holdings here is the same as that of the digwāri holdings in Pānchet. But neither the statement nor the inference is entirely an accurate one in the case of Pāndra, at any rate, which for sixty years before the permanent settlement, was subordinate to Bīrbhum rather than Pānchet; of the other three, it is only in the case of Jhalda that there is any definite evidence of its partial subordination to Pānchet. It is impossible, therefore, to say that the fact that there are digwāri tenures in these estates and not in Kātras, Nāwagarh and the smaller estates of the north, or in Bāghmundi, Jaypur and other smaller estates bordering on Jhalda and Pānchet is due to the connection of the former with Pānchet; as a matter of fact, the origin of these tenures is entirely obscure, and all that can be said with any definiteness is that they differ from most of those in Pānchet in that they were not specifically excluded from the assets of the estate at the time of the Decennial Settlement.

Digwārs in Jharia, Pāndra, Jhalda and Begunkodar.

In Jharia there is a single tenure consisting of two villages, the digwār of which maintains 4 naibs and 2 tabedars; the digwār pays a quit-rent of Rs. 64 per annum to the zamindar, who, it may be noted, pays in his turn Rs. 36 as Digwāri Cess to Government. This tenure has recently been the subject of litigation in regard to the question of mineral rights, and an attempt was made by the zamindar to show that the digwār and his predecessors were mere *ijārādars* and not digwārs or jaigirdārs. The contrary view was, however, taken by the High Court, who rejected the finding that the tenure could only date from some time after 1833 when the zamindar was divested of police powers, and held that so far as there is any evidence it must be presumed from it that this tenure is analogous in origin and nature to the ghātwali tenures of Bīrbhum. The decision is an important one as materially affecting the decision of any future disputes between Government or ghātwal and the zamindars as to the proprietary rights in minerals, its finality is not, however, assured as an appeal has been filed before the Privy Council.

In Pāndra 13 ghātwāli holdings covering 11,069 bighas were demarcated in 1880-83, and according to the registers these maintain a force of 7 digwārs, 2 naib digwārs, 2 village sardārs and 35 tabedars. The bulk of the latter are mere paid subordinates of the digwārs; the two sardārs appear to be independent. Nothing can be asserted definitely of the origin of these tenures, but it is noteworthy that the most extensive of them, *i.e.*, those which comprise whole villages, are found in groups along the extreme southern and northern limits of the estate; the smaller tenures are found here and there in the interior of the estate; the antiquity of the former is undoubted, and also their similarity to the digwāri tenures of Pānchet except in the matter of liability to quit-rent to the zamindar, and it may safely be assumed that their origin was similar to that of the ghātwāli tenures in the adjoining district of Bīrbhum. The smaller tenures differ but little from ordinary chaukidari chākran lands and are important neither from an historical or a police point of view.

In proportion to their size Jhalda and Begunkodar support a larger force of rural police. In Jhalda 7 tenures covering 6,509 bighas were demarcated supporting 2 digwārs, 1 naib digwār, 5 sardārs and 14 tabedars, 22 men in all. In Begunkodar there are eight tenures with an area of 8,973 bighās, maintaining 11 village sardārs and 27 tabedars. Between the digwārs of Jhalda and the sardārs of Begunkodar no practical distinction can be drawn, nor any explanation offered on the difference in title. All appear to be equally ancient in origin and to date from before the Permanent Settlement, and like those of Jharia and Pāndra, and the jaigirs of Pānchet, to be analogous in origin and nature to the Bīrbhum ghâtwâli tenures. The subordinate ghâtwals are in all cases, like their superiors, holders of quasi-hereditary posts, and entitled on appointment to hold lands regularly set aside for the purpose.

Digwārs without tenures. There are also, as already noticed, digwārs without tenures in Mārra and Jaynagar, parganas of the Pānchet estate, and similar digwārs, remunerated either in cash by the zamindar, or by *dasturi* collected from tenants, exist in the estates of Nāwagarh, Kâtras, Jaynagar and Jaypur. The very fact that no lands are attached to these posts suggests a different origin, and there can be no doubt that they are relics of the time when the zamindars had charge of the police as Darogas, and had to find special establishments where necessary, as for example in the early days of the Grand Trunk Road, for the protection of travellers along particular roads. Special police were organised for the Grand Trunk Road in 1863 and the northern zamindars were relieved of this charge, and assessed in lieu thereof to what is now known as Digwâri Cess, the proceeds of which go to the Road Patrol Fund, and the solitary digwārs are left as a relic of the once considerable force supplied by the zamindars along this road. It is interesting to notice that *dasturi* is still paid by the villagers to several of the regular digwārs of the Pānchet estate, and the demand is not confined to those landless digwārs.

Collection was in former days enforced by issue of warrants under the signature of the Deputy Commissioner, but in more recent years the digwārs have been left to their own devices. It is not recorded whether on any occasion they have succeeded in recovering from defaulters through the civil court, but probably they have not.

Service tenures in Mānbhum, Barâbhum, Kailāpāl and Pātkum. There remain now of the service tenures only those of the four parganas Mānbhum, Barâbhum, Kailâpāl and Pâtkum, which are remarkable for their number and extent, and in the case of Barâbhum especially for the intricacy of the questions which have arisen as to their exact origin and status. According to the figures furnished by the Ghâtwāli Survey of 1880-83 Mânbhum contains 117 tenures comprising 76,800 bighas, nearly one-sixth of the pargana area, and supporting two digwārs, 114 village sardârs, and 321 tabedars. Of the tenures 45 are entire villages and the remainder either fractional shares or isolated plots within villages. Kailâpāl, which is a small pargana 25 square miles in extent, has 9 tenures, *i.e.*, three whole villages and scattered lands in six others, with a total area of 2,514 bighas; in each village there is a sardār, and under the nine sardars are 13 tabedars. In Pātkum, with an area of nearly 300 square miles, 38,754 bighas or 20 square miles were demarcated as ghātwāli in 45 villages supporting 3 sardār ghātwals, 31 village sardārs, and 43 tabedars. The largest area of ghātwāli land is in Barābhum where no less than 271 square miles, or 42 per cent. of the whole area of the estate, go to form 336 tenures maintaining a force of 9 sardār ghātwals, 9 sadiyāls, 308 village sardārs, and 766 tabedars.

Kailāpāl. Of the tenures in Kailāpāl it need only be said that they are of comparatively small importance; the estate was not assessed to Government revenue till as late as 1862, and beyond the fact that it was still a wild and almost uncultivated area as late as Ganga Nārāyan Singh's rebellion in 1833 we have no knowledge of its earlier condition; the ghātwāli tenures are probably of comparatively recent origin and they may either represent regular Mundāri *khuntkatti* villages, or, as is not improbable, either maintenance grants to relatives of the zamindar or semi-military fiefs given to his chief retainers. The zamindar of Kailāpāl was a "chuār" of the "chuārs" continually raiding his neighbours, and it is only to be expected therefore that we should find him surrounded by vassals for whose support specific lands were set apart.

Mānbhum. The ghātwals of Mānbhum have not received the same careful study as those of the adjoining estate of Barābhum; all traces of any division into *tarafs* or large semi-feudal estates have been lost, and it is noticeable that a considerable proportion of the ghātwals are Bāuris or Bāgdis and not Bhumij. No distinction can be drawn between the digwārs and sardārs: the latter are not subordinate in any way to the former, and as a matter of fact the titles seem to be interchangeable, as at present the number of superior ghātwals known as digwārs is five instead of two, and that of sardārs proportionately reduced. A few only of the Ghāts consist of more than one village, and there is a much larger proportion of part villages, and scattered small pieces of land constituting the tenures of the sardārs than is the case in Barābhum. Whether this points to a difference in origin or merely in development is a matter of opinion, and the known facts are too scanty to form a basis for any definite decision.

Barābhum. Pātkum and Barābhum are differentiated from other areas by the fact that there is a more distinct and definite organisation of the ghātwals; elsewhere (if we except some of the digwārs and jaigīrdars of Pānchet) the tenure is usually confined to a village or at the most two or three villages, and the subordinate ghātwals are more of the nature of paid retainers of the sardārs or village ghâtwals. In Barâbhum we find the whole series of tenures grouped into large divisions to which the name *taraf* is given. Four of these have a higher status than the rest, *i.e.*, Pancha Sardâri, Satrakhâni, Tinsâya and Dhâdka, comprising respectively 59, 75, 28 and 42 villages; the remaining four, though recognised as tarafs, may be classed as minor. Five of these tarafs, the four major and Bângurda, have a recognised taraf sardâr or sardâr ghâtwal; two others, Sarberia and Kumâripar, have each two who hold jointly; the remaining one, Gartoli, is without a sardâr, though it includes as many as 45 villages. In Gartoli and Kumâripar village sardârs pay their quit-rent direct to the zamindar; in the others the zamindar's dues are paid by the taraf sardâr, who collects quit-rents from the ghâtwals of subordinate degrees.

The origin of these tenures has been the subject of much discussion, and received the particular attention of Mr. (now Sir H. H.) Risley when employed as Superintendent of the Ghâtwâli Survey in Mânbhum in 1880-1883. The circumstances which led to this survey being undertaken were the endless disputes which arose out of the want of definiteness as to the areas which were covered by the quit rents payable by the ghâtwals to the zamindar, and as to their liability to pay rent or increased rent for non-ghâtwâli areas held by them. These disputes were brought to a head when the whole of the ghâtwali tarafs of Barâbhum were leased by the zamindar to Messrs. Watson & Company, who naturally had less compunction in pressing their claims against the ghâtwals than the zamindar, and were in a position to spend, if necessary, large sums in fighting out the various issues in the courts of law.

The Survey of 1880 and following years was conducted by Munshi Nandji and covered the whole area then claimed by ghâtwals, by whatever name known, throughout the district; it disclosed in Barâbhum the fact that the ghâtwals claimed and were in actual possession of large areas in excess of what was professedly recorded as such in the list known as the *isamnavisi* of 1833. Rightly or wrongly, a certain amount of finality had been attached to this document in virtue of a *rubakâri* of Colonel Oakes, Deputy Commissioner in 1862, which stated that on enquiry he learnt that it had been prepared by Captain Nicholson with the concurrence of the zamindar and ghâtwals, summoned in for the purpose, and had been approved by Captain Wilkinson, the Governor-General's Agent. This list was accordingly made the basis of a so-called compromise between Government, the zamindar (or rather his patnidârs, Messrs. Watson & Co.)

The Ghâtwâli Survey, 1880-83.

The compromise of 1884.

and the ghâtwals, the area demarcated as ghâtwâli being strictly confined to that shown in the *isamnavisi*, and the remainder actually held by the ghâtwals described as excess. For the excess land terms were prescribed on which settlement of it could be taken by ghâtwals of different degrees from the patnidârs, the basis of the calculation being certain rates of rent for different classes of lands. When the ghâtwal refused settlement on these terms, the land became the zamindar's *mâl* land, and it was open to him or his patnidârs to settle with any one they pleased on the best terms they could get. *Primâ facie* the terms were fair to all parties, the ghâtwals were confirmed and their rents fixed in perpetuity in respect of all lands which they were apparently entitled to hold as ghâtwals, and they were given the chance of obtaining a regular and permanent settlement of the remaining areas claimed by them on favourable terms. Three out of the four major tarafs were then under management as attached or encumbered estates, and the terms were accepted on behalf of these by the Commissioner; the signature of the taraf sardars themselves were also obtained to the document and also of many of the village sardars.

The results of the compromise. But when it came to give effect to the compromise the ghâtwals were as unwilling as ever to give up any of the lands they held or to take a fresh settlement of them on the terms proposed. In the case of two of the tarafs Government, as Manager, was held to be bound by the compromise to give effect to it, and though it was pointed out that it was impossible to make the tenants pay rents at the rates which had been laid down as those on which the payments by the inferior ghâtwals to their superior and by the latter to the patnidâr were to be based, settlement on these terms was actually made. In one taraf (Satarakhâni) the sardâr was sufficiently powerful to force Messrs. Watson and Company subsequently to give him a permanent lease of his whole taraf on a fixed rent, much smaller in amount than would have been the rent payable on the compromise terms; other sardârs for the most part refused settlement, and at the same time resisted any interference by the Company with the excess lands in their possession. The result in most cases was the same. The ghâtwal, when he had taken settlement, could not pay his rent, was sued and sold up; tenants with whom settlement was made in default of the ghâtwal could not obtain possession, defaulted and were also sold up, and the bulk of the so-called excess land thus came into possession of the Company through the courts. Meantime the ghâtwal has still to pay for his ghâtwali lands the same panchak which formerly covered the whole of the land held by him, and in a considerable number of cases this also fell into arrears, and the ghātwāli holdings, put up to sale with the permission of the Commissioner under Notification No. 1246 L.R., dated 7th March 1903, have also been bought in and the purchaser, generally Mr. Mathewson, who succeeded to the interests of Messrs. Watson and Company, was appointed ghātwal. So far therefore as the ghātwals generally are concerned, the compromise of 1884 has had most disastrous results, though there are still many cases where individual ghātwals have been sufficiently strong to resist the efforts of the Company to oust them, and several cases in which the courts have ruled that their signature to the compromise was obtained by undue pressure and that they are not bound by it. In the most recent case the decision goes further, as it has been definitely ruled by the High Court that prior to the compromise of 1884 the taraf sardār of Tinsāya held as a tenure-holder the whole of a particular village Erka (and the ruling applies equally to other villages of the taraf) in which the *isamnavisi* and the compromise showed only 4 *rekhs* of cultivated land as ghātwali.

The compromise overruled by the Court.

There can be little question that this decision is a just one, and that the theories on which the compromise of 1884 was based were mistaken, and that in attempting to force the compromise on the ghātwals a great injustice was done to many of them. This will be apparent from the following analysis of the documentary evidence of earlier date than 1833 relating to these tenures.

Documentary evidence of early origin.

Though the word 'ghātwal' is not found in any document earlier than the *isamnavisi* of 1824, the existence of sardārs and paiks in Barābhum is frequently referred to in papers relating to the early years of British rule. In 1794 the zamindar Raghunāth Nārāyan asked for military assistance against his brother Lachman Singh who had entered into alliance with "the five sardars" (*Panchsardāri*) and had "brought the *chuārs* of village Berma (to this day the headquarters of Taraf Tinsāya) and five or seven villages under his own influence and has been oppressing the tenants." This rebellion of the Panchasardāri assumed such dimensions that in March 1796 it was proposed to reinforce the local military detachment and attack them in the jungle of Dalma, but before troops were ready, the paiks came in of their own accord and acknowledged the Rāja's authority, promising to restore the cattle they had lifted and pay their rent regularly in future.

Sardārs and paiks in 1800 and earlier years.

Writing a few years later in 1800, Mr. Strachey, Magistrate of Midnapore, to which district Barābhum was then attached, describes the state to which Barābhum had been reduced by the struggles between the parties supporting the rival claims of the

Mr. Strachey's account of Barābhum—1800.

two minor sons of Raghunāth who had died early in 1798. In this dispute the sardārs had taken sides and Lal Singh of Sauri, ancestor of the present sardār of Satarakhāni, headed one party, and Kishen Pathar of Panchsardāri the other. Guman Gunjan of Dhādka had been outlawed for raids in Dhālbhum and was then in hiding to avoid arrest. Writing of these Mr. Strachey says: "Several sardārs of paiks occupy considerable portions of land, and enjoy profits, some of them nearly equal to what the zamindāri yields to the zamindar. The sardārs may be considered the talukdars of Barābhum, and they have commonly acknowledged the zamindar as their chief. Their ancestors have for many generations possessed the land occupied by them. They have, however, of late made very considerable encroachments, and several causes have conspired to increase the number of their followers." In the same report he describes the reasons for the failure of the Daroga system of police introduced by Regulation XXII of 1793, and asserts that the only effective police were the sardār paiks or chuārs. He proposed to abolish the regular police as useless and to offer a general pardon to Lal Singh and the other sardārs and to arrange a general settlement between them and the zamindar, and to engage them "to defend the lands which they have been employed so long in desolating."

Identity of the sardārs and paiks with the later ghātwals. In another paragraph of his interesting report he states that "no tolerable police system can be established in Barābhum without the assistance of the sardārs, and that, therefore, unless they receive sanads as the zamindars have done, empowering them to act as police officers, they must be encouraged to make their peace with the zamindar." Mr. Strachey's proposals met with the approval of Government, and he was authorised to offer the sardārs a general pardon for all past offences, conditional, however, on their future good behaviour, and "to make such use of the sardār paiks in Barābhum as circumstances may appear to render expedient or necessary." Lal Singh and the other sardārs were accordingly pardoned, and it is to be inferred that Mr. Strachey gave effect to the rest of his proposals, and made the sardārs responsible, under the Managers of the estates, for the peace of the zamindāri generally. In a later report it is stated that a number of new paiks were appointed, but whether by this is meant sardār paiks, or merely paiks under the pardoned sardārs, or directly under the Managers, is not clear.

Apart from any other evidence, the above is enough to show that ghātwals, under the name of sardārs and paiks and having a efinite status as police, were recognised very early in the period of British rule, and that certain of the sardārs, the Panchasardār or their chief Kishen Pathar, Lal Singh of Satarakhâni, and Guman Ganjan of Dhâdka held a very prominent position. Mr. Strachey's proposals in 1800 suggest more regularised employment of them as police, and no doubt it was these proposals that originated the present elaborate arrangement, but at the same time they apparently imply that even before this the sardārs had obligations in this respect and were supposed to carry them out through their subordinates or paiks. The general impression conveyed is that the earlier organisation was a semi-military one rather than one of internal police, that the leading sardārs had in the past admitted their liability, but that latterly, in the disturbances arising out of the two disputed successions, had got out of hand and taken to employing their forces against one another and against the zamindar and Government rather than against outsiders. The pardon offered them by Mr. Strachey saved their tenures or estates from the forfeiture, to which their misconduct had rendered them liable, and in return they allowed themselves to be organised into a more or less regular police force with definite obligations to the zamindar as head of the zamindāri police.

Existence of certain of the tenures in 1789.

Of the recognition of their various tenures, even as early as 1789-90, the year the Decennial Settlement was completed with Rāja Raghunāth Nārāyan, there is positive evidence in a list of villages which exists for that year in the shape of the so-called quinquennial papers. These, read with certain papers filed by the Tahsildars and Managers of the estate while under Government management for the years 1205, 1206 and 1207 (1798-1800) and entitled *ekjai mahādad* or *ekjai jamā-wāsil-bāki*, throw a clear light on the early history of the ghātwāli tenures. The quinquennial papers give a list of the rent-paying villages of the estate, 149 in all, and among the entries appear the following :—

			Village.	*Jama.* Rs.	A.
Chalania, etc.	...	...	13	137	8
Dhādka ,,	...	...	14	147	8
Sauri ,,	...	...	17	267	0
Tilsāya ,,	...	...	13	137	8
Bānguda ,,	...	...	2	66	12
Pudara ,,	...	...	6	20	0
Rajda ,,	...	...	5	30	0
Sarberia	...	...	1	20	0

As to the identification of the first four with the four major tarafs of Panchasardāri, Dhādka, Satarakhāni and Tinsāya there can be no question. Bāngurda and Sarberia are two of the minor tarafs, and Punrara and Rajda or Bajra are to this day the respective headquarters of the two sardārs who are jointly classed as the Taraf Sardārs of Kumāripar. There is of course nothing in this list to indicate the nature of the tenures which these groups of villages constituted, but the very fact of their being so grouped, *e.g.*, Dhādka, etc., 14 villages, conclusively shows that they were held in one interest, and that, if it were necessary to sell a portion of the estate in order to realise the revenue (this was the primary object of the quinquennial papers), the group, that is to say the zamindar's interest in it represented by the *jama* disclosed in the statement, would have to be sold as a whole

Their entry in the *ekjai* papers of 1205 as Mahal Bhumi jāni.

The *ekjai mahādad* of 1205 (1798) is signed by Gangā Gobinda Nārāyan, one of the two claimants and eventually the successful claimant to the succession. It gives details of the demand under various heads from 71 villages, apparently those under direct management or held by members of the family by way of maintenance, specifying in each case the name of the holder. There then follows a list of 18 mahals comprising 64 villages and headed "*mahal bhumi jāni.*" Among these the first four are entitled "Lal Singh, Guman Ganjan, Panchasardār, and Tinsāya" with 11, 14, 13 and 13 villages respectively and total *jamas*, including *batta* and *dewāni*, of Rs. 267, Rs. 137-8, Rs. 190 and Rs. 137-8. Lal Singh's villages (Satarakhāni) are reduced from 17 to 11, Guman Ganjan's (Dhādka) *jama* is reduced by Rs. 10, and that of Panchasardāri raised by Rs. 52-8, but in other respects the entries exactly correspond with those of the 1197 list.

Of the other entries Hatu Sardar's two villages on a *jama* of Rs. 67-8 are identifiable by means of the later *ekjai* papers with Bānguda, etc., 2 villages (Bāngurda and Bānd), *jama* Rs. 66-12 of the 1197 list; Birbar Singh's one village on Rs. 12-4 is possibly identifiable with Sarberia. Of the others described by the names of their holders, it may be possible by careful enquiry as to the ancestry of present ghātwals to identify some of the names and attach them to villages. One village name only appears, Atsimul held on a *jama* of Rs. 6, and this is now one of the part ghātwāli villages of Panchasardāri.

And in those of 1206, 1207.

Similar lists of Mahal Bhumijāni appear in the *ekjai* papers of the two following years, which are statements of collections as well as of demands and profess to be prepared on behalf of the zamindar by the two muharrirs of Rāja Nanda Lal Singh, the rival claimants' uncle, to whose management the estate had been entrusted. The list is, however, curtailed and includes only eight mahals, *i.e.*, the four major tarafs, Birbar Singh (possibly Sarberia, *vide* above), Lâya Barga Sinha against whose name appears Bāngurda in Mr. Risley's report, Garwarah or Gemarah held by Bajnath Singh, possibly a village in Sarberia, and Sukhla Sabna Singh, not identified. The number of villages is no longer given and there are further changes in the *jama*, due in part, at any rate, as the details of the statement show, to a difference in calculation of the *batta* and the omission of the cess *dewâni* charged in the 1205 statement. Between the 1206 and 1207 lists also there are differences, and it is only in the latter that we get for the four main tarafs (this word is used for the first time in the 1207 list) the exact *jamas* (exclusive of *batta*) which we know from Mr. Dent's report of 1833 remained till Madhab Singh doubled them some time before the revolt of the preceding year and which appear as 'panchak' in the isamnavisi of 1833, *i.e.* Satarakhāni Rs. 240, Panchasardāri and Tinsāya Rs. 16 each, and Dhādka Rs. 120.

The four major tarafs definitely recognised as tenures prior to and immediately after the Permanent Settlement.

These papers then, by themselves, establish what was reasonably inferred from the less detailed list of 1197 that the four major tarafs at any rate existed as recognised tenures of considerable extent at the time of the Permanent Settlement; that they were of considerable extent appears from the number of villages they comprised, *i.e.*, 57 out of a total of 149 rent-paying villages in the estate. It would also be reasonable to infer that the rents may have been more or less privileged but not mere quit-rents, as for rather more than one-third of the estate as reckoned by villages and even now containing a large area of unculturable hill and jungle and in those days undoubtedly a very wild and hardly developed area, the total rent demand from these four tarafs is put down in 1789 as Rs. 689-8 out of Rs. 2,642-5, the total mufassil *jama* of the estate.

Meaning of Bhumijāni.

Exactly what the title 'Bhumijāni', as applied to these mahals, conveyed at the time it was used, cannot now be ascertained, but it is difficult to account for its use unless it was intended to describe tenures to which some particular incidents attached, and not merely that they were held by Bhumij, though it is an interesting fact that looking through the names shown against the "*Dehat*", "*Khas Khāmar*" and "*Mahal jat*" villages of the estate, the names of Kurmis, Sonthals and others, but only in very occasional instances, of Bhumij appear as the holders of the villages. On the other hand, all the names in the earliest Bhumijāni list (that of 1205), except possibly Madhu

Dīgwār, are clearly Bhumij names, and so also are those of most of the holders of villages shown under *chākran*, except such as are obviously servants, etc., of the zamindar, *i.e.*, Khāwas, Kabiraj, Hukābardar and the like.

Whatever the exact nature, there can be no question that the Bhumijāni Mahals were distinct and separate tenures, and as distinguished from the *chākran* tenures to be referred to later, it is noticeable that the lists in no case give the names of the villages, and that no cesses other than *batta* and, in the earliest list only, *dewāni* also, were charged against them and no *abwab* except in the case of one of the smaller Mahals, Garuara. All these facts seem to point to a class of tenure with the internal details of which the zamindar had little concern, liable to pay a fixed tribute and nothing more except, if such was the case, police or military service.

The Bhumijāni tenure not distinct from the ghātwāli or jaigir.

In Mr. Risley's report the view is taken that these Bhumijan tenures were held by the sardārs as something apart from the lands held by them in consideration of their performing service for the zamindar or Government. It is unnecessary to go into the reasonings on which this conclusion is based; it is sufficient to say that the assumption that the *ekjai* papers are incomplete and that, if complete, there would have been a list of '*Mahal jaigir*' is incorrect. The papers of 1206 begin with an abstract of the different classes of villages giving the total *jama* for each and the details given in the succeeding pages exactly correspond; there can be no question therefore that the papers are complete, and that for the four major tarafs at any rate the only details are those found under the head of 'Bhumijani'. Moreover, the word 'jaigir' actually appears in the heading of one of the columns of this abstract, viz, "deduction on account of *chākran jaigir*", under which an entry appears against the cross heading "*chākran*"; *jaigir* cannot, therefore, be something distinct from *chākran*, and no separate list of *jaigirs* was required. It follows, therefore, that the only tenures held by the four taraf sardārs in the period covered by the 10 years succeeding the Decennial Settlement were those described as Mahal Bhumijāni; how far these were ordinary and how far service tenures will be discussed later.

Origin of the so-called minor tarafs.

Before doing so the results of an examination of the *chākran* lists contained in the *ekjai* papers are worthy of consideration, as these furnish particulars of some of the tenures which make up the other so-called minor tarafs.

Bāngurda.

Bāngurda (which now contains 1 whole village, 4 *rekhs* in three and detached lands in two others) has been identified above with the two villages shown in 1205 Bhumijāni list against the name of Hatu Sardār on a *jama* of Rs. 67-8. His name does not appear in the 1206 list, but under *chākran* of that year is the entry Mauzas Bānd and Bangurda, Chatu Sardār, Rs. 67-8 rent and *batta*, besides various cesses. The isamnavisi of 1833 gives the sardar of Bāngurda only 4 *rekhs* in Bānd but he was still in possession of the whole village in 1880.

Kumāripar (*i.e.*, beyond the Kumāri river) has two taraf sardārs, each of whom has seven whole villages under him; there are besides these 45 villages containing small areas of ghātwāli land nominally within the taraf, but not actually any part of the taraf sardārs' charge. The Mahal Bhumijāni lists contain no entries which can be identified with these two sardārs, but the tenures are clearly identifiable among the Mahal Chākran, the first two entries in which are Bajra or Rajda and four other villages in charge of Aini Sardār and Punrara with five other villages in charge of Asman Sardār; the majority of the village names are clearly identifiable with those of villages now in the two taraf sardārs' possession, and Bajra and Punrara are to this day their respective headquarters. Both groups, as was noticed before, appear as such in the village list of 1789, Pudara with a *jama* of Rs. 20 for six villages and Bajra of Rs. 30 for five. The *ekjai* papers give the detailed *jama* for the separate villages and exclusive of *abwāb* and deducting the allowance for *chākran* the rents for the two tenures in 1206 were respectively Rs. 46 and Rs. 20. The *panchak* now payable, which is according to the isamnavisi of 1833 and includes *mamul khajana* and various cesses, is respectively Rs. 69-3-6 and Rs. 60-13. **Kumāri-par.**

These tenures have therefore continued practically unchanged since before the Permanent Settlement, though they have not apparently enjoyed the same fixity of rent as the four major tenures.

The identification of Sarberia is not so easy but the fact that it has at present two taraf sardārs points, as in the case of Kumāripar, to an origin in two distinct tenures. One of these is apparently the Bhumijāni Mahal Dhuni Birbar Singh, corresponding perhaps to the village Sarberia, the other Gemarah or Garuarah held by Baijnath Singh, which also finds a place in all three lists of Bhumijāni Mahals. The two sardārs were in 1884 in possession of only four *rekhs* of Sarberia, but held the whole of villages Kudlong, Jiling and Mahisādabar in spite of the fact that the isamnavisi of 1834 only gave them fractions of these villages. Now a village list of 1279 Fasli filed by the zamindar, to which reference will be made later, shows Jiling as a *chak* of Gerua (the map name is Garwara), Mahisādabar as a *chak* of Sarberia, and **Sarberia.**

Kudlong as a *chak* of Sinduri, and of the 20 villages in which there are ghātwāli lands in this taraf more than half are shown as offshoots of these three villages. There is every reason, therefore, to believe that taraf Sarberia originated in these two Bhumijāni Mahals of Birbar and Baijnath Singh.

Other ghātwāli tenures in the *chākran* lists.

Other entries also in the *chākran* list related to villages which fall within one or other of these minor tarafs and of Gartoli. Raigara and Chechangdih in which there are now (following the 1833 isamnavisi) only lands requiring 2 or 3 maunds of seed, were held as a *chākran* by Khosal Sardār on a net rent excluding *abwāb* of Rs. 29, Bamu in the same taraf by Chamu Sardar for Rs. 60, Digram by Ranjit Rāy for Rs. 50, Darberia (Kumāripar) and Parasya (Gartoli) by Bauri Sardār for Rs. 9, Hulung (Gartoli) with Padampur by Sagar Sardār free of rent Of these it is worth notice that Raigara, Bamu and Hulung were still in 1880 entirely held by the ghātwal, though the isamnavisi shows portions only as ghātwāli; the last-named village being in fact the only case in the whole of the so-called taraf of Gartoli in which an entire village is held by the ghātwal. In this taraf also is Pargala, of which 2 *rekhs* are now ghātwāli; this through the *chākran* list of 1206 is identifiable with the Bhumijāni Mahal shown in 1205 in the name of Madhu Digwār. Kumāripar would, therefore, appear to be largely made up of a number of distinct *chākran* tenures having no connection with one another; Gartoli, which has no Taraf Sardar and which in Mr. Dent's report of 1833 is the name given to the portion of the estate constituting the Rāja's *khalsa* villages and has now locally an alternative name, viz., Dubrāji, *i.e.*, that part of the estate in which the Dubraj or eldest son's maintenance villages lie (another of Mr. Dent's divisions of the estate), had evidently no separate existence as a superior tenure and its ghātwāli holdings are to this day mere scattered lands in villages spread over the central part of the estate in which the *khās khāmar*, *dehat*, *mahal jat* and *babuāna* villages, *i.e.*, villages held by the Rāja and his relations, lay; in fact there are now ghātwali holdings in many of the villages included in the lists of 1205 to 1207 under those heads. The same applies to those parts of Kumāripar which are outside the two main tenures and the smaller ones referred to in the preceding paragraph.

Vague distinction between Mahal Bhumijāni and *chākran*.

The classification of some of these tenures as Mahal Bhumijāni in the papers of one year and as Mahal Chākran in those of the succeeding years suggests, at any rate, that the distinction between the two was not very great, and in view of what Mr. Strachey writes of the services of the sardārs and paiks as police there can be very little doubt that specific duties attached to the holding of the Bhumijāni tenures as well as to those specifically described as *chākran*. The village list of 1197, moreover, read with the *ekjai* papers, conclusively shows that the four major tarafs, and also what may be called the nuclei of the minor tarafs Bāngurda, Sarberia and Kumāripar date from before the Permanent Settlement. The settlement of the estate was made in the lump, and it cannot, therefore, be said that these tenures were like the Pānchet Digwāri tenures excluded from the Permanent Settlement, but there can be little question that one of the considerations which led to the low revenue, fixed first in 1776, being left as the revenue to be permanently settled, must have been the knowledge of the fact that a large part of the estate was permanently alienated in tenures held at low rates of rent and subject to services which would become renderable to Government in virtue of the terms of that settlement. This view is supported by Mr. Harington who in his Analysis of the Regulations, Calcutta 1814—1817, Volume II, pages 235-236, Volume III, pages 509-512, distinguishes ordinary *chākran* and ghātwāli tenures. "The ghatwāli tenure, however," he writes, "as ascertained from the result of inquiries made by the Magistrates of zillas Burdwan, Birbhum, and the Jungle Mahals, and communicated to the Court of Nizamut Adawlat in the year 1816, differs essentially from the common *chākran* in two respects; 'first, that being expressly granted for purposes of police, at a low assessment, which has been allowed for, in adjusting the revenue payable by the landholders to Government, at the formation of the Permanent Settlement, the land is not liable to resumption nor the assessment to be raised beyond the established rate at the discretion of the landholders; secondly, that although the grant is not expressly hereditary, and the ghātwal is removeable from his office, and the lands attached to it, for misconduct, it is the general usage on the death of a ghātwal, who has faithfully executed the trust committed to him, to appoint his son, if competent, or some other fit person in his family, to succeed to the office'. The above discrimination between the ghātwāli tenure, which being an appropriation of land at a low *jama* for a police establishment, may be considered within the fourth clause of section VIII, Regulation I, 1793; and the common *chākran* assignments in lieu of wages to zamindāri servants, which have been annexed to the malgoozari lands and declared responsible for the public assessment, by section 41, Regulation VIII, 1793, is taken verbatim from a letter written by order of the Nizamut Adawlat to the Calcutta Court of Circuit on the 30th October 1816. It is probable that some specific provisions may hereafter be enacted for defining more exactly the rights of the ghātwals referred to. At present, however, those of Zilla Bīrbhum only are included in the enactments of Regulation XXIX, 1814."

The description given in this paragraph seems to be in every respect applicable to these Barābhum tenures, whether described as mahal bhumijāni or *chākran*, which latter are quite distinct from the common *chakran* given to personal servants, of which, judging by the names Khawas, Kabiraj, and Hukabardar, the mahal *chākran* lists of 1205, 1206 and 1207 contain a number of examples. In connection with the term 'bhumijāni' it may be mentioned that in the leading *digwāri* case of district Hazāribāgh (Nam Narayan Singh *vs.* Tikait Ganjhu, Calcutta Weekly Notes, XII, 178) what purported to be copies of lists of "digwārs, ghātwars, and bhuinhars" for the years 1799 and 1806, said to have been furnished by the Rājas of Rāmgarh to Government, were produced. Between the original meanings of 'bhumij' and 'bhuinhar' there is little or no distinction, and the use of the latter term in the Hazāribāgh district in conjunction with the terms 'digwār' and 'ghātwar' suggests at once that these particular bhuinhars had specific police duties attached to them as early as 1799, and that they were classed, like the digwārs and ghātwars, as service tenure-holders owing service to Government. In another case (Nilmoni Singh *vs.* Bir Singh) it was observed that "there can be little doubt that these rural police were variously named at different times and in different districts, but as guardians of the ghāts or passes they are better known in later times as ghātwals."

It has been necessary to deal at this length with the evidence of the early existence of these tenures because so much has been made of the absence of any trace of the use of the word 'ghātwāli' prior to the *isamnavisi* of 1824, and in conjunction with the statement that after Mr. Strachey's reorganisation of the Pargana new paiks were created by the zamindar, it has been suggested that the ghātwals only became such after the Permanent Settlement, and that their tenures having been created by the zamindar out of his permanently settled estates, they would be resumable by him on the services of the ghātwals being no longer required. Within the 'Ghurtoolee' and 'Dubrāji' of Mr Dent's report, *i.e.*, the modern Gartoli and part of Kumāripar taraf, where the zamindar would be personally responsible for the maintenance of order, it is conceivable that more paiks were required and that some of the small holdings in this area were then created; in the four major tarafs and in the groups which constitute the nuclei of the Kumāripar, Sarberia, and Bāngurdā tarafs, the position of the zamindar must have been taken by the sardār or holder of the Bhumijāni Mahal and any creation of tenures for the support of the necessary number of paiks must have been made by him.

Mr. Risley's original conclusion that the ghātwali tenures—as distinguished from 'Bhumijāni' or ordinary tenures as headmen of Bhumīj villages—date from some time after 1800, is, therefore, untenable; the tenures certainly existed with services attached to them from a much earlier date. The next record available of them is the *isamnavisi* of 1824, which professes to be a list of the ghātwals and the lands held by them and amount of cash remuneration, if any. This list has since 1862 at any rate been treated as superseded by the similar but more elaborate list of 1833, the importance attached to which has already been referred to. The 1824 list is not, however, worthy of the contempt showered on it; it is exactly what it professes to be and its accuracy is probably at least as great as that of any of the numerous later lists which were prepared and submitted by the zamindar as head of the police. The greater elaboration of the 1833 list, the abstracts which are given for the major tarafs, distinguishing between original jaigir villages and others, and splitting up the total amounts payable into *panchak*, rent and various cesses, all suggest more careful preparation, but in spite of the weight attached to this document by the courts in several cases, and the authority given it by Colonel Oakes' statement (29 years later) of his belief as to the manner in which it was prepared, there can be little question that, looked at dispassionately, it is a document which considered only the zamindar's interests, which ignored actual facts, and which, if it be a fact that the ghātwals assisted in its preparation, can only be explained on the supposition that they were reduced to extremities by the suppression of Gangā Nārāyan's rebellion and by fear of the results of their complicity in it and in the murder of Mādhab Singh and were forced to accept on paper a compromise which, if given effect to, reduced their holdings by as much as two-thirds, more than doubled their rents and rendered them liable to further increase. This document is dealt with at great length in Mr. Risley's report of 1884, and on his interpretation of it are based the terms of the compromise of that year. His inferences from certain of the entries are now clearly demonstrable as wrong, and it is a question whether the compromise would have taken the form it did take but for these.

The isamnavisis of 1824 and 1833.

Rent and *Panchak* in the 1833 isamnavisi.

That drawn from the entry of rent separately from *panchak* in the abstracts for the four major tarafs is, perhaps, the most important. In this abstract the entries are "ordinary *jaigir* lands" so many villages, ordinary rent (*mamul khajana*) of "*mal*" lands held besides jaigir lands—so many villages—and against each of these, under the heading "*panchak jama*" is entered an amount, in all cases the same in both. In the margin is a note in the vernacular. "*panchak sewai* .... *taka mamul khajana san san alahida mulgujari kare ebang bastu batir khajana o mulukdar nawa anka jakhan jaha haya sab pargana har san san alahida dei,*" which Mr. Risley paraphrases, "these (number) villages are held by separate payment of regular rent (*mamul khajana*) of .... rupees. Besides this, the holder pays separate rent for *bastu bati* (high land and houses). He also pays, according to the custom of the country, new rent (*naya anka*) from time to time (*jakhan jaha haya*) according to the pargana rate." A more literal translation however would be, "besides *panchak*, Rs. .... is to be paid separately as ordinary rent (*mamul khajana*) annually. Further *bastu* rent as also any new cess or impost (*anka*), provincial or local (*mulukdar*), which may from time to time be imposed, will have to be paid according to the pargana rate year by year." '*Anka*,' literally a number, is a word occasionally used for a cess or impost; it is not, so far as can be ascertained, used for 'rent,' and the entry does not necessarily, as Mr. Risley assumed, imply a tenure held on a variable rent.

Mamul khajana.

The words "*mamul khajana*" have an importance which was overlooked by Mr. Risley. Mr. Dent, to whose report of 1833 reference has already been made, gives in clear terms the historical origin of these double entries of similar amounts as *panchak* and rent. Describing the oppressions of Madhab Singh Babu, to which the outbreak of 1832 was largely due, he writes: "The measures he adopted were these. He commenced an extensive and lucrative trade in which his position in the zamindāri gave him a complete monopoly; this soon brought him wealth, the free and usurious use of which rendered the Rāja and nearly all his subjects his debtors, and it was the merciless severity with which he enforced these claims particularly against the ghātwals, that made these people his inveterate enemies. Our law of debtor and creditor, severe perhaps in itself, was rendered doubly so when applied to these rude and ignorant people, but Madhab Singh did not hesitate to avail himself to the amount of the entire power it gave him over the property of his debtors in compelling payment Not satisfied, however, with the exorbitant profits of his trade, he had recourse to his power as Dewan and Manager of the estate for extorting further sums from the unfortunate ghātwals. The rents as per margin paid by the four principal ghātwal sardārs were very light owing to the nature of their tenures; he doubled them calling the additional cess 'mamuli;' this, as was natural, was resisted and never, I believe, fully enforced in the Satarakhāni.

	Rs.
Dhādka	120
Satarakhāni ...	240
Panchasardāri ...	160
Tinsāya	160

He also established a house tax 'Ghartaki' which was compounded for in many villages by the payment of a fixed sum; other illegal but not altogether unusual (in these jungle estates) 'Cesses' made under the denomination of 'Maugon' or voluntary subsidies, were levied, such as "Hatee Mangon" a cess or rate for the purchase of a horse or elephant. So great, however, is the attachment of these people to their Rāja that any demands of this latter description within moderate bounds, which may be necessary to enable him to maintain a proper degree of state, have always readily been complied with. This, however, was not the case with regard to the 'Ghartaki', 'Mamuli' and other exactions which were permanent taxes."

The identity of the "ghartaki" with the "*bāstu bāti khajana*" of the isamnavisi is undisputed, and there can be no reasonable doubt that the doubling of the *panchak* by means of the tax "*mamuli*" is represented by the double entry of *panchak* and "*mamul khajana*" of the isamnavisi.

The "*mamul khajana*" was, therefore, in 1833, a recent imposition and one which was strongly resented by the ghātwals and yet we are asked to believe that the ghātwals accepted the entries in this *isamnavisi* as correct at the very time when Mr. Dent, fresh from the scene of the disturbances was writing "the ghātwals are throughout loud in their complaints of the encroachment of the zamindars and others and of the exactions and irregular demands to which they are subject," and that it was "of the most vital importance to the general peace of the district and the maintenance of an efficient police that these jaigirs should not in any way be diverted from the purpose for which they were originally granted, either by fraudulent alienations of the ghātwals themselves or the encroachments of the zamindars and others which are now daily taking place". Unless it be a fact that the spirit was entirely taken out of the ghātwals by the measures taken to suppress the disturbances, which were not completed till April 1833, it is inconceivable that, within the few months that remained of that year, they agreed to all the zamindar's demands;

it is still less conceivable when we learn that 50 years afterwards they were still in possession, with nothing to indicate that they had ever been out of possession, of 85 whole villages in which the isamnavisi only assigned them a few *rekhs* or land requiring a few maunds of *dhān* as seed; and this in spite of executive and judicial orders asserting the finality of the 1833 papers.

The village list of 1870. An interesting side-light is thrown on this *isamnavisi* by a statement of the *patit* (*i.e.*, uncultivated) and jungle lands contained in the villages of his estate, filed by the zamindar in 1279 (1870). This professes to be a complete list of then existing villages, and contains entries in regard to 608, of which, however, only 169 are "*asli*" villages and the remainder "*chaks*", *i.e.*, hamlets or offshoots from one or other of the parent or "*asli*" villages. A careful examination of this list shows that the vast majority of the villages in which, according to the *isamnavisi*, so many *rekhs*, or land requiring so many maunds of seed, are ghātwāli, but which were found during the survey of 1880-83 to be held entirely by the ghātwals, are *chaks* of *asli* villages which the *isamnavisi* shows as entirely ghātwāli. The *isamnavisi*, therefore, asserted the zamindar's claim to all new villages which had sprung up within the areas in which the original jaigir or *bhumijāni* villages lay, a claim which, in the absence of any maps or record of village boundaries and in the face of the adverse possession of the jaigīrdars or talukdars, he could never have established in a court of law in 1833, nor, without the *isamnavisi* of 1833 being treated as authoritative, in 1884. Mr. Dent's description in 1833 clearly implies that what he calls the ghāts were self-contained and distinct from the portion of the estate with which the zamindar was directly concerned. He writes: "It is divided into the Rāja's Khalsa villages called Ghurtoolee, the Dubrāji Mahal (or estate for the support of the Rājā's eldest son) which comprise the more open and cultivated portions in the interior of the estate, and ten ghāts or divisions which entirely surround the estate. The principal of these are Dhādka which adjoins Kailāpāl and Dompāra in Dhalbhum; to the westward and adjoining Dhādka is Satarakhāni which protects the estate against Dhalbhum; to the westward of this is Pancha-sardāri which guards that side against Singhbhum and Pātkum; the others are smaller ghāts on the side of Mānbhum. Each of the ghāts is held in jaigir on a mere nominal rent by a sardār who is the captain of the border or lord of the marches, and a certain number of followers called ghātwals who were the old military force of the country and whose duty it was to protect the estate from the predatory incursions and inroads of their neighbours.

At the settlement of the jungle mahals "(*i.e.*, Mr. Higginson's settlement in 1776)," the ghātwals were allowed to remain in possession of their lands and became the police servants of our Government; they were the chief factors in the recent disturbances." He has unfortunately only given the names of the four major ghāts, but it would not be unreasonable to assume that among the others were Bajra and Punrara within the modern Kumāripar, Sarberia and Garuara within Sarberia, Bāngurda, and the tenth, one of the unidentified Bhumijāni Mahal (possibly Sukhla Bir Singh, two villages). These form a practically complete ring round the estate, and the list of villages comprising the estate in 1197 contains, with a single and that a doubtful exception, the name of no village which could by any stretch of imagination be described as lying within the periphery of any one at any rate of the major tarafs.

The ultimate origin of the main tarafs or ghāts, whether classed in the early papers as *mahal bhumijāni* or as *chākran*, must almost certainly have been in the ordinary village system of the Mundas, a race to which the Bhumij undoubtedly belong. Authorities differ on some points, but the generally accepted view is that the sardār of the Bhumij area is the headman or Munda of the Munda village community, *i.e.*, the head of the family which first brought the village under cultivation; other members of the original family would be the *bhuinhars* or *khuntkatti* tenants, and the village might contain also outsiders as ordinary unprivileged tenants. Over groups of five to a dozen villages in Mundāri areas one of the headmen takes precedence as mānki; in the Bhumij area there is the exact equivalent in the sadiyāl, or sardār sadiyāl of whom there are four and five respectively in the two largest tarafs of Panchsardāri and Satarakhāni. The taraf sardār, locally the sardār ghātwal, or sardār simply, as distinguished from a Grāmya sardār, is almost certainly a mere overgrown mānki or Sadiyāl. Thus the name Panchasardāri obviously means merely a group of five sardārs, and in 1795 it was of the insolence of the five sardārs, of whom the ancestor of the recent taraf sardār was the chief, that the zamindar complained. In both this and the Saturakhāni taraf, each sadiyāl and also the taraf sardār has his separate group of villages, not differing greatly in extent, and no doubt they were originally independent of one another, and combined for purposes of mutual protection or aggression on their neighbours, recognising one of themselves as their chief. In Dhādka and Tinsāya there are no traces of smaller subdivisions, but the name Tinsāya possibly arises from

Ultimate origin in the Mundari village system.

there being an amalgamation of three sadiyāls. Rajda with its four villages and Punrara with its five, in Kumāripar, are typical sadiyāli or mānki tenures; Bāngurda, Sarberia, Garwara, either sadiyāli or merely sardāri. When the bigger taraf sardārs acquired their commanding position it is impossible to say, but there is every reason to believe that the zamindar himself at one time held an exactly similar position, and that his elevation to the dignity of overlordship was due to mutual consent rather than to any special superiority in power or rank, and the quit-rent payable to him represented probably the minimum required to support him in his dignity, and to mark the fact that the other sardārs owed him allegiance; the bulk of his necessary income was expected to be realised from his own original *mānkiat* or taraf. Within the other tarafs a similar arrangement would also be the rule, and in the two which have specific divisions we have one out of five or six groups of villages directly under the taraf sardār; and within these groups again, usually one or more villages in which the sadiyāl is himself the sardār, while in the rest there are sardārs who themselves pay a quit-rent and nothing more for the whole village to the sadiyāl. Exactly, however, as the zamindar has claimed as his *khās* the greater part of the areas within the tarafs brought under cultivation since the Permanent Settlement, so also the taraf sardārs and sadiyāls have striven to better themselves at the expense of the village sardār whose quit-rent for the original village might reasonably have been held to cover that of new villages colonised by families from his, the heads of which would in the ordinary course become themselves village sardārs and pay a quit-rent to the sardār of the parent village. But even in the typical Mundāri community there is ordinarily no fixity of rent, though the original clearer is by custom entitled to special terms, and ultimately a portion of the additional rent due for new cultivation must find its way to the mānki, and, it may be, through him, to the superior landlord. Elsewhere, however, in Mānbhum the mānki became at the Permanent Settlement either a recognised zamindar, as for example in the case of Torang, or a shikmi zamindar as in the case of Naro in Pātkum, or at least a permanent tenure holder at a fixed rent as in the case of the mānkis of Bāghmundi. By analogy, therefore, the sardār ghātwals also of Barābhum should have reached one or other of these positions when Barābhum came under settlement, and reasons have been given above for believing that such was actually the case. But the particularly disturbed condition of this area, the notorious tendency of the Bhumij population to pilfering and thieving, besides the liability of the country in the 100 years or so before the Permanent Settlement to be overrun by the Marhattas imposed on the zamindar and the leading sardārs something more than the usual obligations in the matter of external defence and internal police, and it can hardly be doubted that in the very earliest days of British rule, those specifically imposed on the zamindar by the agreement (*vide* page 191 *supra*) taken from him by Mr. Higginson in 1776 must have been partially transferred to his greater vassals and by them again to the village headmen or sardārs under them. The result, if this is so, must have been that conditions of service as well as liability to pay rent must already have attached to these tenures at the time of Permanent Settlement, and it is not surprising that later on what had originally been an ordinary tenure of the type usual in the Mundāri communities came to be looked upon as purely a service tenure, and that the failure to render the required service made the holder liable to removal.

The conclusion arrived at is, therefore, that the tenures of the present taraf sardārs, sadiyāls and village sardārs had their origin in the ordinary Mundāri village system, and that in course of time and on account of the special circumstances of the area they came to be treated as purely service tenures; that the larger tarafs and the nuclei of the others were specific blocks of country and not mere scattered or isolated villages, and that the claim of the zamindar to all new cultivation within their limits was probably unjustifiable, though as a result of their origin being overlooked or forgotten, and their being treated as purely service tenures he has been able, thanks to the interpretations put upon the *isamnavisi* of 1834, to a considerable extent to establish it. Of the lowest rank of ghātwal, the tabedar, it is only necessary to say that, as the village sardār was required to provide so many paiks, those must have been found among his tenants who were mainly members of one or other of the families who originally colonised the village; the tabedar must also, therefore, have been in the first instance an ordinary tenant or *khuntkattidar* of the village who was required to give his services as well as pay a nominal rent for occupation of his holding. As in the case of his superiors, his original status was forgotten and he became a mere service tenant or ghātwal liable to dismissal and, as a consequence, to loss of his holding. At the same time he got the advantage, if advantage it be, that his holding became inalienable and indivisible, going from father to eldest son or next direct heir, except where it was forfeited for misconduct.

The only distinction that can be drawn is, as already noticed, between these *ab origine* tenures, and what may well have been more recent creations in the villages in the centre part of the estate where it is conceivable that definite assignments of land were made to persons who were not village headmen or even khuntkatti tenants of the village as remuneration for service under the zamindar as Daroga of police.

Tenures in Pātkum. Of the Pātkum tenures it is only necessary to say that their origin appears to have been similar to that of the corresponding tenures in Barābhum, though the holdings are much more attenuated. There are numerous *isamnavisis* of various dates from 1816, but these are widely discrepant, and it is difficult, if not impossible, to infer from them what was the original area held as ghātwāli, or by the ghātwals as talukdars or tenure-holders. The three tarafs are traceable to three out of the twelve tarafs or ghāts into which the quinquennial papers of 1798 divide the estate, and it is noticeable that another of these twelve is Naro, an admitted *shikmi* zamindāri. The taraf sardārs have now only one or at the most two whole villages, and in the majority of the villages the ghātwāli land is represented by comparatively small areas, for the most part fixed by compromises filed in suits arising out of the survey operations of 1880-83.

The admission of Naro as a shikmi tenure and the claims of other holders of villages in this estate to the status of mānki or Munda, with more or less exclusive rights in their village or group of villages, combined with the comparatively small number of compact ghātwāli tenures, form a contrast to what has been described as the state of things in Barābhum, while at the same time they corroborate very strongly the view taken of the origin of the ghātwāli tenures in these parganas. As compared with Barābhum, it would appear that in Pātkum the necessity for imposing special services on the headmen or mānkis of the Mundāri village organisation was less imperative, and as a result we get side by side the *murāri* or *mānkiāri* tenure which has remained so, and the similar tenures on which service conditions were imposed and the original nature of the tenure merged or forgotten. By way of further contrast, and at the same time corroboration of this view, the case of the adjoining estate of Bāghmundi, the only major estate in the district in which there are no ghātwals of any kind, is of special interest, as in it the clear division into five mānkiāri tenures, corresponding to the *parhas* of the Mundāri area across the Rānchi border and to the tarafs of Barābhum and Pātkum is extant to this day.

The settlement of the many still vexed questions in regard to the nature and extent of ghātwāli holdings and tenures in these two parganas is one of the problems of the survey and settlement operations now going on; and indeed these are among the special reasons why these operations have been undertaken in advance of the regular programme, according to which Mānbhum, as a whole, will not be dealt with until the work in the other districts of the Division is completed. The protection of the ghātwals from any further encroachment on the holdings, which the compromise of 1884 has left them, the settlement of the relations between the different grades of ghātwals and between them and their tenants, and the manner in which commutation of services can, if at all, be equitably arranged, are among the most important of the subjects with which the Settlement Officers have now to deal. Conclusion.

CHAPTER XII.

GENERAL ADMINISTRATION.

Administrative staff. LIKE other districts of the Chota Nāgpur Division, Mānbhum is a non-regulation or scheduled district, *i.e.*, one to which certain of the general Regulations and Acts in force in other parts of India and Bengal have not been extended From a practical point of view, the main distinction at present lies in the fact that the head of the district is styled a Deputy Commissioner, instead of a Magistrate-Collector; that as such he exercises certain extended powers under section 30 of the Criminal Procedure Code, and that he exercises jurisdiction in rent suits, which were tried under Act X of 1859 till December 1909, and since then under Bengal Act VI of 1908, (Chota Nāgpur Tenancy Act) by Deputy Collectors, or by Munsiffs specially gazetted as Deputy Collectors. Down to the year 1902 the Deputy Commissioner exercised also the powers of a Subordinate Judge, but from 1891 the bulk of the civil work had been done by a separate Subordinate Judge belonging to the Provincial Service.

For administrative purposes the district is divided into the Sadar and the Dhanbaid (formerly Gobindpur) Subdivision, with an area of 3,344 and 803 square miles, respectively, the river Dāmodar forming a natural boundary line between the two. In the administration of the Sadar Subdivision the Deputy Commissioner is assisted by a staff of five Deputy Collectors, one of whom is occasionally a Joint Magistrate, and by one or two Sub-Deputy Collectors, and from time to time an Assistant Magistrate. Besides this regular staff there is a special Deputy Collector in charge of Excise and Income-Tax, and also from time to time a Special Land Acquisition Officer. The Subdivisional Officer of Dhānbāid, who is ordinarily a Joint Magistrate, is assisted by a Sub-Deputy Collector. In the administration of Wards and Encumbered Estates, which at present extend over 969 square miles, the Deputy Commissioner has the assistance of a general Manager. Other local officers are a Superintendent, and Deputy Superintendent of Police, a Civil Surgeon, and a District Engineer. The Inspector, Additional Inspector, and Assistant Inspector of Schools for the Chota Nāgpur Division also have their head quarters at Purūlia.

The Revenue of the District under the main heads increased from Rs. 3,0[illegible],000 in 1881-82, by which date the district had assumed its present dimensions, to Rs. 7,67,000 in 1901-02. In 1908-09 the collections amounted to Rs. 13,45,000, of which Rs. 5,33,000 were derived from Excise, Rs. 3,32,000 from Cesses, Rs. 2,73,000 from Stamps, Rs. 88,000 from Income-Tax, and Rs. 83,000 from Land Revenue. Revenues.

The collections of land revenue have varied very little from year to year during the last 25 years. The current demand in 1908-09 was Rs. 83,126, as compared with Rs. 82,418 in 1881-82, Rs. 80,715 representing the fixed demand from the twenty-seven permanently settled estates, Rs. 2,391 that from two estates settled for periods of 12 and 15 years expiring in 1916, and the small balance the demand from Government Camping Grounds settled from year to year. The total land revenue represents only 5·65 per cent. of the gross rental of the district as disclosed by the Road Cess Returns, and the incidence is barely one anna per cultivated acre. Land Revenue.

Excise is the most important source of revenue. The receipts from this source from a considerably larger district area were, in 1870-71, only Rs. 47,300. In 1892-93 they had increased nearly three-fold, to Rs. 1,38,000; in 1901-02 the receipts were Rs. 2,63,000, and since then there has been a steady increase to Rs. 5,68,773 in 1908-09, a total considerably higher than for any other district in the Division, excepting Rānchi. The net excise revenue in 1908-09 amounted to Rs. 4,085 per 10,000 of the population (approximately 6½ annas per head), as compared with the provincial average of Rs. 3,333 per 10,000.

The greater portion of the excise revenue is derived from the sale of country spirit prepared by distillation from molasses and the flower of the mahua tree (*Bassia latifolia*). The receipts from this source amounted in 1908-09 to Rs. 4,29,000, or more than three quarters of the excise revenue Until the year 1907 the system in force was the outstill system, except in a small area served from the distillery shop at Asansol. In April 1907 the contract supply distillery system was introduced throughout the district, of which the main features are that local manufacture of country spirit is prohibited, and a contract is made with one or more large distilleries (in the case of Mānbhum with Messrs. Carew and Company, Asansol) for its supply. The liquor is sent out from the distillery to three depôts at Purūlia, Dhanbaid and Balarāmpur, where it is blended with water and issued to the retail vendors at various fixed strengths for sale to the consumers. The general issue strengths are 30°, 50°, 70° under proof, but in the case of the Balarāmpur depôt and certain outlying shops served from the Purūlia depôt liquor is also issued at 60° under proof, with permission to still further reduce before sale to 80° under proof. This is a concession allowed on account of the difficulty and expense of conveying liquor to shops situated in hilly and jungly areas, away from the main roads. Maximum prices are fixed for retail vend, varying according to the strength of the liquor and also according to the *locale* of the shop, a distinction being made between ordinary and colliery shops.

The number of retail shops for the sale of country liquor is 140, of which 18 are classed as colliery shops. Approximately, this gives one shop for every 29½ square miles and for every 9,291 persons. The issues from the depôts in 1908-09 represent a consumption of 92 proof gallons per 1,000 of the population, the incidence of taxation per head of the population being As. 6-11.

The income from other exciseable articles is in comparison very small. Ganja is sold at 46 shops, and produces in license fees and duty Rs. 67,700; opium at 16 shops, producing Rs. 36,000, and imported liquor at 14 shops, the fees from which amounted to Rs. 4,200 in 1908-09. In the same year 69 licenses for the sale of pachwai or rice-beer were issued on fees amounting to Rs. 28,000. Pachwai is the ordinary drink of the aboriginal inhabitant of the district, and it is the policy of the administration to encourage him to stick to it in preference to the stronger and less wholesome country spirit. The taste for the latter is, however, readily acquired, and the ordinary cooly, who has returned from a spell of work in the mines where high wages have enabled him to indulge in the more expensive drink, reverts with difficulty to the cheaper but less intoxicating rice-beer of his forefathers. Free-brewing of pachwai for home consumption is allowed throughout the district; the privilege is ordinarily made use of only on the occasion of festivals and family or village ceremonies, and no tendency to abuse the privilege is noticeable.

Stamps. The revenue from Stamps ranks next in importance as a scource of income to that derived from Excise. From Rs. 56,500 in 1881 the revenue rose to Rs. 1,94,500 in 1901-02, and there was a further increase to Rs. 2,73,000 in 1908-09. The bulk of the revenue is derived from sale of judicial stamps, the receipts from which were in 1908-09 Rs. 1,89,000, as compared with

Rs. 84,000 from non-judicial. The figures point significantly to the increase in the volume and value of litigation, due partly to the normal progress of the district but influenced largely by the enormous expansion of the coal industry.

The collections of Income-tax were Rs. 19,900 in 1892-93, and by 1901-02 had increased nearly four-fold to Rs. 74,000 paid by 1,326 assessees. At that time the minimum income assessable was Rs. 500, but this was increased to Rs. 1,000 per annum in 1903, with the result that the number of assessees fell to 639 and the receipts to Rs. 53,000 in 1903-04. Since then the expansion of the coal industry, and an era of great prosperity in the 'lac' trade has resulted in a large increase in the collections, which in 1908-09 amounted to Rs. 88,000, paid by 758 assessees. Income-tax.

Road and Public Works Cesses are, as elsewhere in the Province, levied at the maximum rate of one anna in the rupee. The demand in 1908-09 was Rs 3,20,000 of which Rs. 86,000 was payable by 27 revenue-paying estates, Rs. 4,300 by 57 revenue-free estates, and Rs 1,700 by 549 rent-free properties. Rupees 2,28,000 represented the demand from mines and jungles, of which 319 were assessed in that year. Mines and jungles are valued annually, the basis of assessment being the average profits of the three preceding years, and the increase in the demand from less than Rs. 11,000 in 1896-97 is a striking indication of the enormous progress made by the coal industry during the last twelve years. The last general re-valuation for the purpose of assessing cess on lands was made in 1881-82, but a portion of the district, including the Pānchet estate and Parganas Barābhum and Pātkum, was revalued in 1906, with the result that the assessment was increased by nearly Rs. 20,000. Cesses.

Inclusive of the cess on mines and jungles the figures for 1908-09 represent an average rental value of something less than Rs. 2 per acre of the whole district area. Calculated from the land cess by itself the average rental value of every acre of cultivated land in the district is rather less than Re. 1.

There are 8 offices, of which two, namely those at Hura and Balarāmpur, have only recently been made permanent, for the registration of assurances under Act XVI of 1908. At Purūlia there is a District Sub-Registrar, who deals as usual with the documents presented there, and assists the Deputy Commissioner, who is *ex-officio* District Registrar, in supervising the proceedings of the Sub-Registrars, who are in charge of the outlying offices. The average number of documents registered annually during the quinquennium ending in 1904 was 18,883 as against 16,525 in the preceding five years. Registration.

The marginal statement shows the number of documents registered, as well as the receipts and expenditure of each office for the year 1908. The year was an exceptionally busy one for the Sub-Registrars, as the serious shortage of the 1907 rice-crop, following on a practical failure in the preceding year, forced the cultivating tenants more than usual into the hands of the money-lenders, and their credit being low, practically no money was advanced except on registered mortgages. In many cases also tenants were obliged to sell out-right portions of their holdings in order to get money to enable them to cultivate the remainder.

NAME.	Documents registered.	Receipts.	Expenditure.
		Rs.	Rs.
Purūlia ...	6,037	9,688	5,017
Gobindpur ...	4,458	5,799	2,729*
Barābazar ...	3,829	3,422	2,790
Raghunāthpur	2,682	2,943	2,215
Jhalda ...	4,003	3,044	2,465
Chās ...	3,126	2,921	2,182
Balarāmpur ...	4,408	3,427	2,109†
Hura ...	2,290	2,115	1,682‡

* Now at Dhanbaid.
† Opened on 16th December 1907.
‡ Opened on 18th December 1907.

ADMINISTRATION OF JUSTICE Criminal Justice. Criminal Justice is administered by the Deputy Commissioner, who has special powers under section 30 of the Criminal Procedure Code. There is, besides, at head-quarters, a sanctioned staff of five Deputy Magistrates, four exercising first class powers, and the fifth second or third class powers; there is usually also a Sub-Deputy Magistrate exercising third class powers. The Subdivisional Officer of Dhānbāid is almost invariably an officer vested with first class powers, and the Sub-Deputy Magistrate attached to the Subdivision ordinarily exercises second class powers. There are also benches of Honorary Magistrates at Purūlia, Jhalda, Raghunāthpur, and Adra, and Honorary Magistrates empowered to sit singly at Purūlia, Pokhuria, Jharia, Kātras, and Chirkunda. Of these the Rev. Dr. Campbell at Pokhuria exercises first class powers, and takes cognizance of cases direct both on complaint and on police report. The Judicial Commissioner of Chota Nāgpur was the District and Sessions Judge till March 1910, when a separate Judgeship for the districts of Mānbhum, Singhbhum and Sambalpur with head-quarters at Purūlia was constituted. Prior to this, however, the actual sessions and appellate work of the district had been done, since 1904, by the Sessions Judge of Bankura, exercising powers as an Additional Sessions Judge of this and the Singhbhum district.

Civil Justice. Mānbhum was, until March 1910, under the jurisdiction of the Judicial Commissioner of Chota Nāgpur, to assist whom there was a Subordinate Judge posted at Purūlia. Down to the year 1887 the civil work was done by the Deputy Commissioner, assisted by a Deputy Collector specially vested with the powers of a Sub-Judge Pressure of work during the next few years made it necessary to depute a special Subordinate Judge to the district for several months in the year, and in 1891 a whole-time officer of the Provincial Judicial Service was permanently posted to Purūlia. The Deputy Commissioner continued to exercise the powers of a Sub-Judge with regard to insolvency and succession certificate cases till 1902, when he was finally divested of all civil powers. In March 1910 the district, along with Singhbhum and Sambalpur, was constituted into a separate judgeship, and the District Judge, who has also powers of a Judicial Commissioner under Bengal Act VI of 1908 (the Chota Nāgpur Tenancy Act), has his office and head-quarters at Purūlia. The subordinate civil courts are those of two (occasionally three) Munsiffs at Purūlia, one Munsiff at Raghunāthpur, and one at Dhānbāid. Mānbazar was, till 1879, the seat of a separate Munsiff's Court, which was in that year removed to Barābazar, and this was again transferred to Purūlia in 1898.

The volume of litigation has increased steadily during the last ten years, and the figures for 1908 as compared with those for 1899 show an increase of 32 per cent in the number of suits in the Munsiffs' Courts and of nearly 40 per cent in that of the Subordinate Judge's. The average value of a suit in 1908 in the Munsiffs' Courts was Rs. 114, and in the Subordinate Judge's Rs. 5,184.

EMIGRATION.

The control of emigration to the Tea Gardens still plays an important part in the administration of the district, though Purūlia has ceased to have the importance it had 10 or 15 years ago, when it was practically the centre of the recruiting industry, as the head-quarters of the district in Chota Nāgpur most easily accessible by rail to Assam, and as the station through which practically all coolies recruited in the Division and the Native States adjoining had to pass *en route* to the gardens. The Deputy Commissioner and the senior Deputy Magistrate are *ex-officio* Superintendents of Emigration both for Mānbhum and Singhbhum, and the Civil Surgeon Registering Officer and Inspector of Emigrants. Recruitment is now mainly under Chapter III of Act VI of 1901, *i.e.*, through licensed contractors and recruiters, known as the Arkāti system, and under Chapter IV, *i.e.*, recruitment by Garden Sardārs working under the control of local agents. In 1908-09 five contractors and 64 recruiters held licenses, and 1,532 coolies with 389 dependents were registered and put under contract. In the same year 1,411 Sardārs and 196 Sardārins, working under the supervision of the Tea Districts Labour Supply Association, recruited 3,786 labourers and 2,471 dependents, who, in accordance with concessions recently granted by the Local Government to this and two other Associations, were neither registered or put under contract, but went to Assam as free labourers. Fourteen Sardārs working under Chapter V, recruited 17 labourers with 7 dependents only. Both this and the preceding year were especially favourable years for the various recruiting agencies as the crops of 1906 and 1907, the latter especially, were poor. The Arkāti system, under which each cooly represents a money value of from Rs. 120 to Rs. 160, of which a considerable sum goes to the recruiter, necessarily leads to abuses, as the temptations to entice people away from their homes, or to divert them when *en route* for the coalfields or elsewhere in search of labour are very considerable. The Arkāti is also in a position to tamper with the Garden Sardārs working under Chapter IV or V, to any one of whom a sum of even Rs. 20 would mean a larger profit than he could make by taking a labourer to his Local Agent. Every year there are a considerable number of cases of coolies, usually women, enticed away from their homes, whom the recruiters attempt to pass off under false names and descriptions.

POLICE. For police purposes the district is divided into 16 thānas or circles with 12 outposts; the latter, it may be explained, are treated as thānas for police, though not for other administrative, purposes, such, for example, as the census. The regular police force consisted in 1909 of a District Superintendent of Police, a Deputy Superintendent, 6 Inspectors, 46 Sub-Inspectors, 44 Head Constables, and 358 Constables, representing one policeman to every 9·09 square miles, and to every 2,853 persons. The rural police force, intended for watch and ward duties in the villages, consists of 2,683 chaukidars under Act V (B.C.) of 1887. There are besides 1,974 ghātwals of different degrees, namely, 12 taraf sardārs, 11 sadiyāls, 504 village sardārs, 1,384 tabedars, 40 digwārs, and 23 naib digwārs, whose services are remunerated by service tenures, particulars of which have been given in an earlier chapter. Their police duties are, in the case of the subordinate ghātwals, periodical attendance at the police stations, patrol of certain roads, and general watch and ward in the villages included in their respective "ghāts". From the ghātwals of higher degree is expected an occasional attendance at the thana, general supervision of the inferior ghātwals of their respective ghāts, and regular submission of diaries detailing the actual duties performed, and reporting any facts of interest in respect of their ghāts. From the point of view of the superior police authorities, the services of the ghâtwals generally are of little value; attempts have, from time to time, been made to make more use of them, but of recent years other considerations, of which some notice has already been given, have prevented any serious pressure, which can only be exerted by means of fine or dismissal, being put upon them. The question of commuting their services has been constantly raised, and it is perhaps probable that a solution of the various difficulties in this connection will be found when the settlement operations, now in progress in Barābhum, where the ghâtwals are most numerous, is completed

There is a second class District Jail at Purūlia and a Subsidiary Jail at Dhânbâid. The latter has accommodation for 40 male and 7 female prisoners. The District Jail has accommodation for 281 prisoners, viz., 6 barracks for 211 male convicts, 10 female convicts, 32 under-trial prisoners and 7 civil prisoners, 5 cells for 5 male convicts, and a hospital with 16 beds. JAILS.

The daily average number of inmates in the Purūlia and Dhânbâid Jails during 1908 was 201 and 15, respectively. The industries carried on in the District Jail are oil-pressing, aloe fibre decortication, weaving of cloth and *daris*, and cane and bamboo work. There is a large garden attached to the Jail, in which prisoners, unfitted for other forms of hard labour, are employed.

Land has recently been acquired and administrative sanction given for a considerable extension of this Jail; an additional double storied barrack with accommodation for 192 prisoners is provided for.

CHAPTER XIII.

LOCAL SELF-GOVERNMENT.

DISTRICT BOARD. OUTSIDE the municipal towns of Purūlia, Jhalda and Raghunāthpur the administration of local affairs, such as the maintenance of roads, bridges, ferries and pounds, the control of village sanitation and water supply, the provision of medical and veterinary relief, and the general responsibility for primary education, rests with the District Board which was established in the year 1900, when the provisions of the Local Self-Government Act III (B. C.) of 1885 were extended to the District. The District Board consists of 14 members, of whom six are *ex-officio*, two elected by the Local Board of Dhānbaid, and the remainder nominated by Government. The Board as constituted in 1909 included 6 Government servants, 5 Landholders and Landholders' Managers, 1 Pleader, 1 Colliery Manager and 1 Missionary. By a recent Notification of Government the number of members has been increased to eighteen, and Landholders have been nominated for the vacant places.

Income. The income of the District Board in the first year of its existence was Rs. 96,799, of which Rs. 45,474 was derived from Road Cess. Since then there has been a rapid increase, and in 1908-09 the total income was Rs. 2,38,500 of which Rs. 1,49,000 was derived from Provincial rates, Rs. 26,500 from Civil Works, including a special grant from Government of Rs. 25,000, and Rs. 33,000 from Education, the bulk of which, *i.e.*, Rs. 31,600 represents the Government contribution. The extent to which the Board's resources have been increased by the opening out of the coal fields, will appear from the fact that in 1908-09 cesses derived from mines and jungles amounted to Rs. 1,06,300 as compared with only Rs. 34,700 in 1906-07.

The incidence of taxation is, for the same reason, heavier than elsewhere in the Division, amounting to nearly 2 annas per head of population.

Expenditure. The expenditure in 1908-09 was Rs. 2,16,000 of which Rs. 1,45,000 was allocated to Civil Works, while Education accounted for Rs. 41,000. The maintenance of 123 miles of metalled, and 527 miles of unmetalled roads, besides a large number of village tracks with a total length of 508 miles, is naturally the heaviest charge on the income of the District Board, and Rs. 51,800 was spent on this account in 1908-09, the cost of maintaining these roads working out at Rs. 447, Rs. 59 and Rs. 6 per mile for the three classes respectively. A large part of the additional income due to the expansion of the coal industry has necessarily gone to improve the road system in the colliery areas, and during the five years ending in March 1909 about 27 miles of metalled road, eight causeways and two Inspection Bungalows have been constructed in this area alone, at a total cost of Rs. 1,70,000 besides another Rs. 20,000 expended on improvement of approaches to rivers and stone-metalling portions of previously existing roads.

Advantage has also been taken of the increased income as well as of special grants received from Government from time to time, to improve by gravelling some of the more important roads in other parts of the district, and to link up the main roads with the different railway stations.

After Civil Works, Education constitutes the heaviest charge on the Board's resources; it maintains four Middle Schools and aids 12 Middle Schools, 71 Upper Primary Schools, 588 Lower Primary Schools, 15 Tols and Muktabs and three Technical Schools. For the purposes of supervision it maintains a staff of eight Inspecting Pundits.

On Medical Relief and Sanitation Rs. 6,500 was expended in 1908-09, as compared with Rs. 1,300 in 1900-01, in supporting eight dispensaries of which two are under the direct management of the Board. The principle adopted is that the Board gives one and a-half times the amount raised by private subscription, but in special cases additional grants are made. A contribution of Rs. 200 was also made in the same year towards the funds of the special Sanitary Committee for the Jharia coalfield, and, when required, special measures are taken on the outbreak of epidemic diseases. The District Board also contributes a sum of Rs. 200 annually towards the support of the Purūlia Leper Asylum. A Veterinary Dispensary was established at Purūlia in 1905 at a cost of Rs. 2,800 and a resident Veterinary Assistant is maintained there; since April 1909 a second itinerant officer has been employed with head-quarters at Dhānbaid.

In subordination to the District Board is the Dhānbaid Local Board, the jurisdiction of which corresponds to the subdivisional charge of the same name. The Local Board is composed of 14 members, all of whom are nominated by **LOCAL BOARD.**

Government. It receives allotments from the funds of the District Board, and is entrusted with the maintenance of certain of the District Board roads, all village roads, pounds and some other small functions.

MUNICIPALITIES. There are three municipalities in the district, viz., Purūlia, Jhalda and Raghunāthpur. The number of rate-payers in 1908-09 was 4,403, representing 16·7 per cent. of the population (26,342) residing in municipal limits, as compared with 16·4 per cent. for the whole division. The average incidence of taxation in the same year was annas 13-4 per head of the population, as against the divisional average of annas 14-4, and varied from Re. 1-0-6 in Purūlia to annas 6-10 in Raghunāthpur.

Purūlia. The Municipality of Purūlia, which was constituted in 1869, is administered by a Board of 19 Commissioners, of whom 12 are elected, 5 nominated by Government and 2 are *ex-officio* members. The area within municipal limits in 1909 was 5 square miles, the number of rate-payers being 3,212 or 18·57 per cent. of the population.

Income and expenditure. The average annual income of the municipality during the decade ending in 1901-02 was Rs. 20,300, and the expenditure was Rs. 21,000; during the succeeding five years ending 1906-07 they were Rs. 29,600 and Rs. 27,600 respectively. In 1908-09 the income aggregated Rs. 33,540, besides an opening balance of Rs. 9,576. The chief source of income is a rate on houses and arable lands assessed at 7½ per cent. on their annual value, which in that year brought in Rs. 11,242; while a conservancy rate, levied at Rs. 3-8 per cent. on the same basis, brought in Rs. 5,414; fees from markets brought in Rs. 4,081, receipts from pounds and serais Rs. 949, and a tax on vehicles and animals Rs. 1,343. The total incidence of taxation was Re. 1-0-6 per head of the population. The expenditure in the same year was Rs. 26,565, excluding Rs. 6,520 expended on the repayment of advances and deposits. The principal items of expenditure were medical relief, conservancy and public works, which accounted for 22·25, 34·79 and 17·25 per cent., respectively, of the disbursements.

The Municipality is at present unable to undertake new projects or carry out substantial reforms for want of funds. An ample supply of good drinking water is available in the large tank known as the Saheb-bandh, but to ensure freedom from contamination good tanks suitably situated are required for bathing and culinary purposes, and existing insanitary tanks require to be thoroughly cleaned out, and in some cases filled up. The town is to a certain extent naturally drained, but the growth of the more densely populated parts calls for an extension of the artificial drainage, and with this object a survey is shortly to be made and a regular scheme prepared. Further expenditure is also required for the provision of more public latrines, and the improvement of the lighting system. A detailed survey of the town is now (1909) in progress, and it is anticipated that the new assessment which will be based on the map and record prepared, will result in a substantial increase in income, and make it possible to take in hand some of the needed improvements outlined above.

Jhalda was constituted a Municipality in 1888, and has a Municipal Board composed of 9 Commissioners all of whom are nominated by Government. The area within municipal limits is approximately 3 square miles, and the number of rate-payers is 775, representing 15·88 per cent. of the population residing within municipal limits. The average annual income of the Municipality during the five years ending 1907-08 was Rs. 4,000 and the expenditure Rs. 3,800. In 1908-09 the income of the Municipality was Rs. 3,941, of which Rs. 2,170 were obtained from a tax on persons according to their circumstances and property, levied at one per cent. on the income of the assessees; receipts from pounds amounted to Rs. 350, and from serais and markets Rs. 320. The incidence of taxation was 7¾ annas per head of the population. Jhalda.

The expenditure in the same year was Rs. 4,725, the principal items being medical relief, conservancy and public works, which accounted for 34·21, 16·88 and 15·4, respectively, of the total expenditure.

The Municipality of Raghunāthpur was established in 1888 and is administered by a Board of 10 Commissioners, all of whom are nominated by Government. The area within municipal limits is 4 square miles, and the number of rate-payers is 416 representing 9·9 per cent. of the population. The average annual income of the Municipality during the five years ending 1907-08 was Rs. 3,600 and the expenditure, Rs. 3,200. In 1908-09 its income was Rs. 3,688 besides an opening balance of Rs. 709. The chief source of income is, as at Jhalda, a tax on persons, levied at one per cent. on the income of the rate-payers, which brought in Rs. 1,168. From pounds Rs. 440 was realized, and rents of serais brought in Rs. 280. The total incidence of taxation was 6¾ annas per head of the population. Raghu-nāthpur.

The expenditure in the same year was Rs. 3,750, the principal items being medical relief (35 per cent.) and conservance (27 per cent.).

CHAPTER XIV.

EDUCATION.

PROGRESS OF EDUCATION. In 1855 Mr. (afterwards Sir H.) Ricketts wrote of education in Mānbhum:—"The only school in this district is an English School established at Purūlia in 1852. Though so lately established, the number on the books is 7 and the average attendance is 34." He goes on to quote the Secretary as saying "the demand for education is confined to the middle class of people, who hold it in great estimation. The zamindars and rich people think it below and the poorer classes above their notice. The people generally are averse to contribute to the furtherance of education, thinking themselves entitled to receive from the Government everything necessary about it." Mr. Ricketts adds that "the attitude of the landholders was unfortunate for they possessed extensive estates, inhabited by very wild and barbarous people, whose ignorance has, on more than one occasion, caused very embarrassing disturbances and much bloodshed."

No material advance in the spread of education seems to have made for many years. In 1870-71 the number of Government and aided schools had increased to 23 with 960 pupils, and the creation of primary schools under Sir George Campbell's grant-in-aid scheme swelled the total to 31 in the following year. The next year saw the scheme more fully in operation and the number had increased to 183 with 5,271 pupils by the inclusion of many of the 72 schools returned in 1870-71 as private unaided schools, attended by an estimated total of 1,238 pupils. By the end of March 1875 the total number of Government aided and inspected schools was 244 attended by 6,938 pupils, figures which represented on the then area and population of the district, one school to every 20·13 square miles of area, and one pupil to every 143 inhabitants.

The succeeding 15 years saw a considerable advance in the number of schools of which in 1892-93 there were 622 attended by 15,578 scholars. In the next ten years there was a steady increase, the number of schools in 1901-02 being returned as 727, and of scholars 19,728. The census of that year showed that the total number of persons able to read and write was 47,231 representing 4·2 per cent. (8·0 males and 0·3 females) of the population.

In 1904-05 the figures reached 849 for schools and 28,686 for scholars, but the succeeding years saw some decrease, the latest returns for 1908-09 showing a total of 768 schools with 26,624 pupils on their rolls.

Of the total number of schools, 759 with 26,382 pupils are classed as public institutions, and only 9 with 242 pupils as private institutions. Of the former 13 schools attended by 754 pupils are under public management, 9 being managed by Government and 4 by the District Board; of the schools under private management 625 are aided and 121 unaided. The inspecting staff consists of 1 Deputy Inspector of Schools, 8 Sub-Inspectors, 2 Assistant Sub-Inspectors and 8 Inspecting Pandits. GENERAL STATISTICS.

There is no college in the district. There are 25 secondary schools, the attendance at which is 2,248. Of these six are High schools of which one only, the Zilla School at Purūlia, is maintained by Government. The pupils on the rolls of this school in 1908-09 numbered 272, but it is reported that for want of sufficient accommodation both in the school itself and the hostel attached, a number of applicants had to be refused admission. Considerable enlargements of the buildings have been sanctioned by Government but funds have not as yet been provided to carry them out. Two schools, *i.e.*, those at Chirkunda and Raghunāthpur, with a total of 259 pupils are aided by Government and in the latter case also by municipal funds. Of the three unaided institutions those at Jharia and Pāndra, which owe their existence to the liberality of Raja Durga Prosad Singh and the late Rāni Hingan Kumāri respectively, provide for 88 and 118 pupils respectively. The remaining High School is known as the Victoria Institution and is at Purūlia; in 1908-09 the number of scholars was 366. Of middle schools there were 19 in 1908-09, namely, 12 middle English and 7 middle vernacular. One of the former and three of the latter were managed by the District Board, the number of pupils on the rolls being 45 and 185 respectively. Of the others 13 with 822 pupils were aided and 2 with 93 pupils unaided. The popularity of secondary vernacular education is evidently declining as the present figures show a considerable falling off since 1891-92 when there were 12 middle vernacular schools with 570 pupils. SECONDARY EDUCATION.

The total number of primary schools for boys in the district is 676, of which 73 are upper primary and 603 lower primary. With the exception of 4 upper primary schools attached to the PRIMARY EDUCATION.

guru training schools, all are under private management, 561 being aided and 111 unaided. The attendance at these schools was 22,585, viz., 21,435 boys and 1,150 girls. Upper primary schools are usually accommodated in buildings specially provided for them, but in the majority of cases such buildings are very unsuitable for the purposes. With few exceptions lower primary schools have no regular buildings and are generally held in the common *puja* house of the village, or the verandah of some comparatively well-to-do villager's house. With the aid of a Government grant of Rs. 15,500 and funds subscribed locally the District Board are now constructing 18 model school buildings, of which 12 are intended for upper primary and 6 for lower primary schools.

FEMALE EDUCATION. The education of women has not advanced beyond the primary stage. There were in 1908-09 altogether 29 girls' schools, *i.e.*, 4 upper and 25 lower primary. These schools were attended by 847 girls, and there were also 1,150 girls studying in boys' schools, so that altogether 1,997 girls were under instruction; of these 1,636 were Hindus, 26 Muhammadans, 148 Christians and 187 aborigines. In the majority of cases the girls' schools are taught by male teachers from the neighbouring boys' schools and there are only 13 girls' schools with separate staff.

There is one model primary school for girls teaching up to the lower primary standard. It is under the management of Government and had 42 girls on its roll on 31st March 1909.

SPECIAL SCHOOLS. There are four schools for the training of primary school teachers, all of which are intended for male teachers. Sixty-four *gurus* were under training at the close of the year 1908-09, and during the year 11 passed the final examination.

INDUSTRIAL EDUCATION. Five technical schools are aided by the District Board or Government, of which 2 are for instruction in blacksmith's work at Jhalda, where there is a considerable manufacture of country guns, sword-sticks, and agricultural and household implements. The German Lutheran Mission at Purūlia maintains a general technical school where carpentering and smithy work are taught to the inmates of the untainted children's ward attached to the Leper Asylum; there is also in connection with the same Mission a lace school for girls, at present unaided. A special weaving school is managed by the Rev. Dr. A. Campbell of the Sonthal Mission at Pokhuria. The remaining aided school is at Tanāsi, the industry taught being smithy. Another weaving school at Raghunāthpur was supported for a number of years by the District Board, but was recently abandoned as the local weavers found that the fly-shuttle loom was unsuited for the local industry of silk-weaving. In all these schools arrangements have recently been made to provide teaching in at any rate part of the lower primary course besides the industrial subject.

NIGHT OR CONTINUATION SCHOOLS. There were in 1908-09, 37 night schools with 824 pupils on their rolls. Their object is to give facilities for primary education to boys of the working classes who are unable to attend the ordinary day schools.

OTHER SCHOOLS. Other schools include 7 Sanskrit tols with 119 boys on their rolls, 11 maktabs with 266 students, 3 indigenous schools teaching vernacular only with 97 pupils, and 6 Koran schools (class I maktab) with 145 pupils, on their rolls. These schools were returned as private institutions.

BOARDING HOUSES. There were in 1908-09 9 boarding-houses with 237 inmates. Of these one is attached to the Purūlia Zilla School and is under the management of Government; the rest are unaided and under private management.

EDUCATION OF DIFFERENT RACES. The number of Muhammadan pupils studying in public institutions in 1908-09 was 1,541, representing 5·31 per cent. of pupils of all creeds, almost exactly the same proportion as the Muhammadan population bears to the total population of the whole district. It is noticeable also that the percentage of literates among the Muhammadan population is 5·9 as compared with 4·2 for Hindus, a fact which suggests that the community has realised to some extent the importance of primary education.

ABORIGINAL. The number of aboriginal pupils in the various public institutions is returned by the Education Department as 5,709 of whom 328 are Christians; few of these go beyond the primary stages, and it is a significant fact that none of the Government offices in the district contain a single aboriginal clerk, though attempts have been made from time to time to recruit suitable aboriginals as apprentices. The backwardness of the aboriginal population generally in the matter of education is shown by the low percentage of literates to total population in the thanas in which the aboriginal element is strongest, Bāghmundi 2 per cent., Chāndil and Barābhum 2·4 per cent., and Tundi 2·9 per cent., as compared with the district average of 4·2. The same table shows that the area in which education is most advanced is that which borders on Burdwan and Bānkura, in which the immigrant population from the more advanced Bengal districts is more predominant than elsewhere.

LIBRARIES AND NEWSPAPERS. There is a small public library at Purūlia, maintained in the Town Hall erected to commemorate the Jubilee of the Queen-Empress Victoria. The only private library of any importance is that of Dr. Campbell at Pokhuria, which is largely theological.

Two newspapers, the *Manbhum* and the *Purulia Darpan*, dealing with topics of local interest are published at Purulia. The Sonthal Mission Press at Pokhuria publishes a quarterly magazine dealing with the progress of Medical Mission in India.

CHAPTER XV.

GAZETTEER.

Adra.—An important station and railway settlement on the Gomoh-Kharagpur and Asansol-Sini sections of the Bengal-Nagpur Railway line, situated at 23° 30′ N. and 86° 44′ E. 177 miles from Calcutta, 24 from Purūlia and 26 from Asansol. This rapidly growing settlement has come into existence since 1903, when the Kharagpur-Gomoh branch was opened. The area covered by the station buildings, yard, workshops and residences is nearly a square mile in extent, and more recently a large area (nearly half a square mile) has been acquired as a sanitary zone, and to secure unpolluted the catchment area of the large tank to the east of the settlement which is the source of the water supply. The settlement includes the residences and offices of a District Engineer, District Loco. Superintendent, District Traffic Superintendent, and Assistants, a Medical Officer and a Chaplain, besides quarters for a large number of European and Indian subordinates of the different branches. A fine church has recently been built at the expense of the Railway Company, and there is also a large institute, providing for the recreation and amusement of the subordinate staff. The affairs of the settlement including a market garden and a meat market, are managed by a Station Committee; there is also a Bench of Honorary Magistrates with third class powers, who dispose of any cases made over to them by the Deputy Commissioner. About five miles south, and connected with the station by a metalled road is Kāshipur, the present head-quarters of the Zamindar of Pānchet.

Balarāmpur.—A village 3 miles south-east of Purūlia near the banks of the Kāsai river. A description of a collection of ruins at this place, written by Lieutenant R. C. Money, is quoted in Colonel Dalton's Notes on a Tour in Mānbhum in 1864-65,* and reproduced in Hunter's Statistical Account under the name Palma, which is apparently an error for Balarāmpur. Mr. Beglar describes the principal ruin as a temple of the Baijnath type dating probably

* The Journal of the Asiatic Society XXXV, Part I of 1866, page 186.

to some time after Rāja Mān Singh, but built of the materials of an older temple. The sculptures of perfectly nude male figures, standing on pedestals and under canopies, with Egyptian head-dresses, the arms hanging down straight by their sides, the hands turned in and touching the body near the knees, described by Lieutenant Money and identified by Colonel Dalton as images of the Tirthankaras of the Jains are no longer extant, and had apparently been removed before Mr. Beglar's visit in 1872.

Barābāzār.—A village of considerable size, in pargana Barābhum in latitude 23° 2′ N. and longitude 86° 25′ E. 12 miles south-east of the Barābhum railway station in the Asansol-Sini section of the Bengal-Nāgpur Railway. The village contains the residence and family temples of the zamindar of the pargana, a police station, a sub-registry office, a District Board inspection bungalow, a middle English school, and a post and telegraph office combined. The offices and residence of the Manager of the Midnapore Zamindāri Company, which holds a large part of the estate on a *patni* lease, are situated just outside the village. Barābāzār was also the head-quarters of a separate Munsifi from 1880, when it was transferred there from Mānbāzār, until October 1898 when it was again transferred to Purūlia. The traditional origin of the Barābhum family connects them closely with the adjoining estate of Pātkum and its mythical founder Vikramaditya (*vide* also under Dalmi, Pabanpur, Telkupi); their family legend is given by Colonel Dalton as a specimen of the skill of the Bhumij zamindars in making pedigrees. "Nath Varaha and Kes Varaha, two brothers, quarrelled with their father, the Rāja of Virat, and settled in the court of Vikramaditya. Kes the younger was sawn into two pieces, and with his blood Vikram gave a 'tika'* to the eldest and a pair of umbrellas, and told him that all the country he could ride round in a day and night should be his. Nath mounted his steed and accomplished a circuit of eight 'yojanas'† within the time specified, and a precious stiff line of country he took in riding round what is now Barābhum, but it must be all true as the print of his horse's hoofs are still visible on the southern slopes of the hills." (Descriptive Ethnology of Bengal 1872). Another variant to the earlier part of the story is that the two brothers came to Vikramaditya's court with the fixed determination that they would not bow their heads to any one. To test them Vikramaditya had some swords hung in the door through which they would first pass:

* Mark on the forehead.

† A "yojana" is equal to four "kros" or a trifle over 9 miles, a "kros" being equal to 8,000 cubits or 12,000 feet taking a cubit as 18 inches.

Set or Kes passed through without stooping and his head was in consequence severed from his body, whereupon Vikramaditya stopped the other brother, and took him into favour, awarding him a kingdom in the manner already described.

The name of the pargana and estate Barābhum is beyond question a survival of the Varāhabhumi described in the Bhavishyat Purāna of the 15th or 16th century, as a country "contiguous in one direction to Tungabhumi" (the southern part of Raipur thana in the Bānkura district), "and in another to the Sekhara mountain" (either Parasnath or the Panchet hill) and comprising Varābhumi, Sāmantabhumi (Chātna thana in Bānkura) and Mānbhumi." According to the same account the inhabitants were "mostly Rājputs, robbers by profession, irreligious and savage, eaters of snakes and drinkers of spirituous liquors," a description which remained very true to the facts till a much later date.

At the time of the British accession to the Dewāni of Bengal, Burdwan, and Orissa, and for many years afterwards the area covered by this estate was notorious as the home of the "chuārs," and the zamindar and his chief sardars were little better than leaders of banditti. Details of the organisation of the ghātwals, who are a special feature of the pargana, will be found elsewhere (*vide* Chapter XI and Appendix).

Borām.—A village some four miles south of the police station Jaypur (railway station Garh Jaypur) on the right or south bank of the Kāsai river. Here are the ruins of three large brick temples and several stone temples of which Colonel Dalton* gave the following description:—

"The most southern of the three temples is the largest. The tower rises from a base of 26 feet square. The chamber occupies only 9 feet square of this, and after 9 feet of upright wall is pyramidal in form, the bricks, in rows of first three, then two, and near the top one, gradually approaching till the four sides meet. The remainder of the tower is solid brickwork throughout. Its height is about 60 feet; but the upper portion of it has fallen, and it is impossible to say how it was finished off. The bricks of which these temples are composed, some of them eighteen inches by twelve, and only two inches thick, look as if they were machine made, so sharp are the edges, so smooth their surface, and so perfect their shape. They are very carefully laid throughout the mass of masonry, so closely fitting that it would be difficult to insert at the junction the blade of a knife. The

* J. A. S. XXXV. Part I of 1866.

entrance to all the temples faces the rising sun. The objects of worship, whatever they were, have disappeared from the fanes; but in the southern temple there is a stone gutter through the wall, terminating in a well-carved gargoyle for carrying off the water used in the ablution of the idol. The bricks used for ornamental freizes and cornices appear to have been carefully moulded for the purpose before they were burned; and the design, executed entirely of bricks thus moulded and put together, is, though very elaborate, wonderfully perfect and elegant as a whole; but in some places stucco has been added, and further ornamentation or more delicate tracery attempted in the stucco on the brick foundation, and this tracery, where it remains, is in wonderful preservation. The entrance to the temple is wide and lofty, and arched like the interior; that is, by the projection, till they meet, of bricks horizontally laid. Door, there appears no sign of. The fane must have been open to the world. The only animals I could discern in the ornamentation were geese, introduced in the scrolls. The goose is a Buddhist emblem. The other temples are of similar design, but smaller size. In front of them I observed several pillars of stone; but I found no architraves, and the pillars are hardly long enough to have been the support of a covered porch in front of the fane. These three temples are all of the same type, and are no doubt correctly ascribed by the people to the Srāwaks or Jains. I found, indeed, no Jain images on the spot; but about a mile to the south the remains of a Hindu temple in a grove were pointed out to me, and all the images from all the temples in the neighbourhood have been there collected. The grove temple was dedicated to Siva; but amongst the images were several nude figures like those already described, that were in all probability the Jain figures belonging to the brick temple. Near the brick temples I found, amongst a heap of ruins, a square stone crypt in which was a four-armed female figure, finely carved, in the style of the sculptures at Dālmī, to be presently described. This was worshipped by the women of the place under the name of Sasthī. In the grove there was a similar figure, and the other images of Hindu gods found there appeared to be of the same period. Another mound was pointed out to me, about half a mile from the grove, as a collection of ruins, but I did not go to it."

Mr. Beglar* describes these temples as definitely Saivic; the largest, that described in detail by Colonel Dalton, faces east and the object of worship is a four-armed female presumably

* Archæological Survey of India Reports, Vol. VIII.

Parvati seated on a lion. Another Parvati with a small figure of Ganesha to its right and a female figure to the left lies near the second brick temple; this resembles in execution and style the sculptures of Dalmi (q. v.) and belongs apparently to the same period, *i.e.*, the tenth or eleventh century. The third brick temple faces north, and contains a life-size sculpture of the eight-armed Durga slaying Mahishâshur, and is of particularly fine workmanship. Mr. Beglar describes also a fourth brick temple besides three stone temples, and the numerous mounds and debris scattered about point to the existence of others, which may have been of earlier date. The only inscriptions are the single letter K inscribed on a round-ended flat slab between the river and the largest temple, and the figure 6 on one of the side posts of the entrance to one of the stone temples. The former is ascribed, from the formation of the character, to the ninth or tenth century.

Buddhpur.—A village four miles north of Mâubâzâr on the Hura Road on the north bank of the Kâsai river. There is here an interesting group of temples of which the largest is still in a fair state of preservation and maintained as a place of Saivic worship; in its immediate neighbourhood are the remains of four smaller temples, besides numerous roughly sculptured stones commemorating in all probability "*satis.*" The main temple is thus described by Mr. Beglar, "The temple is placed on a high plinth on the topmost point of a low hillock; in plan, the temple resembles other temples of the kind, with some petty variations, the principal of which is that at the two sides of the entrance into the "antarala" are two recesses, like the recesses at the sides of the westernmost temple at Barâkhar. The windows in the projecting ends of the transept are closed by plain square-holed lattices cut in the same sandstone of which the temple is built; the windows being projecting, the three open sides of each are thus closed. The entrance into the 'antarala' is similar to the entrance into the temple at Buddha Gaya, being formed of overlapping courses of stones. The ornamentation externally consists of lines of mouldings of a plain kind, sparingly used; the mouldings resemble those of the temples at Barâkhar. The pinnacle that surmounted the original tower roof of the sanctum lies neglected on the ground; it is an urn-shaped vessel, supported by four cobras with expanded hoods and forked tongues, and is graceful in outline and design; there can, I believe, be no doubt that it was, as it now is, a Saivic temple."

The lingam of the temple is known as Budheswar and ranks locally, in point of sanctity, with the Gadādhar of Gaya, and Buddhpur is the scene of an annual fair held on the last night of the month of Chaitra, which attracts plilgrims in considerable numbers both from the immediate neighbourhood and from adjoining districts.

Chākultor.—A large village, situated in 23° 14′ N. and 86° 24′ E. about seven miles south of Purūlia, on the Purūlia-Barābāzār Road. The place is chiefly notable for an annual fair held at the time of the *Chhata* festival on the last day of the month of Bhādra. The origin of the celebration of this festival, usually confined to places where local zamindars reside, and of the fair which follows it lies apparently in the fact that at one time this was one of the seats of the Pānchet Zamindar. Some members of the family still reside here, and there are remains of fairly elaborate buildings, both residences and temples. The fair lasts for seven days and is one of considerable local importance attracting large numbers of people, chiefly of the aboriginal or semi-aboriginal tribes, from the southern half of the district.

Charrā.—Village in the head-quarters subdivision of Mānbhum district, situated in 23° 23′ N. and 86° 25′ E. 4 miles north-east of Purūlia. Population (1901) 1,532. It contains some very old stone temples, called *deuls* or *debalayas*. There were originally seven temples, but five have fallen. Some of them were Jain or Buddhistic, and numerous votive chaityas with mutilated figures either of Buddha or one of the Jain hierarchs lie in the village, but the greater number of the remains of sculptures lying about are Brāhmanical. According to local tradition these and some large tanks in the vicinity were constructed by Sarāks (*vide* Chapter III, page 83 *sqq*).

Dalma.—Principal hill in Mānbhum district, situated in the headquarters subdivision in 22° 53′ N. and 86° 14′ E. rising to a height of 3,407 feet above sea-level. It has been described as the rival of Parasnāth, but it lacks the bold precipices and commanding peaks of that hill, and is merely a long rolling ridge rising gradually to its highest point. Its slopes are covered with dense forest, but are accessible to beasts of burden. The chief aboriginal tribes living on the hill are the Kharias and Pahārias.

Dalmi or more correctly **Diapur Dalmi,** the site of an ancient town of considerable extent on the north bank of the Subarnarekha river, in latitude 23° 4′ N. and longitude 86° 2′ E. The actual ruins are now, and have for a long time been, in a very dilapidated condition; a full account of them is to be found at pages 186-*sqq* of Volume VIII of the Archæological Survey of India Reports (J. D. Beglar), and at pages 190-*sqq*, Volume XXXV, Part I, Journal of the Asiatic Society, Bengal, 1866 (Colonel E. T. Dalton). One brick temple alone remains and this also is much dilapidated, but for several miles almost every eminence is marked by debris of temples and other buildings. A few only of the statues described by earlier observers are to be found in situ, the remainder have been removed to various places in the village or to Purūlia. Mr. Beglar identified some of the more northerly ruins as Jain or Buddhist, and the remainder as Brāhmanical. The ruins of a brick fort of no great size, known as Vikramaditya's fort, are still visible to the south of the village, on the bank of the Subarnarekha river; nearer the village is a large tank known as the "Chhata Pokhar" from the singular structure of stone, two small columns supporting a triple umbrella, which marks what was perhaps once the centre of the tank. Tradition has it that this is where Vikramaditya used to perform Puja before bathing; Telkupi some 60 miles away on the Dāmodar was where he rubbed his body with oil preparatory to the bath. The most notable of the extant statues is a colossal Ganesha, who according to Colonel Dalton was the janitor, the heaps of stones round about representing the remains of the river gate of the old city. In the village itself are various statues of Vishnu, and of groups representing Vishnu and Lakshmi, Durga Mayi, the monster Mahisasur, and of Kamdeva and his wife.

The only inscribed statue is one of Aditya, the characters being probably of the tenth century to which period Mr. Beglar, judging from the general style of the sculpture, would date the temples. Some of the sculpture and ornamentation is described by him as very good, and obviously ascribable either to Jains or Buddhists; he infers that there was a large Jain establishment here in the ninth and tenth century, succeeded, say about the eleventh century, by Hinduism.

Of equal interest with these remains of an ancient Aryan civilisation is the enormous collection of "Kistvaens" in the village itself, the sacred burial places of the Bhumij; some of the stones are of enormous size, 10 to 15 feet square, and altogether there must be several hundred, representing originally as many heads of houses or founders of families. The inference to be drawn from their presence here and the ruins alongside is that the Aryan city was conquered, and the followers of Brāhmanism driven out by the incursion of the Bhumij section of the Kolarian race sometime probably between the eleventh and sixteenth centuries. The small extent of jungle for some distance round, the absence of any sign even of earlier forests on the now bare hills, and the very considerable cultivated area all mark the place as a very early settlement of the Bhumij; from the extent of the ruins it might reasonably be inferred that much of the country was already cultivated when they became its masters. Another view, it may be noted, that held by Colonel Dalton, is that the Kolarian tribes were already in possession when the Buddhists, and later the Brâhmans, pushed out missions into the wilder parts of the country. He assumes that when these missions got too aggressive the progenitors of the Kols, Bhumij, and Munda finally after severe and continued struggles extirpated them.

The present reigning family of Pâtkum, six miles from Dalmi, claim descent from Vikramaditya and have the usual stories to account for their presence here. The generally accepted theory is that the Râja or Zamindar of this and other estates is descended from a self-elected chief or mânki of a group of Bhumij, or Munda villages; it may be as Colonel Dalton half satirically suggests that the conquering aborigines "from a lingering admiration for the superior intelligence, higher civilisation and godlike beauty" of the Aryans they displaced, "retained some of them as guides and instructors and in some instances from the remnant heirs retained, elected their chief. We might thus account for the Aryan features and Brâhmanical predilections of some of the chiefs whom we find ruling alike people without any evidence that they had by conquest attained that position."

The chief modern importance of Dalmi is the manufacture of cups and plates from the soft dark coloured slate stone, which crops up in and along the bed of the river here. Some 16 or 20 people are employed in quarrying and about as many in cutting the stone. There are obvious indications all round that a great part of the sculptured or plain blocks, forming the ruins of the temples, have already been used up for the same purpose.

A few miles further up the Subarnarekha, and north-west of Dalmi, is Safâran, which Mr. Beglar identifies with the Kirana Sufalana of Hwen-Tsang, the capital of the Sasangka Râja At Safâran itself are uninvestigated mounds, and near it in Deoli and Suisa fairly extensive indications of early Jain civilisation; in Suisa there is also another large Bhumij burial place.

Dhanbaid.—Headquarters of the subdivision of that name since July 1908. It is an important station on the East Indian

Grand Chord Line, and is the junction for the Jharia and Kātras branches from which radiate most of the short lengths of line which serve the various collieries. The railway quarters cover a considerable area on either side of the line near the station, and quarters have been erected or are in course of erection for a full complement of railway officials besides a very large subordinate staff, both European and Indian. The civil buildings constructed between 1905 and 1908 lie in the village of Hirāpur about half a mile from the railway station and comprise a Subdivisional Magistrate's Court, a Munsifi, Sub-Registry Office, Post and Telegraph Office combined, and police station, with residences for the Subdivisional Officer, Munsif, and Sub-Deputy Magistrate. North of these again is the large double-storied office of the Department of Mines in India, with residences for the Chief Inspector, an Inspector, and a large number of clerks. The purely native town which is still in the early stages of growth consists of a considerable bazar in the village of Dhanbaid immediately south of the Railway line and a rapidly growing residential quarter for pleaders, clerks, etc., between the offices of the Mines Department and the rural village of Hirāpur. The chief feature of the former is the Lindsay market-place recently constructed by private enterprise. There are also several large general merchandise shops and a couple of printing presses.

Dhanbaid Sub-division.—Known till July 1908 as the Gobindpur Sub-division, is the northern sub-division of the district lying between 23° 38′ and 24° 4′ north and 86° 7′ and 86° 50′ east with an area of 803 square miles. In shape it is an irregular triangle between the Barākhar and Dāmodar rivers, their junction just south of Barākhar in the Burdwan district forming the apex. A third river, the Jamuni, forms a part of its western boundary, the remainder being formed by the lower slopes of the Parasnāth Range, and the various spurs and ridges which strike off from it. To the north and east the country is fairly open, marked only by occasional hills of no great height. The population of the subdivision was 277,122 in 1901 as compared with 221,434 in 1891, the density being 345 persons to the square mile. The south-eastern part of the subdivision, comprising the police stations of Dhanbaid and Jharia and the independent out-post of Kātras, constitutes the Jharia coal-field, the rapid development of which between the years 1894 and 1901 accounts for the large increase in the population of the subdivision as returned in the latter year; during the succeeding years the development has been even more marked, and there were in 1908 no less than 281 collieries at work in this area employing a daily average of 72,000 labourers. A portion of the Rāniganj coal-field falls within the eastern part of the subdivision (police station Nirsa and independent out-post Chirkunda). The area covered by the remaining police stations of Gobindpur, Tundi and Topchānchi and out-post Rājganj is almost entirely outside the limits of workable coal deposits, and is consequently purely rural in character. There are no towns, but Jharia Khās, Kātras and Dhanbaid are now places of considerable size and importance. The head-quarters of the subdivision were moved to Dhanbaid from Gobindpur in July 1908; for some years before 1846. Bāgsuma, a small village at mile 167 of the Grand Trunk Road, was the site of the Sub-divisional Officer's residence and office.

Gobindpur.—A village situated in 23° 50′ N. and 86° 32′ E. at the 169th mile of the Grand Trunk Road, formerly (till 1908) the head-quarters of the northern sub-division of the district. Population (1901) 1,293. There were the usual subdivisional offices and a residence and a sub-jail. The last named has now been converted into a guru-training school, and the Subdivisional Officer's residence has been taken over by the District Board for use as an inspection bungalow. The village has now lost practically all its importance with the removal of the pleaders, mukhtears, clerks and most of the shop-keepers to Dhanbaid. A weekly market is held, which is attended by a considerable numbers of villagers from the rural areas surrounding. A single lac factory, and a few big grain merchants' depôts remain to testify to the former importance of the place. There are two fine sheets of water, *bāndhs* constructed at the expense of Government during the famine years of 1866 and by public subscription in 1882-83, known respectively as the Sāhib bāndh and the Risley bāndh. Both of these are maintained by the District Board. There is also a Government camping ground to the west of the village, and a Public Works Department inspection bungalow about 3 miles west on the Grand Trunk Road at Kandra. Good gravelled roads to Tundi and Pokhuria (towards Giridih and Jamtara, respectively) take off from the Grand Trunk Road on the northern side, and on the south there is the direct road to Purūlia viâ Pradhānkhunta station and Sarsākunri Ghāt, and also a metalled road to Dhanbaid and the coal-field.

Jhalda (Jhalida).—A small town in the head-quarters subdivision, situated in 23° 22′ N. and 85 59′ E. Population (1901) 4,877. Since 1908 it has been connected by railway with Purūlia and Rānchi. Jhalda was constituted a Municipality in 1888, and its income, mainly from a tax on persons, averaged

Rs. 4,000 during the five years ending 1908-09; its average annual expenditure during the same period was Rs. 3,800. The town consists of one main street (the Purūlia-Rānchi road) with several small streets leading off from it. There is a regular weekly market, and also a fair number of merchants, shops dealing in grain, cloth, kerosine oil and miscellaneous articles. There are some 43 lac factories owned for the most part by Armenian and Mirzapuri firms, and it is a very important centre for the lac trade, large quantities of the raw material being brought in from the wild tracts, both of Mānbhum and of the Rānchi and Hazāribāgh districts which surround it. There is also a considerable manufacture of cutlery, including sword-sticks and also of guns. Besides the Rānchi-Purūlia road, there is a good metalled road as far as the border of the district, towards Gola, one of the chief trade centres in Hazāribāgh, and there are fair gravelled roads towards Bāghmundi (south) and Begunkodar (east). The public buildings consist of a small Municipal office, a dispensary with accommodation for in-patients, a District Board inspection bungalow, and a police station. Besides the usual middle vernacular and primary schools, there are two technical schools, subsidized by the District Board and Municipality, where boys of the artisan class are taught how to make cutlery and agricultural implements. Jhalda is also the head-quarters of the local zamindar, whose residence, a collection of not very imposing buildings, is surrounded by a high earthen rampart, partly natural, partly artificial.

According to one of the traditions of the Pānchet family Jhalda was their earliest seat in the district, and the sacred cow, Kapila Gai, who nourished the abandoned child of Anot Lal, Rāja of Kāshipur, who eventually became the first king of Chaurāsi or Sekharbhum with head-quarters at Pānchkot, is supposed to have been converted into stone and to have her resting place one of the hills north of Jhalda. The traditional history of the Jhalda Rāj family contains nothing of special interest.

Jharia.—A large village in the Dhanbaid subdivision, situated in 23° 44′ north and 86° 27′ east. Population (1901) 4,623. The village itself, except in point of size, possesses few features of interest; it contains a market place, built by the local Rāja, a charitable dispensary built and maintained by him, and a police station. There are a number of shops of considerable size dealing in grain, cloth, kerosine oil and other necessaries of the large coal-field population; there are also residences, some of imposing dimensions, of Indian colliery owners, managers and others connected with the coal trade. Good metalled roads connect the station, the market, the Rājbāri, etc., with the main District Board roads running from Dhanbaid, Kātras and Pāthardih. The residence of the Rāja, just outside of and to the north-west of the bazar, is of considerable size; most of it is of comparatively modern construction and of no special architectural interest; a large house for the reception of guests is under construction. Between the Rājbāri and bazar is a fine tank, and another large tank, the Rāni bāndh, recently enlarged and deepened at the Rāja's expense lies between the Dhanbaid and Kātras roads and the Dāmodar Branch of the East Indian Railway line. On all sides of the bazar, and working right up to, if not actually underneath part of it, are numerous collieries; some of the best and most easily worked of the Jharia seams underlie the town, which, sooner or later, will probably have to make room for collieries A quarter of a mile from the present residence of the Rāja is a small hill or mound with a few dilapidated ruins on it, said to be the remains of the original fort of Jhariagarh, from which, according to the historians, the whole tract of country including the greater part of Chota Nāgpur and part of Bihar got the name of Jhārkhand, by which it was known in Muhammadan times. The mound also contains traces of having been a Bhumij or Munda burial ground. According to tradition the present Jharia house is an offshoot of Pālganj in Hazāribāgh and was formerly established at Kātrasgarh, the original offshoot having further split up in more recent times into the three houses of Kātras, Nāwagarh, and Jharia. Twenty years ago the zamindar's income was some Rs. 25,000 to Rs. 30,000 entirely derived from rents of land; his present income from rents and mining royalties is some three to five lakhs per annum, over and above which very large sums have been received as '*salāmi*' on coal settlements.

Half way between Jharia (East Indian Railway) and Bhāga (Bengal-Nāgpur Railway) Railway stations is the Jharia Station Club, which is the common meeting place of the European community of the coal-field; nearer Bhāga station is a District Board inspection bungalow, and also a small lecture-hall where the Mining Instructor gives regular courses of instruction to candidates for Mines' Managers' certificates. On the other side of Jharia about half a mile from the town on the Dhanbaid road is a Protestant (undenominational) Church recently erected by private subscription.

Kātras or Kātrasgarh.—A village of considerable size about 1¼ miles from the railway station of that name, and six miles south of the police outpost Rājganj on the Grand Trunk Road. Along with the new bazar which has sprung up near the station and is locally called Pānchgarhi it is now a place of considerable importance being surrounded on three sides by colliery areas Pānchgarhi contains an independent police outpost, an inspection bungalow, post and telegraph office combined, school, and a large market place which is the chief centre of distribution in the western half of the Jharia coal field. The village of Kātras itself contains the residence of the local zamindar, and according to tradition was formerly the head-quarters of the Jharia Rāj before this was split up into the separate houses of Kātras, Jharia and Nāwagarh. There are traces of ruins of numerous temples and other buildings, of which a small temple half ruined, known as the Dewāl is described by Mr. Beglar as an interesting and ancient example of the single-cell type. It stands on the crest of high undulating ground known by the name of Jhinjhi Pahāri, where a fair is held in the month of Chaitra (March-April). The temple faces west; on the architrave of the entrance is a sculptured human head with matted locks, apparently intended for Siva, and within is an argha centrically placed. South of Kātras about 8 miles off on both banks of the Dāmodar river at Chechgāongarh and Belonja are a number of ruined temples, marking the site of a very ancient Buddhist or Jain religious establishment, succeeded by a Brāhmanical. The ruins, for the most part very dilapidated, are principally of Saivic temples, but indications of the earlier Jain establishment remain in a large naked and obviously Jain statue now at Belonja, south of the river, besides various Jain and Buddhistic figures and emblems sculptured on the fragments in situ or scattered about. The ruins are very extensive, traces of 16 temples, large and small, are extant in a space of about a quarter of a mile broad and half a mile in length, besides others half a mile away on either side on the north bank of the river and of one large temple on the south bank, and there is every indication that the buildings were elaborate and profusely ornamented with sculpture, some of which in beauty and delicacy of workmanship vies, according to Mr. Beglar, with the similar work in the superb temple of Udaipur in Central India.

Mānbāzār.—A village or rather group of villages of considerable size, in latitude 23° 03′ N. and longitude 86° 43′ E. some 28 miles south-east of Purūlia, and the chief place in the pargana from which the district gets its name; it is also the seat of the local zamindar, locally known as Rāja of Mānbhum. The family claim to have come originally from Rājputana and settled first in the Burdwan district and later in Bānkura. They are connected by marriage with the landholding houses of Ambikānagar, Khātra, and Bishnupur. Of their Rājput origin they have nothing in the shape of authentic records of ancient date, and in all probability like other zamindars of the district they are actually of Bhumij or possibly in this case of Bāuri origin. The estate is at present heavily involved in debt due partly to an expensive succession suit but mainly to the wholesale alienation of portions of the estate on nominal rents fixed in perpetuity. It is now under management under the Chota Nāgpur Encumbered Estates Act.

Mānbāzār, or rather a small village close to it, Bartoria, was the head-quarters of the Jungle Mahals district from 1833 to 1838. Of the office buildings and residence a heap of bricks is the only remains, but the police station occupies the site of the Munsifi and Sub-Registry Office which were not removed from here till a much later date. The bazar is of considerable extent and is an important centre of the lac trade, which is exported mainly in the unmanufactured state to Purūlia to the extent, it is said, of nearly a lakh of rupees' worth per annum. A large factory was started here a few years ago by an Armenian firm, but owing to the dulness of the lac market and the distance from any railway station the venture has not been successful and the factory is now (1909) about to close. There is one middle vernacular school and also two lower primary schools in the village, and a third lower primary school at Pāthormohara, which immediately adjoins it. There is also a police station and a post office, and a District Board inspection bungalow. A good road connects the place with Purūlia, and there are also roads leading north to Hura, west to Barābāzār, and east to Bānkura and Khātra, besides a fair-weather track leading south to Kailāpāl and Bandwān.

Pabanpur.—A village in pargana Barābhum in latitude 22° 57′ N. and longitude 86° 23′ E., where there are extensive ruins of temples and other buildings, which have not as yet been examined by any archæologist. The ruins extend into the neighbouring village of Bhula, which is a purely Bhumij village and the site of a large burial ground belonging to the Bhumij of the Gulgar sept or Killi. Tradition connects the ruins with Rāja Vikramaditya, the reputed ancestor of the zamindars of the adjoining pargana of Pātkum, whose name is also closely connected with the ruins at Dalmi and Telkupi (q. v.). The carving on the fragments that remain is described as highly artistic and from the specimen recently sent to the Indian Museum, a miniature temple about two feet in height and six inches square at the base, with representations of Tirthankaras on the four sides and apparently a votive offering of some Jain pilgrim, the Jain or Buddhistic origin of these remains is apparent. Closer examination will probably prove, as in the case of Dalmi and other places in the district, that the original Buddhistic civilisation was succeeded by a Brâhmanical dynasty, which was eventually destroyed by the aboriginal population, the Bhumij. The close proximity of a very early Bhumij colony to the relics of an ancient and higher civilisation is here, as at Dalmi, suggestive.

Pākbira.—Two miles east of Puncha and some 25 miles south-east of Purūlia, in pargana Bagda, contains the remains of numerous statues and sculptures principally Jain, a full description of which is given by Mr. Beglar.* The principal object of attention is a colossal naked figure with the lotus as symbol on the pedestal and worshipped under the name of Bhiram which is obviously the Jain Tirthankara, Vira. The figure is 7½ feet in height standing on a low pedestal; it is depicted perfectly nude with the arms stretched out close to the sides and the hair wound up into a knot on the top of the head. The shed in which it now stands contains numerous other figures, two small ones with the bull symbol, one smaller with the lotus, a votive chaitya on the four sides of which are sculptured a lion, an antelope, a bull, and what appears to be a lamb; over each principal human figure on the chaitya is represented a duck or a goose, holding a garland. Mr. Beglar also unearthed from one of the numerous mounds of ruins near by five Buddhist sculptures of late age, the most remarkable being a male and a female figure under a tree, possibly the date palm.

One large brick temple still stands and north of it a line of four stone temples, three standing and one broken. Near this is an irregular line of five temples, two of stone of which one is standing, and three of brick all ruined, and again north of this another line of four temples, three of stone and one of brick, all in ruins. East of the brick temple are other lines of two and three temples all in ruins, and all according to Mr. Beglar probably stood originally on a stone pavement some 100 or 120 yards square.

Traces of other ruins are numerous in the immediate neighbourhood. The hill called Lathondungri near Kharkiagarh, just south of Pākbira was probably the site of one, as there are here numerous votive chaityas and round and oblong cut-stone blocks. It is also the site of an old burial place of the Bhumij.

* Archæological Survey of India Reports, Volume VIII.

Dhādki Tānr, Tuisama are other places just south where ruins of temples, probably Saivic, and later in date than those at Pākbira, exist, and immediately south of these are the temples of Buddhpur (q. v.).

Pānchet or Pānchkot.—Hill in the head-quarters sub-division of Mânbhum district, situated in 23° 37′ N. and 86° 47′ E. half way between Raghunâthpur and the junction of the Barâkhar and Damodar rivers. It is 3 miles long stretching from north to south in a long rounded ridge, and has a height of 1,600 feet above sea-level. At the foot of the hill towards the southern end is the fort of Pânchet, once the residence of the Rājas of Pānchet but now deserted and in ruins. The name is variously explained as meaning that the Râja reigned over five Râjas, or over five crores of people, but the word probably means five forts or citadels and apparently refers to the number of walls surrounding the actual citadel. Of these there are actually four on the west, south, and east, the hill defending the fort on the north, and the fifth, it is suggested, is an outer natural line of ramparts, the ridge-lines of the surrounding undulating country.

"The four sets of artificially built walls of the fort are all of earth, and are each defended by deep and wide moats, now filled up in many places; the moats were so connected with the streams descending the sides of the hill, as to keep them always wet, and to this day they always contain some water; in most places the walls, or earthen ramparts, were also ingeniously led so as to form continuations of natural spurs of the hill itself, thus securing the maximum of defensive power with the minimum of labour in throwing them up. In the walls were numerous gates, now mostly gone, and represented by mere gaps in the walls; four gateways, however, of cut stone, in various stages of decay, still exist, and have names; they are named Ankh Duār, Bazar Mahal Duâr, or Desbândh Duār, Khoribāri Duār, and Duâr Bândh; the last is in the best state of preservation; all of them were built in much the same style, viz., the usual Muhammadan style and with true arches, though overlapping arches were also used: some of these gateways served the double purpose of gateways proper and openings for water, and the Duâr Bāndh still serves the purpose of allowing water to be taken in from the moat outside, when necessary for irrigating the fields within; the fort is very large, the outermost ramparts having a total length of more than five miles, while the traditional outermost defences, viz., the ridge lines round the fort, inclose a space of about 12 square miles, exclusive of the hill itself." (Beglar. Archæological Survey of India Reports, Vol. VIII.)

Within the fort are numerous brick remains, for the most part much dilapidated and grown over with jungle; the outlines of the Rāja's palace, of the female apartments, and of various other buildings are pointed out, and one or two small temples in a fair state of preservation remain. All are apparently post-Muhammadan and of the Lower Bengal type of architecture; moulded and cut brick and terra cotta sculptured tiles are used in almost all of them. On the side of the hill, and overlooking the fort, are a number of temples, all massively built, and marked by the occurrence of the true dome and the true arch as post-Muhammadan. The largest temple is known as Raghunāth's *mandir*, and is ascribed to a Rāja of that name, probably the eighth in ascent from the present zamindar who reigned from about 1590-1626.

The date of the fort is more or less definitely fixed by that of two of its gates, the Duār Bāndh and the Khoribāri, on which there are duplicate inscriptions in the Bengali character referring to a Sri Vira Hamira, and giving the date Samvat 1657 or 1659, *i.e.*, about 1600 A.D. Vira Hamira is apparently the Bir Hambhir of the Bishnupur Rāj, who threw in his lot with the Mughals and rendered good service to the Viceroy Mān Singh when he invaded Orissa in 1591.

It is a matter for question whether the fort was built by him and subsequently captured by the Pānchet Rāja, or by the Pānchet Rāja for his own protection against Vir Hamira and perhaps also against the Muhammadans. The reason for its abandonment is not known. According to one story connected with the name of another Raghunāth, whose period was about 1705-1720, it was on account of some mysterious sickness which affected numerous members of his household. There is nothing, in any case, to show that the family was forcibly driven out, but it has been suggested that it was due to the desire to avoid the notice of the Musalmān Governors, whose aggressions were at that time coming somewhat close; it may also have been due to pressure from Chitra Sen Rai of Burdwan, who conquered Shergarh, once a part of the Pānchet estate, about 1742. Support is given to this theory by the tradition that Mani Lal (also a Raghunāth) who reigned from 1753 to 1791 hid himself for some time at Manihara.

Later the head quarters of the estate was at Chākultor, a few miles south of Purūlia, at Kesargarh in the jungles on the Kāsai river, 12 miles south-east of Purūlia, and finally at Kāshipur.

The history of this great zamindāri, so far as it comes into the history of the district, has been referred to in chapter II.

The legendary origin and establishment of the family is thus described by Mr. Beglar:

"Anot Lal, Rāja of Kāshipur, was going, with his wife, on a pilgrimage to Jagannāth, when the Rāni gave birth to a child in Aruna Vana (the present Pānchet). The Rāja and Rāni, unwilling to delay on account of the child, determined to abandon it, thinking that they could easily get other children, while the fruits of the pilgrimage could not be so easily got so they proceeded on to Thākurdwāra; the fabulous cow Kapilā Gāi, who used to live in Arunban, seeing the child abandoned, took upon herself to feed it with her milk, and thus the child lived on and grew up, and remained in the jangal. One day a party of hunters, who were looking for game in the forest, saw the child, and carried him off, notwithstanding the resistance of Kapila Gāi, to Pāwāpur; when he grew up, the people made him Mānjhi (chief of a clan or village), and finally, when in want of a king, determined to elect him, and he was accordingly elected king of pargana Chaurāsi (Sikhar-bhum); they built him the Pānchet fort, and named him Jatā Rājā; on the death of the miraculous cow, her tail was found and carried to the Rāja, who used it as an ensign, tying it to his horse; hence he was also called Chānwar bāndhā, and the Rājas of Pānchet are said to this day to use the cow's tail, or chānwar, as one of their emblems.

"Anot Lal had two other sons by another wife; they were named Nayān and Asmān; they invaded Jatā Rāja's domains, and he was forced to fly, but his conquerors, in seeking for him in the jangal, lost their way and perished, and Jatā Rāja returned and reigned peaceably.

"Another version says, the child was not deliberately abandoned, but falling accidentally from the elephant on which he was being carried, the Rāja and Rāni left him for dead; then Kapilā Gāi came and fed him; she used to live in Kapilā Pāhār (the range of hills south of Purūlia*), and would come daily to feed the child; when the child grew up, he used to wander in the jangal with the cow, and, eventually, he became king, and built Pancha Kot; as he was made king through election by five Rājas, his fort was named Pancha Kot; he was known as the Gaumukhi Rāja. The Rāja had a cowherd, who one day saw a large snake issue from a hole in the hill side, and the snake vomited forth a brilliant gem that illuminated the whole forests by its light; it fed and then swallowed the gem; then

* Mr. Beglar's geography is at fault; Kapila Pahar is a hill north of Jhalda, Ed.

bands of celestial nymphs and musicians came and performed for some time, and finally all vanished. The cowherd related the particulars to the Rāja, who went to see the wonder, and so great an effect had the sight on him, that he returned bereft of speech, and died in two or three years. During his son's reign, the Rāja of Murshidābad invaded the country, and exterminated the entire race of the Rājas of Pānchet, except one child, who was saved by the headman of the village of Suri Lachhiā, hiding him in a drum ; he grew up and regained his kingdom, and he is the ancestor of the present Rājas. The cow, turned into stone, still exists at Jhalda on the Ajodhya hill.* As there are remains of Saivic temples in Jhalda, the petrified cow is most probably a statue of Nandini (the celestial cow mother)."

According to the zemindar's geneological tree the first Mahārāja of Chākla Pānchkot was Dāmodar Sekhar Singha Deo, described as 12th Mahārāja of Ujjain, about 80 A.D., from whom the present zamindar is the 67th in direct line of descent, the succession having been, according to the tree, direct from father to son, except on two occasions when grandsons succeeded. The value of this tree is discounted largely by the stories told of various Rājas. Thus Abhay Nath Serkhar, 33rd Rāja, whose date is 952—967A.D., is supposed to have provided a fight for the Emperor's son at his Garh Pānchkot and gave so good a show, keeping off the Emperor's army for four dandas (1½ hours), the time stipulated for the fight, that he was rewarded with a *sanad* and the title of Mahārājadhirāj and the whole of pargana Shergarh as an addition to his Rāj. The loss of a portion of this pargana is explained by the following story, the historical inaccuracies in which will be obvious. "About 1688 Sak (1767 A. D.) one Bahuram gave himself out as Ananta Lal, an uncle of the then Rāja Mani Lal *alias* Raghunāth, who had become a religious mendicant, and with the help of Kanta Pal, Dewān of the Nawab of Murshidābad, got himself recognised as Rāja of Pānchet (by whom the story does not say), and gave part of Shergarh to Kanta Pal. The impostor was found out and deposed but Kanta Pal prevailed on the Rāja to let him keep part of pargana Shergarh in consideration of his promising in future to look after the interests of the Pānchet Rāja." This story is no doubt more consistent with the dignity of the family than would be an admission that Warren Hastings found Shergarh a sort of debatable ground between Pānchet, Burdwan, and Bishnupur, and carved off a large portion of it by way of

* Here again the geography is at fault, Ed.

reward for his right hand man Kanta Pal. (*Vide* W. B. Oldham's Some historical and ethnical aspects of the Burdwan District, Calcutta, 1894.)

These stories illustrate the manner in which fanciful and mythical traditions, mainly complimentary to the family, have made it impossible to trace with any sort of accuracy the real history of any one of the great zamindāri families of the Mānbhum district any further back than late Muhammadan or early English times.

Pāra.—A small village in the head-quarters sub-division, situated in 23° 31′ N. and 86° 33′ E., on the direct road between Purūlia and Gobindpur, and about four miles from the railway stations Kargâli and Anāra, on the Kharagpur-Gomoh and Asansol-Sini sections of the Bengal-Nāgpur Railway. There is a police station, but the chief interest in the place lies in the numerous ruined temples which are found in the neighbourhood. These are locally ascribed to the ancestors of the Saráks, an account of whom was given in an earlier chapter, and of whom a considerable number still reside at Jhāpra and other places in the immediate neighbourhood. As a matter of fact, however, according to Mr. Beglar,* the ruins for the most part date from the post-Muhammadan period. The most ancient and interesting objects are two temples, to the east of, and just outside, the village, one of brick, and the other of a soft kind of stone, both much weather-beaten and broken, but full of interesting architectural and archæological features. Both must at one time have been profusely ornamented with mouldings and sculptures, and those on the brick temple, which have weathered better than the soft sandstone of which the other is built, were particularly fine. Extensive repairs appear to have been done to both temples, during the time of Rāja Mān Singh, probably by one Purushōttam Das of Brindāban to whom is ascribed a more modern temple called Rādhāraman dating from that period, which remains in a good state of preservation at the extreme western end of the village, and which, like the more ancient, is profusely ornamented with moulded and cut brick.

"Close to the stone temple is a large mound, on which, and about which, lie several tapering plain pillars; this mound was clearly once the site of a large temple, larger than the existing ones. At the east end of the mound still stand two pilasters, with plain square mouldings; they measure 28 inches in width by 16 inches in thickness. Tradition says they are the side

* Archæological Survey of India Reports, Volume VIII.

supports on which the trunnions of a dhenki used to work, the said dhenki having been set up by an evil Rankini, who was fond of human flesh, which she used to pound in this dhenki; and one of the long stone pillars, lying at the foot of the mound, is pointed out as the dhenki beam; it is said that, by agreement with the Râja, she was allowed one human victim daily. One day a poor cowherd, on returning with his cows to his master's house, saw his master and mistress crying bitterly; and ascertaining on inquiry the cause to be that one of them was to be made over to the ogress, he volunteered to go instead, stipulating only that he should be immediately furnished with some gram made of iron and some ordinary gram; armed with these, the man and his two dogs went to the temple and waited; presently in came the Rankini, and was about to seize him, when he said—"Hold, before you eat me, or I eat you, let us make a trial of strength: here is a handful of gram for you, and here is one for me, whichever of us two finishes eating the gram first, shall also eat the other." The Rankini agreed, but vainly tried to masticate the iron gram she had received, while the cowherd soon got through his share, and made as if he would begin on her next; terrified the Rankini rent the temple and ran out pursued by the cowherd and his two dogs; the Rankini fled to Dhalbhum, where, seeing a washerman washing at the river, she begged him to hide her promising him the Râj as recompense; the man hid her under his "pât" (the piece of wood they beat the cloth on), and the cowherd, after a fruitless search was returning with his two dogs, when, in passing through the Baghal forest, near the village of Baghâlyâ, he and his dogs were turned into stone, and exist to this day! In proof of the truth of this legend, they point to the Râjas of Dhalbhum, who are said to be dhobis by caste, and who are notorious for having practised human sacrifices, till very recent times, in honor, it is said, of this very Rankini, who became their tutelary deity and the principal object of worship in the country; her temple is said (and the site is pointed out at Sarangarh, near Ambikânagar) to have existed till within the last few years, and to have been regularly supplied with human victims till it was destroyed by the British authorities.

"The petrified cowherd is nothing more or less than a Sati pillar, standing by itself, in the Baghâlyâ forest (scrub jangal), near the Baghâlyâ village; it is clear that the name of the village and of the jangal has suggested the identification of the Sati pillar (the real purpose of which was forgotten) with the petrified cowherd; the dogs are said also to be there, but one of them is certainly a lion from some temple, and the other is perhaps another from the same, or some other temple: the Sati pillar is now worshipped, if plenteous libations of milk and ghi be any criterion of worship. The Baghālyā village is a couple or 3 miles off the road, between Kotra and Jhāpra."

Purūlia.—Principal town and administrative head-quarters of the Mānbhum district, situated in 23° 20′ north and 86° 22′ east on the Sini-Asansol section of the Bengal-Nāgpur Railway, and at the junction of that system, with the 2 feet 6 inches gauge line from Purūlia to Rānchi, which was opened in February 1908. Purūlia has been the head-quarters of the district since 1838; it was first constituted a municipality under the old law in 1869, and became a regular municipality under Act V of 1876 from the 26th July 1876. For municipal purposes it includes the villages of Purūlia khās, and Nadiha, and portions of Pālanja, Ketka, Dulmi, Balguma, Bhātbāndh, Mānguria, and Rāghabpur, covering an area of nearly five square miles. The town proper is, however, little more than a mile in length from east to west and rather less in breadth, lying for the most part, between the railway station, and the fine lake known as the Sāhib Bāndh. The population which was only 5,695 in 1872, had expanded by 1901 to 17,291 of whom 14,287 are Hindus, 2,271 Muhammadans, and 684 are Christians.

The chief streets of the town correspond with the old Bānkura, Chaibāsa, Rānchi and Barākhar roads, which radiate from the public buildings, which cover a considerable area about one mile west of the railway station. Of these the offices of the Deputy Commissioner, District Judge, and Superintendent of Police, occupy a single compound, which includes also an English Church built in 1898, and a large school, the Victoria Institution, built on the site of the old Government Middle Vernacular School. The police lines, and jail are about ¼ mile south-east and south, respectively, and the Zilla School with its hostels, about the same distance south-west, on the Chaibāsa road. To the north and immediatly on the banks of the Sāhib Bāndh, is the Town Hall, in which are the offices of the Municipality and District Board, erected by public subscription in memory of the Jubilee of Queen Victoria.

The town proper contains a considerable number of substantial residences of merchants, pleaders and others, and all houses in this quarter are now tiled. The European residences, including those occupied by the German Evangelical Lutheran Mission, and also their Church, lie along the Rānchi road, and on the western and north-eastern banks of the Sāhib Bāndh. A mile beyond the European quarter, and outside municipal limits, in the village of Mānguria, is the Leper Asylum an account of which has been given in Chapter IV.

The town is purely modern, and there is no building of antiquarian interest; there is a picturesque Muhammadan mosque, dating back some 40 or 50 years, but no Hindu temple of any size or special interest. The main business quarter immediately adjoins the public offices, and the Municipality maintains a market which brings in a considerable income. In more recent years, the eastern part of the town, east, that is, of the railway station, has considerably developed, and there are a number of large lac factories and one large oil mill now working in this area.

The climate of the town is dry and healthy, and prior to the opening of the railway line to Rānchi, there was a growing tendency for it to become a regular health resort for Indian gentlemen, principally of Calcutta. The drainage is naturally good, and the town is well supplied with drinking water, the Sāhib Bāndh serving as a valuable reserve, during the months when other tanks and most of the wells dry up. It is well served by roads and those in the station are usually smooth and well kept, the heavy cart traffic from the Rānchi direction to the railway station being for the most part diverted at a point just outside the town. There are pleasant drives in the Barākhar, Mānbazar and Rānchi directions, and a circular drive of about 6 miles, known as the Wilcox *chakkar*, connecting the Rānchi and Chaibāsa roads, besides the shorter circular drive round the Sāhib Bāndh. There is a European Club, to which are attached tennis courts, golf links, and a fine polo and parade ground; and recently some of the Indian residents have started a Union Club, which provides for tennis and also indoor games. Football is played with considerable vigour by the boys of the different schools, and from time to time the Town Club engages in matches with teams from Bānkura, Asansol and other places.

Purūlia Subdivision.—The head-quarters subdivision of the district lying between 22° 43′ and 23° 44′ N. and 85° 49′ and 86° 54′ E., and covering an area of 3,344 square miles. It comprises the whole of the district south of the Dāmodar river; to the east it merges in the alluvial plains of Bengal, but to the west and south the country is more broken and the general elevation rises towards that of the Chota Nāgpur plateau. The south of the district is marked by the Dalma range of hills, the highest peak in which rises to 3,400 feet; in the south-west the Bāghmundi or Ajodhya range is a conspicuous feature. The population of the sub-division was 1,024,242 in 1901 as compared with 971,894 in 1891, the density being 306 persons to the square mile. It contains three Municipal towns, Purūlia (population 17,291), Jhalda (4,877) and Raghunāthpur (4,171) and 4,273 villages. It comprises the police stations of Purūlia, Raghunāthpur, Gaurāndi, Pāra, Chas, Jhalda, Bāghmundi, Chāndil, Barābhum and Mānbāzār, besides the independent outposts of Ichāgarh (Pātkum), Baudwān, Balarāmpur, Hura, Jaypur and Sānturi.

Raghunāthpur.—A small town in the head-quarters subdivision situated in 25° 31° N and 86° 40° E., two miles from Chinpina station, and about 3½ from Adra station on the Bengal-Nāgpur Railway System. Population (1901) 4,171. Raghunāthpur was constituted a municipality in 1888; the average annual income and expenditure during the five years ending in 1908 were respectively Rs. 3,600 and Rs. 3,200, the chief source of income being a tax on persons or property tax. It is the head-quarters of a Munsif-Deputy Collector who exercises powers in respect of civil justice over parganas Bānchās, Bārpāra, Bankhandi, Chaurāsi, Cheliāma, Mahāl, Mārra, Nalichānda, and Pāra, and in respect of rent suits over parganas Chaurāsi, Cheliāma, and Banchās. The Munsif exercises also powers of a Magistrate of the third class, and until 1906 had powers to take cognizance of cases on complaint. There is also a Bench of Honorary Magistrates who exercise third class powers. The public buildings include, besides the munsifi, a sub-registry office, a police station, a dispensary and also a large Inspection Bungalow, formerly one of the staging bungalows between Barākhar and Purūlia, the direct road between which places passes through the town. With the opening of the Kharagpur-Gomoh branch of the Bengal-Nāgpur Railway, and the development of Adra (q.v.) into a large railway centre, the importance of Raghunāthpur has rapidly diminished. It is still a centre of the tasar silk industry, and there is also a considerable manufacture of cotton cloth, but both industries are on the decline. The Pemberanda Faith Mission (an undenominational American Mission) has a station at Raghunāthpur, with one male and two or more female missionaries in residence. The most notable feature of the neighbourhood is the group of bare cone-shaped hills just to the south of the town, one of which is known as 'Phānsi Pahar,' the tradition being that in former days the zamindars of Pānchet executed on this hill their enemies and other malefactors. The unfortunate victim was pushed or dragged up the less precipitous side of the easternmost peak and then pushed over the other, a sheer drop of a couple of hundred feet or more. There is a small temple on the central hill of no special interest, and also the ruins of one of the old semaphore towers which were erected every 20 miles or so along the so-called old Benares Road, Rānīganj viâ Raghunāthpur and Chās in the Mānbhum district to Rāmgarh and on to Sherghati in Gaya, which was the great military road before the completion of the present alignment of the Grand Trunk Road about 1846. Besides this and the Purūlia-Barākhar Road which intersect at Raghunāthpur, there are good gravelled roads to Adra and to Sānturi (police station) in the direction of Rānīganj, and a fair weather road towards Telkupi.

Telkupi.—A small village in the south bank of the Dāmodar river in pargana Cheliāma, about 7 miles north-east of the village of that name. It contains what Mr. Beglar of the Archæological Survey described as "perhaps the finest and largest number of temples within a small space that is to be found anywhere in Chota Nāgpur." They are in 3 groups, the largest being immediately on the bank of the river to the north of the village, a second close to the village towards the west, and a third within the village itself; there are besides several detached temples further south, and numerous mounds some of stone, but mainly of brick, representing the remains of temples which have collapsed. When Mr. Beglar visited the place in 1872-73 the first and largest of the groups consisted of 13 temples, 3 of considerable size, and 10 small; of the latter two have since disappeared, having fallen with the bank on which they stood into the bed of the Dāmodar river which at this point has cut in considerably. All the temples are Brāhmanical in origin, and the oldest probably date from the tenth century; one of the three large temples, which is still kept up as a place of worship, appears to have been considerably added to at a later date, probably, according to Mr. Beglar, about the time of Rāja Mān Singh, the internal evidence of date being a small true arched opening, typical of post-Muhammadan work, in the wall which forms a court-yard round it. More recently the appearance of the court-yard and the general symmetry of the place has been spoilt by the erection of rough stone sheds forming quarters and cooking shed for the resident priest. Of one of the other larger temples, the most interesting from an archæological point of view, Mr. Beglar gives the following description.

"No. 6 is a large temple, facing west; it consists at present of a sanctum, 'antarala' in the thickness of the front wall of mahāmandapa, an ardhamandapa, and a portico. The sanctum with its tower roof is entire, but the inner roof of the sanctum, being the floor of the upper chamber, is broken the chamber above the sanctum has no opening, and therefore is, and always was, inaccessible ; the roof proper of the sanctum (now broken) was formed of overlapping stones ; the original architrave over the entrance no longer exists, having been replaced at some period by a plain one ; this, too, failed, and others were successively put in, till, at this moment, there are four door frames, one within another, thus reducing the original width and height of the entrance considerably ; the jambs which were afterwards put in are not all entire pillars, but are made up of miscellaneous fragments, put together so as to make up the required height.

"The mahāmandapa was roofed also by overlapping courses of stones ; the square corners were gradually rounded off by successive small portions, till it formed an octagon, over which the circular roof proper rested ; the roof has long ago tumbled in but the corners are yet intact, and the constructive expedient used may be seen in the photograph ; the circular roof was further supported, as is done in several instances elsewhere, by four pillars, placed as a square in the centre of the mahāmandapa ; these pillars are quite plain ; the material and execution of the portion external to the sanctum and 'antarala' differ from those of the sanctum, being of plain ; indeed coarsely dressed, granite, while the sanctum is of finally cut and smoothed sandstone ; the line of junction, too, of the mahāmandapa and of the sanctum is quite distinct, proving clearly that the mahāmandapa is a subsequent addition, the original temple having consisted of the sanctum and its attached vestibule alone, which, far from having the manifestly unfinished appearance of the façade of the Barākhar temples, has, independently of the subsequently added mahāmandapa, a finished façade, the portion over the entrance being provided with regular freize, and cornice, and mouldings and sculpture, all which would necessarily be hidden by the roof and architraves of the later added mahāmandapa.

"Externally, the tower is adorned with sculpture and mouldings, carefully and finely cut in the stone itself. At some subsequent period the tower appears to have received externally a coat of plaster, in which was sculptured devices, ornaments, and figures different to that in the stone below, proving clearly that the original stone tower was not covered with plaster when first built. Over this coat of plaster was put on, at a still later period, a second coat, and on this were sculptured figures, ornaments, and devices differing from either of the previous ones.

The ornamentation executed in the plaster coat resembles that used in the plaster coating put on the brick temple at Pāra, and is therefore presumably of the same age, that is, of the time of Mān Singh to whom therefore, I ascribe the extensive repairs and alterations executed in this temple, and in others of the group." (A. S. I. Reports, Vol. VIII.)

The doorway described by Mr. Begler is once more giving way; there are only scanty traces of the external plaster and its sculptured devices, and much of the detail of the tower is now obscured by a mass of creeper, otherwise Mr. Beglar's description is still true to the facts.

Of the temples in the other groups space does not permit any detailed description; all are of more or less similar type, and Brāhmanical in origin, save one to the south of the village which was either Buddistic or Jain, with the remains of a large monastery, in the shape of a large brick mound, close to it.

Tradition ascribes the building of all these numerous temples to merchants or *mahājans*, and not as ordinarily to Rājas and this tends to confirm the inference drawn by Mr. Beglar that the place rose to importance as lying on one of the great traffic routes and at a principal obstaclo, *viz.*, the Dāmodar river. Its name is ascribed to the fact that Rāja Vikramaditya used to come, or on one occasion came here, to rub oil on his body before bathing in the "Chhata Pokhar" at Dalmi, a distance of some 60 miles. The place is considerably frequented now-a-days by Hindu devotees, and a fair, known as the Khelai Chandi Mela, is held in the month of Pous, which is attended by Hindus from considerable distances. Another fair called the Baruni Mela, is held in the last days of Chaitra, which is largely attended by Sonthals to whom the place is specially holy as situated on their sacred stream, the Dāmodar (Nai), into which they throw the ashes of their dead. On this occasion it is said that the Sonthals are rigidly excluded from the main temple enclosure known as the Bhairabthan, and they take no part in any of the religious ceremonies performed at that time in honour of the Hindu deities.

INDEX.

A

Aboriginal races, 76-83; education of, 261.

Abwāb, 147-148.

Administration, land revenue, 187-212; general, 246-253; of justice, 250-253.

Administrative divisions, 246-247.

——— staff, 250-251.

Adra, description of, 263.

Aghani crops, 121; rice, 122.

Agreement 1776; form of, 191-193.

Agricultural Association, 126-127; classes, 157; material condition of, 153-154; statistics, 120-121.

Agriculture, 113-127.

Agriculturists' Loans Act, 156.

Ahars, irrigation from, 116.

Ahriat, tenures, 209.

Ajodhya range, 3.

Akhan Jātra, 97.

Amusements of the people, 96-97.

Animals, wild, 20-23.

Animists, 73-74.

Anorthosite, 44.

Archæological remains, 68.

Area of the district, 1, 69; cultivated, 120-121.

Arkati system, 251-252.

Artisans, wages of, 149-151.

Arts and industries, 157-168.

Aspects, physical, 1-25; medical, 98-112.

Assessment of rent, 143-149.

Asylum, Leper, 111-112.

Auli hill, 4.

Aus rice, cultivation of, 127.

Autumn crops, cultivation of, 125.

B

Bābir bāndh, 8.

Bāghmundi, range, 3; thana at, 286.

Bahāl land, 119.

Baid land, 119.

Bājra, cultivation of, 125.

Balarāmpur, sub-registry office at, 250; description of, 263-264; police outpost at, 286.

Bāndhs, 8; irrigation from, 116; utility of, 116-117.

Bāndwan, police outpost at, 286.

Bāngurda ghatwāli *taraf*, 232-233.

Bānsa hill, 5.

Bānskar, 148.

Barābazar, rainfall of, 25; sub-registry office at, 250; description of, 264-265; police-station at, 286.

Barābhum in 1800, 58-61; settlement of, 190-193; ghatwāli tenures in, 224-244; zamindāri family of, 264-265.

Barākhar Coal Company, 159; iron and steel works, 45, 158-159; river, 6.

Barākhar sub-stage, 31.

Bāri, *bāstu* or *udbāstu*, 119.

Barley, cultivation of, 125.

Basket-making, 167.

Bāstu bāti khajana, 239.

Bāstu rent, 148.

Bāuris, 79-80.

Bedding, 93.

Bengal gneiss, 40.

Bengal Iron and Steel Company, 45, 158-159.

Bet-begāri, 147.

Bhādoi crops, 121; rainfall required for, 114-116; rice, 121-122.

Bhātottar, 209.

Bhokta, hook-swinging festival, 96.

Bhuiyas, 81.

Bhumij, 78-79.

Bhumijāni mahal, 230-232.

Binda parab, 97.

Birds, game, 23.

Births, 99-100.

Blindness, 103.
Boarding houses, 261.
Borām, description of, 265-267.
Botany, 11-20.
Boulder-beds, 31.
Boundaries of the district, 2.
Bowel complaints, mortality from, 103.
Brāhmans, 80.
Brāhmottar, 209.
British administration, early, 55-58.
Buddhistic era, 48.
Buddhpur, description of, 267-268.
Building stones, 45.
Bungalows, staging and inspection, 186.
Burdwan stone, 44.

C

Calamities, natural, 128-142.
Calcareous jasper, 35; schists, 48.
Camping grounds, Government, 187.
Canals, 185.
Cash rents, 143-146.
Castes and Tribes, 76-85.
Cattle, 127.
Census of 1901, 70.
Centres of trade, 167.
Cesses, revenue from, 249.
Chākran, 212, 234-237.
Chākultor, description of, 268.
Chalk, 10.
Charajural hill, 4.
Charak festival, 96.
Charitable dispensaries, 109-111.
Charrā, description of, 268.
Chās, rainfall, 25; sub-registry office at, 250; thana, 286.
Chātam hill, 4.
Chaukidars, 252.
Chhāta parab, 94.
Chirkunda, police outpost, 272.
Cholera, epidemics of, 102-108.
Christians, 75-76.
Civil Justice, 250-251.
Clay, 44, 118-119.
Climate, 24; in relation to health, 98-99.
Coal-fields of Mānbhum, the, 45, 170-182, early discoveries of, 170-171; early developments, 172; the Rāniganj, 172-173; the Jharia, 173-178; geology, 45, 175-178; method of working in, 178-181; labour, 180-181.
Coal, composition of, 177-178, industry, 157-158.
Commerce, 167-168.
Communication, means of, 183-186; development of, 183-184; roads, 184; railways, 184-185; extension of the railway system, 185; rivers, 185; ferries, 186; bungalows, 186; postal, 186.
Compromise of 1884, 66, 225-227.
Condition of the people, material, 153-156.
Configuration of the district, 2.
Conservancy, 256-257.
Continuation schools, 261.
Copper ores, 10.
Cotton weaving, 164-165.
Country spirit, manufacture and consumption of, 247-248.
Courts, civil and criminal, 250-251.
Criminal justice, 250.
Crops, principal, 120-126; rotation of, 118; statistics of, 121; autumn, 125; non-food, 125; outturn of, 126.
Cultivating tenures, 208-209.
Cultivation, system of, 113-114; extension of, 120; extent of, 120-121; improvements in, 126-127.
Culturable waste, 120.
Cutlery, manufacture of, 165-166.

D

Dalmā, range, 3-4; description of, 268; trap, 37-38.
Dalmi, 49, 289; description of, 268-270.
Dāmodar fossils, 32; river, 6, 185, 271, 289.
Dāmodar stage, 31.
Dānga (high land), 119.
Dar-mokrari, 205.
Dasturi, 223.
Deaths, 100; by wild beasts, 21.
Debottar, 209.
Density of population, 71-72.
Dhaba chita soil, 119.
Dhalkisor river, 7.

Dhānbāid subdivision, 246, 271-272; town, description of, 270-271; dispensary at, 110-111; sub-registry office at, 250; sub-jail at, 253; police-station, 271; public buildings, 271.

Dhānkhet or rice land, 143.

Dhārwār system, 35-40.

Diarrhœa, mortality from, 108.

Digwāri estates, 203.

Digwārs, 210, 216-228.

Diseases, principal, 101-104.

Dispensaries, 109-111; veterinary, 127, 255.

Distilleries, 247-248.

Distress in 1908, 140-142.

District, formation of, 67-68; staff of, 250.

District Board, administration of, 254-255; income of, 254; expenditure of, 254-255; roads, 184.

Dolerite dykes, 34.

Domo gneiss, 41; constitution of, 42.

Domestic animals, 127.

Dress of the people, 92-93.

Dulrāji, mahal, 234, 240.

Dudhi chita, 119.

Dumunda hill, 5.

Durgapur hill, 6.

Dwellings, 88.

Dysentery, mortality from, 103.

E

Early English administration, 55-58.

Early history of Mānbhum, 47-52.

Earthquakes, 142.

Education, 258-262; progress of, 258-259; statistics of, 259; secondary, 259; primary, 259-260; female, 260; industrial, 260-261; of Muhammadans, 261; of aboriginals, 261; of different races, 261.

Educational staff, 259.

Ekjai mahadad of 1205, 230.

Embankments, 116-117.

Emigration, 70, 251-252.

Encumbered Estates Act, 201-202.

Epidiorites, 44.

Estates, revenue-paying, 187; permanently-settled, 187-197; probable origin of, 188-189; temporarily settled, 197-199; exemption of, from sale for arrears and debt, 200-201; revenue-free, 202; *digwari*, 203.

European club at Jheria, 274; at Purulia, 285.

Excise administration, 247-248.

Execution hill, 5, 286.

Exports, 167-168.

F

Factories, 158-167; iron and steel, 158, 159; pottery, 158.

Famine, liability to, 128-130.

Famine of 1770, 130; of 1866, 130-135; of 1874, 135-137; of 1897, 137-140.

Fauna, 20-23.

Female education, 260.

Ferries, 186.

Festivals, 75; village, 93-96.

Fever, mortality from, 101-102.

Finance, 246-249.

Fiscal divisions, 187-188.

Fish, 23.

Floods, 142.

Flora, 11.

Food-grains, prices of, 152-153.

Forests, Protected, 199.

Formation of the district, 67-68.

Furniture, 90-91.

G

Game birds, 23.

Ganga-buru, hill, 4.

Ganga Narayan's rebellion, 61-64; causes and results of, 64-65.

Garaya puja, 95.

Gaurāndi thana, 286.

General administration, 246-253.

General characteristics of population, 71-72.

Geological constitution of the district, 26.

Geology, 8-9, 26-46; of Jharia field, 175, 178.

Gharāmis, 149.

Ghartaki, 239.

Ghartooloe or Gartoli *taraf*, 225, 232, 240.

Ghatwāli survey, 1880-83, 225.

Ghatwāli tenures, 210, 223-245; evidence of their early origin, 227-232; their ultimate origin in Mundari village system, 241, 232-245, 252.

Ghatwāls 211, 252.
Girls' schools, 260.
Gneisses, 40-41; of Parasnath, 44.
Gobindpur, description of, 272; police station at, 272; rainfall of, 25.
Gold, alluvial, 10, 40; gold-washing, 10, 166.
Gondli, cultivation of, 125.
Gondwana coal-fields, 30-35; system, 26-29.
Goraiti grants, 212.
Gora land, 119; rice, 122.
Government camping grounds, 187.
Gowai river, 6, 184.
Gram, cultivation of, 125; prices of, 152.
Gramya devata, 74; *Gramya than*, 94.
Grazing grounds, 127.
Guru-training schools, 260.

H

Hānkwa, 97.
Harai river, 8.
Hatee mangan, 239.
Hāts, 168.
Health, public, 98-112.
High Schools, 259.
Hikimāli tenure, 207.
Hills, 4-5.
Hindus, 73-74.
History, of the district, 47-68; of land revenue administration, 187-203.
Holi festival, 96.
Honorary Magistrates, 250.
Hospitals, 109-11.
Hot springs, 69.
Houses, 89-90.
Hura, sub-registry office at, 250; police outpost, 286.

I

Ichāgarh (Pātkum), police outpost, 286.
Ijara, 206-207.
Ijri stream, 6, 184.
Immigration, 70-71.
Imports, 167-168.
Incidence of rent, 143.
Income-tax, revenue from, 249.
Ind parab, 94-95.
Indebtedness, 156.
Industrial classes, 157.
Industrial education, 260-261.
Industries, 157-67; in district jail, 253.
Infantile mortality, 100-101.
Infirmities, 103-104.
Influenza, 102.
Inoculation, 104.
Inspection of mines, 182.
Intrusive rocks, 29; in Gondwāna coal-fields, 32-33.
Iron-ores, 45.
Ironstone shales, 31-32.
Ironware and cutlery, 165-66.
Iron works, 158-59.
Irrigation, 116-17; necessity for, 116; from *bāndhs*, 116-17; from wells, 117; extension of, 117-18.
Isamnavisis of 1824 and 1833, 237.

J

Jahira, 74.
Jaigirs, Pānchet, 210, 218-221.
Jail, district, 258; subsidiary, at Dhanbaid, 253.
Jalkar tenures, 208.
Jalsāsan tenures, 208.
Jamunia river, 6.
Jangalburi tenures, 209.
Jangalkar, 148.
Jantal parab, 94.
Jaypur, police outpost, 286.
Jhalda, rainfall of, 25; sub-registry office at, 250; municipality, 257; description of, 272-273; police-station at, 286.
Jharia coal, composition of, 177; Coal-fields, 26, 45, 173-178; town, description of, 273-274; thana, 271.
Jita parab, 95.
Jobuna-bandh, 8.
Jungle products, 12-19, 128-129.
Justice, administration of, 250-253; criminal, 250; civil, 250-251.

K

Kailāpal, temporarily-settled estate, 198-199; ghatwāli tenures in, 224.
Kālipuja, 95.
Kamiyas, 150.

Kāmars, 80.
Kānāli land, 119.
Kunkar, 11, 119.
Kārū khunta festival, 95.
Karam festival, 94.
Karanti, hill, 4.
Karkari river, 7.
Kāsai river, 7, 184.
Kāthikar, 148.
Kātras, police outpost, 271; description of, 274-275.
Katri river, 6, 184.
Khajana mamul in Barābhum, 238-239.
Kharias, 82.
Khelai chandi mela, 289.
Khesāri, cultivation of, 125.
Khorposh, 207-208.
Khudia river, 6, 184.
Khuntkatti tenants, 209, 241.
Kodū, cultivation of, 125.
Kolarian tribes, 81-82.
Koro, 81-82.
Kumārdubi, Brick and Tile Syndicate, 159; Fire Brick and Pottery Works, 159.
Kumāripar *ghatwāli taraf*, origin of, 233.
Kumāri river, 7, 184.
Kurmis, 76-77.
Kurthi, cultivation of, 125.

L

Labour, supply of, 151; in the coal-fields, 180-181.
Labourers, wages of, 149-151.
Labouring classes, 157.
Lac industry, 159-164.
Lakes, 8.
Lal māti soil, 119.
Land Improvement Loans Act, 156.
Landlords, condition of the, 154-155.
Land revenue, administration, 187-212, receipts from, 247.
Lands, classification of, 118-119.
Land tenures, 203-209.
Language, 72-73.
Laterite, 44-45.
Lāyāli grants, 212.
Lead ores, 10, 46.
Legendary history, 47-52, of Barābhum family, 264-265, of Pānchet family, 273, 280-282.
Leper Asylum, 111-112.
Leprosy, 103-104.
Libraries, 261-262.
Limestone, 46.
Local Board, 255-256.
Local Self-Government, 254-257.
Locusts, 142.
Lohars, 80.

M

Magura hill, 7.
Mahal bhumijāni, 230-231; 234-237; *dubrāji*, 240, *jaigir*, 232.
Mahaljat, 231, 234.
Mahattran tenure, 209.
Mahli, 82.
Maintenance tenures, 207-208.
Maize, cultivation of, 125; prices of, 152.
Maktabs, 261.
Malaria, 102
Mullik, 82-83.
Mamul khajana, 238-240.
Manasa, 94.
Mānbazar, description of, 275-276; thana, 286.
Mānbhum (newspaper), 262.
Mānbhum, origin of name, 1; geological constitution of, 26; early history of, 47-51; Muhammadan rule of, 52-53; early English administration of, 55-66; formation of, 67-68; division into estates, 187-88; police tenures in, 213-245.
Māngan, 147-48.
Mankairi tenures, 204-05, 244.
Manufactures, 157-67.
Marshes, 8.
Marua, cultivation of, 125.
Material condition of the people, 153-56.
Mātha, temporary settled estate, origin of, 197-198.
Means of communication, 183-186; roads, 184; railways, 184-85; river, 185-186; postal, 186.
Measures, 168-69.

Medical aspects, 101-12; institutions, 109-112.

Medicine, indigenous system of, 111.

Meteorological statistics, 24.

Mica-peridotite, 33.

Middle English Schools, 259.

Middle Vernacular Schools, 259.

Migration, 70-71.

Minerals, 9-11; 45-46.

Mines, 157-158, 170-182.

Mission, German Lutheran, 75, 260; Pemberanda Faith, 286; Sonthal, 76, 260.

Mokrari tenures, 205.

Moghuli, brahmottars, etc., 205-206.

Mortality, 99-901.

Mountains, 4-5.

Muhammadan rule on district, influence of, 52-54.

Muhammadans, 75; education of, 261.

Mundari village system, 188-189; 241-44.

Mundas, 82.

Municipalities, 256-257.

Murāri tenures, 204-205, 244.

Mustard, cultivation of, 125.

Mutiny of 1857, 65-66.

N

Natural calamities, 128-142, division of the district, 2-4.

Navigation, 185.

Nayābadi settlements, 145-48; tenures, 208.

Nongsai river, 7.

Newspapers, 261-262.

Night schools, 261.

Nirsa, police-station at, 272.

O

Occupancy raiyats, 209.

Occupations of the people, 157.

Officials, village, 85-86.

Oil-seeds, cultivation of, 125.

Outposts, police, 252.

Outturn of crops, 126.

P

Pabanpur, description of, 276-277.

Pack-bullocks, use of, 168.

Pahira, 83.

Pākbira, description of, 277-278.

Panchak quit-rent of ghatwāli tenures, 225, 238.

Panchaki, brahmottars, etc., 205.

Pānchet estate, 58-64, 187; rents in, 144; suzerainty of, 189-190; during Muhammadan era, 195-196; in early British era, 196-197; jaigirs, 210, 218-221; early police arrangements in, 215-216; description of, 278-282; fort, 278; hill, 4, 278; stage (geological), 30, 32.

Pāndra, estate, 55, 187, 189; partition of, 200, rainfall at, 25.

Pāra, description of, 282-284; thana, 286.

Parasnath hill, 5, 51.

Pasturage, 127.

Pastimes, 96-97.

Pātkum estate, early history, 57-58, 61-62, 194; service tenures in, 223-224, 244; gold in, 10, 166; traditional history, 269, 289.

Patni taluks, 204.

People, the, 69-97; social life of, 86-97; material condition of, 153-156; occupations of, 157.

Permanent Settlement, 190.

Phāgua festival, 96.

Phānsi pahar, 5, 286.

Phosphorus, 34.

Phudi inganu, 97.

Phuni khel, 97.

Physical aspects, 1-46.

Pirottar, 209.

Pitha parab, 96, 97.

Plague, outbreaks of, 103.

Police, administration of, 252-253; early arrangements in Pānchet, 215-216; tenures in Mānbhum, 213-245.

Population, growth of, 69; density of, 71-72.

Porphyry, felspar, 44.

Post offices, 186.

Postal communications, 186.

Potatoes, cultivation of, 126.

Potstone, 35-36, 166.

Prices, 152-153; famine, 131-141.

Primary education, 259-260.

Primogeniture, the rule of, 199-200.

Produce rents, 146-147.

Products of forests, 128-129.

Professional classes, 157.

Protected forests, 199.

Public health, 98-112.

Purūlia Darpan (newspaper), 262.

Purulia subdivision, 285-286.

Purūlia town, description of, 284-285; rainfall of, 25; Church of England at, 75-76; hospital at, 109-110, 255; Leper asylum at, 111-112, 285; sub-registry office at, 250; district jail, 253; municipality, 256-257; zilla school at, 259, 284; population, 284; thana, 286.

Q

Quarries, 10-11, 178.

Quartzites, 46.

R

Rabi crops, 121, 125; rainfall required for, 114-116.

Raghunāthpur town, description of, 286-287; rainfall of, 25; sub-registry office at, 250; municipality, 257; High school at, 59; population, 286; police-station, 286.

Rahar, cultivation of, 125.

Railways, 184-185; extension of, 185.

Rainfall, statistics of, 25; in relation to agriculture, 114-116; in 1873, 135; in 1892 and 1897, 137.

Raiyats, occupancy, 209.

Rājganj, police outpost, 272.

Rāni-bāndh, 8.

Rāniganj coal, composition of, 177; coal-field, 26, 45, 172-174; sub stage, 32.

Rape, cultivation of, 125.

Registration, 249-250.

Registry offices, 250.

Religion, 73-76.

Rent, 143-149; rates of, 143; in Tundi, 143; in Mātha and Kailāpal, 143-144; in Barābhum, 144; in Pānchet, 144; prevalence of customary or quit rents, 145; cash rents, 143-146; produce rents, 146-147; *bāstu* rent, 148; rent for trees, 148-149.

Rent-free grants, 209.

Reptiles, 23.

Reservoirs, irrigation from, 116-117.

Revenue of the district, 246-250; land revenue administration, 187-212; from land, 247; excise, 247-248; stamps, 248-249; income-tax, 249; cesses, 249; registration, 249-250.

Revenue-free properties, 202.

Revenue-paying tenures, 203-207.

Rice, cultivation of, 121-125; price of, 152; varieties of, 122-125.

Rinderpest, 127.

Risley-bāndh, 8.

Rivers, 5-7, 185.

Roads, 183-184.

Rohini festival, 94.

Rope-making, 167.

Rotation of crops, 118.

Rural police, 252-253; population, 72.

S

Sadiyāls, 211.

Sahib-bāndh, 8, 256, 285.

Salt, prices of, 152.

Sands, magnetic, 40.

Sanitation, 104-109; in Purūlia, 105; in the villages, 105-106; in the coal-fields, 106-108.

Sanskrit *tols*, 261.

Sānturi police outpost, 28 i.

Saraks, 83-85.

Sarboria *ghatwāli taraf*, origin of, 233-234.

Sardar ghatwāls, 210-211, 225, 241-244.

Sārul festival, 93.

Sawai hill, 4.

Scarcity in 1809, 137; in 1908, 140-142.

Scenery, 2-4.

Schools, 259-261; High schools, 259; Middle-English, 259; Middle Vernacular, 259; Girls', 260; Primary, 259-260; special, 260; training 260; technical, 260; lace and weaving, 260; indigenous, 261; night or continuation, 261; Koran, 261; other schools, 261.

Secondary education, 259.

Service tenures, 210-245.

Settlement, *nayābādi*, 145-146.

Shikmi taluks, 203-204; tenures, 244.

Silai river, 7.

Silk weaving, 164, 286.

Singbonga, 74.

Small-pox, mortality from, 103.

Snakes, 23.

Soap-stone, 10, 35-36, 166.

Social life of the people, 86-97.

Soils, 118-119.

Sonthal Mission Press, 262.

Sonthals, 77.

Special schools, 260.

Spirit, consumption of, 248.

Springs, hot, 34.

Stamps, revenue from, 248-249.

Statistics, 24; *agricultural*, 120-121; of *education*, 259; *jail*, 2?3; *medical*, 110; *meteorological*, 24; *of occupation*, 157; *of rainfall*, 25; *vital*, 99-101.

Stone-carving, 166.

Sub-aerial denudation, 27.

Subarnarekha river, 7, 184.

Subdivisional administration, 271-272.

Subordinate tenures, 203-207.

Sugarcane, cultivation of, 126.

Sun God, 74.

Supply of labour, 151; in the coal-fields, 180-181.

Surguja, cultivation of, 125.

T

Tābedars, 211, 243.

Talabi, *brahmottars*, etc., 206.

Tālcher fossils, 31; stage, 30.

Tāluks, *shikmi*, 203-204; *patni*, 204.

Tānr land, 119.

Tarafs, *ghatwāli*, 224; origin of, 231-234, 241-244, 232-234.

Tasar rearing and weaving, 164.

Tea Districts Labour Supply Association, 252.

Telegraph offices, 186.

Telkupi, description of, 287-289.

Temperature, 24.

Tenures, *cultivating*, 208-209; *ijara*, 206, 207; *maintenance*, 207-208; *minor service*, 212; *rent-free*, 209; *service*, 210-212; *subordinate*, 203-206.

Tetko river, 7.

Thānas, 271-272, 286.

Til, cultivation of, 125.

Tols, 261.

Topchānchi police-station, 272.

Topography, 1, 28.

Towns, 72.

Trade 167-169; centres, 167.

Training schools, 260.

Trees and vegetation, 11-12; economic uses of, 12.

Tribes and castes, 76-85.

Tundi police-station, 272; range, 3.

Tusu parab, 95-96.

U

Ud-bāstu bāri, 119.

Union Club, 285.

Urban population, 72.

Urid, cultivation of, 125.

V

Vaccination, 104.

Vaishnavottar tenure, 209.

Vegetation and trees, 11-12; economic uses of, 12.

Veins, auriferous, 38; pegmatite, 43; kyanite and corundum, 48.

Vertebrate fossils, 32.

Veterinary relief, 127.

Victoria Institution, 259, 284.

Village festivals, 93-96; labourers, wages of, 150-151; officials, 85-86; *sardārs*, 211; social life, 86-97; watch, 252-253.

Villages, 72; general appearance of the, 86-93.

Vital statistics, 99-101.

W

Wages, 149-151; rates of, 149.

Water-courses, 116-117.

Watershed, 2, 3, 7.

Weaving of silk and tasar, 164; of cotton, 164-165.

Weights, 168-169.

Wells, irrigation from, 117.

Wheat, cultivation of, 121, 125; prices of, 152.

Wild animals, 20-23.

Winds, 24.

Winter rice, cultivation of, 121-25.

Witchcraft, belief in, 74-75.

Women, education of, 260.

Wood-carving, 167.

Z

Zamindar, meaning of, 193-194.

Zilla school, 259, 284.

Zoology, 20-23.

B. S. Press—13 10 1911—2793J—536 —C. A. P. & others.

OFFICIAL AGENTS FOR THE SALE OF GOVERNMENT PUBLICATIONS.

In India.

MESSRS. THACKER, SPINK & CO., Calcutta and Simla.
MESSRS. NEWMAN & CO., Calcutta.
MESSRS. HIGGINBOTHAM & CO., Madras.
MESSRS. THACKER & CO., LD., Bombay.
MESSRS. A. J. COMBRIDGE & CO., Bombay.
THE SUPERINTENDENT, AMERICAN BAPTIST MISSION PRESS, Rangoon.
MRS. RADHABAI ATMARAM SAGOON, Bombay.
MESSRS. R. CAMBRAY & CO., Calcutta.
RAI SAHIB M. GULAB SINGH & SONS, Proprietors of the Mufid-i-am Press, Lahore, Punjab.
MESSRS. THOMPSON & CO., Madras.
MESSRS. S. MURTHY & CO., Madras.
MESSRS. GOPAL NARAYEN & CO., Bombay.
MESSRS. B. BANERJEE & CO., 25, Cornwallis Street, Calcutta.
MESSRS. S. K. LAHIRI & CO., Printers and Booksellers, College Street, Calcutta.
MESSRS. V. KALYANARAMA IYER & CO., Booksellers, &c., Madras.
MESSRS. D. B. TARAPOREVALA, SONS & CO., Booksellers, Bombay.
MESSRS. G. A. NATESAN & CO., Madras.
MR. N. B. MATHUR, Superintendent, Nazair Kanum Hind Press, Allahabad.
THE CALCUTTA SCHOOL BOOK SOCIETY.
MR. SUNDER PANDURANG, Bombay.
MESSRS. A. M. AND J. FERGUSON, Ceylon.
MESSRS. TEMPLE & CO., Madras.
MESSRS. COMBRIDGE & CO., Madras.
MESSRS. A. CHAND & CO., Lahore.
BABU S. C. TALUKDAR, Proprietor, Students & Co., Cooch Behar.
Messrs. Ramchandra Govind and Son, Book-sellers and Publishers, Kalvadevi, Bombay.

In England.

MESSRS. A. CONSTABLE & CO., 10, Orange Street, Leicester Square, London, W. C.
MESSRS. GRINDLAY & CO., 54, Parliament Street, London, S. W.
MESSRS. KEGAN PAUL, TRENCH, TRÜBNER & CO., 43, Gerrard Street, Soho, London, W.
MR. B. QUARITCH, 11, Grafton Street, New Bond Street, London, W.
MESSRS. W. THACKER & CO., 2, Creed Lane, Ludgate Hill, London, E. C.
MESSRS. P. S. KING & SON, 2 & 4, Great Smith Street, Westminster, London, S. W.
MESSRS. H. S. KING & CO., 65, Cornhill, London, E. C.
MR. B. H. BLACKWELL, 50-51, Broad Street, Oxford.
MESSRS. DEIGHTON BELL & CO., Trinity Street, Cambridge.
MR. T. FISHER UNWIN, 1, Adelphi Terrace, London, W. C.
MESSRS. LUZAC & CO., 46, Great Russell Street, London, W. C.

On the Continent.

MESSRS. R. FRIEDLÄNDER & SOHN, 11, Carlstrasse, Berlin, N. W. 6.
MR. OTTO HARRASSOWITZ, Leipzig.
MR. KARL HIERSEMANN, 29, Konigsstrassee, Leipzig.
MR. ERNEST LEROUX, Rue Bonaparte, Paris.
MR. MARTINUS NIJHOFF, The Hague.